INK IN THE BLOOD

First published in 2007 by

WOODFIELD PUBLISHING LTD
Bognor Regis ~ West Sussex ~ England ~ PO21 5EL
www. woodfieldpublishing. com

ISBN 1-84683-039-7

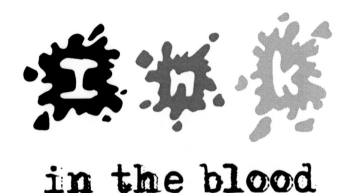

in the blood

Memoirs of a Regional Newspaperman

BARRIE WILLIAMS

Woodfield

Woodfield Publishing Ltd

Woodfield House ~ Babsham Lane ~ Bognor Regis ~ West Sussex ~ PO21 5EL
telephone 01243 821234 ~ **e-mail** enquiries@woodfieldpublishing. com

Interesting and informative books on a variety of subjects

For full details of all our published titles, visit our website at
www. woodfieldpublishing. com

Dedicated to:

Jack Cater, Jim Thompson,
Christopher Pole-Carew and Ian Park.

Without them there would
have been no story to tell.

~ CONTENTS ~

Foreword

THE SPEECHES WERE DONE, the Conference to debate Cornwall's use of EU Objective One status and cash was petering out and I wondered what joys the evening still held as I shuffled up to the conference bar. Leaning on the bar was a man with a lived-in face and a baleful expression. He surveyed the room with disdain, yet behind the expression bright eyes flashed.

There's a bit of swash and buckle here, I thought.

"Where's the *vision*? Where's the *passion*?" said the man. He snorted. Then, unable to contain himself, he fixed me and said: "What sort of man are they expecting to lead Cornwall if they're offering bloody peanuts?"

He drained his glass and offered me a drink. Not sure whether the question was rhetorical or not I decided to introduce myself instead of answering it. "I know who you are," he said. "I'm Barrie Williams." He was angry. He was a journalist but not just any journalist. He was the Editor of the *Western Morning News*, the paper of choice for many of us who live in the West Country. And editors should be dispassionate *shouldn't they?*

So began a long friendship with a remarkable man. He has that most wonderful quality of being interested in absolutely everything and usually has a droll or wicked perspective which, remarkably, is not completely stained by cynicism. Barrie is an optimist who hopes, against all the evidence, that common sense will prevail and good will out. His *Western Morning News* was apolitical and shunned the scurrilous or wilfully damaging view. It was strongly opinionated, yes, but it was the balanced paper of record (except for the odd Quixotic charge against wind farms, which, as a Dutchman, I found mystifying!) and Barrie was passionate that it should remain so.

I could tell you a hundred tales about the man but will instead focus on one...

In June 2005 I had been following closely Bob Geldof's progress leading up to *LIVE8*. A month before the concert came a rash of criticism of the perceived hypocrisy of putting on a global concert with so few African musicians on display. An idea grew and – ridiculously just 17 days before the concert – we decided we would have a crack at turning Eden into Africa for one day.

I called Barrie: "Do you think I'm mad?" I asked him.

He was fantastic.

Every problem the world threw at us, Barrie helped us with.

He found me Geldof's phone number (God knows how!)

When Harvey Goldsmith turned down our approaches to be included in the TV coverage of *Live8* because we weren't international or professional, Barrie called a good friend of his – John Lilley, the regional boss of the BBC. "Bugger that," said Barrie and John – and wheels began to move. John pulled favours. Barrie promised major coverage and a special sponsors' insert.

We had to raise £750,000 in a few short days to pay for the staging, the flights (not to mention 120 visas for African musicians at a time of high terrorism alert) the accommodation etc, etc, etc.

Unbelievably, the momentum built up. Harvey backed down when John found two satellite trucks and persuaded BBC 1 to cover bits of our show and Radios 1, 2 and 3 to come down. Soon, we had every major TV company, every newspaper and just about every radio station in Europe coming. Angelina Jolie was coming... and so it went on.

Barrie commissioned an in-depth interview with Peter Gabriel, the host of the concert, and then dispatched his team to the Press launch in London.

It had all stemmed from that one phone call I had made to Barrie. His commitment was infectious and when July 2nd dawned and the world looked on, Africa **HAD** come to Eden and it was watched by two billion people. Even Bob Geldof admitted it had been a remarkable success.

"That'll teach them to think we're hicks from the sticks!" said Barrie.

He and I share a passion for the doomed cause (such is the lot of the Nottingham Forest supporter!) and a love of the West Country, a region that owes more to Barrie than it knows, for it was on his watch and with his unstinting enthusiastic support that its major transformation began then flourished; the building of the Tate at St Ives; the success of the Lost Gardens of Heligan (I *would* say that!); the boom in good food and drink and the extraordinary changes that have taken place in the outside world's perceptions of the West Country... no longer the cider drinking buffoons of mythology or the last refuge of the bucket and spade brigade, this has turned into a much more sophisticated region demanding a more subtle commentary.

Barrie's tireless support for the Eden Project, from its first imaginings to the day of *Live8*, leaves us forever in his debt. Of all the massive media coverage Eden has attracted, literally world-wide, my favourite headline of all is the one Barrie wrote to accompany a huge *Western Morning News* front page picture on its opening day.

'OUR EDEN' it said.

I welled up.

A special man; an unconventional man; old fashioned yet modern; passionate yet capable of analytic distance; perhaps even a little sentimental at times. A man with a life lived full and of whom one can say the room feels better for his entering of it.

This is a book about the messiness of real life and the joy to be had from it as well as the moments that give you pause to think, to reflect, to despair for a moment... then reach for a beer and put the world to rights all over again.

Enjoy.

Tim Smit CBE
Chief Executive
The Eden Project

Tim Smit CBE

1.   Rabbit and Rhubarb

YOU WERE 'POSH' IF YOU HAD A FRIDGE. And we did... but only because we lived in a prefab. Prefabs were instant pre-fabricated council homes thrown up to ease the housing crisis after the Second World War. They were just single-storey shacks, but for some reason I've never been able to fathom, they came equipped with fridges – in those days a modern luxury usually possessed only by rich people and Americans in films.

Mum and Dad – Thelma and Stanley – had, like hundreds of other struggling young couples, applied to the council for a prefab more in hope than expectation and had been thrilled when they got one. It was an escape from the tiny privately rented Victorian terraced house (no bathroom, tin bath hanging up in the backyard, freezing cold outside toilet) in which they had lived in Oswestry, a town nestling on Shropshire's borders with Wales, since they married. It was a measure of the low levels of early postwar working-class aspiration that a pokey prefab, with concrete panels and corrugated asbestos roof, represented 'luxury' and was occupied with a considerable sense of pride.

Thelma and Stanley had four children in that tiny prefab. We must have been quite poor because Dad earned only a few quid a week, driving a snorting, flat-nosed tanker around the contorted Welsh country lanes, delivering fuel to farms. But thanks to their love, care, devotion and unquenchable spirit, we never *felt* poor – particularly not when Mum made ice cream and ice lollies (with free National Health orange juice) in our posh fridge for pals, who considered themselves fortunate indeed to be friends with prefab kids.

Those postwar years were so austere that virtually everybody was badly off by today's standards. Few of the inessential trappings which were later to separate the haves and have-nots were available, anyway. They must have been grim times, nonetheless, for the grown-ups, with food rationing and queues and continuing wartime shortages of the basics we later came to take entirely for granted. One of my earliest memories is of some poor, undernourished woman fainting in a bread queue and hitting the pavement in front of Mum and me with a fearful thud. She looked dead as she lay there, blood gushing from her nose, stripped of her dignity with her skirt up around her neck... just for a loaf of bread to feed her kids.

What would today's pampered supermarket shoppers have made of that?

Mostly, though, I remember the good times. Like wet Sunday afternoons with the pouring rain playing loudly on the thin corrugated roof of the prefab while we sat inside, cosy and warm by the fire with our mum and dad laughing at *Life With The Lyons* on the old wooden wireless, sharing a paper bag of mixed sweets (facilitated by studiously saved family ration coupons) from old Mrs Bull's corner shop, which was just the front room of her terraced house.

That would follow a Sunday lunch of roasted rabbit provided by Mr Don Evans – a jovial coal miner whose face we never saw white – via his fearsome ferrets, the dreadful stench of which, emanating from their makeshift cages, was readily tolerated by his grateful neighbours in the prefabs because of his unstinting largesse in sharing the spoils of clandestine excursions to the nearby fields. The rabbit, succulent and tender, if modest in portion, was followed by Mum's delicious rhubarb crumble and custard. Later, Sunday tea was piping hot toast, made on the open fire and served with homemade blackcurrant jam and deep yellow farm butter, free from one of Dad's more demonstrably appreciative customers. Then, we would re-visit the bag of sweets, switch the wireless back on and thrill to the exciting exploits of *Dick Barton*.

Poor? We were little bloody princes!

Mum and Dad were not much more than kids themselves, still only in their twenties, and maybe that's why we laughed such a lot. God knows they had their problems and their worries, particularly financial, but their kids were going to have as much fun as anybody else's. There'd always be some sort of rainbow on the horizon and when you think like that you usually find one. Just occasionally when there wasn't, and there was still a lot of week left at the end of the money, we'd hide under the table with Mum, stifling laughter and pretending to be out when the rent man knocked on the door. Next week we'd pay him double. Fair enough.

York Fields, which was what this block of prefabs was called, was a great little community in which everybody (all young couples with children) pulled together, sharing and caring for each other. Very little money. Few possessions. We didn't even have enough bedclothes to go round and overcoats doubled as blankets when the wafer thin walls were no match for the mid-winter frosts and ice formed on the *inside* of the bedroom windows at night. But we were happy. There was real pride among those prefab people, living in their flimsy little shacks. And loyalty. And camaraderie. And friendship. And fun. So much fun.

Our Rita, me, Derek and Les had the best Mum and Dad in the world. We could not have had a better start in life.

When four growing children ceased to be compatible with a two-bed roomed prefab, Mum and Dad moved to a bigger council house – a 1930s semi at the top of Coppice Drive, a steep hill on the outskirts of Oswestry. Immediately behind our back garden, with its air raid shelter cum kids' den, was a big, wild, wooded hill known to everybody in the town as "the coppie". It is said that, in those days, at least half the population of Oswestry lost its virginity "up the coppie". Beyond "the coppie" lay Oswestry's famous Roman earthworks – a source of deep delight to archaeologists and big fat succulent blackberries to the local children.

No. 39 Coppice Drive was an antique compared with the prefab (and it was to be several years before we had a fridge again!) but it was a great environment for energetic youngsters and we loved it. Mum and Dad, though, were sadly less happy here. Dad lost his job after the giant ShellMex, for whom he had been so proud to work, sold off its petroleum distribution operation in Oswestry to a smaller company, which turned tanker drivers into driver/salesmen, which some of them were never cut out to be, then made those who inevitably failed to meet their sales targets redundant. It was what I was later to come to know as 'business development' but it was a cruel fate for proud, strong, working men and though, after a couple of unsatisfactory attempts at other things, Dad did eventually find a factory job, he was never really happy in his work again.

It had been bloody hard having to manoeuvre that wilful, heavy old beast of a tanker around inhospitable Welsh hills and cart tracks, then unloading its booty of essential farm fuels in often atrocious weather, but Dad was respected and admired by those farmers who knew they were stuffed if he had failed to get through to them. It was tough, dirty, smelly and sometimes even dangerous work, but Dad had loved that job. It had given him pride and freedom and individuality; a feeling of indispensability; a sense of importance. He never got any of that being just one anonymous cog in the robotic wheel of a mind-numbing factory process, churning out plastic doors. Dad deserved so much more from his work, for he was the most decent, generous, honest, life-loving and humorous of men.

The move to Coppice Drive was to be hugely significant in my own evolving life too – but in an altogether more positive way…

Next door but two lived the Hawkins family. Rod Hawkins was a gregarious railway worker who, with the not insignificant assistance of the rotund and jolly Mrs Hawkins, had produced two extremely bright offspring, Marion and Bobby. Marion was so gifted that she had made it into university – a genuinely rare and momentous achievement for a working class kid (particularly a girl) in the early 1950s, when only exceptionally clever youngsters took that route. Bobby was equally successful. He'd become a journalist on the local weekly paper, the *Oswestry Border Counties Advertiser*, also a rare feat for a council house kid.

It would have been easy to understand if the Hawkins brood had considered themselves a cut above their neighbours. On the contrary. Probably due to the influence of their very likeable parents, they were a delightful pair. Bobby was one of the kindest, most unselfish and considerate chaps you could ever wish to meet. I hero worshipped him. Bobby and I spent hours playing "*Owzat!*" – a cricket game with a simple little metal cylinder which you rolled like a dice. It had singles, boundaries, bowled, caught, stumped and lbw as the options on whichever of its surfaces landed upwards. In these games Bobby would be Australia (always Australia) and I would be England. Each of us "batted" and "bowled" two full test match innings and our carefully kept scorecards used the names and batting orders of the international teams from each nation.

As we played these leisurely matches, sitting on his doorstep, Bobby would tell me all about his job, about the stories he had written, the assignments he'd been on and the people he had met – and about how one day he was going to go and be a journalist in Australia. I was totally absorbed in all this. Enthralled, captivated and excited by this young man's life and ambition.

I was just nine-years-old but I told my mum and dad, "I'm going to be a journalist, like Bobby."

Bobby did go to Australia as a journalist. Then on to Papua New Guinea, helping the impoverished, emerging (and not too long since, still cannibalistic!) natives to set up their own newspaper for their primitive communities called *Newspeppi Bilong New Guinea*, written in pidgin English and edited by Bobby Hawkins. Typically unselfish, characteristically kind and thoughtful, he was allowing his own career to be subservient to his desire to help others. What a great bloke. And still only in his twenties.

I was worried and thought "I hope they don't eat him." His Mum and Dad then left Coppice Drive. We lost touch completely. And I never did know what happened to my hero after that. I like to think that life gave him back as much as he put in, because that was the very least he deserved.

Spurred on vicariously by the example of Bobby Hawkins, I developed a real passion for the English language, but some of that must have been inherent, because much earlier in my primary school days, writing compositions for the kindly Miss Bawden, I would take flights of fancy – on imaginary holidays (which we could never have afforded) on exotic journeys and on the most unlikely adventures, all written as fact and truth – good training for a journalist, some would say!

It wasn't all fiction, however. I would also describe the days spent with my dad, riding (illegally but perfectly safely) in his tanker, kept as warm as toast by the engine, which was *inside* the cab; watching him wrestle with huge, reluctant serpent-like pipes, which he had to unleash from his vehicle and attach to the farmers' tanks in order to disgorge his loads. Sometimes, somewhere between tanker and tank, these defiant "serpents" would escape Dad's custody and with a projectile vomit, spout diesel spectacularly in the air while he grappled to bring them back under control. When he'd done and the farmer had signed for proof of delivery and amount of fuel received I'd wave in one movement with my Dad, "Cheerio, Mr Jones" (they were *all* called Jones, it seemed) "See you next time."

I wrote and told Miss Bawden how very important my dad was because if it was not for him the farms could not run at all and if the farms did not run at all none of us would have any food and then we'd all die and then what? I wrote and told Miss Bawden about Dad taking me to watch Oswestry Town play football. Good non-league clubs like Oswestry would, in those pre-television days, attract really impressive crowds. Dad loved his football. Very well-known locally as "Curly" Williams, he'd been a good goalkeeper, tipped for a professional career, until the day a flying boot with a whopping centre forward inside it made permanently injurious contact with his upper body and stopped him playing at a decent level ever again.

Dad's loss was my gain, because it meant he could take me to matches instead of playing himself on Saturday afternoons. Kids rarely paid to get into Oswestry's Victoria Road ground (a boring bloody housing estate now – but that's another story) even though the match posters said "Minors – 4d"; Dads just lifted them up and over the turnstiles while the attendants merely nodded benignly. Inside, I would stand, proud as Punch, with the men as they shouted, cheered, jeered, swore and smoked cigarettes.

The half time pee was a parlous pursuit for one like me, who stood no higher and frequently lower than the huge, mysterious wrinkly appendages out of which would roar great steaming torrents of recycled *Border* bitter, consumed in copious quantities in the *Black Lion* before kick-off. (I never wrote about that bit, though. Miss Bawden wouldn't have approved.)

One day, Miss Bawden told my mum that she thought I was a smashing little writer. I don't know who was more proud, Mum or me. Both fit to burst, we were.

I might just have settled for being a professional footballer if I was not going to be a journalist! In junior school I formed a close friendship with one Alan Ball. He was tiny, red-haired, hot-tempered and freckled – and even thinner than me. He was from Lancashire, so he spoke funny – as did his dad, also called Alan Ball. Alan Ball Senior was player/manager of Oswestry Town FC and also kept a local pub, the King's Head. Such was the close rapport between clubs and fans back then that I recall a match in which Alan Ball Senior – as he lined up for a corner – was asked by one of a couple of hundred supporters standing behind the goal which Oswestry were attacking:

"Why haven't you picked Edgar Cornes today?"

"He's got the flu," replied Ball – before rising to head the corner kick goalwards. Roy Keane, fierce critic of today's mercenary capitulation to the distanced, corporate "prawn sandwich" soccer watcher, would have been so approving of that!

Alan Ball senior had been a decent Football League player with clubs like Southport. As manager and inside right of Oswestry Town he was a local star. For some reason, though, my dad didn't like him.

"Big 'eaded bugger," was all I ever heard him say on the subject of my best pal's father.

I'd better keep that to myself, I thought, because I didn't think it was altogether fair!

I would see Alan's dad often when we'd go round to his pub after school and he'd give us impromptu training sessions in the yard among the empty crates and beer barrels. He was very strict, it seemed to me, but a good man who wanted the very best for his lad.

Some 50 years later I would hear Alan Ball junior, who became a World Cup winner with England in 1966, give an after dinner speech which was a moving and funny tribute to his father (who died in a car crash) and the role he had played in the young Alan's life. Alan described in that speech how impossible to please his dad had been throughout his career (only grudgingly conceding that he'd "not had a bad game" after winning the World Cup!) but how he came to recognise and appreciate that without that feet-on-the-ground discipline from his greatest critic, he would never have made it to the pinnacle of international football fame.

More than 200 people in that banqueting hall wiped away tears as Alan spoke from the heart about his father that night. Fond memory transported me back to that pub yard "training" with Alan and his dad – and I shed more tears than most.

Alan and I had also left an indelible mark on No. 39 Coppice Drive where, on the brick shed in the back yard, we painted a heading target – a solid circle in turquoise lead paint that we'd nicked from the shed. When my dad's theatrical wrath over the theft of the paint and the permanent desecration of the council's shed had subsided (he'd bollocked us with a huge grin on his face and only because mum had told him to) he would watch as Alan and I threw a ball up into the air for the other to head at the target. When either of us "scored" Dad would burst into exaggerated applause and shout "Just like Tommy Lawton!"

Tommy Lawton: one day that name would mean so much to me.

Along with others, Alan Ball and I passed the now infamous 11-plus exam and graduated to the hallowed halls of the local grammar school – Oswestry Boys' High School. There, Alan became inside right (like his dad) and captain of our team. I was outside right. This was "big time". Now we played on full sized, lush grass pitches with proper goalposts and nets. Now we wore, with immense pride, the green and white quartered colours of our school and had proper football boots, made of thick brown leather with wooden toe caps and studs. Alan was never less than brilliant. I was. With Alan in our side we never lost a game. After he had left to move back to Lancashire we did. Often.

The last time I saw Alan (apart from at that dinner in 2005) was at a dance at the Plaza ballroom in Oswestry. We were both 17 and he wore the smart club blazer of Blackpool FC, where he had become an apprentice professional. That night I reminded him of the last match in which we'd played together... He'd threaded an inch-perfect pass through to me on my wing, with an instruction to "GO!" but as a huge, pimply, hairy monster of a full back bore down on me I had chickened out of the tackle, leaving the great lummox free to charge down the field and pass to his centre forward, who scored.

"That was Barrie Williams fault!" Bally bellowed, over and over again, as he jumped up and down in rage, leaving the watching pupils, staff and parents in no doubt whatsoever that my captain questioned his right winger's membership of the human race.

I wouldn't have minded so much – but we were winning 29-0 at the time!

Alan and I laughed as we recalled that incident and concluded in agreement that I had better stick to journalism for *my* ambition. Alan stuck to football, of course, and became an enduring star – mourned by millions when a sudden heart attack killed him in April 2007. Fame never changed him. God bless you, Alan.

The style of Oswestry Boys High School and the conduct of some of its teachers would beggar belief today. To say that some of those schoolmasters indulged consistently in brutality towards their pupils is not to exaggerate in any way. We were frequently beaten about the head and body and even kicked. One evil old sod called George Peacock, who taught physics, would, if you had offended him, which was very easy to achieve, make you bend over his desk, then literally run at you before aiming a fierce kick at your backside. It was serious assault and would today be prosecuted as such.

That's not to say that we did not often deserve punishment. We played the volatile masters up at every opportunity, shouting their very rude nicknames into cupped hands when they turned their backs on us to write on the blackboard. Despite the physical assaults that this bad behaviour often provoked, we never entertained any thought of making a complaint. This was a war with its own rules of engagement. If they caught you and thumped or kicked you, that was fair enough. It hurt like hell but you'd asked for it, and there was an unspoken honour if you returned to your desk without tears after they had administered your beating in front of the rest of the class.

The teachers we targeted for this systematic provocation were the bullies and the weak – our conduct towards the latter being particularly reprehensible…

A beautiful young Frenchwoman on secondment to teach us her native language was never allowed to complete a lesson without frequent loud and lewd exhortations to *"Get 'em off, Fifi!"* We knew that was not her real name, of course, and we didn't really expect her to remove her undergarments for us. but stereotypes were too readily embraced by ignorant, badly behaved 14-year-olds.

When "Fifi" tried to retain our interest by playing Edith Piaff records we sang along, not in French as she had requested, but with our own English lyrics, all relating to the naughty bits of Fifi's anatomy. How intolerable it must have been for the poor girl and how we deserved it when the Headmaster Alf Exton burst in during one of these renditions and caned the lot of us.

But there were also beatings that we did *not* deserve…

Bert "Thud" Fisher was universally feared and taught maths, at which I was worse than useless, in total awe and silence. "Thud" would knock seven shades out of me in a pointless attempt to beat his subject in to me. His favourite form of assault was to "screw" my head to my desk using the knuckle of his index finger. It would make me feel sick. *The bastard!* One night, years later, I saw him in a pub and only the intervention of my mates prevented me from returning the treatment. It would have been fitting revenge if I'd screwed *his* head to the bar!

The teachers we didn't goad were those we liked and/or respected and I suppose the difference was that *they* respected *us* so there were no grounds for warfare. There was never any appalling misbehaviour in *their* lessons. And fortunately for me two of those – Fred Chapman and Norman Hunter – taught English. Another, Fred Dickinson, taught History and a fourth, Geoff Mott, taught Geography.

These were subjects at which I excelled and which I knew were relevant to the ambition I took to school with me every day; to become a journalist. I told myself that it what I was going to do every time I walked through those school gates. I wanted nothing else.

English periods were an absolute joy for me. I would analyse Dickens, Shakespeare and Austen with Fred Chapman, a kindly, elderly man nearing the end of his career. Despite his many years in the job he had retained an almost child-like enthusiasm for literature. Once, when he was reading aloud from Chaucer's *Canterbury Tales*, I was the only one in the respectfully silent classroom to burst into a fit of raucous laughter. For a second or two I thought I'd be in trouble for that, but instead Mr Chapman laughed along with me, nodding in unspoken approval of my understanding of the naughty nuance. Now *that's* teaching, I thought.

Norman Hunter, a young teacher in his first post, was my mentor. He took a special interest in me and my writing – coaching and coaxing me with great skill and patience. I lived for my lessons with Mr Chapman and Mr Hunter. How much I was later to owe to those men – my relationship with whom shone like a beacon out of the thick mists of destructive mayhem and obstructive tomfoolery which passed for the rest of my grammar school education.

When I left school to pursue my avowed intent to be a journalist, the reference provided by the Headmaster, Alf Exton, might just have got me a job sweeping the streets. This document, so vital to my future, so crucial to the rest of my life told potential employers merely that I was *unenergetic* and *ordinary* but that given some encouragement I might make a reasonable employee. This was desperately unfair. *Unenergetic?* I might not have been as gifted as Alan Ball, but they'd had to drag me off the football pitch; I'd been an enthusiastic ever-present in the cricket second XI as wicketkeeper and, according to the sports master in charge "the only boy in the second team who knows how to keep a straight bat" – and I'd been a keen and willing also-ran at athletics. In short, I'd loved school sport and joined in everything. *Ordinary?* By far the worst omission in this dreadful reference was to make no mention whatsoever of the fact that my performance in English Language, English Literature and History had consistently excelled through every one of my five years at that school. True, I'd been pretty useless at everything else, but surely, given that I had made well known to the school my consuming and passionate journalistic ambitions, that performance *plus* the writing ability which was so well recognised and applauded by the relevant teachers *had* to be mentioned?

It wasn't. None of it.

It was as if Alf Exton had got me mixed up with somebody else.

2.   In Spite of Alf

SO THERE I WAS, AGED 16, with a huge, burning ambition but no supporting evidence whatsoever from my school of the essential skills and energy required to even begin to fulfil it. Stuffed by Alf Exton, who barely even knew me. This was so bloody unfair.

I had taken my GCE 'O' Level exams and I was confident of securing the passes I needed to get me a start as a trainee journalist, but the so-called careers advice given to me before I left school had been to forget all about journalism "because very few trainees are taken on" and try for the civil service.

Bollocks! I was going to be a journalist. And *nothing* was going to stop me...

I had a Saturday and weekday evenings job for pocket money (delivering groceries on one of those inverted Penny Farthing bicycles with a huge basket at the front like those in the *Hovis* ads on TV) and that would have to keep me going for the time being. I was determined that I was not going to drift into some nothing job and prove that bugger Exton right about me. The lovely people with whom I worked in that *Irwin's* shop were well aware of my ambition, shared it with me and had a touching faith in me.

That big grocery emporium – the forerunner of the supermarket – was an absorbing place, smelling of delicious coffee and soap powder. Sides of bacon and giant hams hung on huge hooks from the ceiling. An extraordinary device resembling a mini cable car system sent the customer's money in a canister hurtling above your head across the shop to the cashier who would return the change and receipt by the same method.

The manager, Mr Evans (nobody ever knew his Christian name) was a pink and porcine little pudding of a man, shiny bald with thin wire spectacles on the end of his nose. He would seek to assist customers, carefully placing their weekly orders, to be sent round on my bike, by prompting constantly: *"Rice? Tapioca? Missus Ahhhhh...?"* We never heard any of the *"Missus Ahhhhh's"* actually ever *order* any rice or tapioca, so Mr Evans' repetitive reminders for them to do so were a mystery to all but himself.

To the rest of the shop's staff – the Assistant Manager Mr Bob Roberts, a trainee manager called David Williams (to whom – and how the poor lad must have hated it – I was consistently held up as some sort of paragon whose virtues he should aspire to attain) and an assortment of lovely ladies, I was the *Irwin's* protégé … a star in the making, just passing through and destined for something so much better than groceries. They were wonderful folk – a second family to me – and how I wish that I had taken them all a little less for granted.

Disgusted by my school reference, Bob Roberts wrote an alternative one for me on the back of a sheet of thin *Irwin's* paper used for listing your weekly order. It was unsolicited. It was a glowing reference. It was a lovely thought, bless him. He shoved it surreptitiously and self-consciously into my hand as I left work one night, avoiding eye contact as he whispered in his strong Welsh accent, "*Ere, boyo, 'ave this… And sod that bloody 'eadmaster!*"

What was Alf Exton's problem? I had a theory, shared by a couple of my schoolmates but almost certainly induced more by the chips on our shoulders than the facts, that he didn't like working-class kids. We reckoned he preferred the boys with posh parents.

That was probably nonsense, but the perception bugged us, and I had used the opportunity of a school essay competition to pen my first piece of campaigning journalism and get it off my chest. "*Prejudice Becomes Remorse*" was the ludicrously pretentious title of this piece, which was intended as a warning to Alf Exton. It was an entirely fictional account of how an un-named headmaster of a grammar school had persecuted a black pupil until the poor kid killed himself. Given that this was 1960, Oswestry had never had a black inhabitant and race issues nationally were, at most, only embryonic, it was, I suppose, an article ahead of its time!

English teacher Norman Hunter liked it, gave it literally 10 out of 10, declared it to be a sensitive piece of writing and submitted it forthwith for the essay competition, with the confident prediction that it was going to take some beating.

Alf Exton read and judged all the entries. Mine came nowhere. Had I touched a nerve? It gave me huge comfort to think so, but the truth was far more likely to have been that old Alf just had an aversion to precocious teenage boys with an unattractive penchant for bellowed invitations to voluptuous visiting female French teachers to take their knickers off in the classroom!

Undaunted, and armed with my *Irwin's* reference, I wrote to the local weekly newspaper, offering my talents. My excitement and anticipation reached fever pitch the day a letter arrived at No. 39 Coppice Drive, addressed to 'Mr Barrie Williams' and bearing the legend *OSWESTRY BORDER COUNTIES ADVERTISER* on the envelope. I was invited to make an appointment with the Editor, Mr Ted Parry-Jones, for an interview regarding the possibility of a position as a trainee journalist. This was the paper upon which my hero, Bobby Hawkins, had learned his trade before going off to Australia. Could this really be true? Was this letter *really* for me? I read it over and over and over again…

Mum was ecstatic and couldn't wait to tell the neighbours. Dad seemed much less impressed. No doubt he was just trying, like Alan Ball's dad, to keep my feet on the ground. No doubt he feared how badly rejection would hit me. This was, after all, he pointed out, just an interview, not a job. Dad was just being Dad. It was his way of looking out for me, of trying to make sure I didn't get hurt. But I was well pissed off with him at the time.

On the appointed day, with heart thumping in my chest, my best and only suit well pressed, my suede shoes brushed and my quiff well Brylcreemed, I walked into the Advertiser offices to meet Mr Ted Parry-Jones. The unique aroma of hot metal printing and fresh newsprint – so distinctive and later to become so addictive and evocative – permeated the old building called, splendidly, *Caxton House*, as I was led up the creaking wooden stairs to the Editor's office.

By now, my heart was about to burst with excitement and pride. I sat down in front of Mr Ted Parry-Jones, a neatly dressed, silver-haired man of late middle age, convinced that it was now only a matter of time before I became the next Bobby Hawkins. How proud mum was going to be – and all my friends at *Irwin's*.

"So why do you want to be a journalist?" asked Mr Ted Parry-Jones, for whom the word *conservatism* could have been invented.

I blurted out the ambition I had cherished since I was nine years old, namedropped my hero Bobby Hawkins, and told Mr Ted Parry-Jones how my English teachers all thought I was a very good writer. Then I waited anxiously for the dreaded request for a reference from school. Bob Roberts was a good man and spotless of character and reputation, but would Mr Ted Parry-Jones be sufficiently impressed by a reference from the Assistant Manager of *Irwin's?* Immediately a feeling of deep shame engulfed me. I was betraying my class and belittling a fine man like Bob Roberts. How *could* I do that? Bugger it! If he asks for a reference I'll give him Bob's with pride.

I need not have bothered. Mr Ted Parry-Jones suddenly launched into a lecture about Teddy Boys and how there would never be a place on the *Oswestry Border Counties Advertiser* for such delinquents.

Teddy Boy? Did he mean me?

I was no Teddy Boy! I'd seen plenty of them around town on a Saturday night and at the Plaza jive club. They wore big, black, brothel creeper shoes, pink luminous socks, drainpipe trousers, drape jackets with velvet collars and bootlace ties. Some of them carried cutthroat razors and knuckledusters (metal weapons with holes in which fingers were inserted so that a punch caused maximum injury) and fought bloody battles with the squaddies from the local National Service camp.

I was wearing the grey/green checked suit my mum had bought me from the mail order catalogue and for which she struggled so hard to keep up the weekly payments; the gleaming white shirt she had lovingly laundered and the neat, striped, green and white tie which had been part of my school uniform. Yes, my shoes were suede – also out of the catalogue – but they were light brown and conventional, not big black brothel creepers with four-inch soles. I did have a quiff in my hair and it was combed into a 'D.A.' (Duck's Arse) at the back, but this was just fashionable, like Elvis and Cliff Richard, not the symbol of a criminal lifestyle!

I was shocked into silence. The day I had dreamed of for nine years was here – and I was being dismissed as a Teddy Boy! The rest was just a blur but what was very clear was that there was going to be no job for me on the *Oswestry Border Counties Advertiser.*

I left the office of Mr Ted Parry-Jones with my life shattered, wiped the tears from my eyes and went to *Irwin's* to work.

"Stuffy old sod!" said Bob Roberts.

"We'll give him 'Teddy Boy' if he comes in 'ere," said the girls on the counter.

I couldn't bring myself to tell Mum and Dad that Mr Ted Parry-Jones thought I was a Teddy Boy. Mum would have been mortified in shame and Dad might well have gone round there and thumped him.

"Don't be too disappointed, love," said Mum. Dad said nothing but I felt he thought I was aiming too high and if you did that you fell and got hurt. But I soon recovered. I was still the budding star to my good friends at *Irwin's* and they were right... *no prickly old puritan was going to stop Barrie Williams becoming a journalist!*

My next target was the *Shrewsbury Chronicle.* Now, if applying for a post on the *Oswestry Border Counties Advertiser* had been aiming too high, the *Chronicle* – a much bigger weekly paper 18 miles up the road, serving Shropshire's county town and its environs – was off the scale.

"Nothing ventured..." I told Mum and Dad, as I sat down to write to the Editor.

"Christ! – They want me to go for an interview next week!"

What I had been convinced was going to be another rejection letter brought news I simply couldn't believe.

So it was off on Vagg's bus – the trusty old 1950s red and green charger, which coughed and spluttered up and down between Oswestry and Shrewsbury, calling at every village en route – to meet Mr Jack Cater, the Editor of the *Shrewsbury Chronicle*. I wore the same clothes and shoes. I had no choice. They were all I had. And the hairstyle? Bugger it. It looks good, the girls at *Irwin's* said – and not *all* editors can be puritans.

How right that was!

Mr Jack Cater, Editor of the *Shrewsbury Chronicle*, looked up from the pile of papers on his desk, pushed his spectacles down his nose and barked, "Now then, boy! – What the fuckin' 'ell are *you* doing 'ere?"

"I want to be a journalist, sir. You asked me here for an interview."

"Did I? Bloody 'ell! You're terribly thin, boy. Shouldn't you be wearing boxing gloves in bed?"

"NO sir!"

"You're lying to me, boy. It makes you go blind, you know." Then he roared with laughter. Head thrown back. Spectacles bouncing. Red braces struggling to contain his heaving chest. He was a big man, Jack Cater, in every sense.

Having tested my reaction to his somewhat unconventional opening, he got serious…

"Tell me precisely why you want to be a journalist."

I told him what I had told Mr Ted Parry-Jones. But this man *listened.* And his eyes twinkled. And I saw kindness in those eyes. Beneath his fierce, bluff, rude exterior there was a kindly man, I was sure. I was not the least bit frightened of him – even though, with his bark and bite, most 16-year-olds would have been terrified. I just felt immediately at ease with this great snorting bull of a man.

"So you can write, can you boy. How do I know?"

"Well, you don't, sir. But you will if you give me a chance."

"Have you passed your 'O' Levels?"

"I don't know yet, sir. I'm still waiting for the results."

"Will you pass your 'O' Levels?"

"Yes, sir. I will."

"Bloody good show, boy! Now, tell me all about this Barrie Williams…"

And I told him. Everything I could. And he listened. And his eyes twinkled. The more I talked, the more I relaxed. I talked and talked. I got to the bit about working at the shop and about my good friends at *Irwin's,* about how if the delivery orders were a bit slow I'd clean out the warehouse rather than stand around doing nothing and how they really appreciated that, especially Bob Roberts. And I pulled Bob Roberts' crumpled reference from my pocket and threw it on to Mr Jack Cater's desk and – yes – I was bloody proud of that reference, I told him.

He read it.

"This chap thinks you're a good lad. An all-round bloody good egg. Is he a good judge, this Bob Roberts?"

"Yes, sir. He is." (Oh, Christ – did that sound arrogant?)

"Now, when can you start?"

"Pardon?"

"Start, boy. Start. I'm giving you a fuckin' job!"

And so it was that in September 1961, Barrie Williams – council house kid, "failed" grammar school pupil, part-time *Irwin's* errand boy – became a journalist.

Me! A journalist. I'd done it! I'd bloody done it!

I walked into the offices of the *Shrewsbury Chronicle* – much bigger and much more imposing than those of the *Oswestry Border Counties Advertiser* but with that same unmistakable smell – to start work as an indentured trainee journalist for a weekly salary of £4.11s.6d. My intense feeling of pride, achievement and excitement is, to this day, indescribable.

3. Jack's the Lad

JACK CATER WAS A GENIUS. He had arrived at the *Shrewsbury Chronicle* via Fleet Street papers and the Manchester *Evening News*, the biggest evening paper outside London, of which he'd been News Editor. He had also been a Captain in the Army. Jack was a curious, eccentric mix of strict military bearing, sensitivity, deep intellect, common touch, erudition, gutter language and wicked sense of humour. He looked and sounded fearsome as he bellowed and barked from his office, which was under a permanent smog of thick smoke from the foul-smelling pipe that never left his mouth save for lunch – invariably a cheese and pickle sandwich from the *National Milk Bar* across the road.

The senior reporters – all much older than me – were absolutely terrified of him. And with good reason. He could reduce them to quivering wrecks with withering critiques of their work. They would jump with fright when he summoned them to his smelly inner sanctum by simply bawling their surname...

"Turner... Ford... Wilson... Get in 'ere. NOW!"

That shout easily permeated the closed door of his office and could probably be heard in the street. He could never remember the name of his new junior (either that or it was a game to him) and whenever he yelled for me it was for *"Boy"* or *"Marmaduke"*.

It was not for my journalistic contribution that I would be summoned to the smoke-filled torture chamber, but to bring him yet another mug of tea, or to go for a box of *Swan Vestas* matches, or to fetch his sandwich from the Milk Bar, or to run a piece of freshly edited copy to "the works".

On Thursdays – the day the *Chronicle* went to press – my job was to spend all day running back and forth to take copy and instructions to the printers. On Thursdays Jack was especially fierce, loud, irritable, foul-mouthed and unapproachable. It was also pay-day, so all the senior reporters would take refuge in the pub next door, leaving me alone with the fire-belching monster.

I would sit in a corner of his office while he edited the copy for the bulk of the paper, culminating in the biggest job of all – the front page. The pipe would be stoked and sucked even more violently, the smoke would be even more dense and acrid, and the air even more blue with filthy language than usual...

"Fuck me!" he would bawl at every bit of grammar, punctuation, spelling or writing style which offended him, which was most of it.

"Fuck me!" "Fuck my old boots!" "Fuckin' 'ell!" "Fuckin' Norah!"

Each expletive was accompanied by a vicious assault on the offending piece of paper with a violent thrust of his pencil and a puff of smoke from his pipe.

Every time his out-tray was full he'd shout: *"Marmaduke! Get this off to the works and be quick about it. Go boy! Go, fuckin' GO!"*

Every so often I would be sent racing to the pub to fetch one of the reporters with a *"Go and get me that silly bugger Turner"* or *"That bloody idiot Wilson"* and every time I appeared at the door of the pub I was the most unpopular human being in Shropshire.

Out of this Bedlam every Thursday emerged a newspaper of real quality, massively superior to its contemporaries; bright, lively, packed with good stories and controversial, well-written articles, including Jack's own column, which was every bit as irreverent and colourful as the man himself. It all stemmed from Jack. All the journalists were moulded and perfected in his image, and to his incredibly demanding specifications and standards.

On Thursdays I ran all day. In and out of Jack Cater's office, along the corridors, up and down the stairs to "the works", where men in khaki smocks sat at giant typewriters with six feet tall machinery attached to them, out of which would drop sticks of hot metal type with the carefully crafted words on them. 'Linotype Operators', these men were called, and a mere boy like me had to treat them with the utmost respect.

Beyond the linotype machines was "the stone" – huge metal slabs onto which the metal type, the picture blocks (metal impressions on wood) and the leads (column rules) would be hammered in to create a page by men in leather aprons – the compositors – who could read upside down and were to be even more respected and revered. Then the pages would go to "processing", from which would emerge paper-mache "formes" of the pages to go onto the press, where they would be attached to rollers and smothered in ink. Here the press hands would take over – men in dirty overalls who looked like miners because they were always covered in black ink – and with much rushing around, shouting and swearing, followed by ringing bells the monster press would grind into life, slowly at first, then ever faster and ever noisier until it was disgorging completed newspapers by the thousand.

Before any of those pages got onto the press they had to be "proofed up" for the Editor and on my return trips to Jack's office I would be laden with armfuls of proofs, still wet with ink. When Jack had carefully read each page proof I had to return them to "the works" with his big tick and signature in red ink (a code because only the Editor was allowed to use red ink) to testify that the page was safe, approved, and ready to go. Simultaneously, "blacks" – carbon copies of the journalists' stories – had to be taken to 'the Readers', stern-faced men and women who read every word to make sure that not even the Editor had missed a spelling, grammar, punctuation, factual or geographical error.

Sitting incongruously among the middle-aged and elderly readers, with their hunched shoulders and spectacles on ribbons around their necks, in the library-like silence and cathedral atmosphere of the Readers' Room, was Shirley – a gorgeous, leggy girl in her late teens with a Helen Shapiro hair-do and skimpy, ribbed, pastel-coloured jumpers accentuating perky breasts.

I had a monumental teenage crush on Shirley. While waiting for the kettle to boil in the newsroom I would fix a love-struck gaze on her through the glass partition into the Readers' Room, hoping that she would notice and respond.

Quite how she was supposed to react in these circumstances, I never really knew. Perhaps she would jump from the high stool around which she curled those sensational legs, come rushing into the newsroom, knock the giant teapot from my hands and cry, "Take me – I'm yours!"

That never happened. But on Valentine's Day I received a card in the internal office mail. It read: "*Though friends we two must be, I'm fond of you I will agree. Be My Valentine*" It was Shirley's handwriting. I knew it so well. Absolutely no mistake. Joy of joys!

"I'm in love…" I confided to one of the senior reporters, Tim Wilson, when I took him his tea "… with Shirley from Readers."

"You bloody fool!" said Tim, "She's engaged to a bloody big farmer from Dorrington. He plays rugby for Shrewsbury. He's built like a brick shithouse and can be a nasty bugger if he's riled."

I never stared into the Readers' Room again.

As the clock struck five on Thursday evenings, Jack Cater's in-tray would suddenly be empty. He'd sit back in his enormous chair, twang his red braces, heave a huge sigh of relief, put his feet up on his desk, re-light his pipe for the umpteenth time, and hurl a silver coin in my direction. It was half a crown (two shillings and sixpence), always half a crown.

"Ere, boy. Take this and fuck off – and don't go spending it on dirty women."

Dirty women? Some chance! Even if a 16-year-old had known where to find such a commodity in Shrewsbury, I was totally exhausted. I would drag my weary limbs on to the Midland Red bus, go back to my digs, have a bath to remove the printers' ink that seemed to block every pore, have a cup of tea – and crash out.

Bobby Hawkins never told me there'd be days like these!

When he was in a good mood, Jack would sing Gilbert and Sullivan at an intolerable decibel level. He had a voice like a broken cement mixer but he was word perfect. His command of G & S lyrics was phenomenal. If the strains of *"A wandering minstrel, I, a thing of rags and patches"* or *"To make the punishment fit the crime, the punishment fit the crime"* or any one of dozens of others in his extraordinary repertoire were emanating from the fog-bound inner sanctum it was a signal to the senior reporters that it was reasonably safe to knock and enter and ask for a day off or even a pay rise.

Sometimes, without warning, he would burst from his office, leap like a 16-stone ballerina into the newsroom and deliver a virtuoso Gilbert and Sullivan performance for several minutes before looking straight at me with those twinkling eyes and demanding, *"Your turn Marmaduke – Sing up boy!"*

Gilbert and Sullivan aside, Jack's other consuming interest, apart from his children, on whom he doted, was fine art. This big, boisterous, boorish man with a vocabulary like a sewer and the overbearing manner of a despotic military dictator, was also warm, caring, kind, articulate, musical, deeply artistic and clever.

I loved him. And I never met anyone who was anything even remotely like him.

At weekends I would go home to Oswestry and over illegal pints of bitter my pals – like me, all under 18 – would quiz me about being a reporter. They imagined it to be glamorous, exciting and romantic. I said nothing to correct the misconception... but if they could have seen me on Thursdays!

Over the rest of the week I was making decent progress. In the firm but kindly custody of Percy Kaye, the Chief Sub-Editor, I was learning well the basics of my chosen trade.

First thing on Monday mornings I had to call in person on all the undertakers of Shrewsbury – a suitably lugubrious bunch of Uriah Heap type characters – to find out who had died. Then I had to visit the homes of all the deceased to question widows or widowers. Career details, education, personal achievement, military service, sporting interests, hobbies, surviving relatives, ages of children... all had to be included in the obituaries. And God help you if you got anything wrong. A mistake in an obituary report brought the combined wrath of the deceased's relatives, the undertakers and Percy Kaye down on your hapless young head and if it was a particularly serious error you suffered the ultimate sanction of being reported to Jack Cater – a fate worse than the deaths upon which you were reporting! If the deceased was of even moderate local importance you then had to attend the funeral at which your task was to collect the name and relevance of every mourner and to say who they were also representing when that was appropriate. Miss out a mourner from your report, or spell a name wrongly, or fail to mention who they were "also representing" and your head was on the block.

I had also to call on local churches, schools, clubs and organisations, talking to vicars, head teachers, secretaries and events organisers – all for the purpose of collating the *pot pourri* of parochial paragraphs which filled the pages of run of the mill "news" – all to be avidly consumed by readers of the *Chronicle*.

I learned very early the essential importance of getting *everything* right and I was tutored in that discipline by Percy Kaye, an elderly silver-haired Lancastrian – a gentleman and a *gentle* man – who was the custodian of this less dramatic but absolutely essential part of the newspaper. Percy would guide, nurture, cajole and sometimes chastise me. He was a stickler for 100 per cent accuracy, propriety and polite good conduct.

It was from Percy that I learned the hard way that most fundamental of journalistic disciplines… *never to assume.*

At the end of one exceptionally long, exhausting day's work I dropped my last piece of copy – an obituary report – in Percy's in-tray and waited for the obligatory clearance that it was OK and I could, at last, knock off and go home to my digs for supper. I was dog tired. And I was hungry.

"How are you spelling Davies?" asked Percy.

"D-A-V-I-E-S" I replied.

"Did you check that?"

"Well, no – but."

"No buts, lad. Supposing it's D-A-V-I-S? Get back to them and check it properly."

The deceased's family lived some three miles from the office. Juniors were not allowed to use telephones (indeed, *seniors* were strongly discouraged from doing so except in emergencies and on Thursdays) and even so, telephones were by no means to be found in every home. So all your calls had to be made using the buses, or on foot. You claimed your bus fares back on expenses, but that process took a week. This was a Wednesday evening, the day before payday. And I was skint. Penniless. Checking my spelling of "Davies" meant a six-mile trek – not to mention the acute embarrassment of having to knock on the door of the grieving family for a second time and admit that I had failed to check my spelling.

And it *had* been D-A-V-I-E-S all along!

But the lesson was well and truly learned – and never forgotten.

Percy's son Peter was the *Chronicle's* Sports Editor – dark, brooding, muscular and handsome, all the women in the office wanted Peter's body and his babies. Mother Kaye would send Percy and Peter off to work every morning with a peck on the cheek and a tin box full of tasty Lancashire cheese sandwiches, made with crusty home-baked bread. Occasionally, Percy or Peter would offer me one of those sandwiches. I can taste them to this day. *Delicious!* I would strive to find some reason to visit Percy's desk with a query about my work just as he'd opened up the tin box...

"Those butties look very nice, Mr Kaye."

"Would you like one, lad?"

"Ooh, yes please!"

No shame. No shame at all.

Percy Kaye – gradually and with contrived grudging – came to the conclusion that I was a good enough lad, that I was doing OK and that I might just make a journalist one day. It was the equivalent of high praise and when he told Jack Cater so in my presence one day I waited with immense pride for the great man's agreement and confirmation. Jack said: "There's bugger all of you, boy! Are you wearing those boxing gloves?"

With Percy's sage advice on how best to handle the situation, I went to Sundorne Avenue in Harlescott to see a Mr and Mrs Morris in order to prepare an obituary report on a girl of 16 – the same age as me. God only knows what an ordeal it must have been for that poor dead girl's mother and father to talk to just a slip of a lad about something so bloody tragic and life shattering as the death, from illness, of their only child. But talk they did.

I took even more care than usual over that obituary which, because it was the death of one so young, had been allocated more space than the others. I had been so moved by the whole experience and I was really anxious not to let that lovely family down. After it had been published in the paper the girl's mother wrote to the Editor to say: *"My sincere thanks to your young reporter Mr Barrie Williams for his nice concise way in which he wrote my daughter's obituary report. It was indeed a tribute to her memory."*

Percy was pleased.

"You'll make a journalist, lad," he told me.

In next to no time after that I was "flying". Released from Percy's custody and Jack's Thursdays (there was a new "Marmaduke" now, poor little bugger) I came under the direction of the News Editor, Bryan Fogg. A striking, urbane, blond man in his early 30s, Bryan was impeccably well-dressed – the legacy of his time on *Tailor & Cutter* magazine in London – and seemed to me to be on another planet of knowledge, experience and maturity. He had a mind as neat and well ordered as his clothing and he ran a newsroom to match.

With Bryan's meticulous guidance I was now trusted with reporting courts and council committee meetings and doing off-diary stories – good, mostly human interest stuff, which did not come from the daily round of institutionalised news gathering and particularly rewarding if you dug it out yourself.

I got to do the police calls... a vitally important process in which reporters from all the newspapers and agencies in and around Shrewsbury descended on Shropshire Police HQ every morning to be briefed by the genial Inspector Peter Minshall on all the crime, accidents, sudden deaths and mixed mayhem from the night before. This *really* meant that I had "arrived" – and I was only 17.

I was so proud. But something was wrong. I was being shunned by most of the other reporters. Ignored. Ostracised.

Why? What could make them treat a 17-year-old kid like that?

The answer was that in 1956 there had been a national strike over a NUJ (National Union of Journalists) pay claim. Journalists on some newspapers – and the *Shrewsbury Chronicle* had been one of them – had broken the strike call and carried on working. The newspaper and all of its journalists had been "blacked" by the NUJ and its supporters ever since.

Thus, a teenager who had been running around the school playground in short trousers at the time of the dispute and could not be expected to know, let alone understand anything about it, could be "sent to Coventry" for the "crime" of working for that paper.

The senior reporters on the *Chronicle* were a tough, thick-skinned bunch (they had to be, working for Jack Cater!) and they'd seen off the vicious victimisation by treating it with the utmost contempt, but anybody new on the scene got the full treatment. I had heard the senior blokes talking about it once or twice, but I'd given it no thought and I certainly wasn't prepared for the intensity of it.

It was cruel and thoroughly unpleasant. And it hurt and upset me to the point that while I did my very best to hide it, I was often close to tears. One day, I left my notebook on the court reporters' bench while I nipped out to take a break from a long, complicated case to find upon my return the words *Black Bertie* scrawled in huge capital letters all over my carefully taken notes, rendering them useless and my court report buggered. There was absolutely *no* chance of any of them allowing me to use *their* notes, even if I'd been daft enough to ask.

Childish. Nasty. And these were grown men.

It was my introduction to the trade unions that were to dominate the newspaper industry for the next two decades.

Gradually, like the rest of the *Chronicle* reporters, I saw it off by making it appear that I didn't give a damn, toughing it out, giving as good as I got and laughing in the faces of the bullies. Although it was the very last thing they had sought to achieve, they actually did me a huge favour by thickening my very thin, young skin.

There were two very notable exceptions among those NUJ reporters – Doug Morris, who worked in the Shrewsbury office of the Wolverhampton *Express & Star* and Keith Parker from the *Wellington Journal*. Their refusal to be part of the callous blackballing of a 17-year-old boy meant so much to me, much more than either of them realised. Keith was always friendly and helpful and Doug, in particular, would go out of his way to make a point of his defiance, offering me a lift from police calls in his car.

My career path was to cross those of Doug and Keith many times in later years and we are pals to this day. Keith rose, through the editorship, to become Managing Director of the *Wolverhampton Express & Star* group – about as high as it gets in the regional newspaper industry. Doug retired as Assistant Editor of the *Nottingham Evening Post*.

The scrapbook of Barrie Williams' by-lined stories that my mum was keeping was growing more impressive by the week. Soon I was producing regular front-page splashes and features – the non-hard-news content which only those who could write, as opposed to merely reporting, got to do.

Sent to cover the 'topping out' ceremony of Shrewsbury's new General Market Hall, I chose not to produce a straight, boring account of the mayoral proceedings like everybody else but to describe instead the absurd mandatory ascent by ladder and scaffolding to the top of the 220-foot tower by a bunch of quaking, unfit, inappropriately-clad journalists, hanging on to each other for grim life and pretending not to be scared shitless. It was so funny that it cried out to be described in humorous and (only slightly!) exaggerated terms and it offered the irresistible added incentive of an opportunity for me to take the piss out of the NUJ blockheads.

My copy had been sent through to Jack Cater and I was enjoying a cigarette and that special feeling journalists get when they know they've written a bloody good piece when from inside the smoke-filled sanctum came a burst of raucous laughter.

"Williams – get in 'ere!"

"Yes, Mr Cater."

"This is only fuckin' brilliant, boy! You can write! You can really fuckin' write!"

I could not have felt more elated if I'd been told I had won a million pounds.

The Beatles happened so quickly that the phenomenon of completely new music and fashion they inspired had arrived before most people over 30 had even heard of them. I went to see Jack Cater...

"This is just amazing," I told him, "It's not just happening in Liverpool – there are groups springing up all over Shropshire and thousands of kids in our county are going wild."

"Let's have it, then," said Jack.

The result was a two-page spread with pictures of John, Paul, George and Ringo and their Salopian imitators doing the *Yeah, Yeah, Yeah* bit in front of gyrating Shropshire lads and lasses from Oswestry to Ironbridge. Better still, Jack was so impressed that he decided to make my story the front page splash as well.

This was incredibly racy stuff for a stately county weekly like the *Chronicle* to publish so prominently, but Jack loved to shock people.

Out of that grew *TEENBEAT* – my own weekly page of news, views, record and theatre reviews and pictures of the Merseybeat-led revolution in popular music and culture, which was as immense in Shropshire as it was everywhere else.

The bands and solo artists appearing on one-night-stand tours at Shrewsbury's Music Hall and Granada Theatre were a Who's Who of the phenomenon – and I got to interview them all. The Rolling Stones, The Hollies, The Dave Clark Five, The Fortunes, The Kinks, Gerry and the Pacemakers, Wayne Fontana and The Mindbenders, Herman's Hermits, The Searchers, Freddie and the Dreamers, Dave Berry, Sandie Shaw, Marianne Faithful, Cilla Black – the list of early 60s stars I met and interviewed was endless, though sadly it never included The Beatles themselves.

Often, after my interviews had been completed in unbearably hot, stuffy, sweat and smoke filled dressing rooms, the stars would seek the benefit of my local knowledge to discover where best they could go for a decent meal without being mobbed by the crowds of screaming girls who besieged the theatres. I obliged – and was frequently invited to join them. And every Friday in the *Chronicle's*

TEENBEAT section, which was astonishingly innovative for a local newspaper, Barrie Williams would bask in their reflected glory.

Suddenly, my clothes were Carnaby Street inspired and my Merseybeat hairstyle would have sent old Ted Parry-Jones hurtling in deep shock to an early grave! I was Shrewsbury's chronicler of the beat scene and as such enjoyed a vicarious local "stardom" of my own. I got to go free to all the gigs, more often than not with a cute "bird" on my arm for – just as suddenly – I was popular like never before with the fairer sex of this fair town.

On one such visit to the Music Hall I was on the lookout for the best six girls (best looking, best dressed, best dancers) for a *TEENBEAT* competition I was running with one of the record companies. One of our chosen six was a girl from Nesscliffe, a little village between Oswestry and Shrewsbury. She had fabulous eyes, incredible bone structure, stunning legs and gorgeous, shiny hair. Like a beautiful little doll. She was exquisite. Considerably younger than me – she was still in school – but she had the serenity of a lovely older woman and an untouchable allure.

I took down her name and address for the picture caption... *Pauline Stealey, Bank View, Nesscliffe.* In stark contrast to all the others, this girl was singularly under-impressed with my "scribe to the stars" reputation and credentials.

"Oh, really," she said, with genuine indifference, as I introduced myself and offered the revelation that, "I can get you in anywhere."

The patter was pointless. No effect whatsoever. She was just not interested in me and only mildly curious about the competition for which I had chosen her. She was clearly different... and so lovely.

I was smitten.

"One day," I told myself. "One day..."

Unable to get her out of my mind, I peeled Pauline Stealey's picture off the *TEENBEAT* page and put it in my wallet.

As a consequence of another 60s revolution you now *could* peel pictures off pages after they'd been printed, because the old 'hot metal' process had been replaced by the cut-and-paste of clean, modern Web Offset printing. The quality of reproduction was vastly improved, especially the photographs, which now seemed to jump from the pages. The old hot metal stone had been replaced by lines of drawing boards, on which those wonderfully skilled compositors now just put wax on the back of strips of photographic paper and rolled them onto the page. The foundry in which the metal had been melted down and re-cycled had gone, so had those huge linotype machines. This was quieter, cleaner and produced a much clearer newspaper, but those proud, skilled men now looked like sad wriggling fish out of water, their skills – truth to tell – no longer necessary but their jobs retained through a combination of management sympathy and union insistence. Another victim of this printing revolution was that addictive, evocative smell. Gone forever. Replaced, now by the pong of hot, melted wax.

The proprietor of the *Chronicle*, Morley Tonkin – an ugly, beached whale of a man with enormous ears – seemed to me to be terminally grumpy, but along with Woodrow Wyatt he was an early UK pioneer of modern printing methods. Like other visionaries who followed these men in the regional newspaper industry, they were light years ahead of their contemporaries in Fleet Street in identifying and pursuing truly radical new processes.

While all that was going on, my formal journalistic training – via day release every Friday at Birmingham College of Commerce – was nearing completion. For all Jack Cater ever knew I might not even have obtained my statutory 'O' Levels, because he never asked, but I had. And now I had also studied Law, British Institutions, Current Affairs and 'A' Level English at Birmingham and the dreaded obligatory Shorthand at a local Shrewsbury night school – the only male in a class full of gauche, giggling girls who wanted to be secretaries – and me a showbiz personality!

I had been indentured (apprenticed) to the *Shrewsbury Chronicle* for three years – the time allotted formally for me to complete my on-the-job training and fulfil all the academic requirements of qualification through the *National Council for the Training of Journalists*. Now, at the age of 19, I was fully and formally a senior reporter.

My three years at the *Chronicle* seemed at once to have been a lifetime and the mere blinking of an eye. That skinny, bright-eyed, hopelessly naïve 16-year-old boy had both metamorphosed and degenerated into a wild-living, hard-drinking, heavy-smoking but (though I said it myself, and why shouldn't I?) bloody good all round journalist, writing more front page splashes than anybody else on the paper, digging out exclusives, writing features – even covering football matches.

Ink was in my blood now.

And it was time to move on…

Jack Cater, to whom I was deeply indebted for the rest of my life, gave me a reference to help me make my way in the tough journalistic world into which he had delivered me. It read:

> "Barrie Williams came to the *Shrewsbury Chronicle* as a junior reporter at the age of 16. From the start he rapidly developed into a first class young reporter and news feature writer. He quickly proved that

he was a natural so far as news sense is concerned and he has since gone on to become an outstandingly good and versatile journalist. He has a lively and inquiring mind and can make it work. He can produce ideas that lead to lively and compelling news stories. You can tell a Barrie Williams hard news or feature story by the freshness and crispness of the writing, the sure grasp of the essentials and the inclusion of those telling little details which lift a piece out of the ordinary run of reportage and make of it an attractive piece of journalism.

I should like to add a word about his very pleasing personality generally. This, coupled with recognition of his journalistic ability, has secured for him innumerable friends and a host of influential contacts. It gives me pleasure to wish him the best of good luck in his future career and to commend him for what he is to any Editor who may employ him in the future – a thoroughly competent journalist full of drive and initiative."

Now then, Alf Exton – *THAT's* a bloody reference!

4.   Spit and Polish

ERIC MACKERETH WAS EVERYTHING lesser men (and that was virtually the entire male population of Shrewsbury!) hated. Astonishingly good looking, very successful, blond, athletic, captain of Shrewsbury Rugby Club and a minor counties' fast bowler for Shropshire. If that were not quite enough, he was rich, drove a brand new Jaguar, owned a big house in an exclusive suburb of the town, was married to Margaret, a stunning, statuesque blonde beauty from the Welsh borders, and had two lovely children, a boy and a girl – both blond(e) of course.

Mr Bloody Perfect… and still only 28!

Eric owned a news agency serving Shropshire, Herefordshire and Mid-Wales for the popular national newspapers, TV and radio. He started the agency after leaving the *Daily Express*, on which he had been a brilliant reporter. The mere mortals of the local papers knew that if *Eric Mackereth* turned up on a job it must be a bloody big one.

Eric's partner – just as envied, considerably older but every bit as dashing and charismatic, and richer still, with an even more expensive Jaguar, was John Rea. John had been a very highly-rated photographer on the *Daily Express*. He provided the Fleet Street standard pictures to go with Eric's words. John also owned a plush, trendy and hugely successful photographic studio (staffed by fabulous, feisty, fashionable girls) alongside which, in Shrewsbury's scenic Tudor heart, was Eric's office.

Not to be outdone by his partner, Eric was expanding. His agency was making a great deal of money but suddenly, in the soaraway sixties, there was a lot more to be made out of freelance public relations – and with his abundant charm and panache there was nobody in Shropshire better suited to exploit that opportunity than Eric. His plan was to build up a PR company – to be called *Impact Information* – while hiring a sharp young journalist to look after the news side of the business.

He called me at the *Chronicle*.

"Barrie. You know where we are. Come round and have a natter."

Soon afterwards I was telling dear Jack Cater, "I owe you and the *Chronicle* so much, Mr Cater, but this is a great opportunity for me and I really feel…"

"Of course it's a great opportunity for you lad! Stop fucking about. Get back round there sharpish and tell Mackereth you'll take it. And make sure the bugger pays you what you're worth!"

"Twenty quid a week – plus bonus," said Eric.

Just three years earlier I had started on less than five quid a week.

The bugger seemed to be paying me well enough. It was a deal.

As I pondered my new salary I recalled Alf Exton telling us – a motley crew of fifth formers for whom he held out little hope:

"When you're earning *a thousand pounds a year* you'll be able to say you've made it."

We could tell by his sarcastic tone that he didn't think any of us had a cat in hell's chance of doing it.

Well, up yours, Alf! I thought to myself. *It's taken me next to no time – and I'm only nineteen!*

Eric's smart little office was such a contrast to the clatter and clutter, old furniture and even older typewriters of the *Chronicle* newsroom. A devout non-smoker at a time when just about everybody did, Eric's *Impact House* was pristine and polished – sparkling and smelling of expensive carpet and freshly percolated posh coffee from a machine which made our old 1940s Army-issue giant green teapot look positively prehistoric.

Eric sat behind a grand modern desk in the middle of the room, the new addition *"My reporter, Barrie Williams"* at a much smaller one, alongside and his prim, proper and ultra-efficient secretary Cynthia in the corner.

This was truly a different world; slick, sophisticated and first-class. If only Mum could see the office I was working in now!

Now, when a story was ordered rather than just offered, I was able to say with as much validity as pride when introducing myself: "I'm from the *Daily Mail* or the *Daily Mirror;* the *Daily Express*, the *Daily Herald* or the *Daily Sketch;* the *Sunday Express*, the *News of The World* or *The People;* the *BBC* or *ITV* – for we worked for them all.

Now I stood ten feet taller. Now, those nasty NUJ buggers who used to blackball me were as jealous as hell. Now, the mere mortals of the local papers knew that if *Barrie Williams* turned up on a job it must be a bloody big one!

Jack Cater had dug me out of our council house, made a journalist and a young *man* of me. Eric was to polish me until I shone as brightly as any reporter on any national newspaper. I thought my copy was as good as it got on the *Chronicle*. I was wrong. For the nationals, it had to be even crisper, shorter and more dynamic. Offering stories to the busy Manchester offices of the popular nationals meant that you had to grab and hold the newsdesk's attention and interest with your *first* paragraph – or it went straight onto the spike. This was excellent discipline and skill to acquire, because the same thing goes for the reader... if you hook 'em in Paragraph One they'll stay with you. If you don't, they might not.

Before your copy got to the newsdesk, however, it had to run the gauntlet of the copy takers – ranks of blunt Northern men to whom you dictated your stories over the telephone. No-one would dare to suggest that these fellows were merely copy typists. Like the linotype operators and stone hands of the hot metal production processes, these chaps had to be treated with the utmost respect and were worthy of the highest admiration. The phenomenal speed of their typing was exceeded only by that of their wit – and they were never short of wry observations on your work as you read it over to them.

Sometimes they would tell you, just as you were in mid and fully optimistic flow, "*This'll never make it in a month of bloody Sundays!*"

And they were never wrong.

Here I was also to learn and perfect the freelance art of making something out of nothing or, as Eric and John called it, *applying a bit of "top spin"*. Living, literally, off your journalistic wits, as this highly successful duo did, it was never enough to rely merely on natural breaking news. "Top spin" brought in the steady money, while the murders, the rapes, the bank robberies, the fires, the train crashes, etc, came as a bonus. That way, you were not so much a hostage to fortune.

The "top spin" process began by acquiring *every* local newspaper – no matter how small and seemingly inconsequential – circulating in Shropshire, Herefordshire and Mid-Wales and that was a hell of a lot of newspapers! There were dozens of them to be read from cover to cover every day. Every item on every page – including all the classified advertisements – read with a pair of scissors, a clean sheet of A4 paper and a paste pot at the ready.

Any local story which had the potential for a bit of "top spin" would be snipped out and pasted onto a piece of paper, with notes on how to achieve the spin written carefully alongside, then dropped into an in-tray to await the visit, at 9. 30am sharp – never a minute either side – of John Rea. Over cups of Cynthia's posh coffee and several of Eric's very best shortbread biscuits, John and I would go through the pile of cuttings from the in-tray and identify which stories might be worthy of his own extremely valuable and expensive time as well as my own. The ideas would then be prioritised and the working day would begin at around 10. 45am (most of the nationals would take copy up to 10pm, so there was plenty of time to perfect the "top spin"). Then it would be off out in John's gleaming

Jaguar, if there was a picture with the job, or on my £25 Vespa motor scooter if there wasn't, to secure the day's earnings.

So what was "top spin" and how did it work?

EXAMPLE: Buried away in the *Oswestry Border Counties Advertiser* (Up yours, Ted Parry-Jones!) a story told how a little old lady living in Ellesmere had been housekeeper to French President General Charles De Gaulle when he was evacuated and tucked away out of harm's way of the Germans occupying his country during the war.

At that time, De Gaulle was refusing stubbornly to sanction Britain's entry into the European Common Market and we were desperate (believe it or not!) to get in there. De Gaulle's infamous "*Non, Non, Non*" had become a national catchphrase and with his long nose and silly hat he had become a cartoonist's dream.

His obduracy was legend.

So… supposing we could persuade Mrs Ex-Housekeeper to write to General De Gaulle, pleading with him to repay Britain for the sanctuary we had given him during the war by relenting and letting us in to the Common Market?

Off I go to see little old lady. She's lovely.

Would she write to the President?

"Well, yes dear – if you think it might do some good…"

I'm on a roll. But John's not so happy. He leans across for a word in my ear.

"It's not quite there yet. We need a bit more."

Sudden inspiration…

"When you used to cook for the President, what was his favourite dish?"

"I really can't remember any particular dish, dear, but he was very partial to my home-made pickled beetroot."

"Do you have any?"

"Lord, no. I haven't made any for years."

No problem. A quick trip to the local corner shop, swift purchase of a jar of pickled beetroot, nifty removal of the manufacturers' label with steam from the old lady's kettle. Lovely picture of smiling old lady holding "her" jar of "home-made" pickled beetroot in one hand and "her" letter to De Gaulle in the other…

Dear President De Gaulle,

Remember how fond you were of my home made pickled beetroot when I looked after you during the war? Well, here's a jar of it sent with my love to remind you how kind we all were to you when you needed us most.

Now it's our turn to need YOU. Please stop being beastly to Britain and let us in to the Common Market.

Jar of beetroot and old lady's letter safely posted off to the President in Paris; story written; pictures sent. Next morning – *Bingo!* Page leads in every paper and lots of lovely lolly made.

And the pay day was repeated when the lady later phoned me, thrilled to bits, to say that she had received a reply from De Gaulle, who said he remembered her and her pickled beetroot with great fondness and had so enjoyed the jar she had sent him!

No mention of the Common Market, though.

"Lying old bugger!" said John... as if *we* had caught *him* out in some wicked act of subterfuge!

EXAMPLE: Out for lunch with John in the Granada Theatre restaurant I order bacon, egg, sausage and chips. When it arrives there's only *one* sausage – and I'm very hungry, so, I ask the waitress for another sausage and she duly obliges.

But when the bill comes, we've been charged an *extra* 1s 6d ... for *one* sausage! This is daylight robbery! Our protests at the till fall on totally unapologetic ears.

"That's what we're told to do, sir and that's that."

Next morning over coffee John and I are still incensed.

"That was so outrageous it's worth a story," he said.

True. But they'll not be interested without some *top spin*...

This gross exploitation of the humble banger must be brought to the attention of the Government at the highest level, we resolved. We'll send them a one and sixpenny sausage with a letter of complaint. But how?

Half an hour later I'm on the phone to headline-loving local Liberal Councillor Basil Baldwin.

"Do you fancy lunch at the Granada Theatre restaurant, Bas?"

"Rather!"

"Good. Now, here's what we're doing..."

In the whole of the next morning's popular national press, under a variety of headlines such as the *Daily Sketch's* **TO BROWN BY POST – A DEAR SAUSAGE** the following story appeared:

> COUNCILLOR BASIL BALDWIN is very fond of sausages. And yesterday he decided to have two with his bacon, egg and chips at a restaurant.
>
> But when he was told that an extra sausage would cost him 1s 6d he was angry. So angry that, instead of eating it, he wrapped it up and posted it to Mr George Brown, the Economic Affairs Minister.

With it, Councillor Baldwin, of Shrewsbury, enclosed a letter telling Mr Brown to place the sausage before the Prices and Incomes Board.

Councillor Baldwin's letter added:

"Just imagine my surprise to learn that the price of the hitherto lowly sausage rockets to no less than 18d when grilled and carefully put on a plate to make a meal just that little bit more substantial.

"On what can we blame its introduction into the expense account class?

"Is it the seamen's strike?

"Is it Jim Callaghan's unfortunate payroll tax?

"Is it deliberate sabotage on the part of the caterers who dislike your prices and incomes policy?"

Councillor Baldwin said later:

"People in Shrewsbury are conditioned to high prices but 1s 6d is ridiculous. This size retails at 3s 3d a lb. This means that one sausage would cost the caterer 4d – 300 per cent profit."

The restaurant manageress Mrs Frances Davenport said: "All the prices are fixed by our head office in London."

The story was accompanied by John's splendid picture of the obliging Basil holding the offending sausage on a fork (we'd smuggled it out of the restaurant in my pocket) and looking at in absolute disgust.

Lots more dosh for Eric and John, some of which was spent on buying me a slap-up meal… at the Granada Theatre restaurant!

EXAMPLE: On Page 36 of the *Wellington Journal* a little story about an old lady of 78 who had failed her test on her tiny moped for the umpteenth time contains a gem of a quote just crying out for *top spin*:

"I don't care, anyway," she had said. "I'm fed up with the moped. *I want something bigger.*"

In Shrewsbury were to be found the motorcycle showrooms of one Fron Purslow, former racing champion and a mate of Eric's, who had dreamy 750cc super bikes for sale.

"Lend us a bike for a picture, Fron."

"What's the story?"

"Just a bit of fun. There's this old dear says she wants a bigger bike – at 78 years old! We'll put her in leathers and a skid lid and sit her on a really big bike. Great picture, Fron. What do you think?"

"OK, let's do it. But she must only *sit* on it, mind…"

So, we call on the old dear at her little terraced cottage in the countryside just outside town.

"We're going to take you into Shrewsbury to Fron Purslow's – get a nice picture of you on a big bike – just for a bit of fun. OK?"

"Oooh, yes please! Can we call at our Vera's on the way back?"

"Course we can – the very least we can do."

In a convenient car park, Grannie Nell is kitted out in full racing leathers and a magnificent gleaming crash helmet. Carefully, I lift her onto a huge motorbike. John and I had decided that just *sitting* on the bike would be no good. Too static. We'd let her move just a tiny bit. And I would make sure she stayed safe...

"Now on the photographer's signal I want you to let the clutch out *very slowly* and twist the throttle *ever so gently*. OK? Just move off *really, really slowly*. I've got hold of you, but remember this is *much, much more powerful* than your moped, so be *very, very gentle...*"

Down comes John Rea's hand... Out goes the clutch... Twist goes the throttle... Except none of it is gentle! Anything but.

The turn of the wrinkled little wrist on the ultra sensitive throttle is far too much. The release of the clutch is far too sudden. Grannie Nell is airborne. And I'm hanging grimly on to her and her bike.

John's shouting: "Great! Great! That's great!"

When the engine inevitably stalls and the monster bike stops roaring, the old dear is just fine. Calm as you like. Not the slightest bit concerned.

"That was lovely," she says, "Thank you ever so much!"

Me? I'm a quivering nervous wreck!

Back – via her Vera's – to the darkroom and John is delighted.

"I'll just remove this twat on the back of her bike and we'll be in business," he said.

Next morning. Marvellous. Grannie Nell's made it really big. Great pictures of our 78-year-old "*in high speed action on a racing super bike*" and thanks to John's picture editing dexterity "the twat on the back" has become her slipstream.

Another big pay day.

And so it went on. And on...

A page lead (the main story on a page) would yield between £90 and £120 per paper for the words alone. John would never say how much he got. Whenever he was asked he would just flash his endearingly charming smile and say, "Enough." But I reckoned it would have been a minimum of £50 per picture and with his quality and reputation John was not a man to deal in minimums.

This was 1965. This was big money. And it was a bad week if we didn't get at least two page leads in every popular national paper. No wonder Eric and John drove big brand new Jags.

Me? I just had my old motor scooter.

It wasn't all "top spin" by any means. There were plenty of real hard news stories to be done and, then, only the biggest and best.

And sports stories, too – which I enjoyed immensely. And yet... as the novelty began to wear off, I felt there was something vaguely unsatisfying about this plum job.

I had grown close to John Rea and I once confided in him when we were out "top spinning" together that I was sometimes a bit uncomfortable with the process. John had his own pragmatic and inarguable way of rationalising that concern.

"Look, mate," he said. "You're just helping it to *happen*, just giving it a bit of *polish*. Right?"

The logic was faultless. But I was a precious young thing and I couldn't help thinking that the principle was somewhat less so. Then there was the money. Twenty quid a week had seemed a fortune when I joined him, but more than a year later I knew just how much I had made for Eric. I was often covering my £20 in not much more than an hour's work, and I was on call seven days and seven nights a week. The promised bonus had never been paid, but I was too proud to challenge Eric about it. Eric had sharpened me up all right. No longer was I the grateful kid just so privileged to be able to call myself a journalist. I was now highly-rated by the national newsdesks. I knew my worth. And in youthful, hasty judgment I thought I was being way under-paid. Eric could have paid me more, yes, but the impetuosity of youth also clouded proper appreciation of what a priceless service he had done me in knocking the rough edges off the boy, as well as off my copy. Money couldn't buy that.

Now, I was comfortable – if not cocky – in *any* company. There were two big aristocratic families in Shropshire: the Bridgemans, the heirs and offshoots of the massively wealthy and highly respected Lord Bridgeman and the Heber-Percys, just as seriously rich and steeped in the county's history. The lads on the *Chronicle* would tell the story about how one hapless hack incurred the wrath of the former family when, in a feature article for the county magazine, he had written, "*...it is in this palatial hall that Lord Bridgeman holds his balls and dances.*"

John Rea picked up, from some posh friends of his, a smashing story about how relatives of Lord Bridgeman – Lord and Lady Boyne – had built a swimming pool in the *library* of their stately home, Burwarton Hall, because it got more light than the rest of the house.

The pool, 25 feet by 12 feet, heated and six feet at the deep end, took up a third of the huge library, which was also stocked with an art collection, antique furniture and thousands of priceless books. Despite the vast value of the library's contents and the incongruity of the pool's surroundings, Lord and Lady Boyne's children, Caroline, nine, Sarah, six and Lucy, four, splashed happily around in it – as did their parents.

It was a situation heaven-sent for John's great camera work and my storytelling – and while they had at first been extremely reluctant to co-operate, we had talked Lord and Lady Boyne around.

With the story and pictures nicely in the bag, John and I were sitting amidst all this opulence, having coffee with Lord and Lady Boyne, when there was one of those embarrassingly long gaps in the conversation (inevitable given the equally cavernous gap in our backgrounds. I believe John, too, for all his own acquired wealth, had grown up with no arse in his trousers) so I decided to break the silence...

"Do you see much of the Heber-Percys?" I asked them.

John choked on his coffee, unable to stifle a laugh.

On the way back to the office in his car John was still laughing uncontrollably.

"What?" I said.

"*Do you see much of the Heber-Percy's!* Have you any idea what a complete PRAT you sounded?" he chortled, "*Do you see much of the Heber-Percy's!* Oh, Christ. That was bloody priceless!"

Some considerable time had passed before I realised why John had laughed so much that day. And then I cringed in retrospect.

In the time that had passed since my *TEENBEAT* exploits, Pauline Stealey had grown into a lovely young woman – and we two had become very good friends. In her later school years, and after she had started work in a bank, we would often share Vaggs bus journeys to and from Shrewsbury and chat about all that was going on in our lives. She would confide in me, and me in her, when our respective love affairs went awry. We'd talk, also, about work, music and all that was wrong with the world, in the youthful but cock-sure way in which we viewed it. The friendship was platonic, but her picture was still in my wallet (though she never knew it) and had been ever since that night at the Music Hall.

The maturity she had displayed as a 14-year-old had become even more impressive for one still so young, but she also had a great sense of humour and we laughed at the same things. We were getting ever closer. If she was not at the bus stop when the bus got to Nesscliffe I would experience a feeling in the pit of my stomach that was more than mere disappointment. Gradually, slowly but surely, these two very good friends were falling in love.

That genuine friendship, built on mutual respect and real enjoyment of each other's company, came first and love later is, I'm convinced, why we are still together, so happily, nearly 40 years later.

Nobody called it being "soulmates" in those days, but that's what we were and still are. By the time I was at the peak of my professional performance as a reporter for the national newspapers, Pauline and I were lovers as well as inseparable pals and making plans to marry.

All that stuff about the loose sexual morality of the swinging sixties was mostly mythology – in Shropshire, at least. If you wanted to live together, the only socially acceptable way to do so was to marry and marriage remained – desperately old-fashioned though it must seem today – the ultimate affirmation of your love for one another.

As Pauline and I planned that huge step in our lives, I was getting more disillusioned with my professional role. I was just not finding it fulfilling. Apart from helping to keep Eric Mackereth's bank manager the happiest man in Shropshire, I did not feel that my sweat and toil was achieving much at all. The earlier excitement and "glamour" of working for the nationals had largely receded now and I was taking all that pretty much for granted.

On the really big stories we would play host at *Impact House* to national newspaper reporters – and too often I found them to be shallow, self-obsessed individuals to whom pursuit of a story – no matter what the effect on the people involved – was the only source of real satisfaction in their lives. That didn't seem much to which to aspire for a young man with his whole life before him. Few of them seemed to have secure relationships and several of them talked with what seemed to me to be false bravado about broken marriages. The next hotel room was their home, the nearest bar their comfort. Apart from the transient success of the next "exclusive", what was their contribution to their own lives and those of others, I wondered?

In short, what was being a reporter on a national newspaper – an ambition I had cherished – really worth?

It was dawning on me, too, that working for a national was a levelling process. I was good. Bloody good now. And it was not immodest but sensible to realise that in my local environment there was nobody better. Locally I was a "star" – a really big fish in that relatively small pond – but on national papers they were all at least as good as me and probably, in many cases, better. But then, locally I'd done it all as a reporter.

So where did I want my career to go from here?

The only thing I knew for certain was that I wasn't certain. Then came an incident over a story which provided the answer I needed...

One of the popular Sundays had been tipped off about a Welsh vicar who had allegedly disgraced himself on a cruise ship by dancing naked on deck with a toilet seat around his neck. A good story if you like that sort of thing. My brief: to find this poor sod, check it out and nail him. It would ruin him, of course.

Hours after they'd called I rang back the newsdesk.

"I've drawn a complete blank on the vicar, I'm afraid."

"OK, Barrie. We'll try elsewhere."

But the truth was that I had not even tried. I had not even picked up a telephone in pursuit of that poor sod. I had told myself that somebody else could have this one. I had no appetite for and no interest in such a story. Even if it was true. Who had he hurt? Who **cared** about this? I just didn't want to know. And yet, having made that decision, I did not feel good and worthy. I felt weak and unprofessional.

I went to see Jack Cater.

"Anything for me back on the *Chronicle?*"

"As it happens, old son," said Jack, "your timing is bloody impeccable. We want a new News Editor."

When I gave Eric my resignation I told him I was leaving because he had never paid me the bonus he had promised me when I was appointed. Actually, it was only a tiny part of the reason, but I wanted to make the point and I was not going to admit to him that I had lost my desire for the glittering prize of Fleet Street. That would have sounded like failure. (As indeed, in a way, it was. And if I had not been so rash in my youthful judgment, I could have sought a job on one of the serious nationals.)

Eric was shocked and looked genuinely hurt. It was a terribly ungracious and ungrateful way in which to tell him that I was leaving, because he had done much, much more for me and my career than at that time I had the maturity to understand, let alone articulate.

Yes, I had made a lot of money for him, but what he had done for me and my development was beyond price. He owed me nothing and by comparison I was deeply in **his** debt. I was too full of myself to appreciate that at the time and it was to be many years before I thanked Eric Mackereth properly for all that.

But I was so glad that I did, and I do to this day.

5. Onwards and Upwards

NEWS EDITOR of the *Shrewsbury Chronicle* at 21. Now that was some achievement. The *Chronicle* was a big paper by weekly standards. Reporting to me was a team of 16 journalists, all but two of them older than me and one or two old enough to be my grandfather.

The attributes I had gained with Eric and John – the slick, swift turnover of copy; the clever writing; the polished news sense; the sharp eye for a good picture, the top flight professionalism (minus the 'top spin') – were now being employed for Jack Cater. And he really appreciated it.

I had resolved – even at that tender age – to build an executive career in the regional newspaper industry. I had tasted the thrill of the chase on the nationals. It had often been exciting and exhilarating. It was different class, certainly, and it could be great fun. But there were also barrowloads of trivia and too often what I had been doing seemed so pointless.

Now, I was no longer just one of a highly talented national newspaper cast of hundreds in which excellence was the norm. Back in the regional press I was *the* "star" again. The *leader* of the pack. The *boss* of the reporters. *Nice.*

But there was something far more important than that. There was now a *point* to what I was doing. I was *involved* in the community of Shropshire. I had ready access to the movers and shakers in the local authorities, in business and commerce. The *Chronicle* was my vehicle for keeping thousands of people fully informed of events and decisions that were relevant and often crucially important to their lives. I was forming opinions on the right and wrong way to control those events and make those decisions and I was expressing them in the newspaper. I now shared with Jack Cater the responsibility for writing the paper's leading articles – berating or praising the local politicians as we saw fit. Now this mattered. And as a consequence *I* mattered. I now started to practice campaigning journalism – though back then it had not become universally known as such...

When the council decided to name a road in a suburb of Shrewsbury after a local man named Eric Lock, there had been some snooty protests from a few people, because Lock was also the name of a well-known local gipsy family. The council had been obliged to point out that *this* Lock had been an extremely brave and much decorated war hero – a World War Two fighter pilot – nothing whatsoever to do with the gipsy family (as if that really mattered, anyway!) and 25 years overdue for some hugely well deserved recognition by his home town.

I was incensed by this snobbery and intrigued by the story of Eric Lock DSO, DFC & Bar which – amazingly – had not been told since 1941. I tracked down his sister, who was living in the village of Baschurch. She had lovingly kept Eric's medals, newspaper cuttings telling of his heroism, pictures of him with his Spitfire and his letters home. This was a veritable treasure trove of emotive, historic material – and none of it ever published. Eric's sister – a lovely, serene woman – guarded his memory and his memorabilia with quiet, dignified determination. She had no comment to make about the road naming controversy and her contemptuous silence was condemnation enough. She was, though, very happy for me to tell Eric's story – neglected for so long – in full. I felt genuinely honoured that she was prepared to entrust it to me. And what a story it was.

This incredibly brave young man, when he was just 21 – the same age as me – had shot down 16 German planes and become a national hero, honoured by the King, but as I read his letters they revealed that he was anything but a warmonger. He was a sensitive, caring country boy and there was a deeply moving irony to those descriptive letters. In one, he enquired how the harvest was coming along at home and, recalling that he had flown over harvesters in France a day or two earlier, he confided that the sight had made him realise *"how bloody stupid this war is"*.

He was frequently wounded and had no less than 16 hospital operations, but always went straight back into action. His exploits and decorations made the world's headlines. The name of Eric Lock became famous. The American magazine *Life* named him "Britain's greatest air ace of the war" All the newspapers of the time loved the youngster they dubbed "the pocket pilot" – but his letters home complained that he didn't like the publicity…

'I have only done my duty,' he wrote.

Like his contemporary hero, Wing Commander Douglas Bader, Flight Lieutenant Eric Lock fought back from serious injury after being shot down and returned to the fray yet again – only to be reported missing presumed killed after leading a fighter sweep over Northern France in August 1941.

Earlier that summer his recuperation had afforded the luxury of some prolonged leave, which he had spent in Shropshire. Many local organisations had entertained and honoured their war hero and, in response, he had overcome his natural reticence for public speaking to make several speeches to raise money for the Spitfire Fund. Grateful local folk had collected together to buy him an inscribed silver cigarette case and an airman's watch, but before he could receive the gifts at a presentation planned in his honour, he had been recalled to operational duties.

Twenty-five years later, some inconsequential suburban snobs had been bickering over whether a road should be named in his honour... *Bloody hell!*

Telling the Eric Lock story in full for the first time – with the benefit of his sister's personal mementoes – was a thrill. Above the story, published with pictures of Eric provided by his sister, which had never been seen outside the family, I wrote a leader, calling for a proper honour for this brave son of Shropshire. It read...

"The name of one of the great 1939-45 war heroes once hit the world's headlines. So did the news of his heroic death in action. Now it has been recalled, briefly, in Shropshire because his native place has decided to name a cul-de-sac in a housing estate after him. There was a flurry of controversy before that decision was agreed. But, in the event, the *Chronicle* believes this to have been to the good for it focuses attention on the fact that *nowhere* in Shropshire is there a public memorial to this man who was one of the greatest of those immortal few of the RAF who saved this country in the Battle of Britain days.

There is not a painting of him in Shrewsbury Guildhall, not in the Castle or in the Public Library. Nor does he appear in the Shirehall's gallery of portraits of men whose names are famous in the county and beyond. There is not even a simple plaque in a public place to commemorate him. Read the story below, of his heroism and courage, and ask yourself if this omission should not quickly be rectified. The *Chronicle* says that Fl. Lt. Lock is deserving of a more worthy memorial than a name plate to a cul-de-sac. That is not nearly good enough.

He was only 22 when he died but into his short service in the RAF he had packed the heroism of ages. His story should be an inspiration to the youth of today. If they read it they will know something of the calibre of the young men of a few years ago who sacrificed all so that future generations might know freedom. A memorial in a form which would benefit the youth of today would, perhaps, be one that he himself might have wished to be remembered by.

The *Chronicle* makes this suggestion in the hope that, perhaps, the chairman of the County Council, the Mayor of Shrewsbury, the chairman of the local parish council and the RAF Association might consider getting together to discuss the possibility of launching such a project.

Eric Lock's heroism as a fighter pilot was a war time legend 25 years ago. The years have passed and – except among his family – the memory of him has dimmed. Late though it is, Shropshire should act now to see that his name is not forgotten for ever."

Reading that 40 years later, it seems a bit pompous for a lad of 21 to have written but it is illuminating in that it represents the type of journalism upon which I was to build a career and a life. *And at the time it sure beat the hell out of smuggling one and sixpenny sausages out of the Granada restaurant!*

There were other campaigning issues for the *Chronicle's* new News Editor – like the threat to Shrewsbury's future of the proposed Dawley (later Telford) New Town; the woeful waste of the wonderful natural assets of the River Severn; the decline of the old "borough" of Frankwell and whether Shropshire County Council could afford to enter the new age of the computer. It was at a cost of £112,000 – and I concluded not! Not one of my most forward thinking editorial stances.

On September 30th, 1967 Miss Pauline Florence Anne Stealey of 3, Bank View, Nesscliffe and Mr Barrie Charles Williams of 20,Chaucer Road, Oswestry (the Williams clan had moved to their *third* council house) were married at Great Ness Parish Church, a beautiful rural Shropshire setting.

My lot (the townies) nearly never made it. They couldn't find the bloody church!

The family of the groom gasped, spluttered, puffed and panted their way self – consciously down the aisle with the ceremony already underway while Pauline's lot (the country folk) glared at them in disgust and disdain convinced (apart from her dear mum and dad with whom I shared mutual affection) that she had made a thoroughly bad choice.

'CHRONICLE NEWS EDITOR WEDS' proclaimed the headline above our picture in the paper. It also made the *Oswestry Border Counties Advertiser*, which kindly refrained from referring to the groom as a Teddy Boy!

For our honeymoon we took a train to St Ives in Cornwall, a marathon journey in those days, there to stay in the spare bedroom of a Mrs Lander, who did bed and breakfast.

I was 22 (by just one day) and Pauline was 18. We were just kids but, paradoxically, I believe youngsters matured much earlier in those supposedly less enlightened days and we certainly did not think of ourselves as kids. I was, after all, running a newsroom and Pauline had a very responsible and demanding job with an insurance company.

For a year we lived in a rented furnished house by the River Severn, owned by a couple who were visiting their daughter in Canada.

It came complete with an appalling spoiled and arrogant cat called "Whoppsie", who one night caught her tail in the fire, causing me to dive around the room after her, trying to put out the flames, then to apply copious quantities of Vaseline on the bald appendage in the hope that it would heal and re-grow fur before her doting owners returned!

Then, we moved to a big flat in a Tudor mansion, the ground floor of which was a shoe shop, in the middle of Shrewsbury and only yards from both our offices. It was a beautiful flat but it had a strangely spooky, cold atmosphere and we were convinced that it was haunted.

Having survived the early difficulties, uncertainties and rows which beset all newlyweds (though they seem dramatically unique to you at the time) we were growing even closer by the day.

But professionally I was now not so happy. The job was easy. Too easy. I was getting bored with it. Jack Cater had stepped up to become Editor-in-Chief of Morley Tonkin's *Powysland Newspapers Ltd*, publishers of the *Chronicle*. He was like a captain without a ship and that induced a mellowing – which most who worked with him welcomed – but I didn't. I missed so much the obstreperous, cantankerous, demanding old devil who had been such an influence on my life. The place was just not the same without him.

A new Editor was now in charge of the *Chronicle* – Derek Bourne from London, a thoroughly nice man who was to die tragically early from a brain tumour – and my ex-minder from the police calls Doug Morris was Deputy Editor. Both were relatively young men so I could see no light at the end of my professional tunnel.

Jack and I would have a few beers together every Thursday night. My enormous respect and admiration for this giant of a man had not diminished – never did – but I was no longer in awe of him. We were pals now. Real pals. He would confide in me about the frustrations of his new role – more exalted, better paid, but "fuckin' boring, old lad" – and I would do likewise. "Nothing against Derek and Doug, Jack. Nothing at all. They're bloody good blokes. But it's just not the same now you're not there."

One night, over a pint, I told Jack, "I'm getting stuck in a rut. I've outgrown this job. I need to move on."

"Where to?"

"I don't know. I've done the nationals. Don't want that. I want to be an editor – and a bloody good one like you."

"You know what that means," said Jack. "You'll have to learn sub-editing and design for a start…"

"Yeah, but not on a weekly. I'll need to be really stretched."

And so it was that I came to be hired as a trainee sub-editor on the *Wolverhampton Express & Star.*

This was a vast step up. Along with the *Manchester Evening News* – where Jack had been News Editor – and the *Birmingham Evening Mail,* the *Express & Star* was in the top three of England's regional evening newspapers – selling comfortably more than 350,000 copies a night, compared with the *Chronicle's* 50,000 a week. The Editor, Clement 'Clem' Jones was an icon.

Our flat was only a few hundred yards from Shrewsbury Railway Station and Wolverhampton seemed to be reasonable commuting distance. The more predictable nature of a sub-editor's hours would assist that process and if I was to be an editor one day this was the best possible training ground for the production experience which was essential to that mission.

On my first day at the *Express & Star* I walked nervously through the huge open plan news room to report to the Chief Sub Editor George Phillips. A granite-hard northerner with a thin chiselled face, pale complexion and curt manner, George snapped, "Right... Desk Number Eleven!"

The set-up was like nothing I had ever imagined or have ever seen since. I can best describe it as an industrialised words factory.

George Phillips, flanked by two deputies and a copy taster, sat at the control centre of a T-shaped sub's desk. In front of George was a panel with the numbers 1 to 22 and a red light and a green light against each number. It looked like the technology of a Blackpool bingo hall. Stretching out from the control centre were 22 desks – 11 each side of a two-way conveyor belt. Each desk had its own green light and red light set into the desk side of the conveyor belt. George would send a piece of copy down the conveyor belt without looking up from his control panel, simply shouting the sub-editor's name. At this shout, the sub would press his red button. That would release a small mechanical arm, which would shoot out and stop the copy at the appropriate spot on the conveyor belt. At the same time, the light against the sub's number would shine red on George's control panel, indicating that this desk was busy, and it remained red until the copy had been subbed and dispatched via the "out" stretch of the conveyor belt down to the "works". Then the sub would press his green button, causing his number light on George's control panel to change from red to green, which let George know that this desk was now ready for more copy. This automated process went on at head-spinning speed, with barely a word being spoken.

For the uninitiated (and for *some* sub-editors I've known!) I should explain here what a sub does... The reporters' raw copy has to be carefully checked and, where necessary, corrected for grammar, spelling and punctuation. It must also adhere to "house style" – the preferences, where there is a choice, laid down by the Editor. It must also be free from libel, defamation and contempt of court – the former carrying the risk of costing the newspaper hundreds of thousands of pounds in damages; the latter having the potential to put the Editor behind bars. The story must be clear, concise, accurate and well-written and if it's not it has to be remedially treated. And it must never offend the newspaper's standards of taste and decency.

When all that has been done and the copy is squeaky clean, it has to be tailored to fit the shape on the page – and thus, the number of words it contains – working to the instructions of the design subs. The correct required variation of type-sizes also have to be employed. Finally, working similarly to instructions, the headline must be written. This has to fit exactly the pre-determined word count – or disaster will ensue. The headline must also be a concise, accurate, legally safe but compelling and lively précis of the contents of the story.

"Barrie – this is for you!" shouted George Phillips, as a pile of copy was conveyed to Desk No. 11 before I'd barely had time to sit down. I picked it up, got up and walked sheepishly up to George's control centre where, head down, he ignored me completely.

Very gingerly, I tapped him on his bony shoulder.

"I'm sorry... I'm just a trainee... I've never actually subbed any copy before..."

"Bloody hell!" bellowed George Phillips. "Nobody tells me a bloody thing! I thought you were a sub!"

"No. I'm sorry. Clem Jones took me on as a trainee. He knew I'd never subbed."

"Oh, for God's sake!" shouted George, loud enough for the whole newsroom to hear. "Go and sit down. I'll talk to you at lunchtime."

It was only 8. 30am. And there I sat at Desk No. 11, doing absolutely nothing, feeling extremely foolish, while the frenetic activity of the words factory reverberated around me.

Humiliated? I can't begin to tell you...

At 10. 30 am, after I had been sitting in embarrassed inactivity for two hours, I heard a slow handclap coming from the top end of the newsroom, where the reporters sat. Looking up, I saw that the handclap was synchronised to the stately march of a huge matron, resplendent in crisp blue and white tunic and big white cap. Ignoring the journalists' ever-louder handclap, and looking intently ahead like a Royal guardsman on parade, the matron marched forward towards the sub-editors' area. When she stopped at George Phillips' desk, so did the slow handclap, and one of those eerie silences, like the lull before a storm, ensued.

George didn't look up.

"The lad on number eleven," he barked.

Matron beckoned me forward with a withering glare and, like a lamb going to whatever slaughter awaited, I walked pathetically towards her.

"Medical," she said. "This way…"

As Matron marched back through the newsroom, with the lad from desk number eleven trotting respectfully behind her, the slow handclap resumed, growing to a crescendo as we reached the door at the top end.

Matron led me along the forbidding corridors, down which I'd walked for my interview with Clem Jones, until we came to a surgery. When inside she ordered, "Right… Nip behind those screens. Remove your clothes and give me a urine sample in here," handing me what looked like a wine decanter wrapped in a spotless white cloth.

Behind the screen, stripped down to my Y-fronts (and of what little dignity I had remaining) I wondered how much more humiliation could be heaped on a bloke in this place…

Don't they know I've worked with Fleet Street's finest! What the bloody hell is going on here?

I was so pre-occupied with my plight that I hadn't noticed how big a sample I was providing for Matron. There'd been a farewell piss-up for me the night before with the gang from the *Chronicle* and I had been too self conscious to ask the industrious words factory workers where the toilets were, so I'd not been near a loo since 6am. When I stepped sheepishly out from behind the screen, practically naked, shoulders slumped in shame, holding in my sample "decanter" a pint and a half of Worthington 'E' with a perfect deep head of froth on it, Matron looked at me with utter contempt.

"*A drop or two was all I required!*" she scolded, as she tipped the foaming ale disdainfully down a sink with an exasperated shake of her head.

"*Oh, Christ – just let me go home to Pauline,*" I thought, "*I don't want this bloody job **that** much!*"

A doctor duly arrived, conducted his various tests on me and declared me fit… but "very thin".

"You need a few plates full of our canteen chips," he concluded.

What would today's medics have made of such advice!

Back on Desk Number Eleven, it was now 12 noon on my first day on the famous *Express & Star* and I was still being completely ignored by everybody as the frantic conveyor belt process began to reach fever pitch. Some sort of zenith (a major edition deadline, I later discovered) was obviously approaching.

Suddenly, the elderly, grey-haired, wire bespectacled sub-editor sitting on the other side of the conveyor belt from me threw a pile of copy paper up into the air and as it fluttered to the floor he jumped up and down on it, cursing like a demented witch at an occult orgy.

"Isn't somebody going to fetch that doctor?" I thought, desperately concerned about this poor man's dreadful state, but no-one else was batting an eye lid and George Phillips, without even looking up from his control panel, said simply: "Settle down, Jim."

"Sorry George," said the old sub-editor, picked up his scattered pile of copy paper, sorted it back into order, sat down and carried on subbing.

"What bloody mad house is this? I thought. *I'll not last a day!"*

At lunchtime, George Phillips seemed only marginally less exasperated to have me on his staff.

"When the heat's off, at about three o'clock, I'll get my deputy Gerry to talk things through with you," he told me, then turned to his copy taster and – loudly enough for me to hear – complained, *"They take these bloody people on. They tell me half a story. Who needs bloody trainees?"*

"Welcome to your new job..." I told myself.

Following medical advice, I went to the canteen for a plate of chips. And with the chips, a Black Country delicacy... faggots and peas. Piping hot and absolutely delicious. Amazingly therapeutic, good food can be. Suddenly, I was feeling a lot better about it all.

"Mind if I join you?" The question came from a quietly spoken young sub-editor wearing a sports jacket and fawn cavalry twill trousers. I'd noticed him during the morning mayhem and observed how remarkably calm he seemed. Maurice Moorcroft was his name. He came from the Potteries and he was just two or three years older than me. A kindred spirit?

"You mustn't mind George, you know," volunteered Maurice, clearly sensing the deep discomfort I had endured during the morning's events and sympathising. "He's a really good bloke. Salt of the earth. It's just that he's *so* short of subs at present. I came in as a trainee too and he wasn't too happy about that at the time – but he's fine now. You'll be OK, I'm sure."

Maurice's considerate words were as warming and comforting as the faggots and peas and back at Desk No. 11, after lunch, I was ready to take on whatever grumpy George wanted to throw at me.

Gerry Link, George's deputy, looked more like a farmer than a journalist. Rosy cheeked, chubby and healthy, he seemed out of place in the words factory. He was friendly and patient as he talked through the basics of the job with me. I picked it up very quickly and by the end of the week I was making a contribution, albeit a modest one.

"You've done OK. Well done, Barrie," George Phillips told me. "Have a good weekend and we'll see you on Monday."

"It's a piece of cake!" I told Pauline, when I got home.

But it wasn't. It was bloody hard work. The hardest job I ever had in journalism. Learning, mastering and then performing the daunting demands and disciplines of sub-editing under intense pressure was tough enough. But that was the relatively easy bit. The volume of work which then followed was enormous. George's conveyor belt seemed to me to be merciless. The huge success of the *Express & Star* was built on intensive editionising. Every significant area of the Black Country got its own edition – packed with stories and avidly consumed by the paper's hundreds of thousands of readers. That, in turn, meant thousands of stories – all to go through the sub-editing process. Here, there was none of the finesse of fancy design which goes into your papers today. It was all about moving masses of words through that factory. The design, such as it was, of the pages was pre-set and predictable. The mountain of material would be taken off the conveyor belt in "the works" and turned into galleys of hot metal type (no time for the new web offset methods in *this* system) to be laid out geographically and sorted by a wizard of a "stone sub" called John Ogden, who shared the compositors' mystical ability to read upside down and worked with them at a speed which had to be seen to be believed to churn out edition after edition after edition...

When he wasn't earning the admiration of everybody with whom he came into contact at the *Express & Star*, John Ogden – dark-skinned and long-haired – played in a rock band. The man's stamina was phenomenal, yet his approach to everything he did, work included, was so deceptively laid back as to seem almost lethargic. John Ogden was a rare and truly exceptional talent – and the last I heard he was *still* at the *Express & Star* and *still* plying the sub-editor's trade. Incredible!

After three months I had become a fully fledged member of George Phillips' highly professional team – shifting as much copy just as fast and just as accurately as anybody else. George, who I was to discover was a thoughtful and considerate boss under the bluster, *was* short of sub editors. *All* the best newspapers were back then. The *Express & Star*, a superb employer, would gladly have hired more – but you just couldn't get 'em. So we were all working extremely hard. This included extra voluntary shifts, for which we were paid excellent overtime rates, on the Saturday night sporting pink paper – which carried reports and results of just about *every* football match played in the Black Country. Such was the obligatory pace of this particular operation that the sub-editor had to write his headline on each match report after only *forty minutes* of play, then complete the report and finally add the score at full time. I had many testing tasks in my career, but none more difficult and challenging than trying to write a lively and compelling headline when Moor Green were drawing 0-0 with Atherstone after 40 minutes of a match in which absolutely nothing worthy of note had occurred. On such occasions – and they were frequent – you were always grateful if the reporter had mentioned the weather in his copy and given the frequency with which it rains during a West Midlands winter, headlines like MOOR GREEN MUDBATH were a life saver!

The demands of the brilliant *Express & Star* and the intense pressure under which the daily production of the paper was being achieved were hardly lessened in my case by having to get up at the crack of dawn every day for the first leg of a return rail journey of some 120 miles, then, when I'd finished a shift, having to wait for a train before I could get home at night.

"Gruelling" was an understated description of what I was doing to myself, often six days a week, but I didn't mind. I was very proud of my newly-acquired skills and I was enjoying the hard work. What I was not realising, however, was that my body was not appreciating it quite so much. There were warning signs, unrecognised as such and so unheeded at the time, like some nights I would be desperately tired and on days off all I wanted to do was sleep. Once, as Pauline and I lay in bed at our flat a fire engine raced past outside, siren wailing in the still of the early morning. "There's a fire somewhere," Pauline observed quietly. To which I jumped up and shouted loudly and irritably: "*I know. I know. I subbed that half an hour ago!*"

Not a good sign, that.

It was Good Friday and typically I was working a shift at the *Express & Star* but George had promised us we'd get off a bit earlier and I'd arranged with Pauline to nip over to the fish stall in Wolverhampton market – a relatively short walk from the office – to pick up some nice fresh fish for dinner.

I'd bought the fish and I was walking through the market to go on to the railway station to catch my train home when suddenly, with absolutely no warning, I experienced an indescribable feeling and everything went black. I shook my head and walked on but realised that I was sweating profusely. And my legs had turned to lead. Putting one foot in front of the other had suddenly become a massive effort. *"What on earth is happening to me?"*

There was no way I was going to make it all the way to the station so I headed back to the office. That moderate distance seemed like 50 miles and every step felt like it was going to be my last. It was a monumental effort. When I eventually reached the sanctuary of the newsroom everybody had gone home. I slumped into my chair, drenched with sweat from head to toe, convinced that I could not move.

I rang Pauline at home... *"I'm not at all well, Paul. You'll have to come and get me."* It was a profoundly stupid thing to say. Neither of us possessed a car. The buses and trains were operating a restricted Easter holiday service and Pauline was some 60 miles away. Sensibly, she talked the situation through with me. Calmly and reassuringly.

"If you feel you're seriously ill you must ring for an ambulance," she said. "Otherwise, sit for as long as it takes to compose yourself then walk slowly to the station, catch your train and I'll be on the platform to meet you when you get here."

"Seriously ill? Me? No. Never. Get a grip, lad. Have a cup of tea then go and get your train," I told myself.

I walked over to the drinks vending machine, put my coins in, leaned forward to press the button and WHAM! Again, the world around me suddenly turned to a black nothingness and my legs to lead. Again, I shook my head to clear it. Again sweat poured from every pore. *Christ – what IS this!* Home – I've got to get home.

The walk to the station seemed to take hours. I had to drag my legs through every step along the way but I got there, boarded the first available train and sat at the window. The usual commuters, unlike crazy journalists, were all on a day off. I had a compartment virtually to myself. With every mile nearer to Shrewsbury we travelled, I felt better. When we got there, I had recovered. Pauline, bless her, was on the platform. No mobile phones, back then and she'd had a long, anxious wait, not knowing what to expect.

"I feel a prat now," I told her.

"Off to the doctor with you, my lad," she replied.

"It's your nerves," said the doctor. "They're shot."

He prescribed Valium and a few days' rest. It was the first time I had been off sick since my first day at work – but I wasn't arguing. Pauline did her best to get me out and about, but I didn't want to know. I was fearful of those "blackouts" returning and I didn't want to leave the flat. After a week I went back to work, but every time I feared that awful feeling returning it did. I was having what today are recognised and rationalised as 'panic attacks'.

My doctor kept on trying to reassure me that I was not the only person in the world ever to experience these symptoms and kept repeating the tablets, but I was not improving and I had got into what seemed like a comfort zone, but was in fact a dangerous rut of my own making. I would get in to the office, do my work well enough and get home again, but that apart, I would do nothing and go nowhere. And I would keep convincing myself that I needed more time off sick.

One day, Jack Cater called to see me.

"Come and have a snifter with me, old son."

"Thanks Jack, but I won't, if you don't mind. Don't really feel like it."

One night Eric Mackereth knocked on our door.

"Thought you might like to come and have a chat over a pint, mate,"

"Nice of you to call Eric, but no thanks."

She's never admitted it but I've always suspected that Pauline had secretly contacted my two mentors, for whom I had such respect, in the hope that they could re-ignite my interest and talk me out of what was now becoming a serious bout of depression.

I was now taking two days off sick for every five or six I was working. It couldn't go on and at Pauline's insistence I went back to the doctor to tell him so.

This time I was given extremely thorough examinations and tests, at the conclusion of which I was told, "Look... there is nothing physically wrong with you at all – but you are completely exhausted. You have two choices. You move to Wolverhampton to live, so that you're not piling tiring commuting on top of your work, or you give up that job and find something else."

He was right, of course. The other blokes on the *Express & Star* subs' desk, all living reasonably locally, were absorbing the workload well enough. I had been daft to think that I could combine a long commute with this job and I had been piling one pressure point on top of another ever since the day I became a journalist. My progress from Day One had been at breakneck speed, never stopping for breath. This was, quite simply, overload. And it was entirely self-induced.

As ever when there's a big issue in our lives, Pauline and I sat down and discussed the doc's ultimatum very thoroughly. We concluded that in the time (nearly a year) I had been at the *Express & Star* I had fulfilled completely the purpose of going there. I had been fully and expertly trained and then gone on to succeed impressively as a news sub-editor in the toughest environment on one of the biggest and best newspapers in the regional industry. My exhaustion aside, I had passed the test I set myself with flying colours and I had acquired a vital string of an Editor's bow. Having a stint on a great regional daily newspaper like the *Express & Star* on my CV was worth its weight in gold.

Apart from a handful of good people on whose confidence and discretion we knew we could rely *nobody* – not even our close families – knew that I'd had any problems.

So, yes, It was time for the next career move.

But first, on doctor's advice, we needed a really good holiday and a proper rest. We took a caravan at Clarach Bay, near Aberystwyth, just yards from a big, bracing beach. My dad drove us there in the old green van, which was the only transport the family possessed, and arranged to pick us up two weeks later.

It was April, freezing cold, deserted... *and bloody wonderful!*

The old caravan we'd hired had a wood-burning stove. Very early every morning we walked miles along the beach, collecting driftwood for the fire. Then we'd walk over the cliffs into Aberystwyth, explore the town, buy fresh provisions and have a splendid lunch by the fire in a local pub, with friendly, interesting people to talk to. (The Investiture of the young Prince Charles as Prince of Wales was imminent, so there was no shortage of lively debate in Welsh hostelries, particularly if the presence of "the English" presented the opportunity!)

Then we'd trek back over the cliffs to our cosy little caravan, light the stove, cook dinner and sit, warm and snug, listening to the radio, reading and chatting. It was one of many times in our lives which reminded me how very lucky I am to have lovely, lively Pauline for my wife and what a true and loyal friend she is, too. And how very much I love her.

Every day for two weeks our routine was the same. By 10pm every night I was tired out. But this was a different sort of tiredness; this was fresh air and exercise, calm and contentment induced tiredness. When my dad came to pick us up, I was fit and full of energy, refreshed, renewed, recharged.

I went back to work at the *Express & Star* firing on all cylinders and enjoying my work as much as ever.

But the decision we had made was the right one.

I was looking for the next move.

But where was *this one* going to take me?

6.   So What Now?

THERE WAS NO GREAT RUSH to leave the *Express & Star*. My brief and uncharacteristic period of ill-health and depression banished by the restful quietness and re-energising air of the Welsh seaside, I was coasting through my work again. I had resolved that, with the skills of a sub-editor now added to my portfolio, I needed to return to news editing – the thing I did and liked best. But there did not seem to be a suitable opportunity anywhere.

Then, at home one evening, I got a phone call from one Trevor Buckley. I had known this fellow, from a distance, when he was an editor of one of Morley Tonkin's lesser-known publications and he was, by reputation, a really nice bloke who enjoyed a good laugh. Very easy to get along with.

Trevor Buckley had left 'Tonkin Towers'[1] to become the Managing Editor of the *Stoke-on-Trent City Times* series.

"I hear on the grapevine that you might be looking for a news desk job," said Trevor. "Is it true? And if so, can we talk?"

Yes it was and yes of course we could, I told him. "But time is difficult, what with the hours I'm working on the *Express & Star* and all the travelling. I'm afraid I don't know when I'll be able to get over to Stoke."

"Then let's meet in Shrewsbury," said Trevor.

"Fine – where? In one of the pubs?" I suggested.

"No. We're both too well known and I need to be discreet at this stage," said Trevor, "Why don't I come to your home?"

And the next evening I had the most bizarre and unlikely "interview" of my professional life. Trevor Buckley sat on the sofa in the lounge of our flat and it soon became obvious that *I* was interviewing **him**. This guy desperately wanted me to join his outfit and that made me realise that the temporary problems I had endured while toiling away at Wolverhampton had led me to overlook that I was a pretty hot property.

Still only 23-years-old, I had crammed a hell of a lot of achievement and experience into my seven years as a journalist (when I

---

[1] As Jack Cater used to call Morley's *Powysland Newspapers* group.
"*It's Turkey Time at Tonkin Towers…*" *he* would sing, loudly, in mock reverence at Christmas.

took stock, there was no wonder I'd had that period during which I was absolutely knackered!) and I had a great deal to offer an editor like Trevor.

In retrospect, I was under-selling myself professionally by even showing interest in Trevor Buckley's approach, but it was a ready-made opportunity to get back to news editing and although the *Stoke-on-Trent City Times Series* was a small weekly outfit it was part of a big company (Tillotsons', owners of the *Bolton Evening News*) and the surprisingly good salary Trevor was offering me was much better than I expected – in fact, it was marginally more than I was being paid for my sweat and toil as a sub-editor in the huge Wolverhampton words factory.

Besides, Trevor's reputation and popularity was obviously well justified. This was a genuinely nice chap: good looking, in his late 30s, with a strong accent from his Warrington roots, oozing natural, unaffected charm and possessing the most infectious laugh I have ever encountered, he was extremely difficult to reject.

We shook hands on a deal.

Pauline was pleased. She'd been more worried than she'd ever let me know about that bout of exhaustion and depression which had laid me much lower than I had realised at the time and she wanted me back at my best. As has been the case so often in our partnership it meant sacrifices for her, which I was far too personally preoccupied to appreciate. She had to leave her Mum and Dad behind, as well as her job at the insurance company – at which she was very highly-rated and well-liked – and her many friends in and around Shrewsbury. But there was not one word of complaint from her.

Having no car (not even, at that time, a driving licence) made Stoke-on-Trent pretty inaccessible for us. Consequently, we never so much as saw the place until the day we arrived to live and work there. We found accommodation (a rented, "partly furnished" house through an agency without seeing it and we travelled to the Potteries in the back of a van hired to transport our own few bits of furniture. We had made the journey to our new abode in excitement and anticipation – as you always do when moving house – and when it's to one you've not previously seen those feelings are heightened.

The small detached property at Normacot, on a main road into Stoke, was unremarkable from the outside. Inside, it was horrendous. It had been unoccupied for months but its most recent tenants had been a bunch of students – and they had left behind the *House From Hell!* It was filthy. It stank. There was rubbish all over the floors; the furniture, such as it was, was wrecked; soiled curtains hung in tatty strips over windows so dirty you could hardly see through them; there were muddy footprints on the *ceiling (!)* in the lounge; used condoms under the beds and in the bathroom lurked an evil *wc* which you would not have wanted to stand on in thick Wellington boots, let alone entrust your naked nether regions to.

Pauline wept. I felt dreadful. I had brought her away from our beautiful Tudor flat in posh Shrewsbury – *to this.*

In next to no time, Pauline had recovered her composure...

"Right..." she said. "No time to lose. If we're staying here tonight we've got to get this place cleaned up." We would, she resolved, try to get the kitchen, one bedroom and that unspeakable toilet habitable by nightfall. A hotel was out of the question because we had our lively young Labrador cross *Brandy* with us. I was dispatched to the nearest shop to purchase gallons of bleach and disinfectant while Pauline filled every suitable receptacle she could find with water to boil. We located the oldest clothing we had – and set to.

Soon after the clean-up had commenced there was a knock on the back door and there stood a tall, blond boy, aged about 12.

"Hello, I'm Paul," he said with an engaging smile. "I live next door. This place is filthy, yeah? Could you use some help?" And with no more ado he rolled up his sleeves and pitched in. It was an impromptu introduction to the people of the Potteries – the friendliest, warmest, most kind-hearted and considerate folk you will find anywhere in the world.

Pauline's appetite for hard work and her ability to make a home anywhere saw to it that the *House From Hell* was soon spotlessly clean and comfortable and, two days after arriving in the Potteries, I set off for work at the *Stoke-on-Trent City Times Series.*

Trevor had explained that this was a group of weeklies serving the Potteries towns plus Newcastle-under-Lyme and Alsager. It had sounded a substantial operation and within its own context it was – but when I eventually found the office in Hanley, from where it was produced, I could not believe my eyes... It was a corner shop!

The paper was printed in Bolton, so there was no publishing activity at all. Downstairs in the corner shop there was a reception area – with just one receptionist to take advertisements, sell photos, etc, and a photographic darkroom. Upstairs was the Editor's office, an Assistant Editor's office and a tiny newsroom. Small as it was, it didn't have to be any bigger because the *Stoke-on-Trent City Times Series* had just *three* reporters, *two* photographers and a News Editor (me) who doubled as Chief Reporter. This tiny team, aided only by a sprinkling of amateur correspondents who were paid a few pence a line, had, between them, to produce enough material for *six separate broadsheet newspapers.* All the sub-editing and designing of pages was done by the Assistant Editor, one other senior journalist (who was *also* called News Editor because Trevor Buckley had been too nice to tell him that I had taken his title!) and Trevor himself, who was also in sole and total charge of all the commercial and financial elements of the business.

This was an operation run on the slenderest of shoestrings. I had come from a massive evening newspaper, occupying both sides of a big street in a major city and employing more than a thousand people. I knew this was going to be smaller, but nothing had prepared me for just how *much* smaller!

"Bloody hell, boy, you've made a big mistake, here," I thought. "I'm going to have to get out of this place as soon as I can!"

In the meantime, there was no alternative. I just had to get on with it.

"What's it like?" Pauline wanted to know when I got home after my first day's work in the Potteries.

"Well… let me put it this way, luv… This will not be a long posting. I've come down so fast I've got the bloody bends!"

Next day I enrolled with a firm of editorial executive headhunters to find me a bigger and better job, but that didn't mean that I was not going to make the very best of things for as long as I was in Stoke-on-Trent…

Pauline got a job managing the stock control of a major furniture store in Hanley. Mr and Mrs Williams were, for the time being at least, Potteries' people.

If anybody had told me on that first day how happy Pauline and I were going to be in Stoke-on-Trent and how much I was going to enjoy working on the *City Times Series* I would have laughed at them. But we *were* and I *did*. Apart from the Assistant Editor, Reg Tomkinson (a lugubrious old bugger who'd had a sense of humour by-pass) that little team was the happiest I ever worked with because the job was fun. Journalism should *always* be fun.

The reporters Phil Chadwick, Clive Steele and Susan Davies were all local kids who loved their work and treated every day as something to be enjoyed and savoured. A fourth, Mandy Wormold, was added to the team by Trevor and between us we produced bloody good local newspapers, which often gave the big local evening paper, the *Sentinel*, a pasting.

I was back doing what I always liked best – creating ideas, digging out stories, writing, working contacts, getting involved in local issues, campaigning. Stoke-on-Trent was just beginning to discuss the need for the regeneration, which has made it such a very different place today, and that was right up my street. We threw the support of the *City Times* so enthusiastically behind the politicians and city planners, who were not even yet at embryonic stage but grappling with the principles and problems of moving the old town towards a re-born future, that they repaid us with scores of exclusives on the issue.

Phil, Clive, Susan and I became a really close little unit. We thought as one. We worked as one. We shared the same sense of humour. And, boy, did we have some laughs together.

On the opposite corner to our little "shop" stood a tiny back street pub, *The Victoria*, run by a splendid Liverpudlian landlord called George, a jovial giant whose lunchtime speciality was a wonderfully tasty Scouse Pie... a concoction of meat, gravy, potato, onions and pastry which stuck to your ribs and warmed your cockles on the coldest of days. There we would gather most lunchtimes, when Pauline would join us. George loved dearly a song which was a huge hit for *The Hollies* – and so did we. We would play it time and time again on the old juke box in the corner and sing loudly along with Alan Clark: *"He 'aint heave-e-e-e... He's my brothe-e-e-r"*

Nobody would sing it more loudly or enthusiastically than big George, but he could never remember what it was called and he would have us in stitches when he frequently tossed a coin for the juke box over the bar to us with the request to "Put that good one on... *"Put 'im down, 'e's too 'eavy!"*

Big George had an extraordinary employee, a little old lady known only as *Dickie Mint* because she looked so very much like Ken Dodd's Diddyman character of that name. *Dickie Mint* would report for duty at the pub early in the morning and clean and polish the whole place until it sparkled. Then she would go into the kitchen to prepare and cook the *Scouse Pie*... all of those duties performed without ever removing her hat, which was secured in place by an enormous "jewelled" hatpin, or taking off her permanently buttoned-up camel coat. At lunchtime, when all the *Scouse Pie* had been served, she would retire to *her* seat (and heaven help anybody else who dared to sit upon it!) where she would remain, sipping stout, until closing time at 10. 30pm. Then she would walk regally down the road to catch her bus home, happily and gloriously inebriated – but hat and coat still immaculate – before repeating the entire ritual again the next day.

I have this enduring imaginary vision of *Dickie Mint*, who was said to have been in her eighties, being eventually laid to rest, still wearing that hat and coat, with a bottle of stout in one hand and a *Scouse Pie* in the other, under a tombstone proclaiming: "*Here lies Dickie Mint – So don't you **dare** bloody sit here!*"

At work, Phil, Clive, Susan and I were like four musketeers – fiercely loyal to each other and inseparable no matter what. We put up with *"old Reg"* – whose miserable aura was acceptable because we thought he was a bloody good journalist.

With Trevor Buckley it was different, in that we all liked him enormously, really enjoyed his company and admired the way he ran the business but (while it may have been just typical youthful journalistic intolerance of editorial authority) we didn't really rate him as a journalist. We always referred to Trevor as *"Imasrunsus"* because that was what he was called by Sheila, our delightfully disrespectful receptionist, who had **Stoke** stamped through her like a stick of rock.

In a leader about a forthcoming local election Trevor once wrote: *"Who will win? Nobody knows. And it's our guess that nobody will know until all the votes are counted."* We were a hyper-critical bunch but we didn't think that was the best thing we had ever read!

Over a pint and *Scouse Pie* one day we had been joined by *Imasrunsus* (which didn't often happen because Big George's wasn't really to his liking) and I had been holding forth about the things I had learned as a sub-editor on the *Express & Star*. I had told of a tip the Deputy Chief Sub Gerry Link had given me, which was that a headline was always a good one if you could *sing* it. Gerry's meaning and message were subtle: If your selection and use of words for a headline were *right* it would have a lyrical lilt and quality to it. But *Imasrunsus* must have taken what I said too literally. A dreadful Des O'Connor song called *"One, Two, Three O'Leary"* was a big hit at the time... and the editor's headline over a report of a routine local planning inquiry in the next issue of the paper read *"One, Two, Three O'Leary – Knutton Garage Query."*

A miserable Reg Tomkinson read the "musical" headline out loud to the assembled newsroom in deadpan tones and utter contempt.

"I don't bloody **believe** it!" he moaned.

Twenty five years later I was to meet up again with Trevor Buckley, who moved on from Stoke to become a successful Managing Editor of the *Warrington Guardian* group and then, in semi-retirement, to create the concept of a big print edition of newspapers for the partially sighted. (A typically thoughtful project and a bloody good idea, which several newspapers adopted.)

I reminded him of his *"One, Two, Three O'Leary"* headline – for I knew that one of Trevor's many endearing qualities was that he never took himself too seriously – and we both roared with laughter. He might not have been the best journalist I ever met, but Trevor Buckley was the very best of people, spreading warmth, kindness and good humour everywhere he went and the happiness which epitomised that tiny newsroom in Stoke-on-Trent was as much his creation as it was that of the tremendous team of young journalists with whom I have always considered it a privilege to have worked.

The happy and positive memories which Pauline and I cherish still of our time in the Potteries are down entirely to the **people.** In the late 1960s the place itself was a shit hole. The pottery factories were still going strong and seemed to employ virtually everybody in the five towns. The kilns spewed out massive clouds of smoke and when it rained it rained soot. The factories were surrounded by rows of Victorian terraced houses, the red brick of which had long since been blackened by the all-pervading industrial pollution. It was an unremittingly bleak, grey, dull environment in which collective depression and huge chips on shoulders would have been entirely understandable and forgivable.

Yet nowhere in the world have I met more warm, welcoming, happy, upbeat, sharing, caring people.

In the streets, in the shops, in the pubs and the clubs the people of the Potteries were *always* cheery and friendly. In Normacot, the *House From Hell* became, incongruously, an abode of many fond memories. Our neighbours' doors were always open to each other and so – for this warmth was infectious – was our own.

Next door lived John and Lily, mum and dad to young Paul, who had been such a willing and welcome helper on the day we moved in. They were a lovely, gregarious and amusing couple. John was a very big muscular man, well over six feet tall, who looked like a professional wrestler but actually drove a truck for his living. Lily was petite and attractive. Unlike us, they possessed a motor car – a smart blue Rover which was John's pride and joy – and on Sundays he would take us all out for a trip through the Manifold Valley and into the Derbyshire countryside and we'd laugh all day.

John's best pal was another Normacot neighbour, a delightfully polite Indian who we called Ray. He was something important in the offices of the Wedgwood factory but had the most diffident and charmingly self-effacing manner.

Every Friday night, John, Ray and I would go out on a pub-crawl, starting at the British Legion Club then wending our way through the back street boozers in a circle that ended up back at "the Legion" – by which time we were as pissed as *Dickie Mint*. Pauline and Lily perfected an hilarious description of this unlikely trio – John six feet four and seventeen stone; Ray barely five feet tall and eight stone; me six feet tall and as thin as Ray – as we tottered home from our

Friday sessions, supporting each other against the ravages of our indulgence. It must, indeed, have been a rare sight.

It was on one of our Friday nights out that John came up with the "perfect" solution to a problem at the *House From Hell* which had been much occupying Pauline and I. The back garden was as badly neglected as the rest of the dump. It hadn't been touched for years and was completely overgrown with long grass. It had gone much too far to be tackled by a lawn mower, even if we had one, which we didn't. We were not, at this young stage in our lives, gardeners. Nothing like. And we didn't have a clue how to tackle this jungle.

As I bemoaned this problem over our fifth pint, John sat bolt upright and proclaimed: "JASON! He's your answer."

"Who's Jason?" I asked – imagining some philanthropic gardening expert who would come and do the job for nothing.

"JASON the donkey!"

Halfway down the road on which we lived, there was another pal of John's, who kept a donkey for the kids' amusement. Finding fresh pasture for this beast was a never-ending problem for John's mate, it seemed. And he would be only too pleased to let Jason graze away our own problem.

"Perfect," John concluded with an air of great satisfaction. "Jason'll 'ave it all looking like a bloody bowling green in no time!"

By the following Sunday lunch time Jason was at work, his "dad" having tethered him to a post by a length of rope carefully measured to be long enough to allow him access to all areas of our garden and short enough to ensure that he went no further.

Perfect. John was right.

Two weeks later the back garden might not have been looking like John's promised bowling green but Jason was doing a grand job. The grass was short and tidy. We were well pleased. It was Sunday afternoon and John and Lily had called round ready for our customary ride out in the Rover when young Paul banged on the back door in a great panic.

"Mum, Dad, Pauline, Barrie!" the lad shouted. "It's Jason. He's legged it!"

John and I raced out to see the ample rear end of this large donkey careering down the main road towards Hanley, rope and stake rolling and rattling in his wake. Soon, this pantomime scene was completed by one very large man and one very thin man, plus a 12-year-old boy in panting hot pursuit, shouting, **"Stop! Jason! Stop you bugger!"**

But Jason was unreceptive. His new-found freedom was great fun and he was stopping for nobody.

After chasing the stupid animal for miles, we eventually cornered him, in the small front garden of a neat terraced house where he was making a meal of some very nice roses.

"Next time," observed John as we walked back with an unrepentant Jason being dragged along behind us and our Sunday afternoon in ruins, "…. we'll borrow a bloody scythe!"

Often in the years that have followed, Pauline and I have reflected with great fondness on the friendships and fun we enjoyed in the Potteries and when ignorant people say – as they do – "Stoke? Who the hell would want to live *there?*" we say, "*We* would … gladly."

7. Nottingham ~ Round One

WE HAD BEEN IN THE POTTERIES for just a few months when the headhunters with whom I had enrolled came up trumps and the *Nottingham Evening Post* beckoned. Much as I'd enjoyed life on the *Stoke-on-Trent City Times Series* and happy though Pauline and I had been among those lovely people, this was the route back to the regional newspaper industry's "Premiership" after a brief spell in the fourth division.

The *Evening Post* was a big paper in a big city. Selling around 180,000 copies a night, it wasn't quite up there with the *Wolverhampton Express & Star* but it was one of the biggest in the UK.

The job the *Post* was offering was an interesting one that would take me into new areas of journalism and add a few more strings to that expanding bow which would one day shoot me into an Editor's chair. As **Diary Editor** I would be responsible for organising, collating, writing and sub-editing the paper's daily Diary (or gossip) column. I would also chip in as a general Features Sub-Editor. Both elements of the job would give me invaluable experience of page planning and design, which I lacked and of subbing in a different, more creative journalistic environment to the head-down, hard news, every-second-counts pace of the *Express & Star.*

I was interviewed by the laid-back, likeable and impeccably mannered Editor-in-Chief, Ken Burnett. He explained that my immediate boss would be the *Post's* Editor, Bill Snaith. He also informed me (and a few years later *this* would have been unthinkable for an employer!) that I would be required to join the National Union of Journalists, because this newspaper was a closed shop. I had never joined the union after the experience of my early days in Shrewsbury, I told him, but if that had to be a condition of the job, fair enough.

Just how different Nottingham was to Stoke, Wolverhampton and Shrewsbury struck me as soon as I walked out of the railway station to report for that interview. This was a *special* place. The city had a buzz to it, the like of which I'd never experienced. I felt excited and privileged to be there. There was an air of anticipation; an atmosphere of sophistication. I could not explain the intense feeling that being in Nottingham for the first time induced, but I did sense that it was unique.

It was big and bustling but it was also beautiful, with breathtaking architecture – nowhere more so than in the grand central Square where the splendid domed Council House with its imposing pillars looked down graciously on glorious high dancing fountains, this whole scene gleaming bright and light against a blue summer sky.

I had known big cities – like Liverpool, where lots of my mum's relatives lived – and Birmingham, where I'd been a student, but Nottingham was, quite simply and splendidly, something else.

Mr Burnett's offer accepted, new job in the bag, back on the station waiting for the train to Stoke, I rang Pauline at work. I was like an over-excited child, trying to describe so much at once that I did none of it justice.

Nottingham here we come…

No *House From Hell* here. The *Nottingham Evening Post* – or rather its proprietors, the seriously wealthy Forman Hardy family – owned a stunning stately home called Wilford House. It stood amidst its own beautiful grounds on the outskirts of the city, just a couple of miles from Trent Bridge, and had once been the much-loved home of an elderly female member of the family. When she died she had, with an old-fashioned philanthropy that I would come to know as typical of the Forman Hardys, bequeathed Wilford House to be used for the benefit of the newspaper's staff. It had duly been turned into 14 flats, which were let to employees for inexpensive rents. The glorious, secluded, tree-lined grounds of Wilford House had been converted into a magnificent sports centre for the staff, with football and cricket pitches, bowling greens, tennis courts and a social club.

"I'll see if one of the flats might be available for you," Ken Burnett had said when we'd discussed accommodation at the interview. And it was. So, on the day we moved to Nottingham, we were in proud and extremely grateful possession of the keys to Flat Number Four, Wilford House.

If Nottingham was unique, so was the *Evening Post*. Produced from a huge Victorian building in the middle of the city, this newspaper had a culture like no other I experienced, before or since.

The family of the proprietor, Lieutenant Colonel Tom Forman Hardy (a much decorated war hero) had owned daily newspapers in Nottingham since 1848. Until 1953 Nottingham had supported *four* local newspapers – the *Evening Post* and its sister morning paper *The Nottingham Guardian* (both owned by T. Bailey Forman Ltd, ie the Forman Hardys) and the *Evening News* and its sister morning paper *The Nottingham Journal* (both owned by a national company, Westminster Press). The arrival – or rather threat – of commercial television had led to a major contraction in Britain's newspaper industry and Westminster Press sold its two Nottingham titles to T. Bailey Forman Ltd. Such was the benevolent nature of T. Bailey Forman Ltd back in 1953 that when the subsequent amalgamation reduced the four newspapers to two, the company had promised that no job losses would ensue, so nearly 300 people had been absorbed and when I arrived in the Autumn of 1969 the *Nottingham Evening Post (and News)* and the *Nottingham Guardian Journal* were, to say the least, still exceptionally well-staffed. It was, as a consequence, a sheer joy to work there, because you had what seemed like all the time in the world to do your job.

The paternal approach of the Forman Hardy family was a throwback to a different age. They demonstrated hugely commendable appreciation, care and sense of duty towards their employees and that, plus the military background and style of the chairman (who was known to all with genuine affection as "Colonel Tom") induced, in turn, a deference and respectful protocol which equally belonged to times long since past. The result was a culture which would not have seemed out of place in the pages of a Dickens' novel and you felt that if it *had* been the great writer would have cast the Forman Hardys in an entirely favourable light – kindly and thoughtful rich folk, much to be admired and loved.

This Victorian culture revealed itself, among other manifestations, in the staff's habit of addressing every boss in the building as "Sir" and everybody but their closest colleagues as "Mister", "Missus", or "Miss". Thus – incongruously and rather absurdly it seemed to me – at the back end of the swinging sixties and aged only 24 I became known, at work, as Mr Williams!

The Editor of the *Evening Post* was Mr W. W. (Bill) Snaith. A dapper little Geordie with a shiny bald head, Mr Snaith was in his mid-50s... a very nice man but very conscious of his position and of the protocol. The Editor of the *Guardian Journal* was Mr K. L. (Ken) Macmillan. Another little man, with a shock of white hair and a white beard, he too was in his mid-50s. This was the age at which most editors were appointed. Mr K. E. (Ken) Burnett had become Editor in Chief at the same time (May 1969) as the two editors were installed, so I was one of the first appointments made by this new team of top editorial executives.

The features department, where I was to work, was shared by both papers and known respectfully as "The Brains Room." It had a studious, sombre atmosphere, the near silence of which matched that of the library, which, by deliberate design, was next door. I was very flattered to have been considered worthy of a place in The

Brains Room and wondered mischievously what some of my schoolmasters would make of such a thing, but in truth it was a very staid and dull environment for a 24-year-old.

The other occupants of The Brains Room were Wilf Berry, the Features Editor of the *Post;* Ian McKenzie Scott, the Features Editor of the *Guardian Journal;* Harold Mount and Don Taylor, features sub-editors who worked for both papers and Jean Bell, who did the administration and secretarial work for the department. Wilf Berry was middle-aged, Ian McKenzie Scott wasn't but seemed to be; Harold Mount and Don Taylor were elderly, as was "Miss" Bell – a heavy smoking, fond-of-a-drink gem of a woman loved dearly by all. Wilf was a thoroughly pleasant, considerate, gentlemanly bloke, a bit fussy; Ian was a sullen Scot who kept his head down; Harold, who had returned to journalism after a spell in public relations with a top firm in London, was a gentle, genial man with a great sense of humour; Don Taylor was a nice, well-meaning chap but a depressive hypochondriac who would, if you let him, talk for hours about his assorted ailments.

It was a small team, considering that the company employed around 200 journalists, but these were the days of thin (12 to 20 pages) broadsheet newspapers and it was easily big enough to do all that was required of it. None of the feature writers worked out of The Brains Room. They preferred the comparative pace of the news room and Jean Davey, the jovial, colourful Women's Editor told me one day: *"When I'm ready to be embalmbed, luvvie, I'll go to an undertaker – not in there!"*

For most of the time, The Brains Room team worked steadily on in complete silence but that would be broken just occasionally by some quiet small talk which would occur without the participants looking up from the pile of copy they were subbing and for some bizarre reason, I've always remembered every word of one such exchange...

Don Taylor – in a tone of deep personal loss: *"And the doctor's told me I can't ever eat broad beans again."*

Wilf Berry – in a tone of deep sympathy: *"Oh, I say Don. That's such a shame. You're really going to miss your broad beans?"*

Don Taylor: "No. I can't stand them."

Harold Mount: *"Bloody Hell."*

In the middle of The Brains Room stood an enormous table and every day began – at 7. 45am sharp, never so much as one minute earlier or later – with a ritual, the origin of which I never did fathom. One of a squad of spotty youths called "messengers" would struggle in with a massive wicker basket containing every piece of mail deliv-

ered for the entire Editorial Department and dump it in a moun-
tainous pile on the table. That was a signal for Mr Wilf Berry and Mr
Barrie Williams – both having already reported for duty at 7. 30am –
to march in silence up to the table, at which point they would be
joined simultaneously and with military precision by the editor, Mr
Bill Snaith, who, upon entering the room would say:

"Good morning, Mr Berry."

"Good morning, sir."

"Good morning, Mr Williams."

"Good morning, sir."

In complete silence, the three of us would then proceed to open
every piece of mail, placing it into a line of trays for the appropriate
recipient. Quite why this menial task had to be performed by the
Editor, the Features Editor and the Diary Editor was a complete
mystery to me – but such was the protocol of this well-ordered and
disciplined regime that I never thought it proper for me to ask!

My work as Diary Editor/Features Sub Editor on the *Nottingham
Evening Post* was absorbing and enjoyable. Features subbing and
page design was *(is)* very different from hard news work. I learned
new skills under the excellent and patient guidance of Wilf Berry and
there was a real quality to the journalism on this newspaper. My
Diary column was a daily half page of Nottingham gossip – a sort of
regional *William Hickey* – titled *On The Square*. It had been a much
loved feature of the *Evening Post* since Adam was a lad and the
Square referred to in that title was the busy, beautiful heart which
had so impressed and enthralled me on my first visit to this wonderful city known, not without very good reason, as the **Queen Of The
Midlands.** Every reporter on the staff was under standing instruction
(frequent failure punishable by dismissal) to provide a minimum of
two diary items a week.

My role was to choose, from all those offered, just half a dozen a
day to be polished and presented to the *Post's* many thousands of
readers. When I wasn't doing that, I would sub and lay out other
feature pages. After a while, I volunteered to take over the paper's
entertainment pages and the weekly women's page, which I welcomed because these allowed freedom to experiment and break
with the otherwise very strictly controlled page design of the paper.
It also brought me into regular contact with some exceptionally
talented specialist writers in theatre, pop, jazz and classical music
and with the inimitable Jean Davey, who always made me laugh.

Jean Bell was another who made me laugh. A little, elfin woman
with a gruff, smoker's voice and a blue boozer's nose, Jean was a
beacon of intelligent, sometimes smutty, humour and a purveyor of

unladylike language, which would occasionally liven up "The Brains Room" to the distinct discomfort of Wilf Berry, who was a paragon of politeness and proper protocol and had never been known to swear.

The *Nottingham Evening Post,* as befitted such a big, fine newspaper, had many excellent journalists: the News Editor Bill Ivory; the Chief Sub-Editor George Hunt and his young Deputy Tony Moss; the Sports Editor Harry Richards were all executives of Fleet Street standard; Jean Davey was a fine writer surpassed only by Emrys Bryson, a legend in Nottingham who had also written some much-admired books.

But the *Post* also had more than its fair share of lead-swingers, abusing the largesse of the proprietors and able to get away with it because the paper was so generously staffed. Harold Mount and I shared a bus journey home every night and we would sometimes fume with anger as we discussed the conduct of some of those rhino-skinned wastrels, full of bullshit and deference when under observation but bone-idle buggers when not. Most of them had never worked anywhere but the *Nottingham Evening Post* or (if they had moved across the city in the merger) the *Nottingham Evening News* and when, like Harold and I, you had travelled around a bit, you had a genuine appreciation of what marvellous employers Colonel Tom Forman Hardy and his family were. It filled us with rage to see people taking that for granted and – worse – taking the piss.

Away from work, Pauline and I would take full advantage of life in Nottingham. We were frequent visitors to the marvellous theatres, cinemas and lively pubs – as were my mum and dad when they came to stay with us at Wilford House, itself a source of the most enjoyable recreation. We spent hot summer Sunday afternoons sunbathing in the gardens while listening to John Peel playing ground-breaking music from previously unknown bands. T-Rex, with the fabulous Marc Bolan, were one of many to get a first airing on that innovative radio programme and even now, when I hear the ageless *Ride A White Swan* being played it transports me back to that time and place.

At work, I went from strength to strength, all the time growing in confidence and ability and particularly enjoying my latest acquired skill – designing pages. Time here just flew by and we were soon heading for our second Christmas in Nottingham. Every Christmas, Colonel Tom would add a very generous Christmas gift to everybody's weekly pay packet. The percentage of salary paid as this Christmas gift was loosely based on the company's performance during the year, which would be reviewed in the Colonel's annual message to the employees. That review occupied the first page of the two page message – with the Colonel's good wishes for *"A very merry Christmas and a happy New Year to you, your wives, husbands, sweethearts and families"* preceding his announcement of the gift on the second page. He was an extraordinarily shy and diffident man and it was said that he agonised for weeks over every word of that review so it would have been a source of great disappointment to the sweet old boy had he ever discovered that it was only the second page that ever got read! To the best of my knowledge, nobody ever told him – and that's just as it should have been.

Towards the end of 1970 there was much office gossip about the arrival on this tranquil scene of one Mr C. G. (Christopher) Pole-Carew, the man chosen as heir apparent to the Managing Director Mr F. G. (Frank) Cragg, who was due to retire. Like the Colonel and the Editors, Mr Cragg was rarely, if ever, seen by the vast majority of employees, but the Managing Director-in-waiting, Mr Pole-Carew was a dramatic wave maker in this placid "Victorian" pool. For one thing, he was amazingly striking physically. He was blond and six feet five inches tall. A former submariner, he had all the charisma and drive you would expect of a dashing young naval officer and *dash* he did. Everywhere. He would race from one department of the newspaper to another, determined to get to know every nook and cranny, every custom and practice of the place. In his wake would trail his assistant, Wing Commander Theo Kearton, recently of the RAF and nicknamed "the Winco."

This pair frightened the bloody life out of everybody!

Clearly, Colonel Tom was no fool. He had sensed a wind of change blowing through the regional newspaper industry and he was far too astute to get left behind. After leaving the Navy, Christopher Pole-Carew had been a management trainee and blossoming executive with an innovative national company *Thompson Regional Newspapers*. *TRN* were the recognised and highly respected trailblazers of a new dawn of much more profitable regional newspapers, led by a boom in classified advertising. The colonel had chosen Mr F. G. Cragg's successor wisely and – it was later to transpire – extremely *bravely*.

But rumours of what enormous change C. G. Pole-Carew was to bring to the *Nottingham Evening Post, Nottingham Guardian Journal* and assorted Nottinghamshire weekly newspapers were as near as I would get to experiencing it. While browsing through the journalists' trade magazine, *UK Press Gazette*, over a coffee in the canteen one morning I saw a recruitment advertisement that I found irresistible. It was a big ad with a drawing of a daft cow chewing a daisy chain. *COME WHERE THE GRASS IS GREENER* it implored. The *Kent Evening Post* wanted a Deputy News Editor, but it was the additional line *"with the ambition and talent to make further career progress"* which caught my eye and my imagination.

The *Kent Evening Post* was a new newspaper, one of a cluster launched in the 1960s. It had come out of the stables of the *Kent Messenger* – one of the biggest and best weekly newspapers in the country. It was much smaller than the *Nottingham Evening Post*, with a circulation that was a mere fraction of the size, but I was drawn inexorably to this opportunity. I felt instinctively that it was for me – that this was a job I *must* have.

I knew absolutely nothing about Kent, but a visit to the library for a surreptitious browse through the reference books served to heighten my interest. Within commuting distance of London yet boasting lovely countryside and seaside resorts, it was enormously attractive. The interviews were to be in London. I got one, arranged a mid-week day off with Wilf Berry, donned my Nottingham-best fashionable black suit with matching pink shirt and tie and hopped on a train – with no doubt whatsoever in my mind that I was going to come back with the job in the bag.

I was interviewed by the *Kent Messenger Group* Editorial Director, Michael Finley, and the Editor of the *Kent Evening Post*, Andy Hughes. These men were chalk and cheese. Michael Finley was smooth, impeccably and expensively dressed, with a broad striped shirt and multi-coloured bow tie. His thick brown hair was expertly groomed; his fashionable spectacles squeaky clean. He looked admiringly at my trendy suit as I sat down. Andy Hughes was dressed in an ill-fitting, crumpled suit with a row of Bic biros protruding from the breast pocket. His thinning hair was badly cut and unkempt and in his mouth was the biggest pipe I'd seen since I parted company with Jack Cater.

As the interview progressed, with Michael Finley leading and Andy Hughes occasionally looking exasperated by his line of questioning, I gained the impression that these two fellows didn't see eye to eye – but I liked very much what I was hearing.

The *Kent Evening Post* was clearly going places – and I could go with it. It was clearly going to grow – and I could grow with it. Compared with what I had in Nottingham it would be 'big fish in small pond time' again – but *this* pond was going to get bigger.

Despite the tensions I detected, I liked both these men, different though they were.

Yes… I'd like this job.

"It's yours," said Michael Finley.

8. Kentish Times

IT HAD BEEN A BLOODY GOOD PIECE of national newspaper investigative reporting which had exposed "Rachmanism" – corrupt slum landlords, mostly in London, who had made millions out of miserable people desperate to get a roof over their heads. But it didn't do me and my lovely wife any good at all! To stop crooks like Rachman ever being able to exploit people again the Government had passed the Rent Act, a piece of legislation which successfully controlled the business activities and standards of private landlords.

The trouble was, it had the effect of throwing the baby out with the bathwater. Letting out property privately became such a minefield of prohibitive rules and regulations that it drove the good private landlords out along with the bad. The result was that accommodation available to rent privately became extremely scarce – particularly in London and the South East.

Ever since we were married, Pauline and I had rented privately owned property. Now Williams, typically without giving where we were going to live a thought, had decided to move to an area in which privately rented property had virtually disappeared! We had no savings. Buying a house was simply not an option – nor, of course, for people in our sort of situation was council accommodation, for which there was a long enough waiting list of indigenous residents.

We placed a "wanted" ad in the local papers in Kent but it drew a complete blank. With just a few days to go before my month's notice at Nottingham expired and I was due to start work on the *Kent Evening Post*, we had nowhere to live.

I rang Editorial Director Michael Finley in Kent.

"What are we going to do?" I asked.

"Well…" he replied, "that's largely up to you."

Charming!

There's always been something of the *Micawber* in my approach to life. I took the view that *something* would turn up. And – such as it was – *something* did. Michael Finley, obviously having had second thoughts about his earlier response, rang back to say the company would put Pauline and I up in a hotel while in the meantime exploring the possibility of re-opening some accommodation they once had above a district office.

"If it's habitable, you might be able to rent that from us," he said. We did not have our own transport so this solution meant rapidly arranging to put our dog *Brandy* into boarding kennels in Nottinghamshire and with a truly good friend David Lowe, a reporter on the *Nottingham Evening Post* – who *did* have a car – to drive him all the way to Kent after we'd found a roof over our heads. Then we took a train to our new destination.

That cow chewing a daisy chain in the advertisement which had tempted me to these parts was, it transpired, just a tad misleading. The *Kent Evening Post* was based in and served the Medway Towns, known to locals as "the arsehole of Kent". These were four towns, Rochester, Chatham, Gillingham and Strood, all running into each other, much like the Potteries' towns make up Stoke-on-Trent. They were populous urban conurbations with large numbers of London commuters. The River Medway linked them all. Chatham, a naval town with a big, busy Royal dockyard; Rochester, Dickensian, historic, with a cathedral and rightly considering itself a cut above the rest; Gillingham, an uninspiring dormitory town surrounded by massive housing estates in which dwelt most of the commuters; Strood, an industrial mass and mess with a huge cement factory at its heart. Not a bloody cow to be seen, with or without a daisy chain!

And as for that *grass* which was supposed to be *greener*...

This could not have been further removed from the lush pastures, fruit orchards and hop fields of the much better-known rural Kent, nor from the white cliffs of Dover, the sandy shores of Broadstairs, Margate and Ramsgate, the coastal grandeur of Folkestone, the affluent Weald and posh Tunbridge Wells. By comparison with all that, the locals' description of the Medway Towns as the fundamental orifice of the county was entirely appropriate!

Yet, as Pauline and I explored our new environment on that first weekend, we fell immediately in love with it. And although there was no way we could have known it then, these dirty old towns were to play an enormous part in our future.

It was February 1st, 1971 and it was freezing cold (a condition not improved by the fact that we had nowhere to live!) as I left our hotel to report for duty at 256, High Street, Chatham, the Medway base of the *Kent Evening Post*. The office was quite small but as big as it needed to be, housing just reporters, photographers and the News Editor. The Editor, his Assistant and the rest of the staff were based in the *Kent Messenger's* HQ in Maidstone, where the *Post* was printed. I was greeted by the News Editor, Peter Edwards, a happy and very humorous man in his mid-30s, with jet-black hair and a luxurious black beard. Working under Peter was a team of eight young (but all fully qualified) reporters, who, I soon learned, were very talented and hard-working.

They were an immediately likeable bunch – friendly and good-humoured. This was an office that laughed a lot. Great. Suited me. As did being back doing what I did best, news editing, creating and writing. I was to cover and deputise for Peter as News Editor while at the same time tackling major reporting and writing assignments. My first job was to describe how the Medway Towns were prepared (or not!) for the arrival of decimalisation of the UK's currency... the end of pounds, shillings and pence; of big brown pennies, half-crowns, sixpences, threepenny bits and halfpenny pieces.

The conclusion was that the good folk of Medway wanted this massive change like a hole in the head and despite the Government's protestations to the contrary they were convinced that the money in their pockets and purses was going to be worth less.

"The buggers are conning the bleedin' lot of us," a market trader told me to the instant affirmation of his customers. It was a majority view and while I didn't believe that the Prime Minister Ted Heath or his very recent predecessor Harold Wilson planned it that way – in next to no time those cynics were to be proved absolutely right!

With my first day enjoyably completed, I joined the reporters for a pint before going "home" to Pauline at the hotel and with a lot of week left at what was very nearly the end of my money I asked them:

"What day is pay day?"

In the 10 years since my first week's wages I had only ever been paid weekly in cash and it had never crossed my mind that here it would be any different – but I was in for a shock.

"We don't get paid weekly and it's not cash," I was told. "We get a monthly salary cheque paid straight into the bank."

"Oh, Bloody Hell – It's only the first of the month!"

"And don't tell me," laughed chirpy Cockney reporter Terry Greenwood. "You're already brassic!"

Well, we weren't exactly brassic (ie. boracic lint – *skint)* but I'd anticipated a Thursday pay day, which I'd always had and the money we'd got left was not going to last much more than a week

Terry's next comment brought no comfort, either...

"It's no use asking them if they'll pay you weekly for the first month. We've all tried that and they always say no. Don't like establishing a bleedin' precedent, do they!" Then he slapped me on the back. "Don't you worry, mate. We won't let you starve. Ave anuvver pint!"

So it was back to the hotel to tell my wife that not only were we *homeless* – we were also about to be *penniless!*

Her reaction was typical.

"Oh, well," she said. "I was going to get a job, anyway!"

After a week in the hotel it was confirmed that the firm's accommodation, suggested by Michael Finley, could indeed be made available. It was a flat over the district office in Canterbury Street, Gillingham (another corner shop!). It had a lounge, a tiny kitchen, two small bedrooms and a toilet. Pauline took control of it all while I was at work, cleaned the place from top to bottom and organised delivery of our furniture from the flat we'd left behind in Nottingham. On the first night I went back there instead of to the hotel she had made it warm and welcoming. Our own three-piece suite was arranged around the glowing gas fire and the enticing aroma of piping hot stew wafted from the kitchen.

"Oh, and Dave and Mavis are driving down with *Brandy* at the weekend," she told me over our first dinner in our latest abode. "They've even been to see him in the kennels and they say he's fine. Wasn't that nice of them?"

It was indeed. True friends they had been, in an hour of need.

This flat was nice. It had a big bay window which looked out over the *Westcourt Arms*, the pub across the road (so handy!) It was in a respectable residential area of Gillingham, with everything you could possibly require within convenient reach. By the weekend Pauline had made it even more comfortable and cosy and when *Brandy* bounded up the stairs and flew into our arms we knew we had found a home. With Dave and Mavis, we took *Brandy* to the beach at Whitstable, our first visit to the Kent coast and we all walked for miles in the crisp, cold sea air, the dog, bless him, clearly convinced he had found seventh heaven. Late that night, sitting snug, sound and secure around the fire in the Canterbury Street flat, I told Pauline: "We're all right now, mate – even if we *are* brassic!"

"Of course, we are," she concurred.

But I knew full well that it was no thanks to me and that without this remarkable young woman at my side I'd get myself into all sorts of predicaments.

Pauline *did* get a job very shortly, and a very good one. She joined the Civil Service in the Department of Employment at Chatham. It paid well but there was one bit of bad news… she was to be paid *monthly* too. There was only one thing for it. We'd simply have to manage on what we'd got until the end of the month. We searched every pocket, every handbag, rustled up all our small change and found that we had quite a bit more than I first thought. But it was still going to be extremely tight.

"Thank God February's a short month," said Pauline.

"Is it a Leap Year?" I asked.

As the desperately needed end of the month neared, I was downstairs in the Canterbury Street office one day talking to Arthur Potter, the *Post's* Circulation Manager, whose job included management of the district offices.

"Do you know," said Arthur, looking puzzled, "I can't for the life of me understand where the bloody soap keeps disappearing to."

I looked the other way – and said nothing!

Six weeks into my new job I picked up an exclusive story, which was one of the best I ever wrote. I was in the *Westcourt Arms* enjoying a quiet pint before going down to the Chinese take-away to pick up *three* portions of Chicken Fried Rice for our Saturday night supper (dog lovers will concur that there's nothing at all silly about bringing your pooch a Chinese meal, but I digress) when I noticed the landlord Laurie, to whom I'd become well-known, pointing a customer in my direction. This swarthy little man of forty-something with a battered face, somewhat the worse for drink, introduced himself.

"My name's Bill Applegarth, I'm a merchant seaman," he said. "They tell me you're a journalist."

We sat down in a quiet corner.

"Look mate, I'm pissed, I know," he continued, "but I'd tell you the same stone cold sober." And he went on to explain that he had just been to visit the widow of a shipmate of his who had died from malaria while on a voyage. He was distressed and angry having just left his pal's woman and her three kids, aged seven, six and one and he wanted to expose what had been going on. Drunk or not, I just knew this man was telling the truth. We arranged to meet the next morning so that he could take me to talk to the widow. We did. He was sober. And my hunch about the veracity of what he had told me in his cups the night before was confirmed.

Three weeks later, after a good deal of research and careful checking, the *Kent Evening Post* carried a two-page special investigation. On the front page under my picture byline, was the headline '**THE SHIP OF SHAME**' and a strapline saying '*BARRIE WILLIAMS tells the shocking story of a seaman who should not have died and calls for justice for the widow he left behind*' a condensed version of the story Bill Applegarth brought to me in the pub that night read:

"Today the Evening Post can tell the disturbing story of the Shell tanker SS Vitrina and of the shocking circumstances surrounding the death of a 40-year-old seaman serving aboard it.

It's the story of how a crew were subjected to appalling conditions on THE SHIP OF SHAME.

David Maytum, whose home was in Rock Avenue, Gillingham, died in a New York hospital from malaria. He should not have died.

The ship's hospital, where David Maytum should have been kept and cared for, was used as a dirty linen locker.

After suffering at sea for almost a week, he was left in his bunk for 36 hours when the ship reached New York.

Then he was WALKED ashore to a car to be driven to hospital.

Shipmates of David Maytum, who are doing all they can to help his widow and three young children, have described to me in great detail the conditions aboard the SS Vitrina. They have done so because they believe his life was lost needlessly. They feel it must never happen again.

They told how, even after David Maytum's death, no anti-malaria tablets were issued to the crew, even though they were trading in the Persian Gulf where the quantity of tablets is supposed to be increased by 100 per cent.

They told how, before David Maytum's death, when the ship broke down off Nigeria, they were stuck for two and a half days with no sanitation, no running water and no air conditioning.

Since David Maytum died, on March 7th 1970, solicitors hired by the National Union of Seamen have been negotiating a settlement for damages to be paid to his widow. We hope they will be very substantial. And we hope they will be paid soon because since her husband's death Mrs Pauline Maytum has had a severe financial struggle.

In the meantime, we feel the story should be told because, like those seamen, we believe David Maytum should not have died. And, like those seamen, we believe it must NEVER be allowed to happen again.

Evidence given to me independently and at different times by men who served with David Maytum on SS Vitrina paints a clear picture of what went on. Men like 46-year-old Bill Applegarth, who is doing more than anyone to seek justice for Mrs Maytum and her children.

Bill told me: ' SS Vitrina had visited malaria areas such as the West Coast of Africa. It is laid down in the Merchant Navy Medical Scales Act that the ship's company should be issued with anti-malaria tablets. These tablets were not issued on the Vitrina. '"

Inside the paper, Bill's evidence and that of others I had tracked down and spoken to was published in full, along with pictures of those witnesses. They told true horror stories about the dreadful conditions they had been forced to endure aboard this old rust bucket of a ship. On the front page there was a moving picture of David Maytum's widow and children, along with a picture of him – a big, strong handsome man he had been – and of the ship at the centre of this scandal. The ship's owner, Shell, to its great credit, took my exposé on the chin and made no attempt at a cover up. A Shell spokesman told me frankly:

"It is terribly regrettable but regulations are laid down and we have no way of knowing if they are being followed at sea. Everything was not as it should be on this ship. We have taken disciplinary measures but I'm afraid I can't elaborate on that. This was an isolated case and we hope to God it doesn't ever happen again."

When I look back at that statement 35 years later I realise just how rare the sort of honesty Shell displayed that day in 1971 has now become.

My story was picked up by all the national newspapers and by national and local television and radio. Mrs Maytum was then paid a suitable sum in compensation. She took the trouble to call at our flat, with her lovely kids, to thank me. The next time Bill Applegarth came home on leave, he too contacted me to thank me and we enjoyed several jars of ale together at the *Westcourt Arms*.

This was local journalism at its best.

It was also the brand of journalism much favoured by the Editor of the *Post* Andy Hughes. Andy was a brilliant editor who took the community campaigning role of his newspaper very seriously. He was a disciple of Harry Evans, who, as Editor of the *Sunday Times,* had famously exposed the Thalidomide scandal. It was from Andy Hughes that I learned the enormous value of campaigning on local issues; how a well chosen, well directed campaign conducted with passion and genuine belief can *change* the lives of people for the better; how a relatively small newspaper can punch above its weight and influence thinking and decision-making in the corridors of power; how effective pursuit of good campaigns can raise your profile and build a positive reputation for your paper – and how using the power your paper gives you to benefit your community is *the* most rewarding form of journalism.

It was Andy Hughes' adherence to those principles that led to the *Kent Evening Post's* 'Fighting For Dignity' campaign. Andy had read in the *Sunday Times* how the Chronically Sick and Disabled Persons' Act, passed in 1970, was being virtually ignored by many local authorities a year later. This was the legislation which was ultimately responsible for all the provisions (access to public buildings and public transport; wheelchair-friendly streets; ramps, adaptations to the home, stair lifts, etc, etc) taken pretty much for granted now but practically non-existent then.

Andy rang me in the Chatham office: "Let's find out how Kent County Council is fulfilling this obligation," he said.

A week later, I launched our campaign with a Page One article under the headline '**Record Of Shame**'. It read:

"Kent has an appalling record in caring for disabled people. Does it shock you to learn that more than 2,000 severely handicapped people in Kent have no service whatsoever from the local authority? It shocks us.

Kent had a disabled register of 3,250 in 1969 – yet the total number of disabled people in the county who should be registered is estimated at 18,000. That shocks us, too.

The county spent £90,000 on the disabled in 1969. . . . That is a miserable amount.

Last year, the Government introduced the Chronically Sick and Disabled Persons Act. Its aim was to make sure that counties like Kent pulled their socks up. It sought a completely new deal for disabled people. It was designed to give disabled people dignity and self respect. It set out to ensure that they would no longer be cut off from the rest of society, cruelly ostracised because of their disabilities.

The Act has not worked in Kent. Why? Because little or nothing has been done to make it work. The Post feels that this state of affairs has existed long enough. It is time that serious, concerted attempts were made to implement the Act as fully as possible. The Post now pledges itself to getting this done.

If we fail, it will be a shameful indictment upon Kent County Council and every elected representative of it.

From today, we want to know about those 2,000 people who are not getting what they are now legally entitled to. We want to know, too, about the hundreds who may be receiving some services – but nowhere nearly as many as they should. If you have a relative, friend or neighbour who is disabled and in need of help, let us know. If you are disabled yourself and particularly if you are living alone write to us and tell us how you are living.

The Post's campaign Fighting For Dignity begins today. Inside you will find a simple, easy to read guide to exactly what the Chronically Sick and Disabled Persons Act means and to what it entitles you. Every disabled person, all relatives, friends and neighbours of disabled people should read it. Then ask...HOW MUCH OF THIS IS BEING DONE IN KENT?"

The reaction to that clarion call was amazing. Considering that the *Evening Post* was at that time only three years old and selling around 16,000 copies a night, the number of people who responded was phenomenal. It prompted a hasty response from the chairman of the social services committee at Kent County Council, one Mrs Dorothy Elvy, a Tory alderman, who, in a long and detailed Press statement to the *Post* and the rest of the media, denounced my articles as "painting a false and misleading picture" and declared my conclusions to be "much too harsh".

That was a foolish tactic. I had *really* done my homework on this one. I knew more about this Act of Parliament and what by then it should have been doing than she and her officers did. I had them bang to rights and in a follow-up article I demolished her statement line by line and without mercy.

The picture my articles had painted had not been a "false and misleading" one, I countered, but a demonstrably true and deeply disturbing one. Point by point, statistic by statistic, figure by figure, I proved her wrong and concluded...

Tell me Kent County Council is going to take a fresh look at its methods of registering disabled people; List the provisions of this admirable Act of Parliament one by one and tell me precisely how you plan to deliver them; Tell me that you will enlist the aid of local voluntary organisations for the disabled in order to help make the Act work in Kent; Tell me that you will form a special committee with co-opted representatives of the voluntary disabled associations and co-opted members of the disabled community to look closely at the whole concept of the Act and how it is best implemented in Kent. Then – and only then – will I concede that your council's record is one of performance, not shame.

Every day thereafter the *Post* carried moving stories and pictures revealing how disabled people in the Medway Towns were living or, rather, merely *existing*... for that was the truth of it. Yet for every story that was heartbreaking there was another that was heart-warming – stories of great courage and fortitude, of good humour and incredible patience, of sacrifice and selfless devotion of families, of loyal friends prepared to give up so much themselves to try to bring a little light to these poor, blighted lives. Every story moved you. And every one ended with an assessment of what the new legal entitlement under the Act would mean to these people – if only they had it.

Two months later, when it met for its monthly meeting, Kent County Council had changed its tune. Having just been presented with a petition bearing 10,000 signatures in support of our campaign, senior Alderman Edward Moore paid tribute to the work of the *Post*, to which he referred, somewhat patronisingly, as "... a gallant little evening paper circulating in the Medway Towns." He went on: "I would criticise, in the kindest way possible, the paper's inference that this council has ignored the rights of disabled people as human beings." Then he added: "I warn members that if we are to carry out our mandatory responsibilities under this Act it will cost money."

At last, the truth! Like so many well-intentioned Acts of Parliament, the Chronically Sick and Disabled Persons' Act had hit the reality buffer of how much it was going to cost. It had been a Private Members Bill, pioneered through the House by Alf Morris, the Labour MP for Manchester Wythenshawe. Alf's dad was disabled. He had grown up with the immense difficulties, which his Act sought to ease and he had observed poignantly: "When a member of your family is disabled the *whole* of your family is disabled."

Given the Act's status, the Government, probably cynically, had decreed that there was not an obligation on local authorities for 100 per cent implementation. That had given the less-inclined local authorities (ie most of them!) a legal loophole and the result was that only 10 per cent were seriously even trying to make it work.

Alderman Moore went on: "I would say to the *Evening Post* that it is no use campaigning today for extra money to be spent on this and that and then next February to campaign for the reduction of the burden of the rates."

Bullshit! Our next edition promised the alderman that if the council **did** begin to implement the Act properly we would not complain about the rates come February and alongside more moving local cases of disabled people in distress I wrote another scathing attack which began...

"The charter that never was. That will be the pitiful epitaph for the Chronically Sick and Disabled Persons' Act unless many more local authorities are shamed, bullied, cajoled or somehow forced into action on its widespread provisions."

The campaign was relentless; its unremitting assault on the county council was merciless. A year later, it had still not abated. We were winning. And our crusade was attracting national attention. Our editor Andy Hughes was invited to write an article about its progress. Andy wrote:

"When the *Evening Post's* campaign was mounted in June 1971 the Chronically Sick and Disabled Persons' Act was being virtually ignored by many local authorities...and Kent had one of the worst records in the country.

"Kent's local authorities as a whole – and the county council in particular – had done little or nothing towards implementation of the Act. Indeed, most disabled people had never even heard of it. The first task, then, was to inform; to let disabled people know exactly what they were entitled to under the Act. They were implored to fight – and to keep on fighting – for their rights. Since the Act was basically about bringing dignity to disabled people *Fighting For Dignity* was adopted as the campaign's title.

"The campaign has been conducted throughout by the *Evening Post's* Deputy News Editor Barrie Williams and has demanded his total involvement, working relentlessly for and closely with disabled people while continuing with his normal duties and other assignments. His interest in the cause of the disabled has extended beyond his professional duties.

"If the campaign was to succeed at all it had to be one of sustained effort and pressure rather than short-lived, sensational beligerance. Its criticisms had to be as constructive as they were pungent – and so did all its actions.

"The initial series of articles had more than the desired effect. In the ensuing weeks disabled people throughout the *Post's* circulation area were constantly in touch with Barrie Williams for advice and guidance on their entitlements. This was given and with very few exceptions these people began to get some of the things to which they were entitled.

"The campaign was so successful in its early stages that it soon became apparent that a committee, formed of representatives of the local societies and organisations for the disabled – something which was suggested in the first *Fighting For Dignity* article – was vital to its progress. So many enquiries were coming into the *Evening Post* office that it was becoming impossible to deal with them all. In addition, it was felt that a group which was independent of the *Post* could achieve a much stronger bargaining position than a newspaper could ever hope for. Williams decided the best way to get the group off the ground was to call a public meeting. He hired a hall and lined up eminent speakers. The meeting was an unqualified success. The Action Group was formed that night. The group was unique in bringing together various societies and organisations for the disabled under one banner and its formation aroused national interest and publicity.

"To achieve maximum impact for the campaign Williams had decided, prior to the formation of the Action Group, to petition Kent County Council. Copies of the petition were delivered with the paper, junior delivery agents collected signatures – as did newsagents, members of local societies, clubs, church groups and youth organisations. Thousands of signatures were ultimately presented to the county council by members of the newly formed Action Group…so many signatures, in fact, that it took two burly attendants to carry them all into County Hall.

"The formation of the Action Group is probably the greatest achievement of the campaign so far. Kent's disabled people now have a collective body to act on their behalf. The group is daily dealing with cases – obtaining proper entitlements under the Chronically Sick and Disabled Persons' Act for disabled people who seek their help.

"Another major achievement is the growth of the campaign – spreading as it has, all over Kent and way beyond the *Post's* circulation area. Local councils all over the county have now livened up to their responsibilities under the Act. They are now carrying them out and in some cases even joining in the campaign's constant badgering of Kent County Council. Despite the fact that the county council has not yet carried out its duty to publicise the Act, very large numbers of Kent's disabled population are now aware of their entitlements. They are now pushing for them, either independently or through the Action Group…and getting them. Many more will get their entitlements when the county council improves its register and increases its expenditure on the disabled and the county is beginning to move in the right direction. The Action Group, backed to the hilt by the *Post*, will go on fighting for dignity until the day they are completely satisfied that all that can be done **is** being done. When the campaign started, that day seemed an intolerably long way off. Now it is very much nearer."

When you're working as hard as you live and living as hard as you work as a journalist, it's often difficult to step back and see the big picture. Andy's article on our campaign did that for me. And I read his words (carefully chosen, for he was not given to hyperbole) with immense pride.

That pride was heightened tenfold when, on November 30th, 1971, Alf Morris MP wrote to Andy from the House of Commons:

"I am writing to convey my warmest congratulations to Mr Barrie Williams and your newspaper for your admirable campaign to help severely disabled people in your circulation area.

*As the author of the Chronically Sick and Disabled Persons'
Act, I have had Mr Williams' articles drawn to my attention by
many people. All of them have expressed the highest praise for
his articles and I know, from many sources, of the major impact
they have had throughout Kent.*

*These articles are a fine example of campaigning journalism
and I shall be grateful if you can convey my warmest congratulations to Mr Williams."*

On December 1ˢᵗ, 1971, Mr George Wilson, Director of Britain's
Central Council For The Disabled, wrote to Andy...

*"The Central Council For The Disabled is extremely grateful
to the Evening Post for its efforts on behalf of the disabled and
the weight added to their cause by your Fighting For Dignity
campaign.*

*It represented the first efforts for a sustained campaign on
behalf of the disabled in a specific area and was able to deal
with problems and difficulties on a more personal basis than
any national campaign. Since the launching of your campaign
similar projects have been forthcoming in many parts of Britain
and it has produced a realisation that the problems of the disabled, which are to be solved by local authorities, are best aired
at local level.*

*One of the most heartening features of the campaign has
been its end product of an action committee which can continue to press for improvements in the care of the disabled in the
knowledge that the local press are behind them. The local press
have a major part to play in the pin- pointing of local problems
and "Fighting For Dignity" and its results admirably demonstrate this role."*

And on December 13ᵗʰ, 1971, Mr A. M. Kinnear, Senior Regional
Officer of the Spastics Society, wrote to Andy...

*"I am writing to express my admiration for the "Fighting For
Dignity" campaign waged by your newspaper. As the officer responsible for the affairs of the Spastics Society in South East
England I am only too aware of the enormous problems facing
handicapped people in Kent.*

*For many years the voluntary organisations in Kent have
been pressing the county authorities to increase their services to
the handicapped which, to say the least, were minimal. It was
obvious that this policy was to continue, despite the publication
of the Chronically Sick and Disabled Persons' Act. Your timely*

intervention and the hard-hitting character of Barrie Williams'
articles shattered the oft-expressed complacency of the county's
elected representatives. It is too early to assess the full effect of
this impact but I can report a more co-operative attitude from
my opposite numbers at county level. I also know that the indi-
vidual cases which you have highlighted were dealt with post
haste!

It will interest you to know that my Society has recommended
your campaign to all my fellow regional officers as an example
that they might follow in their respective regions.

I look forward, with you, to the day that dignity for the
handicapped is finally won."

It took a long, long time before Alf Morris' dream of dignified lives
for the disabled came to full fruition – even now you can come
across examples of thoughtlessness. But the attitude of local authorities all over Britain changed for the better after our campaign
and Kent went from being one of the worst to one of the best. The
example we set and the structure for concerted action that we put
into place was copied with successful effect in many other parts of
the land and to this day when I see disabled people enjoying proper
facilities I feel a twinge of pride.

It was a good campaign and an object lesson in tenacious journalism. It also taught me, through sustained close contact with
disabled people, so much about them, their needs and their aspirations and above all else of the crucial need never to patronise them.
You can take away their limbs and their mobility; their sight, their
hearing and their speech. But you should never take away their
pride and their dignity.

That campaign lasted several years and I remained a member, as
Press and Public Relations Officer, of Kent's Disabled Action Group
in a personal capacity. As the only able-bodied member of the
group, *they* took the piss out of *me!* Their resilience and their unquenchable sense of humour never ceased to amaze me... none
more so than that of Len Heale, the group's irascible but very amusing chairman. Len, an ex-sailor, had lost both his legs in an accident
as a young man. He had resolved to make the very best of the two
limbs that remained and developed incredible upper arm strength
and dexterity in his hands – so much so that he became a champion
archer.

Len drove a specially adapted Morris Minor motor car, with **all**
the controls, including the brakes, on the steering column. He always insisted on giving me a lift to meetings and I never liked to

refuse for fear of offending him, but sitting in the passenger seat of that car was an absolute nightmare. Quite simply, Len drove like a bloody maniac! Too fast. Too close. Too late braking. Too soon cornering. You name the driving misdemeanour, he did it. And whenever he had a close-to-disaster encounter with another motorist, which was at least a couple of times on every journey, it was always the other guy's fault. Len would drop his window and yell *"Watch what you're doing you twat. I'm disabled!"* while the entirely innocent recipient of his wrath would look totally bemused, terribly upset and deeply embarrassed.

After one such encounter, and being close enough to Len by then to say what I thought without concession to his disability, I told him:

"Len, it's YOU! You're a bloody awful reckless driver!"

He roared with laughter. "What do your expect?" he said. "I'm only half the man I used to be!"

Andy Hughes and I shared an understanding and agreement about what made good local journalism that was almost telepathic. Between us, we were producing good stuff. I had enormous respect and admiration for him as a journalist and as an editor. He, equally, respected my talent and genuinely appreciated my contribution and work rate. The *Kent Evening Post* was doing exceptionally well and enjoying really impressive circulation growth. This, then, was a professional "marriage" made in heaven.

At a time when Rochester Borstal was getting a very bad Press, including from the *Kent Evening Post,* Andy met the new Governor, who protested that the stories published about his institution were biased, exaggerated and out of context. Essentially, it was being alleged that the regime was brutal, that the young "trainees" were treated more like main line adult prisoners than young offenders and that the underlying culture was one of detention and punishment rather than rehabilitation and education. There had been some well-publicised incidents in which the lads had rebelled against the system – including one major riot – and it had become routine for youngsters leaving the Borstal to slag it off in the local media. A couple of headline-seeking MPs had asked questions in the House of Commons about the Rochester regime and Home Office assurances that there was no cause for serious concern had failed to stem the bad publicity both locally and nationally.

When Andy met the new Governor he was told that there **had** been some problems caused by a handful of backwoodsmen among the Borstal's officers but they had been sorted. However, it was proving impossible to get that across to the media, who still believed every bad word that came out of the place.

"What do I have to do?" he asked Andy.

Smartly, Andy replied, "Let a journalist in with complete freedom to look at everything and talk to everybody."

Between them, they agreed that there was no point in sending a journalist in for a couple of hours. Whoever went had to live, eat and breathe the place.

And that's how I came to spend a week behind bars...

The deal was that I was to have genuine freedom inside to go where I liked, see whatever I wanted to see and talk to anybody I chose. I had to experience conditions for myself.

The Governor was true to his word and I became a Borstal boy for a week. The free reign I was given by a Governor, whose attitude towards Press relations was years ahead of its time, and by the Home Office, which must have approved it, was extraordinary – so much so that I would have known if anything was being covered up.

I was able to produce some great articles. They pulled no punches. I did not like everything that went on by any means, but at the end of my week inside I was able to conclude that Rochester Borstal was tough but properly run and that the inmates themselves, talking to me privately and without fear of recrimination, were able to confirm that most of the stories coming out of the place were out of all proportion to reality.

It had been one hell of an experience.

And to this day, I can still taste the bloody awful food!

Pauline and I loved our new "posting" in Kent. She really liked her job and was beginning to see it as a good career. Everything was rosy... except we still didn't have a proper home to call our own. The Canterbury Street flat was nice now, but we felt it was time we had something better. The problem was that we had moved to the most expensive housing area in the UK and it was going to take ages for us to save enough money to put down a deposit on a home of our own. Browsing through the small ads one day, Pauline saw the offer of a 100 per cent mortgage. It was from a broker in Bromley and boasted "a home of your own without the need for a deposit."

A couple of phone calls and a visit to Bromley later we had a mortgage. The broker – a flash bloke in a very expensive suit – told us: "Just make bloody sure you keep up the payments."

The payments were hefty. Even with two decent salaries it was not going to be easy, but Pauline and I were in total agreement.

"We've GOT to do this."

It was to turn out to be the best decision we ever made.

We found a house we liked in Rainham Mark, a suburb of Gillingham. A modern, five-year-old town house in a quiet tree-lined cul-de-sac, for sale at £6,300. It seems laughable, now, but that was bloody expensive! A similar house in Nottinghamshire would have cost around £2,000.

By September 1971 we were the proud owners (well – in theory, at least!) of No. 7, Phillips Court, Rainham Mark. And we were blissfully happy. We furnished the house "payment by instalments" in black leather, white wood and purple décor – all very trendy. Our neighbours were all roughly the same age as us – youngsters mortgaged up to the neck – and we made our own fun as cheaply as we could, taking it in turn to throw parties.

Now it was time to tackle another hurdle…

"You *really* should get yourself a driving licence," said Andy one day. "If you did, I could get you a company car."

Four attempts at the test later a brand new Fiat 127 in duck-egg blue sat on our drive. It was a small car with an engine that sounded like a sewing machine, but it was OURS. We now had our first home and our first car. When we added our first colour TV (hugely prestigious – albeit only by courtesy of a rental company) we felt like we had really arrived. For council house kids all this was something else and when the parents came to stay our pride was exceeded only by theirs!

Very soon after that, I was promoted to News Editor of the *Kent Evening Post*. The paper was going from strength to strength. A bright tabloid, it was doing things others had not even thought of. Andy Hughes had a natural rapport with the sort of readers we wanted to reach. He knew what they wanted. But selling our paper was never easy. We were only 30 miles from London, where ruled the mighty *London Evening News* and *London Evening Standard* – and both came into our patch. Our Circulation Manager, Arthur Potter, a crafty Cockney with an inherent streetwise cunning, was brilliant. He perfected a foolproof way of dealing with the competition from London. He and one of his reps would stand on Chatham railway station when the relevant train from London arrived; wait while the guard threw the piles of *News's* and *Standards* onto the platform, look around to make sure nobody was watching… **then chuck them back onto the train!** However, he *always* ensured that he left a couple of bundles on the platform – so that newsagents thought that was all they were getting. In time it dawned on our competitors that Chatham wasn't getting nearly enough papers and Margate far too many and 'Arf Pot' – as he was affectionately known to all of us – was rumbled. But the ruse had been very effective.

Recognising that most of our thousands of Medway commuters were going to pick up a *News* or a *Standard* in London, read it on the train and bring it home, we aimed the *Evening Post* at the indigenous working-class population of the Towns and at the *wives* of the London commuters, who were captive on the big housing estates. It was a bizarre reader mix, but it worked, as the very impressive circulation growth – helped along considerably by the energy and innovation of Arf Pot – proved for all to see. We were a good team.

The *Kent Messenger* had always had a really strong reputation in the regional newspaper industry. Now the *Kent Evening Post* was being talked about in similarly admiring terms. There were those in Nottingham who hadn't been able to understand why I chose to move from one of the biggest evening papers in the country to a tiny three-year-old one, but I'd never doubted that it would be the right thing to do. Now I *knew* it had been.

The set-up was not without its friction for others, however. It appeared that the tensions I had detected between Michael Finley and Andy Hughes when they had interviewed me in London had not been a figment of my imagination. These two did not get on well. Andy was quiet and studious. A well-read man who never wasted words, he was also single-minded, fiercely determined and could be infuriatingly obstinate. His dress and demeanour were almost schoolmasterly. In sharp contrast, Michael was a flamboyant extrovert. Extremely intelligent and politically cunning, he could also be very charming. He took great pride in being impeccably well mannered and well groomed. His dress was individualistic and scrupulously smart, his demeanour demonstrative. And he had a legendary short fuse and hot temper.

Andy was never happier than when he was at the sharp end; hands-on, sleeves rolled-up, sitting on the subs' desk editing the paper; smoking his pipe and sipping tea from a huge cracked mug. Michael was a front man; a smooth image builder. He preferred to be out and about. He was an excellent public speaker and a very gifted performer on TV and seemed happiest when doing all that, smoking expensive Dutch cigars and drinking fine wines and brandy. In different circumstances there could have been a perfect partnership between these two men, and for their different qualities, I liked them both very much. But it seemed they could barely stay in the same room together for an hour without disagreeing.

In a move that baffled a lot of us, when the editorship of the *Kent Messenger* became vacant Michael Finley appointed Arthur Potter to the post. Arthur had, in fact, been a journalist years previously in south London, but his forte was Newspaper Sales. He was just brilliant in that role. Peerless and matchless was our Arthur when it came to selling papers ... but editing one?

Not many of us could see Arf Pot as the editor of a prestigious county weekly newspaper serving all the posh bits of Kent. But there it was. About a year later, Michael announced that Andy Hughes was to become editor-in-chief of the *Kent Messenger* Group. A new editor of the *Kent Messenger* was to be appointed and Arthur Potter was to be editor of the *Kent Evening Post*. In the same announcement, I was promoted to deputy editor of the *Kent Evening Post*. I was delighted. It was just three years since I had left Nottingham and the promise of further career progess made in the advertisement that had attracted me to Kent had been honoured much more quickly than I had ever imagined. I was now just **one step** away from my dream of an Editor's chair and still under 30. I was so chuffed with my own place in this re-shuffle that I didn't dwell too much on Arthur Potter's appointment. Some thought it a bit bizarre – but what the hell! Arf-Pot was a good mate and a good man. We'd be fine.

Mr and Mrs Williams were doing very nicely, thank you. Pauline was making career progress in the Civil Service and as the "gaffer" of our financial affairs (she **had** to be since in matters monetary I was feckless) she felt we should be investing in the rapidly soaring property market. It was time to sell No. 7, Phillips Court and move to something bigger and better while getting in on the housing boom that was particularly strong in the South East. In the short time since we had bought our first home it had increased in value to £9,500 and such was the demand for that sort of property among first time buyers that selling it would be no problem. A local house-building firm called Wards was offering splendid mock-Georgian detached four-bedroomed houses. State of the art; *en suite* to the master bedroom, when such a facility was the pinnacle of luxury; imposing solid oak front doors with brass fittings; red-bricked opulence. They were much in demand, but in Gillingham, where we viewed one, they were, at £14,000, outside our price limit. However, the same house, built by the same firm on the Isle of Sheppey was priced at £12,500, which, with a £9,000 mortgage, we **could** afford.

With all due respect to the Isle of Sheppey, it was emphatically **not** a place to which, under normal circumstances, you would have been drawn to live. Of the island's component parts, Sheerness was a dock town, run-down and depressed, Minster was the relatively posh bit, OK with some nice sea views, and Leysdown was a working-class holiday resort, much loved by London's Eastenders. It was at Warden Bay, Leysdown that these fine Wards' homes were being built, the top end of a development that included preposterous white "Spanish" houses, laid out in rows on banks overlooking the sea. There were only a few of the top-of-the-range "Georgian" detached houses and our choice was one of two set aside from the rest of the development and only yards from the sea.

Warden Bay was a drive of just under an hour from Chatham, where we both worked, and we figured that the daily commuting was a small sacrifice for the opportunity to own one of these fabulous homes – and to live literally at the seaside.

The location of our new home was a real conversation-stopper at posh do's but we didn't care. We loved it. Our move came in time for us to enjoy two of the best summers on record – 1975 and 1976 – and driving home, particularly on a Friday, was like going on holiday. In summer, the population of Leysdown grew from around 300 to 6,000 or more. The East End of London would descend upon us to enjoy their holidays in row upon row of hundreds of chalets, laid out claustrophobically in camps with names like "Ponderosa" and "Buena Vista". There was much that was mock Spanish about these settlements, which was fine until you looked at the sea, which, even in mid-summer, resembled a mass of Brown Windsor soup. The camps offered a complete holiday with their own shops, cafes and night clubs, the entertainment at which had to be fit to lay before an Eastender and as a consequence was top-notch. From May to September the residents of our Warden Bay housing development, almost entirely youngsters like us, would join the Eastenders most nights of the week, dancing to the brilliant bands, laughing at the blue comedians, eating the jellied eels and the pie, mash and liquor – East End delicacies not to be knocked until you've tried them – and drinking till we dropped with these wonderfully warm, friendly and amusing people.

If there had been Queen's Awards for Stamina, Mr and Mrs Williams would have been up at the Palace to get one! We would get up at 6. 30am for the drive into Chatham to start work at 8 am. After a full, hard day's work we'd leave Chatham at 6 to 6. 30pm, drive home, cook and eat dinner (a masterpiece in minutes, thanks to Pauline's pressure cooker) Then I'd go out on the piss with the Eastenders – Pauline, too, sometimes – before crashing out in our big posh bedroom with *en suite* at around 1am and getting up again at 6. 30am to repeat the whole barmy process.

It was madness. But it was such fun!

The Eastenders were priceless. Just around the corner from our home stood the Warden Bay Hotel – a misnomer since it had no bedrooms, it was best described as a massive London boozer by the sea. Several hundred holidaymakers would cram into this huge fun temple every night, for it always boasted, with ample justification, the best band on the island. It was packed with flash Jack-the-Lads smothered in pungent aftershave and tasteless gold jewellery, with no apparent means of income but enormously expensive cars outside and ostentatiously thick wads of cash in their back pockets. They would be accompanied by peroxide blondes wearing fur coats (in the middle of sweltering summers) over pretentious evening gowns with cleavage down to the navel, plastered in thick make-up, monstrous earrings gleaming under the neon lights... way over the top yet at the same time incredibly attractive. They would drink just as much as the fellas and when – as was frequently the case – the holiday bonhomie was temporarily suspended for the hostilities of a punch-up it was often the *girls* who were fighting.

Andy Hughes, who had endured a very strict, Godfearing upbringing in a quiet Lancashire town and led a Catholic life, liked nothing better than to come over to our place with his wife for dinner on a Saturday then join us for a night out at the Warden Bay Hotel, where he would sit quietly drawing on his pipe and – like some TV anthropologist – delivering a running commentary on the behaviour of this alien species going about its recreation rituals.

Andy had a quiet pomposity which would manifest itself in carefully considered critical appraisal of everything he observed. One Saturday night at the Warden Bay Hotel the fight which broke out between a bunch of these expensively-clad ladies escalated to mass warfare involving just about everybody in the place. The landlord had swiftly shuttered up the bars, the band had fled the stage and the locals were beating a hasty retreat to the exits – but Andy didn't move. While flying beer glasses whistled past his ears he sat motionless in the mayhem, sucking his pipe and continuing his anthropological dissertation, apparently oblivious to the urgent evacuation of his companions. When the police had arrived in force, stopped the battle and restored order, we went back inside to find him still sitting, sipping his beer and puffing on his pipe. Throughout the ferocious fracas he had not moved an inch.

"Ah, *there* you are," he said, "I wouldn't have missed that for the world." Then he proceeded to describe the entire brawl, from start to finish, in every fine detail. Now that's a *real* journalist!

A cynical, hard-to-please journalist should never have admitted it, but I'd never been typical and I didn't give a damn who I told... we *loved* Leysdown. We loved every minute of those two crazy hot summers; we loved crossing the Kingsferry Bridge to the island every night; we loved our clifftop walks with the dog; we loved the people with whom we shared our little housing estate. Like the young docker – whose name I deliberately omit! – with a heart as big as the capacious duffle coat under which the occasional item of contraband left the dockyard, who would gather marvellously delicious mushrooms on early morning walks across the marshes and leave some on our doorstep for our breakfast; like gas engineer John – surname deleted – who, during the big conversion to natural gas, inadvertently gassed an old lady's budgie then Sellotaped it, dead, back on to its perch because he couldn't bring himself to tell her; like John's inseparable mate Martin, with whom he ran a market stall knocking out dodgy shirts, an amateur boxer who, on the one and only occasion I ever found myself in *real* difficulty with a gang of drunken holidaymakers, stepped between me and them and sent them packing – the ringleader with a thick lip; like Roy, the 24-stone landlord of the Warden Bay Hotel, one of the most generous men you'd ever meet, with whom we ran the hugely successful *Kent Evening Post* Summer Talent Show and discovered some tremendous acts; like Roy's head barman Larry, who, when I walked into the pub for the first time in five years after we'd left the island, said simply *"Light and bitter, Bal?"* as if I had never been away; like Jean, the large vivacious housewife who lived next door and often looked after our dog *Brandy* for us with as much care and affection as if he were her own; like Danny, once a child actor who'd played the Artful Dodger in a top London production, who made a good living as a versatile entertainer around the camp clubs, a handsome, funny, intelligent, sensitive young guy who became a firm and faithful friend. They were all larger-than-life yet *real* and genuine people and, diverse though they were, they all had one thing in common; they made you feel that your friendship was the most important thing in the world to them.

That camaraderie was especially important in the winter, when the population of Leysdown reverted to the handful of locals and we'd stand in the vast Warden Bay Hotel like dots on the horizon, swapping tales of the day's happenings. We were such an odd mix that the conversation was invariably fresh and interesting. The journey to and from Chatham in those winter months was often a nightmare, driving through freezing fog (so bad I once ended up in a farmyard miles from home, thinking we had arrived at our house) on seasonally under-used roads, treacherous with black ice. Those journeys were so dangerous that there was a sense of real pioneering achievement in reaching your destination – and there would *always* be calls from neighbours to check that you'd made it safely.

When people who didn't know us asked where we lived, the reaction to the answer was a blend of incredulity and sympathy.

Totally misplaced. Wholly unnecessary. *We* knew how happy we were on that crappy old island, even if it *was* impossible adequately to explain to people who were never going to be lucky enough to share our experience.

1975 and 1976 – our Isle of Sheppey years – were special. These were the years of **Rod Stewart, Noddy Holder, David Bowie and David Essex;** of **Lionel Richie, Neil Sedaka, Johnny Cash** and the revived **Elvis;** of great bands like **Emmerson, Lake and Palmer** and **The Eagles;** of superb singers like **Jack Jones** and **Charles Aznavour** (Terry Wogan called him **Charles Aznovoice** – but he was a brilliantly emotive and innovative performer); of wonderful cult TV shows like **The Sweeney** and **Starsky and Hutch.** Pauline and I bought LP records by the dozen. Today, they fill an attic – hundreds of them, a testament to a really memorable decade and of far too much sentimental value to be thrown out.

Throughout the seventies I was a dedicated follower of fashion. My hair was shoulder-length; my shirts had giant collars; my ties were of the kipper variety; my trousers were hip-hugging and flared; my jackets had huge lapels and my heels were Cuban, adding several inches, even though I was six feet tall without them (a workmate who was devoutly fashion-resistant once asked me, "Tell me... how long have you had this problem with your height?" *Smart arse!)* My best suit was white, worn with a scarlet shirt and cream tie. Pauline was more beautiful than ever and on our frequent nights out she looked stunning. Those amazingly long, hot summers produced deep suntans. Though I say it myself (and this is *my* bloody story so I'm going to!) we were a handsome young couple. And we loved our lives.

Andy Hughes – as keen on football as I was – had introduced me to Gillingham Football Club. I became a real fan of *The Gills* and counted directors, managers and players among my close friends.

My work had never been so stimulating and enjoyable. I had built a marvellous team of journalists around me in Chatham; we were producing a good little newspaper that was continuing to grow in circulation, at the instigation of the station's charismatic news editor Langley Brown, a good and much valued friend. I had become a regular broadcaster on *BBC Radio Medway* – a new skill which I enjoyed immensely; I had built up a superb list of top local contacts, always ready to oblige with a good story; Pauline was loving her own job, had become an invaluable and highly-rated member of her Department of Employment team and was daily helping unemployed people back to their feet, hugely rewarding work for which she had a natural aptitude. These truly were the best of times.

Arthur Potter was the easiest editor I ever worked with. And that, bless him, was probably his downfall. He was a lovely man... oozing with the best character traits of his beloved London. He was good looking, charming, invariably happy and funny. He never took life – or himself – too seriously and he was totally without cynicism.

On one of a number of occasions when he fell foul of top management – after he had turned his office into a market stall selling trendy clothes – he protested to me in all innocence, *"But it was bloody good gear, Bal!"* Clearly, to Arf Pot, if the gear was *kosher* there'd been no offence!

Arthur and his gorgeous blonde Cockney wife Sylvia had an occasionally volatile relationship but it was clear for all to see that this most endearing of couples were utterly devoted to each other and both of them were equally devoted to their two beautiful daughters. There were so many pleasures to be enjoyed during this wonderful phase of our lives, but of them all few were better for Pauline and I than visiting "Arf and Sylv" for Saturday dinner at their home – Sylvia was a sensational cook – followed by drinks in their local pub, where at closing time Arthur would be persuaded, with very little effort, to bring the splendid evening to a rousing finale by playing the spoons – a skilful Cockney party trick, virtually extinct nowadays, which he performed with great dexterity and aplomb.

Arthur and I had an immediate and natural rapport and we were great pals who understood each other – the explanation for which, if any were needed, became apparent when we went off together one Saturday to watch Millwall FC (his team) play Gillingham FC (my team) at the infamous Den. This was Arthur's territory. He showed me around, introducing me to his mates in the local boozer with a child-like pride, as if *I* was *his* boss and after a lunch of the best fish and chips I'd ever tasted he took me to meet his mum, who lived in a council flat several floors up in one of those enormous London skyscraper blocks which idiot architects and planners had deemed the solution to slum clearance in the sixties.

Mrs Potter, who was widowed, was a splendid woman – that sort of elderly lady who is teak tough, having had more of life's shit thrown at her than you and I could ever have endured; never materially blessed yet rich beyond measure in indomitable good humour, abundant kindness and eternal femininity. I realised, that day, that working-class people have an inherent bond and are basically the same no matter where they live. The only difference between Arf Pot's mum's London home and my own mum and dad's small town council house was that ours wasn't in a skyscraper block. And I knew many Mrs Potters in Shropshire. They just had different accents.

It was often tempting for people like Arthur and I – mixing, as we did professionally, in the most exalted of company and with the cream of local society – to desert and disown your working class background. The alternative was to be entirely open about your humble origins and proud of them, without wearing them on your sleeve – because that was tiresome. We had both chosen that option and it made kindred spirits of us. For all I liked about the guy, I never did think that Arthur was the best editor I ever worked with, but somehow that didn't matter because he was a good "gaffer" and he looked after his team. He was based at Larkfield – the modern plant near Aylesford to which the *Kent Messenger* had moved after fire had destroyed its old Maidstone HQ – while I directed the news gathering operation in Chatham. Over at Larkfield, the subs' team was so experienced, competent and talented that it needed little or no bossing and so far as the content of the *Kent Evening Post*; its editorial stances, its campaigns, its choice of stories were concerned I was making most of the day by day decisions. If it had been anybody but Arthur in this situation I might well have rebelled, but he was such a decent man and such a good pal. I knew that he was not deliberately exploiting me and he never once sought to claim credit for something he had not done himself. So I just got on with it.

Meanwhile… a bombshell. The grapevine between Larkfield and Chatham offices was soon buzzing with the news: *"Andy Hughes has gone!"*

There had been a titanic clash between Michael Finley and Andy over something or other, at the height of which Michael had allegedly told him: *"I'm suspending you."*

"Oh, no you're not," Andy was said to have retorted *"…because I bloody well resign!"*

This had been a disaster just waiting to happen and it was such a shame because if these two huge, disparate talents had continued to work together they would have been unbeatable. But such is life, and so big are newspaper executives' egos that there was no way either of them was going to back down.

So Andy Hughes, without question one of the most gifted editors of his generation, was out of work.

Several times in the months that followed, Pauline and I went to visit Andy, his wife Gloria and his five kids at their home in Maidstone. He tried to put a brave face on things, talking about the book he was writing, but you could tell that he was still simmering under the surface.

Andy had launched the *Kent Evening Post* against fierce and bitter competition. There was no love lost between Edwin Boorman, the dashing young heir apparent to the *Kent Messenger* kingdom and his contemporary Graham Parrett of Parrett & Neves, owners of the rival

Chatham News stable of Kent papers, and when one (it was always at issue as to exactly *who* was first) got to hear about the other's intention, **two** new evening newspapers were launched in the Medway Towns on the same day! This meant that with both the London *Evening News* and the London *Evening Standard* also coming in, this comparatively small bit of England had *four* evening papers fighting on the newsstands and street corners for the custom and coppers of the Medway Towners every day.

It couldn't possibly go on. Clearly, only one of the two local newcomers was going to survive and this survival was going to be of the fittest; the best; the one most people wanted to buy. That's where Andy and his brilliance had come in. He had seen off the rival publication, which folded after several months of head-on competition, then gone on to steer the *Post* to really impressive circulation growth.

Andy was such a stubborn bugger and Michael Finley so volatile that the objective among observers of this sad state of affairs were inclined to think that the big bust-up had probably been six of one and half a dozen of the other, but it was, nonetheless, a dreadfully disappointing manner in which to end this very talented editor's exceptional contribution to Kent's newspaper industry and history.

It was quite a long time before Andy got back into the business but he did, when Sir Richard Storey, proprietor of *Portsmouth & Sunderland Newspapers* made him Editor of the *Sunderland Evening Echo* and there he stayed until he retired, living happily in Durham – where he's still to be found.

Not long after the Andy Hughes episode, the grapevine was buzzing again. This time it was *"Arthur Potter's gone".*

A high-flying regional newspaper executive, Grant Millard, late of Scunthorpe, had been recruited by Edwin Boorman as Managing Director. Grant himself was not long in that position but he was there long enough to decide that Arthur shouldn't be an editor. Off went my mate Arf Pot, with a typical shrug of the shoulders and a big toothy grin. "The job should be yours now, Bal," he said, as we shook hands and hugged each other on the day of his departure.

He was right. It should have been. But it wasn't.

Michael Finley decided that **he** was going to take the title of Editor of the *Kent Evening Post* and combine that with his role as Editorial Director. He didn't think I was ready for the top job but he wanted me to become his Associate Editor.

"Bloody unfair," was the verdict of many to comment upon this arrangement, including Andy Hughes. But they were much more bothered about it than I was. What the hell! It was only five years since I joined the paper. My rise had been meteoric. We were blissfully happy in Kent and I'd just witnessed the catastrophic conclusion to Andy's fit of pique. And Michael Finley had put a good pay rise on the table alongside the slightly unsatisfactory title.

Sod it. It would do very nicely for now.

"OK, Mike. It's a deal!"

Michael Finley wanted me to spend a lot more of my time in Larkfield and that presented a problem. Commuting back and forth between Chatham and the Isle of Sheppey was just about acceptable. A trip that now included going on another 15 miles or so to Larkfield and back began to look stupid. I was taking Pauline in to Chatham first, which meant an even *earlier* departure from Warden Bay and picking her up on the way back, which meant getting home even *later*.

I was now getting much more involved with production and administration, in addition to all my other responsibilities, and some nights it would be 8pm before I got to Chatham to pick up Pauline, who had been waiting patiently since 5pm, meaning that we did not get home until some time around 9pm.

The nonsense of all this came to a head one dark, dank winter night when, after a particularly demanding day with lots of difficult issues to resolve, I found myself turning the key in the front door at home on the Isle of Sheppey at around 8pm and suddenly realising that I been so preoccupied that I had *forgotten* to pick up my wife!

After an embarrassed phone call to her office I turned around and drove back to Chatham to fetch her. When I got there she had been waiting for more than *four* hours. She had no alternative but to wait. One of the downsides to life at Warden Bay was that there was no public transport beyond Sheerness – and even that was sporadic.

Most wives would have been bloody furious. Pauline laughed and called me a prat. But the conclusion was as unavoidable as it was regrettable... our mad, marvellous love affair with the Isle of Sheppey had to come to an end.

"Windswept" was the apt and descriptive name of the property we bought on the top of Bluebell Hill on the North Downs, nicely placed between Maidstone and Chatham. It was a precisely planned and perfectly proportioned little house, built by a local builder for his own occupation in the 1950s with – as one would expect from a professional creating his own home – immaculate attention to detail. He was reputed to have adored the place so much that now, some years after his death, he haunted it! It was said he had been seen (on the seat in the bay window, looking out at the beautiful view over the Downs) by a number of our neighbours and it was claimed that his ghost had frightened off two recent owners in rapid succession. Pauline and I both heard these tales separately and independently – me in the local pub (where else?) and Pauline on the bus going into work, but neither of us could bring ourselves to mention it to the other! We never saw the ghost and the house always had a warm and welcoming atmosphere and that, Pauline confided in me only after we'd moved on, was (according to what his widow had told our neighbours) because he liked us and was happy that we had bought it!

The whole area, we were later to discover, was subject to ghostly goings-on. Kitts Coty, woodland at the foot of the hill, having been an Anglo Saxon battle ground and burial site, was prone to weird and chilling noises and halfway up the hill on the Maidstone-Chatham road, at the spot where a lovely young girl had died in an horrific crash, her ghost was reported at least once a year by terrified motorists, many of whom were not local, had never heard the story of the "Bluebell Hill ghost" and had no reason to make it up.

I suppose if we'd heard about all this supernatural activity before we bought "Windswept" we might have been put off, but we were very glad that we hadn't been. Bluebell Hill has now been outrageously carved up to cope with all the extra traffic created by the Eurotunnel, but back then it was unspoilt and idyllic and it was often joked that hang-gliding from the top of the hill would have been my most effective form of transport into work, since Larkfield and the Kent Messenger HQ nestled beneath it. Chatham was equally convenient, just a 10-15 minute drive from home. Perfect.

We had sold our house on the Isle of Sheppey to a delightful young family from Yorkshire. Dad was a highways engineer expecting to spend a number of years in the South East working on motorway projects; Mum was a lovely raven-haired girl. They were a charming, quietly spoken couple with three beautiful little children. Pauline and I liked them so much that when another potential buyer attempted to gazump them by first offering us £2,000 more than we'd agreed with them then asking us to "Just name your price," we refused.

Only one thing concerned them about living so close to the sea…

"Do you ever get flooded?" they asked.

I was able to tell them entirely truthfully: "No. There hasn't been a flood here since 1953, after which they radically improved the sea defences." Some 18 months later, early in January 1978, I was called in the middle of the night by one of our reporters.

"Massive story," he said breathlessly. "There's terrible flooding…"

"Where?"

"All over the Isle of Sheppey!"

It was indeed a massive story. I decided to print a special morning edition of the *Kent Evening Post*. At 5am I was on the sub's desk going through dozens of pictures of the floods drama when I saw a house (or at least just the top half of it, for the rest was under water) which I recognised.

Bloody hell! It was our former Beach Approach residence! And there was that nice chap, to whom I'd given a firm promise that he'd never see a flood, hanging out of a bedroom window passing his kids to some marines in a boat!

The special edition of the *Post* that morning had a huge headline proclaiming WORST FLOODS FOR 25 YEARS above a story which read:

> *"Hurricane force winds and freak tides left parts of Kent battered and waterlogged today with many people marooned, roads swept away and homes flooded. Most of the damage has been caused by flooding from the sea. Worst affected areas are east Kent and the Isle of Sheppey. Flooding was deepest at Leysdown, the island's holiday centre, where water was up to five feet deep."*

At once I felt relieved that we'd decided to get off the island and guilty about the assurances I'd given, albeit in absolutely good faith, to those lovely people. They recovered from their traumatic experience, I discovered later and went on to *enjoy* life by the seaside!

There were many good stories during this time and the *Kent Evening Post* continued to go from strength to strength. I ran some good campaigns, too, notably with Clive Morman, who was the Leader of the local council for the Medway Towns.

Clive was a local businessman in his late 30s who ran the council on interesting, often exciting and frequently controversial entrepreneurial lines. He was a newspaperman's dream and we struck a firm friendship which endures to this day. Clive would call into my office in Chatham at least once a week and bounce ideas off me. Our friendship ensured that the *Post* was never short of good exclusives from the council. I had built excellent relationships and contacts in other areas of Medway's community, too. I had a firm grip on my patch. And we were producing bloody good newspapers

Michael Finley's fraught dealings with Andy Hughes had not been his only mercurial relationship in the Kent Messenger empire... his clashes with Jim Thompson were also legend. Jim was a charismatic Geordie with a temper every bit as hot as Michael's. Both men were the same age, in their personal and professional prime, and both had egos as big as the building they worked in.

Jim had done a brilliant job for the Boorman family, building up the commercial side of the business, and was, for most of the time, the KM's Managing Director. When he was not Managing Director it was because he'd fallen out with Edwin Boorman temporarily, upon which Edwin would appoint Michael Finley to the post, only to reinstate Jim when they made friends again! (Or so it all seemed to those of us who could only guess at the workings of the top corridor!)

The Big Three at the top of the empire – Edwin, Jim and Michael – all under 40, were a handsome, hugely impressive and dynamic trio and they made the *Kent Messenger* the most innovative and consequently one of the leading newspaper companies of the decade, punching way above its weight in the industry. Edwin, whose elderly father Roy Pratt Boorman (his son had wisely dropped the Pratt!) remained chairman of the company, was a **true** newspaperman. The business was – and still is – in his blood, in his heart and in his soul. Edwin Boorman could be impetuous and impatient, difficult and unpredictable but he was utterly devoted to his role and to his newspapers. Michael Finley brought a presence and a polish to the editorial operation which ensured that the newspapers had a huge reputation and top class status way beyond Kent. Jim Thompson was a highly motivational driving force, a passionate professional. He was fiery, forthright and intimidating. His presence filled a room and he frightened the life out of people, especially the journalists who believed, wrongly (mostly!) that he didn't like them. Having coped with Jack Cater when I was a 16-year-old, men like Jim Thompson never frightened me.

Inspired by them? Yes. Often. Intimidated by them? No. Never. With Jim, like so many of his ilk, the only way to stop him crushing you was to give as good as you got. He respected that. And I was good at it!

It was the tenth anniversary of the *Kent Evening Post* and it was resolved that we should produce a special anniversary edition. Michael Finley had been away through a minor operation and recuperation period and that meant that **all** of the due credit for the special, which was a monumentally splendid edition, was mine. The excellence of the issue was not lost on Jim Thompson, who was fulsome in his public praise of my editorship qualities. At the end of a week of *Kent Evening Post* anniversary celebrations Jim rang to ask me to ensure that I remained in the Chatham office with all the staff until 5. 30pm because he was coming over with Michael Finley to make "a special announcement".

I assumed this would be something to do with the anniversary and it came as a complete surprise to me when Jim, having gathered all the staff around him, announced: *"Barrie Williams is appointed EDITOR of the Kent Evening Post with immediate effect."*

I had made it! I was an Editor! And I was only 32! And when I left the impromptu party which followed, I was also drunk!

I couldn't wait to be with Pauline to share the news. The rest could party on. And they did. But I wanted to be alone with my wife. Later that night we just sat quietly by the fire in the peaceful privacy of our cosy home and cuddled. This was the goal I had worked so very hard to achieve and Pauline, with her unstinting faith and belief in me and her support, love and comfort had played such a huge part in getting me there. No words were necessary. We just sat in the flickering firelight and the warm glow was one of deep satisfaction.

The many letters of congratulations from the Medway community were such a joy to read and there were those who made no secret of the fact that they thought this appointment was overdue. . .

The Mayor of Medway, Jim Wells, wrote:

"It is evident that this outcome has resulted from the considerable contribution you have made to the Post's success and in your case it is good to know that fortune has favoured the brave."

BBC Radio Medway's Langley Brown wrote:

"Well done, mate – and about bloody time! Heartfelt congratulations. If ever a good lad deserved a good title in a good job being professionally done, it's Barrie Williams."

Divisional British Railways PR boss Peter Ellis wrote:

"What splendid news that I no longer have to put Associate in front of Editor!"

And my good friend, Council Leader Clive Morman, wrote:

"Justice prevails! Congratulations. I'm pleased that your patience has been rewarded – not that I ever had any doubt that it would be."

There were those who felt that Michael Finley had deprived me of the editorship for two years but I was not one of them. I had never complained and I had no hard feelings whatsoever. I *liked* Michael

Finley enormously and he'd never been anything but honest, open and up-front about the situation. Some said that was because he had a skin like a rhinoceros but I had no problem at all with Michael because there is always *something* to learn from being close to talented people and I learned much from Michael Finley. I so admired his strong personality, his panache, his motivational oratory, his supreme self-confidence. Some of his distinctive style undoubtedly rubbed off on me ... particularly the self-confidence!

So it was properly *my* newspaper now. And 'Barrie Williams, Editor of the *Kent Evening Post'* (how I loved saying it!) carried on working for and with the people of the Medway Towns – though now with even more zeal and gusto.

It occurred to me one day, having commissioned an article on Charles Dickens' very close links with the area, that Medway in general and Rochester in particular did not make nearly enough of this connection. So I launched a campaign to persuade the Towns to "Make more of Charles Dickens." It was, I argued, a potential goldmine of tourist potential going untapped

There should be an annual Dickens Festival, I wrote, and a Dickens Centre to commemorate the great man. Clive Morman agreed.

"You're on to something here, boy," he said.

And between us we set about making it happen.

It was with enormous pleasure and pride that in the *Kent Evening Post* of June 2nd 1979 we reported the huge success of Medway's first **Dickens Festival.** The three-day festival had attracted thousands of visitors from all over Britain and beyond. There had been dozens of events, big and small, from Dickens trails of conducted walks to book readings; from a professional performance of Lionel Bart's *Oliver* to school plays; from Victorian markets to a Dickensian evening of Victorian Fayre in food and entertainment – all culminating in the Grand Parade... a carnival procession of people dressed as Dickensian characters. Hundreds of men, women and children took part in the most colourful and exciting pageant you could wish to see... scores of Fagins, Bill Sykes, Olivers, David Copperfields, Scrooges, Miss Havershams, etc. Thousands of people lined the route for the procession, which filed through Rochester to finish at a gala day of more Dickens events in the grounds of Rochester Castle.

It was a phenomenal success and it became a nationally renowned annual event, bringing hundreds of thousands of pounds into the local economy.

Not content with that, the Morman and Williams partnership then exclusively unveiled Rochester's new Dickens Centre – a permanent exhibition/tourist attraction featuring the great man's life story, his local connections and his famous works, using the very latest techniques in life-sized models, sounds and smells to transport the visitor back to Dickensian times. This attracted rave reviews from national and foreign newspapers and television.

In 2007 a much bigger Dickens tourist attraction – a huge re-creation of Dickensian England in the former Chatham Dockyard – opened in a blaze of laudatory national publicity and it grew from a legacy of which Messrs Morman and Williams can feel justifiably proud.

Most of the ventures in which Clive Morman's council responded to the cajoling of my newspaper's campaigning were successful – contributing much, we believed, to the good of the Medway Towns and their people. But not all of them...

After I had published a series of articles complaining about the lack of good entertainment facilities for the youngsters of the Towns, I persuaded Clive to back an event at which a rock band would play throughout a Saturday afternoon inside The Pentagon, Chatham's posh new shopping centre. The kids would enjoy the music while at the same time gathering signatures for a petition calling for more to be done for them.

The shopping centre management and the traders were not at all keen on the idea, fearing a detrimental impact on trade on their busiest and best shopping day, but the combined strength of the Leader of the Council and the Editor of the *Kent Evening Post* gradually wore them down and we secured their reluctant agreement, subject to the noise levels of the band being suitably controlled so as not to disturb the shoppers. It was **my** responsibility to provide the band and to make sure the event was properly managed.

Along with the newspaper's Promotions Manager, Barry Reynolds, I identified a promising young local rock band and set the event up. The band had a very lively and ambitious young manager – a personable Asian lad known as Raj – with whom we made all the arrangements and agreements. Paramount among the latter was the issue of the noise levels. Barry Reynolds and I stressed time and time again the importance of restraint, the basis upon which we had secured the use of the shopping centre. Raj saw no problem. Of course they would control the noise levels.

"You can trust us," he promised.

Come the Saturday of the event and the *Post* had done it again. The Pentagon was packed with kids. Barry Reynolds had done a great job with the stage set, leaving nobody in any doubt that this was a *Kent Evening Post* production. There were a dozen pretty girls in *Evening Post* uniforms armed with petition forms. All was set fair for another campaigning triumph.

Until the band started playing...

The music was intolerably, excruciatingly **loud!** Shoppers were stopped in their tracks, shocked, stunned and horrified by the incredible noise. You feared the roof of the Pentagon would explode.

"Christ almighty!" gasped Barry Reynolds. "Where's Raj?"

The little bugger was nowhere to be seen. Meanwhile his band was in an unbreakable trance, playing louder and louder while hundreds of head banging kids jumped up and down like devil-possessed pagans. Soon we were being berated by a delegation of furious traders, all threatening to sue unless the catastrophic cacophony ceased forthwith.

"We'll get it sorted as soon as we can locate their manager," Barry spluttered – but they were not impressed.

"Give us half an hour and it'll be under control," said Barry, which seemed to appease them temporarily and they returned to their shops.

But then...

"Oh, bloody hell – that's all we need," said Barry Reynolds.

"What?" I replied.

"That smell," he said.

"Oh, Christ – that's not tobacco, is it?"

"No – that's *not* bloody tobacco!"

"Oh shit!"

The *Kent Evening Post*, aided and abetted by the Leader of the Council, had turned Medway's pride and joy, state of the art, plush new shopping centre into a deafening drug crazed rave from which shoppers were fleeing in their hundreds.

At this point Raj appeared, butter not melting in his mouth, which I felt inclined to fill with my fist...

"Going well, innit?" he said with a broad smile.

"Going well? Going bloody well? What about our agreement you little shit?"

"You agreed to help the youth of the Medway Towns and that's what you're doing. You should be proud of this. I am," said Raj – then promptly disappeared again. And now the band was even louder and the kids even wilder. It was sheer pandemonium!

Re-enter the shopkeepers' delegation, now incandescent with rage. Their spokesman shoved a piece of paper in my hand...

"This is to inform you officially that the traders will be taking action against you and the council," he said. And they stormed off to their empty shops.

Defeated and dejected, Barry Reynolds and I sank into our seats at the side of the stage while the mayhem proceeded for another hour. It couldn't possibly get any worse. Or could it...?

With the bouncing kids now totally out of their heads and the decibels at eardrum-bursting levels the band reached its finale and – as the guitarists and the drummer got to that state of climax at which rock musicians lose all contact with the human race – Raj appeared on stage with a bloody cannon and after a massive explosion the shopping centre was filled ... with millions of feathers!

The floating feathers were immediately sucked upwards by the shopping centre's air conditioning system, which was soon completely knackered.

"...and we'll be adding *that* to the cost," said the traders' spokesman.

Clive Morman had missed the event, having had to be away on business that Saturday but – anticipating another glorious success story – he rang me at home on the Sunday morning for a progress report.

"Right..." I began. "Are you sitting down, Clive..."

Clive Morman had endured a bad start to his life. His dad was an alcoholic, he told me, and the family had lived in poverty in Devon, where Clive was born. Clive had worked desperately hard to better himself and set up his own dry cleaning shop in Chatham. It grew into a large operation specialising in industrial cleaning but the fact that the rapid growth of his business had coincided with his advancement through the ranks of the Tory council to become its Leader had led to lots of nudge-nudge, wink-wink sniggering and innuendo which, inevitably, reached the ears of the Editor of the *Kent Evening Post*. It was alleged that Clive's position on the council might be giving his company an advantage when it came to securing cleaning contracts for the new businesses that were proliferating in the Medway Towns at this time.

This was a suggestion I could not ignore. We had to investigate it.

My friendship with Clive made the decision to do so extremely difficult on a personal level, but to ignore the gossip because we were mates would have been seriously unprofessional, so I put a team of my strongest, most experienced and most reliable reporters to the task. They spent several months working to my instructions to leave no stone unturned... eventually coming up with nothing more serious or significant than a couple of minor infringements of protocol. I decided to publish our investigation so that everybody could see how precisely and thoroughly we'd looked into the rumours.

As a wiser, more experienced editor, later in my professional life, I would not have published anything, because mud sticks and my best investigative team had uncovered absolutely nothing of substance, nor indeed had any members of Clive's political opposition, despite much effort to do so. But I was so determined to prove my own shining impartiality in all this that I ran everything we had looked into.

A lesser man than Clive Morman would never have forgiven me but he merely scribbled some comments of his own in the margins of our rather pompous two-page spread and dropped them into my office. The next time we met the episode was not even mentioned.

The sniggering allegations ceased and Clive's council leadership went on from strength to strength, so I suppose some good came from a piece of editorial judgment of which I was far from proud.

Investigating was the right decision. *Publishing* was not.

I had put my desire to prove my own impartiality above the risk of causing damage to Clive's reputation. That was wrong. But this most affable of men never once blamed me for making him part of my learning curve!

Clive Morman's unstuffy, entrepreneurial style of council leadership was years ahead of its time and brilliant. Rochester and Chatham (Gillingham retained its own separate authority) owed a very great deal to his flair and vision. Eventually he retired to Australia, where he soon got bored with inactivity and started a completely new business, which succeeded even more than the one he'd built in Britain… this time with no involvement whatsoever in local politics and therefore free from unfounded gossip, jealous innuendo and the over-zealous attentions of young newspaper editors obsessed with the notion of their own integrity! Now retired for a second time, Clive, with his family, still resides happily in Australia and he and I remain the best of friends, keeping in touch to this day. [2]

---

[2] Had Clive Morman's position on the council in Medway helped his business? Quite likely – but not illegally or improperly – and he gave the Towns massively more than he ever got in return. Of course, proper declarations of interest and constant public scrutiny of the conduct of politicians via a vigilant local press are essential and should never cease, but at the same time it seems to me that it's only in this country that we're so over-sensitive about *theoretical* conflict of interest, so cynical about the motives of those who elect to give up a huge chunk of their lives to public service, so ungrateful for their efforts and so hastily inclined to the belief that they're all only in it for what they can get out of it. I was later to encounter this same syndrome with other people in other places and I've often thought that the risk of being subjected to the sort of mud slinging Clive Morman endured so undeserv-

Clive Morman and I shared a passionate support of Gillingham Football Club. I had by now become very close to the club, its people and its players, one of whom, the genial Eire international midfielder Damien Richardson, I counted among my best friends. With another good pal, the *Kent Evening Post's* Circulation Manager Peter Crouch, I travelled to many away games, as well as watching every home match. But it was in the company of the Gills' Club Secretary, Richard Dennison, that I made one of the most memorable away trips. Richard, whose dad had been Coventry City's top-flight goalkeeper, rang me at work early one deep mid-winter Wednesday morning...

"Fancy the match tonight? It's Blackburn Rovers away. I'm driving up. It's a very long trip and I'd appreciate your company."

"Count me in," I said. "It's quiet today and it'll be a good game."

It was easy to understand why Richard wanted some company on this journey. Blackburn was one of the longest away treks and back then the drive from South to North was very much more difficult and time-consuming that it is now. The kick-off was not until 7. 30pm but, given that the Club Secretary was expected to be in the home side's boardroom at least half an hour before the start, we left Gillingham at 11 am.

The journey was an absolute nightmare. Not only was the traffic intolerably heavy but winter threw every known hazard at us on the way. Snow. Sleet. Freezing fog. Ice. We had been so badly delayed that we decided not to stop for lunch. With any luck we'd be there in time for a sandwich before the game. But we weren't. By the time we got into the ground it was 7. 25pm and protocol dictated that we **must** take our seats in the Directors' Box before a ball was kicked; failure to do so would be thoroughly bad form, no matter how good the excuse. You have to experience the polite ritual and disciplined procedures of professional football club boardrooms to fully appreciate how strictly they are applied and adhered to. There's something of the military Mess about it and you break the rules at your peril. So from 7. 30pm, neither of us having eaten a thing since breakfast 12

---

edly for a time must have deprived many a local council – and therefore its people – of many a good business brain and that the quality of local government has suffered badly as a consequence. Real corruption is one thing and must be rooted out publicly whenever it is discovered. But unashamedly and overtly making a compatible involvement in local politics and local business mutually beneficial is, surely, another matter entirely and should be carefully accommodated – even encouraged – rather than sniggered and sniped at.... *Discuss!*

hours earlier, we sat respectfully captive until half-time... *and we were famished!*

The ref's half-time whistle seemed like the relief of Mafeking for two young men with huge appetites at the best of times, who by now were positively bloody starving. We raced to the Blackburn Rovers' boardroom, not stopping, like all the other occupants of the Directors' Box, to chat about the first 45 minutes of football and remove coats, hats and scarves. We were desperate for **food**! Richard threw open the boardroom door and gasped with pleasure.

"Just 'ave a bloody look at THOSE, mate!"

The object of his ecstasy was a huge silver plate bearing a pile of freshly-baked, piping-hot pork pies – as only Lancastrians can make. The jelly and juices ran down our chins as we gorged ourselves on a feast for which the word *delicious* had been inadequately invented. By the time everybody else was making for the plate of pies, Richard and I had wolfed down *five* each...

The tell-tale jelly and crumbs were clinging to our chins when two of the Blackburn directors arrived at our side.

"By 'eck, the pies look good tonight, Bert," said one.

"Yes, they do," replied his companion, "... and there's TWO each!"

So to all latter day footie fans who think the immortal chant *"Who ate all the pies?"* is meant for fat players, I say... *I know better!*

As I continued to grow into my role as Editor of the *Kent Evening Post* Edwin Boorman was changing things at the top of his empire. Jim Thompson had become very much involved in football. As chairman of Maidstone FC he pioneered the Conference – the division through which non-league clubs gain promotion to the Football League and Maidstone made it into the Fourth Division, a tremendous achievement for a club he took over as a piddling amateur outfit in a fit of pique after failing in a takeover bid for Gillingham FC. Jim decided to leave the *Kent Messenger* Group – now much diversified with a subsidiary named *South Eastern Newspapers* – upon which Edwin appointed Peter Edgley as Group Managing Director.

I owed Jim Thompson so much. Without his influence and intervention I would probably not have been Editor. I also admired and respected him enormously. Peter Edgley was chalk to Jim's cheese – a calm, cultured and impeccably spoken officer and gentleman to Jim's noisy, brash Geordie street fighter – yet in no time I was getting on superbly well with him. I like to think both men, in their very different ways, appreciated my ability and professionalism.

Peter was "old money." His family had owned *King & Hutchings*, proprietors of the *Kentish Times*, *Gravesend & Dartford Reporter* and other titles before selling them to one of the big groups and, it was said, Peter didn't *need* to work at all, but desperately missed newspapers. He was middle-aged but still played cricket to a high standard and was the most charming and amusing of men. I liked him immensely and we became very good friends as well as close colleagues. Peter was fond of gin and while I never once saw him anything but 100 per cent sharp, sober and ultra-professional he never missed an opportunity, including my visits to his office, to get out the bottle.

"I normally take one about this time of day, old boy," he would say (no matter what time it was!) "Will you join me?"

Well… it would have been rude to refuse!

I grew to love this bloke. He was gentle, kind, warm-hearted, generous and always impeccably courteous. He had a great sense of humour and despite the huge difference in our backgrounds, he and I laughed at the same things and thoroughly enjoyed each other's company. Working for Edwin Boorman's company had never been less than exciting but it had also been mercurial and Peter Edgley brought with him an aura of stability and surety. An absolute professional who knew every aspect of the newspaper business inside out.

I also got on very well with the group's Marketing Director Malachi Doyle, a handsome, urbane, silver-haired Londoner of Irish (obviously!) origins. Malachi, too, had a wonderful sense of humour and though we worked as hard as ever there have been few times in my life when I laughed as much. Malachi was the originator and exclusive organiser of what became the infamous "Directors' and Editors' Christmas Silly Breakfast". All we were told about what these annual Yuletide events entailed was an early morning time and a place upon which we would board a minibus which would transport us, blindfolded, to the secret "silly" destination where we would be served breakfast.

On the first occasion it turned out to be on board a submarine in Chatham Dockyard where, in considerable discomfort and embarrassment, we shared a Naval breakfast with submariners who had no idea who we were or what we were doing there. On the second occasion it was sitting in the main shop window of Debenham's department store in the middle of Maidstone, where bemused Christmas shoppers stopped, stood and stared at these crazy businessmen eating bacon and eggs.

But it was for the third (and for some reason the last!) Silly Breakfast that Malachi saved his most dastardly plot… When the blindfolds were removed from the baffled Directors and Editors we realised we had been deposited in the canteen at Maidstone Prison, to share a horrible greasy breakfast with the inmates. There, among the prisoners in their overalls sat these prats in their expensive suits – including our exalted proprietor Edwin Boorman, bless him, who joined us every time in case, perhaps, we thought him a Scrooge at Christmas. Malachi had arranged for us to share our breakfast with several of the prisoners and had placed inmate and director alternately around a large table in the canteen.

Edwin Boorman had a coat which was as well known in the company as he was himself. It was every inch a proprietor's coat. Sleek fur, it had a huge collar which turned up to cover the back of his head and it was ankle length. He had acquired *The Coat* in Canada and it must have cost him a fortune. *The Coat* was a legend among the staff and among Maidstone high society and it was Edwin's pride and joy. Whenever he arrived anywhere wearing *The Coat* it had to be very carefully hung up where it was safe from theft or damage; where he could be sure it would come to no harm of any sort.

We had all been dumped in the canteen at Maidstone nick wearing our top coats because it had been a very cold morning and Edwin had chosen to wear *The Coat*. The rest of us had given our coats to a friendly trustee to hang somewhere in the prison for us but Edwin had insisted that *The Coat* should remain within sight. So, he had folded it up neatly and tidily then very carefully placed it on the floor in a quiet corner of the canteen not far from our table. The prisoners who shared our table were great. They'd been told who we were. They were in on the Silly Breakfast joke and were going along with the fun of it all in splendid good humour. We were all getting along famously and chatting away over our breakfasts when I spotted Malachi laughing uncontrollably. Tears were streaming down his cheeks and his whole body was shaking with mirth when, as I caught his eye, he gestured towards the corner where Edwin had so carefully deposited *The Coat*. It was no longer meticulously folded but lay in a crumpled heap – underneath the biggest tomcat you will ever see. That was bad enough, but it was much worse... *The Coat* was being unceremoniously and furiously *shagged* by the prison cat!

Soon everybody around the table was convulsed in helpless laughter. Everybody, that is, except Edwin. He leapt from his seat, raced to his beloved coat, knocked the tomcat off and loudly inquired of the animal: *"Don't you know that's MY bloody coat?"*

The cat didn't answer... and Malachi had left the building!

My accounts of the silly Christmas breakfasts found much mirth and favour with a great friend I made in Kent... the famous entertainer Rod Hull. Rod was splendidly eccentric and what became a marvellous relationship between us started on a hostile footing.

Searching for good features ideas one day it occurred to me just how many famous people lived in Kent. How about persuading, say, half a dozen of them to write us an article explaining why they chose to live in our county and what they liked about it? On the premise that the take-up rate was likely to be no better than one in ten or thereabouts, when I wrote to a long list of local celebrities I had my secretary type the letter just once, photocopy it, and leave the *Dear* blank for me to write in the name.

This absolutely incensed "Dear *Rod Hull*" and he wrote me a stinking reply in which he informed me that lazy buggers who sent photocopied letters were an enormous pain in his arse and demanded to know how I dared to be so bloody rude.

As soon as I read Rod's tirade I realised that he was absolutely right. It *was* lazy to send *anybody* a photocopied letter when asking for a favour – let alone a man who at the time was one of Britain's biggest stars.

I immediately wrote back with an apology...

> *Dear Mr Hull,*
>
> *I hope you can accept my profuse apology for sending you a photocopied letter asking you to write an article for my newspaper. On reflection I cannot believe that I could have been so rude and thoughtless.*
>
> *You were absolutely right to reply in the manner in which you did and I accept your bollocking with much contrition and not a little embarrassment.*

Rod then replied:

> *Dear Mr Williams,*
>
> *While photocopied letters are a major aversion to me, I have the highest regard and respect for people who are big enough to apologise. I will be pleased to write an article for you as requested. My fee will be one large pack of Clan pipe tobacco, which I smoke incessantly.*

Rod's article duly arrived and it was superb; very well written, eloquent and amusing. A large pack of *Clan* pipe tobacco was duly dispatched with a letter (NOT photocopied!) of thanks, to which he replied by telling me that he had always wanted to write a column in the style of *Beachcomber* in the *Daily Express* and inquiring if, for the same fee, I would like such a contribution from him weekly.

I could not believe my luck. A top TV star writing a weekly column for me for the price of a bag of baccy. Brilliant! I rang him immediately – to discover that there was just one snag. He wanted to write his column, which would be mischievous and irreverent, entirely anonymously. I was disappointed, obviously, not to be able to use his big star name, but still delighted by his offer because his first article had demonstrated that he was, among his many talents, a very accomplished writer.

And so the deal was done. Rod Hull became a weekly columnist for the *Kent Evening Post* under the pseudonym of **QWERTY** ... and it was wonderful stuff.

Every week, he wrote splendid sardonic spoofs, fictional parodies, but always with a ring of truth to them, about imaginary incidents and issues in the life of the county of Kent. **QWERTY** was hilarious and controversial – everything Rod had hoped it would be and more and we were both especially pleased when pompous pillars of local society who identified themselves in his copy (but didn't dare to admit it publicly!) rang the Editor, as they frequently did, to complain "off the record" and demand to be told the identity of their tormentor. Invariably they assumed that it was a journalist on my staff and invariably I told them, politely, that I could not disclose the name of the writer.

The relationship between Rod and I developed into an enduring friendship. We would watch cricket (which was the third greatest love of his life, after his beautiful wife and his *Clan* pipe tobacco) together and we enjoyed putting the world to rights and having a laugh over more pints of real ale than was good for us. I got to know that Rod, who was born in Sheerness, was very much deeper intellectually than his stage and TV image suggested. In fact, he grew to hate the Emu that brought him fame because he was so frustrated that only 'that bloody bird' got him the work and stardom that he deserved for much wider talents which were rarely, if ever, seen publicly. At the same time, he recognised and respected the great British public's affection for his fractious feathered friend and forced himself to smile and wave cheerfully to people incessantly shouting "Where's Emu?" when, he confided, he really wanted to shout back something very rude.

Rod and I managed to keep the identity of the increasingly controversial **QWERTY** a secret for nearly a year – until the week he wrote an hilarious piece in which he "reported" that a posh, pretty picture postcard village in east Kent, which was clearly identifiable from his description, was to be buried under millions of tons of concrete and turned into a nuclear waste dump. Some prat on the parish council had been so disturbed by the column that he'd called an emergency meeting to discuss it – and I got a call from a reporter on the *Sunday Express...*

"Could you confirm, Mr Williams, that this column is actually written by Rod Hull?"

I was so taken aback by the unexpected question that I uttered the two words that NO journalist should EVER speak…

"No comment."

Then I rang Rod to alert him.

"Oh, bugger!" said Rod. "Me cover's been blown."

We'd been as careful as we possibly could be but given the very nature of the newspaper business it had been bound to get out sooner or later and the outraged reaction of those posh pillocks in that village had given the *Sunday Express* a smashing story which despite the fact that *"both Rod Hull and the Kent Evening Post's editor refused to comment"* they ran with great gusto.

Rod was caught red handed and he never wrote another column. Once his identity had been revealed all the mischievous fun had gone out of it. But we remained friends for years. I was so sad when he died after falling off a ladder while fixing the roof at his home, but at the same time, I could imagine him laughing at his own demise and saying: "What a bloody silly way to go!"

The *Kent Evening Post* was now a fine newspaper. When I was appointed Editor, Andy Hughes who, understandably, still regarded the paper as his "baby" had sent me a nice note of congratulation to which he had added: "Give it back its heart and soul." And I had.

We were a tough, bright, brash, gritty little tabloid… campaigning, punching above our weight, respected by the community, highly rated and at the same time feared by the local politicians (rightly – because that's the way it always should be!).

Decent editors always have clearly defined editorial policy – that way the journalists know exactly what's required of them and the paper has a discernible character to it – and my policy was to be *local, local, local*. We carried national and international news but it was pointless trying to compete with the nationals, particularly so close to London. We had to play to our strengths, recognise and exploit our unique selling point, which was to be *local* to the Medway Towns. That's why a 'phone call I got from Edwin Boorman one day mystified as much as it angered me…

It was the Queen Mother's 80th birthday and, true to editorial policy, I had carried the picture and story in late editions inside the paper on the national news page. Edwin rarely rang me and had never tried to interfere in the Editor's role, so the nature of his call was the last thing I was expecting when my secretary put it through to me…

"Hello, Edwin – what can I do for you?"

"Do you call yourself a fucking editor?"

"Well, yes, of course I do."

"So why isn't the Queen Mother's birthday in your bloody newspaper?"

"It is. In the later editions. There was nothing worth running for the first edition."

"Not worth running? The Queen Mother's birthday? Are you bloody serious?"

"I'm perfectly serious. Early on it was just a holding story which we'd run yesterday. As soon as today's stuff dropped we put it on the national news page, which is where our readers would expect to see it."

"Why the hell isn't it on your front page? The Queen Mother's eightieth birthday should be on your front page. I want you to know I take a very dim view of this."

And with that he hung up.

I was livid. More angry than I had ever felt at any time in my professional life. I was working my balls off for that bloke and his company and producing a bloody good newspaper. How *dare* he speak to me like that.

That's it! I thought. *I'm not having it. I'm resigning. I'm off.*

When I rang Peter Edgley he could obviously detect the emotion in my voice. "Don't do anything hasty, old boy. Edwin shoots from the hip but he means well. He was out of order but my advice is to forget it. It'll blow over."

"No way. I'm resigning. He can stuff his bloody newspaper!"

"That will achieve bugger all, old son. Go and have a pint and calm down. I'll talk to him and I'll ring you in the morning. Don't shoot yourself in the foot over this, old lad. It just ain't worth it, believe me."

Back home I related the incident and my anger and sense of injustice to Pauline.

"Oh, dear," she said. "Am I packing again?"

"We might well be. I'll see what the bugger has to say tomorrow."

Early the next morning Peter Edgley rang. He had arranged a meeting between Edwin and me... but wisely not for another week.

"You both need to cool off," said Peter. "In the meantime, come over here and have lunch with me."

Peter Edgley would have made a superb diplomat. He took me to a very expensive restaurant and bought me a fabulous lunch with some not inconsiderable liquid accompaniment. It was his way of saying "We DO appreciate you, old son." It was nice and typically thoughtful of Peter but I was not consoled – and after the meeting with Edwin Boorman I was even less so.

Edwin and I had a polite but strained chat. There was not the slightest hint of the apology to which I believed I was entitled. It was no good. I felt our relationship, which had never been close anyway, had gone. I could not work for a proprietor who was capable of talking to me with such little respect and consideration. My working class pride and principles had kicked in. I had calmed down sufficiently not to risk my entire career by walking out in a grand gesture, but I had resolved to quit as soon as I could secure another job as an editor. That was going to take time, but I could wait. In the meantime I would be 100 per cent professional about doing my job to the very best of my ability. And that's what I did...

It was the last job I had expected to see advertised:

> The *Nottingham Evening Post* seeks an Editor Designate to replace Bill Snaith, who retires next year. The salary will start at £20,000 pa rising upon confirmation as Editor and your company car will be a Jaguar. This outstanding remuneration package reflects the importance of this position on one of Britain's top regional daily newspapers. Applications to Christopher Pole- Carew, Managing Director, T. Bailey Forman Ltd.

This advertisement really was a huge surprise. I had always believed, knowing Nottingham as I did, that the Editor to replace Bill would be an internal appointment, reflecting the paternalistic nature of the company. George Hunt, the Chief Sub-Editor was the local bookies' favourite. George was an exceptionally talented operator who was highly respected within T. Bailey Forman. His succession had been deemed a foregone conclusion.

This was a great job. The best.

But by far the most striking aspect of this exciting advertisement was the *salary* on offer. This was 1981. £20,000 a year was a great deal of money. But that was only for starters. A top of the range Jaguar! Bloody hell! The ink was barely dry on the copy of the *UK Press Gazette*, the industry's trade journal, containing the advert before the phone lines between the country's regional editors were buzzing...

"Have you seen the Nottingham job? Have you seen that *salary!*"

A good salary for a regional daily editor then was £12,000 to £13,000. I was by no means badly paid by Edwin at around £11,000. No editor in the regional industry was earning anything like £20,000. And that was just a brief, temporary starting salary! My company car in Kent was more than reasonable – a Fiat Super Miafiori – but a

Jaguar was in a totally different league. All that ... plus, I'd fallen out with Edwin.

My application was in the post the next morning. Even so, though I had never been short of confidence, I expected to be no more than an also-ran for the Nottingham dream job. I knew that most of the top editors in our industry would be in for it. And then there was the competition from within T. Bailey Forman... I had to be a rank out-sider, but hell, they've been known to win, haven't they? You never know...

I told only Pauline that I had applied. No-one else knew.

The *Kent Messenger's* Editorial Director, Michael Finley, was not so circumspect...

"I'm off to Nottingham at the weekend," he told me one day. "I'm in for the editor's job there and we're going looking at houses."

Bloody hell!

So when I got a letter from Christopher Pole-Carew inviting me for an interview it was a genuine surprise. At that stage, I confided in Peter Edgley, in whom I had complete trust.

"You can get it, old son," he said.

"Come off it, Peter!"

The interview was a unique and fascinating experience... and enough to make me think that Peter was not so far wrong, after all.

Because I was, at that time, the youngest editor in the country I had been asked by the Newspaper Society – the organisation repre-senting UK newspaper owners – to head up a committee looking at Newspapers In Education, an imaginative way of getting youngsters to read newspapers, which had been pioneered in the USA, Canada and Australia. These were the early days of growing disquiet about decline in readership of newspapers and youngsters were obviously important to the future of the industry. Along with Jim Black from Burton, who was the youngest Managing Director in the industry, I had started work on a project that was to culminate in delivery of a report to the Newspaper Society. Christopher Pole-Carew was in-tensely interested in what I had to say on this subject and it enabled the interview to get off to a cracking start.

It soon became evident that Christopher Pole-Carew was one of life's natural enthusiasts. The man couldn't sit still for a second. He had pioneered the introduction of new technology in the UK news-paper industry. In 1976 the *Nottingham Evening Post* had become the first newspaper in Europe, let alone the UK, to introduce direct input by journalists, with computers linked to the printing processes replacing time honoured typewriters. This man was a trailblazer. A true innovator. And, boy, was he inspirational! This interview was like nothing I'd ever experienced... mainly because for most of the time he danced around his office in a flurry of incredibly long legs and arms, enthusing like nobody I'd ever met before about everything we discussed. Then he took me on a whistle-stop tour of his domain – dashing from one department to the next with me literally *running* behind him.

The grand old Victorian building hadn't changed in the 10 years since I had left and neither had most of the people – who responded to this gyrating giant with equally energetic and enthusiastic responses, some of which seemed suspiciously pre-programmed and some with the vacant terrified expression of startled rabbits. The technology was mind-blowing and there was an audible buzz around the commercial departments – most of which hadn't even existed when I had moved on to Kent in 1971.

I left the interview with my head in a whirl of excitement and anticipation. It had gone extraordinarily well; better than I had imagined in my wildest dreams. I had struck a real rapport with the man known as "the mad Carew".

"Maybe I'm mad, too," I told Pauline when I got home, "...but I could work with that guy and – as arrogant as it might sound – I got the feeling that he wants me to!"

That feeling soon dissipated the next weekend, when Pauline and I attended the bi-annual conference of the *Guild of British Newspaper Editors...*

The talk of the entire conference weekend was who was going to get the plum Nottingham job with its huge salary. And everybody's money was on Colin Brannigan, the Editorial Director of a group of newspapers which included the *Colchester Evening Gazette* in Essex. Colin, a recent President of the Guild, was a big name in the industry and had previously been Editor of the *Sheffield Star.* He was 50, vastly experienced, highly respected and much admired. The message reverberating around the conference was that the job was his and that he'd beaten off every other big name in the regional industry, including Michael Finley. All bets were off now and it was apparently confirmed when at lunch on the final day Colin and his wife sat alongside Bill Snaith and his wife and were engaged in deep conversation throughout the meal.

"Well, that's it, mate," I said to Pauline as we drove back to Kent. "It's clearly Brannigan's job. I was daft to think it would not be somebody of his calibre and experience."

The following Monday morning I was at work on the sub's desk preparing that day's *Kent Evening Post* with all thoughts of Nottingham behind me when I received a phone call.

"Hi, Barrie, Chris Pole-Carew. The Chairman would like you and your wife to join him here in Nottingham for lunch."

"Fine. When?"

"Today."

"But it's half past nine and I'm a five hour drive away."

"No problem. We'll send the helicopter for you."

A phone call to Pauline, a brief chat to her obliging boss and a quick change of clothes later we were sitting at Rochester Airport waiting for "our" helicopter.

Now, *this* was doing things with *style!*

The pilot, Colin Bond, a friendly, genial man, put us immediately at ease, chatting away as he whisked us to the East Midlands. The helicopter was but a part of the *Nottingham Evening Post* "air force" Colin explained. There was also the company jet.

Just a bit special, eh?

In what seemed like less than no time we were sitting at the highly-polished table in the plush boardroom for lunch with the Chairman Colonel Tom Forman Hardy, the MD Christopher Pole-Carew (both distant legends when I was last in Nottingham) the Editor Bill Snaith (my boss last time I was here) the Chairman's charming wife Mrs Marjorie Forman Hardy and his son Nicholas.

For the first (and last) time in my career I was momentarily over-awed. This was a *smalltalk* occasion. Obviously the Chairman wanted to test the cut of our jib in the social sense. Talk of business and especially THE job was clearly off the agenda.

Without shop-talk I was stuffed!

The places were carefully arranged... Colonel Tom at the head of the table with me on his right and Pauline on his left. I sat looking back at the whole fresh salmon which gazed up at me from the table and I was totally lost for words. What the bloody hell do I talk about? For the first time in many years I felt like the council house kid, out of my depth, nervous and speechless in such company.

The silence around the table was excruciating and exaggerated tenfold by my acute embarrassment. Then, mercifully and not for the first time in my life, Pauline – who was looking stunningly attractive – rescued the situation. She knew Colonel Tom was a farmer and farming was something my wife knew a bit about because her dad had been a farm worker for many years. Suddenly she was discussing the Colonel's herd of pedigree cattle with him as if to the Manor born. And soon they were deep in conversation about every aspect of agriculture you cared to think of.

God bless you, Pauline. I love you to bits!

Mrs Forman Hardy then engaged me in conversation, telling me she had once worked for the BBC. And what did I think of today's Corporation? Easy! The silence was broken. The embarrassment ceased. The rest of the lunch flew by amidst relaxed chattering and at the end I just knew that it had been a success.

"How did it go?" asked pilot Colin as he flew us back to Kent.

"Well... I think," I replied. "Thanks to Pauline."

"The Chairman's so nice, but he's a terribly shy man," said Colin. "He can be very hard work."

"He's a sweetie," said Pauline.

Did I marry wisely?!

Lunch with the Chairman and his wife and son meant I was on the shortlist for the dream job, but I was still convinced, like everybody else, that it was going to be given to Colin Brannigan... until my work on the *Kent Evening Post* was interrupted by another call from Christopher Pole-Carew.

"Hi, Barrie, Chris Pole-Carew. Do you still want the job?"

"Bloody hell! Of course I do!"

"Well it's yours. And you might like to know that you came top out of 73 very strong candidates."

"Christ!"

"There'll be a letter in the post... Bye."

It was June 1981. Less than 20 years since that timid working-class kid – so pale and thin that Jack Cater reckoned he'd seen more meat on a butcher's pencil – had walked nervously into the offices of the *Shrewsbury Chronicle* with nothing going for him but determination. Less than 20 years to land the best and most coveted job in British regional journalism. Less than 20 years to achieve the biggest editorial salary and the best employment package in the business. Me! Barrie Williams, late of Coppice Drive, Oswestry, appointed Editor of the mighty *Nottingham Evening Post* at only 35 years of age... with another 30 years of my journalistic career ahead of me.

It was almost impossible to take in, which was why, when Christopher Pole-Carew's letter arrived, I read it so many times that I memorised it:

Dear Mr Williams,
This is the formal confirmation of my telephone call of this morning to tell you that our Chairman, Colonel Forman Hardy, has asked me to offer to you the position of Editor of the Nottingham Evening Post upon the retirement of the present Editor, Mr Snaith.

I understand that you are pleased to accept and so I can only say how delighted we all are that you will be joining us. For formal details, perhaps I should make one or two points:

The precise definition of the job is initially Editor designate with the expectation of Mr Snaith retiring some time in the first half of 1982, upon which you would take over as Editor of the paper.

The date is flexible and is very much concerned with ensuring not only a satisfactory turnover time but also allowing you to complete your current contract arrangements with the Kent Evening Post. We would wish, obviously, that you make such arrangements with your present employers as not to cause undue disruption of their affairs.

Furthermore, we wish to allow some time before you take over as Editor for you to take such trips abroad as you would like to visit various newspapers and generally to widen your experience and to devote some time working within the non-editorial departments of the company in a role which, once you have been appointed formally, you will never be able to occupy again. This should all be extremely valuable experience.

When you have been appointed Editor it will be a matter of probably a few months before you would expect to become Editorial Director since the Chairman holds that the Editor must be a Director of T. Bailey Forman, the Company which owns the Evening Post.

The salary, as stated, commences at £20,000 a year which will, of course, be increased on your taking up the post as Editor. All removal and out of pocket expenses concerned with having to sell a house and buy a new one are taken care of by the Company.

Meanwhile, we have a flat in Wilford House, a property the Company owns, so that you and your family can come up and stay for long or short periods without having to be concerned with hotels. It is quite comfortable.

I think that covers all the formal details and so it only remains for me to say many congratulations and that I hope it feels nice to have beaten 73 other high-powered editorial people into first place!

Pinch me again! It just got better and better. All that time to settle in, trips abroad, a seat on the board. Me – a bloody company director! And all that money! Was I dreaming?

The first person to be told was Peter Edgley.

"Bloody brilliant, old boy!" said Peter, with excitement that was obviously genuine. "I told you you'd get it, didn't I? I knew it! Oh, I'm so pleased for you, old son. I really am. Get over here. I normally take one about this time of day!"

The large gin and tonic in Peter's office never tasted better.

He dug me in the ribs and with his wicked grin fully engaged and a huge wink told me: "Now Edwin *knows* you call yourself a fucking editor, eh boy!"

In fact, Edwin's response was kind and courteous. He sent me a letter saying:

> *"Congratulations on your appointment as Editor designate of the Nottingham Evening Post. Naturally I am disappointed you are leaving the Kent Messenger Group of Companies but I am very glad that you have done so well. The Kent Evening Post has prospered under your guidance. Chris Pole-Carew has made a good choice. I have written to tell him so!*
>
> *Please may I say the same to you that I say to everybody that has served us well, which is:-*
>
> *(1) Good luck in your career*
>
> *(2) If ever you see or hear of a position which attracts you back to this Company please do not hesitate to contact me*
>
> *I hope you will always be kind enough to speak well of the Kent Messenger Ltd. We do not have the resources that many other companies have. Our only ability is to recruit good staff (which you have so ably proved) We are, therefore, always on the search for new and good talent. It helps us considerably for people to know that we are a good company to work for.*
>
> *Congratulations. Good luck to you and Pauline."*

Edwin was forgiven. Our row over the Queen Mum's birthday now seemed irrelevant and trivial. And he need not have doubted that I would always speak well of the *Kent Messenger* Ltd. In the years that were to follow, in which one private family-owned newspaper company after another was eaten up in a feeding frenzy by the predatory profit-driven corporate big boys, Edwin Boorman stood firm and resolute in his determination not to sell-out, despite some extremely turbulent times. There are only two or three independent family owned newspaper companies left now and the *Kent Messenger* stands proudly among them because Edwin has been strong and principled; a genuine and devoted guardian of Press freedom and the epitome of the nearly extinct breed of proprietor who is in the business not to make massive amounts of money but because he *loves* newspapers. If ever a man deserves a knighthood for loyal and selfless service to an industry it is Edwin Boorman.

In January, 2006 Edwin stood down as Chairman at the age of 70 to be replaced by his daughter Geraldine – the **fourth** generation of his family to run the *Kent Messenger* Group. The official company statement announcing his retirement added that Edwin would remain involved for at least five more years. I bet he will!

Edwin's father, Roy Pratt Boorman, also wrote to me:

> *"I would like to congratulate you on your promotion to Editor designate of the Nottingham Evening Post; wish you every success in it and at the same time thank you for the good work you have put in on behalf of the Kent Evening Post which is continuing to gain in prestige – largely due to the work you have been good enough to put in. Members of the Board wish to express their thanks to you for all you have done while you have been with us."*

On June 30th 1981, the *Kent Messenger Group Ltd* issued the following Press statement:

> *Kent Evening Post* Editor Barrie Williams is leaving the Kent Messenger Group to take up a new appointment as Editor designate of the *Nottingham Evening Post.*
>
> He begins his new job on November 2nd, succeeding Bill Snaith, the present Editor, who is retiring next year.
>
> The move to Nottingham will mean a return to familiar territory for Barrie. He worked there earlier in his journalistic career and is now going back to run the paper he once served in a much more junior capacity.
>
> In due course, he will become Editorial Director of T. Bailey Forman Ltd, the Company which owns the *Nottingham Evening Post.*
>
> Barrie joined the *Kent Evening Post* 10 years ago and held a variety of posts, including those of Deputy News Editor, News Editor and Associate Editor before his appointment as Editor in 1978, which coincided with the 10th birthday of the Post.
>
> His campaigning style of journalism helped to establish the *Post* as a newspaper which cares about the community it serves. He always believed that a newspaper has a duty not just to report the news but to strive to improve the fabric of life in that community. That belief was reflected in the many campaigns which Barrie carried in the *Post*. Most were aimed directly at improving the lives of the old, the infirm and the under- privileged. The *Post's* Fighting For Dignity campaign was designed specifically to expose the shortcomings of care for the disabled in Kent but led, also, to national recognition of that scandal and action to end it.

Many other campaigns followed, together with numerous pieces of effective investigative journalism.

Peter Edgley, Managing Director of South Eastern Newspapers, which owns the *Kent Evening Post*, said: "I would like to publicly congratulate Barrie on this well-deserved senior appointment in the regional newspaper industry. I have had the pleasure of working with Barrie for the last two years and I know that in his area he has been known as "Mr Evening Post". He has served his paper so well and I am sure he will be a great benefit to the *Nottingham Evening Post*. I would like to wish him personally and also on behalf of the Board and all the staff of the *Evening Post* all the success he deserves."

In all the excitement and activity at the time I never discovered who wrote that in order to say **thanks.** I should have done. More often than not, when they write about YOU it makes you realise how inadequately newspapers write about others! But that Press statement was more than adequate. It brought a lump to my throat.

There ensued a farewell lunch in my honour with Edwin Boorman and the directors at which Michael Finley made a typically honest speech, forthright and very gracious.

"Everyone here knows that I didn't think Barrie would make an editor," he said. "Now he's got the glittering prize. He's proved me wrong – and how!" Then, putting his arm around my shoulder Michael told me: "I wish you all the good fortune in the world, mate."

When all the directors, as one, then added: "And so do we" my eyes filled with tears.

It was then that I realised that good companies such as the *Kent Messenger* are just like families. You can squabble, fight, kick and bite between yourselves; you can sometimes dislike each other; occasionally even *hate* each other – but when you've battled side by side through the bad times, laughed together and loved the good times, shared the successes and the failures, agonised together and triumphed together, there's a bond between you which you never forget. And I never forgot the Kent Messenger.

Before I left Kent, there were two massive stories to report:

Prince Charles married his gorgeous young Diana and the Medway Towns, like the rest of Britain, celebrated in style. This was a great opportunity to sell a lot of newspapers and the *Kent Evening Post* planned the big day meticulously. Our souvenir edition was destined to give the newspaper a record circulation on the day and we planned our coverage, printing schedules and distribution with military precision. It all went superbly well. Our pictures were brilliant, our stories and features exceptionally well-written and displayed. Our *Royal Wedding Special* was a cracker – and the timing meant that we could be out on the same day – beating the national newspapers with the story everybody wanted to read and the historic pictures everybody wanted to see.

With the editorial job done and dusted I called to see our Newspaper Sales Manager, Peter Crouch, a genial young man and a close friend, for an early report on how many papers we were selling. Expecting his characteristic beaming smile and noisy welcome I was shocked to find Peter sitting silently at his desk with his head in his hands. When he looked up I could see that he was crying. Sobbing, he told me that one of the schoolboys delivering the paper had just been killed in a road accident. It was devastating news. Like everybody else involved in the big Royal day the lad had been doing his own bit with great enthusiasm when the accident occurred. It was nobody's fault but Peter irrationally blamed himself and our sales performance on the day became a matter of complete indifference to everybody involved.

The day which began with such excitement and anticipation of great success for our newspaper ended in devastating tragedy. A 14 – year-old lad had been killed getting *our* Royal Wedding Special to *our* readers. We could think of nothing but that poor boy and his parents and we all felt guilty and responsible.

There was a feeling of guilt to be endured with the second of those big stories too ... this time that I was deserting the Medway Towns in their greatest hour of need.

There had been rumours for some time that Chatham's Royal Dockyard might close. The Tory Government was rationalising its defence spending and it was feared that one of the three naval yards – Chatham, Plymouth or Rosyth – would go. Chatham's dockyard workers were intensely proud of their record for highly-skilled and rapid work and they believed that would protect them from the axe.

It didn't. And news of the closure came as a huge shock.

Henry the Eighth built that dockyard and at a stroke Margaret Thatcher destroyed it – and with it, 7,000 local jobs. When Defence Secretary John Nott came to the yard to discuss closure details he refused to meet the local Press. I was incensed and my anger led to one of the best front pages I ever produced. It featured a startling cartoon of John Nott sneaking surreptitiously out of the dockyard. Over his shoulder was an axe dripping dramatically with blood. In each pool of blood there was a number or a letter and the blood spelled out **7,000 JOBS**.

The loss of those jobs, plus many more in ancillary businesses, knocked the Medway Tows for six. And irrational though it was, I felt ashamed that I was leaving when those people needed a battling newspaper like never before. It made me more determined than ever to fight their case with energy and flair and this meant that throughout my last weeks on the newspaper I was so pre-occupied with the dockyard issue that I barely gave Nottingham a thought.

We produced some brilliant campaigning newspapers in a bid to ensure that the Government accepted its responsibility to do everything in its power to offset the impact of its defence policies.

Having had the posh farewell lunch with the directors of the *Kent Messenger* it was now time to arrange my own farewell piss-up and I wanted it to be a good one. No formality. No pomp. No ceremony. Just a monumental knees-up in the biggest room we could find. Aided and abetted by my lovely, efficient secretary Geraldine Walker (who I nicknamed "Geoff" because of her Geoffrey Boycott accent) and our long-serving editorial assistant Mrs Phillips (nobody knew her Christian name and such was the respect she commanded that nobody ever asked) I set about the task of organising the event. The venue we chose was the Victoria Hotel, a pub in the centre of Chatham which had an enormous "top room" and a landlord almost as big! Dick Saunders was also Chairman of Chatham Town FC and President of the Medway Football Association. Dick was a jovial giant of a man with a smashing "lady wife" to match. Her name was Vi but she was known to all as *My-Vi* which was what Dick always called her. They were a wonderful larger-than-life, almost Dickensian, couple who ran their pub brilliantly and put on the best spreads in the Medway Towns.

No expense was to be spared on the food; drinks were on me until the cash I was putting behind Dick and *My-Vi* s bar ran out; music was by Medway's top DJ Mike Speake and Cabaret was by a supremely gifted young local singer, Tony Frost – a blind boy who played guitar and harmonica and sang James Taylor classics beautifully. He had been a winner of the *Kent Evening Post's* annual talent contest on the Isle of Sheppey then turned fully professional and he was a class act. His mum, who was also his manager, steadfastly refused to accept a fee for his appearance so Pauline bought him a splendid silver medallion, which we presented to him on the night.

Virtually every contact I had made in 10 years in the Medway Towns, from businessmen to police officers, was invited; every journalist I had worked with through those years; all the local TV and radio broadcasters; local politicians; all the players, officials and directors of Gillingham Football Club and many friends from all walks of local life. And they all turned up!

Young Steve Bruce – who went on to play for Manchester United and now manages Birmingham City – was chosen by Gillingham FC to present me with an inscribed silver tankard and with remarkable maturity made a little speech in which he said: "The Chairman and everyone else at the club who knows how hard you have worked for the paper and for the Medway Towns join me and the rest of the players in giving you our very best wishes."

Bless him. He was only a kid.

There were more presentations and impromptu little speeches throughout the evening – including one poetic offering from Peter Ellis, the British Rail PR boss, which is memorable because it was so bloody awful! It went...

> *It isn't often that we hear*
> *News so free of scandal*
> *That come late Autumn, you'll be off*
> *To the land of Clough and Randall*
> *Bidding farewell to the Medway banks*
> *And all the joys of Kent*
> *To swap them for a fresh success*
> *By the side of the sacred Trent*
> *We'll miss you, Barrie, that's a fact*
> *But ere you speed away*
> *Let's all here present raise a glass*
> *And listen while I say...*
> *I always knew you'd reach the top*
> *(They say I'm good at spottin 'em)*
> *And trust that all your future strings*
> *Arrive without a knot – in – em!*

The groans from the assembled company could be heard in Dover and Peter was universally implored not to give up his day job. But none of that meant that I didn't appreciate the sentiments he was expressing.

It was humbling and deeply moving for me to see so many people from so many different aspects of Medway life gathered for that wonderful party. It was truly a night to remember for the rest of my life... and it almost lasted that long!

It was deep into the early hours as Pauline and I stood outside the pub waiting for a taxi home with Fred "Seth" Jones (one of the closest and dearest friends I had made in Medway) and Damien Richardson (Gillingham's FC's most talented and popular footballer) Seth was 20 years my senior but we were great pals. He was the Deputy Headmaster of an extremely tough comprehensive school in Strood where all the kids adored him. He was a well-read, articulate and very funny man. Damien and I, always good mates, had become even more so after I had worked on his testimonial committee with him. It was not by coincidence that these two very good friends were the last to leave my marathon party – nor that all three of us were by now considerably well imbibed!

We were obviously making far too much noise for the landlady. *My-Vi* had retired to her rest well before the end of the party and much as we liked her, she did not exactly inspire lascivious longing as she threw open an upstairs window and bellowed: *"Aint you lot got no bleedin' 'omes to go to!"*

As we all looked up at the ample and somewhat less than alluring *My-Vi* there was far too much comic potential in the moment for Seth to resist. He dropped to one knee and proceeded, very loudly and with much theatrical aplomb, to recite the balcony speech from *Romeo and Juliet!*

When this was greeted by *My-Vi'*s response – *"You go and wash your bleedin' marff out with soap"* – Seth collapsed in a helpless heap of hysterical laughter. Immediately, Damien then dropped to one knee, picked up where Seth had left off and proceeded to recite more of Shakespeare's lines with word-perfect accuracy and Gielgud standard delivery. *"...Goodnight, good night. Parting is such sweet sorrow. That I shall say goodnight till it be morrow."*

The performance was marred only by Damien's extremely strong Irish accent and *My-Vi's* increasingly vociferous hostility to this performance, but as she invited him to depart in no uncertain terms Damien was undeterred and – still on one knee – responded with: *"See how she leans her cheek upon her hand. Oh, that I were a glove upon that hand; That I might touch that cheek!"*

Seth, Pauline and I were lost in disbelief and admiration. When, where and how did a professional footballer from the Irish Republic learn to do that, for heaven's sake!

With wonderful *My-Vi* still imploring us to *"buggah awff 'ome"* we burst into a round of spontaneous applause and lusty cries of "Bravo" for our most unlikely thespian.

Damien remained enigmatic as he boarded his cab.

"Never underestimate an Irishman," he said.

And we resolved that we never would!

We were not the last to admire the eloquence of Damien Richardson. When his playing career ended he became a high profile manager of Cork City and Shamrock Rovers and a TV soccer pundit with TV 3 in Ireland, where the papers dubbed him "The Zen Of Soccer" after such comments as:

"Football is a ballet of wondrous beauty choreographed by highly skilled performers dramatising the conflict between good and evil that takes place in every heart. At the same time, it reflects the impa-

tient immediacy of modern society in that success breeds immortality while the procurement of second place begets anonymity."

Bloody hell, Damien!

When Pauline and I left for Nottingham and our sparkling new life, it was with huge excitement (how could it *not* be given all that awaited us there) but also with great sadness to be leaving behind the Medway Towns, the great county of Kent and so many wonderful, colourful, larger-than-life friends.

And, oh, what memories we took with us...

9.   Nottingham ~ Round Two

GRAHAM GREENE WROTE that Nottingham "is like a book you can't put down – like a woman you can't forget." I know exactly what he meant. This city keeps pulling at you like a magnet. And on my first day back at the *Nottingham Evening Post* it was as if I had never been away.

Not that it was long before I was off on my travels.

I had not even officially started before "Captain Bond" and the company jet were flying a group of us to Seville for a conference of the International Newspaper Promotions Association. This was at the invitation of David Teague, the *Post's* Marketing Director.

Malachi Doyle, his counterpart at the *Kent Messenger Group* had sent me a note in which he'd told me: "You'll be working with a great bloke in David Teague."

Malachi was right. Christopher Pole-Carew had tempted David out of Fleet Street, where he worked for the *Sunday Times*, in Round One of his revolution in Nottingham. Chris was a good judge. There was *nobody* better on the burgeoning marketing side of Britain's regional press. David Teague was brilliant. And he had the considerable added advantage, for me, of actually *understanding* journalists and appreciating them and what they did. This might have had something to do with the fact that he was married to one (his wife Raye was a reporter on the *Nottingham Evening Post)* but it was rare among most of his contemporaries, many of whom were jealous of the power and independence vested in editors and resentful of the way (as *they* saw it!) in which editorial departments spent lots of the money raised through *their* commercial departments' sweat and toil without contributing anything themselves to the financial health and wellbeing of the company.

This was green-eyed balderdash; demonstrable drivel, but it was a surprisingly common perception among commercial executives. I'd been fortunate in that Malachi hadn't swallowed that crap. David Teague, even more so, would have none of it. Hence, when putting together a *Nottingham Evening Post* delegation to attend a five-day marketing conference in sunny Seville, he invited the new Editor without a moment's hesitation.

When we arrived in the blistering heat of Seville I had not known what to expect of the conference – but I was hugely impressed. This was five-star stuff – and not just the hotel. The conference was slick, superbly well organised and gave marketing executives from newspapers all over the world the opportunity to share new ideas, methods and marketing techniques.

What came across loud and clear through all the presentations – whether from Amsterdam or Alabama, Melbourne or Madrid, Venice or Vancouver – was that maintaining the circulations of newspapers had become bloody difficult and that a stable sale was no longer a right earned by producing and investing in the best publications but a long, hard battle, with no guarantee of success.

Welcome to the world of declining newspaper sales!

What was also very evident – from the unremitting grilling I received from David's team of executives on the flight to Seville and throughout the conference – was that everybody on the *Nottingham Evening Post* was expecting a very great deal from the new Editor!

David intervened in this at one point and told them: "Look – it's not going to make a blind bit of difference what *he* does if we don't get *our* bit right."

Hey, I thought. I'm going to get on with this bloke!

And I did. Brilliantly.

Despite the huge pressures we were both to work under in all the years that followed, David Teague and I never once exchanged a cross word. That has to be unique in our industry.

David had been instrumental in putting together, with Christopher Pole-Carew, the itinerary for my "once in a lifetime" study trip of newspapers abroad, upon which I was to depart only two weeks after joining *T. Bailey Forman Ltd.*

The first port of call was to be Sydney, Australia to spend three days with the *Sydney Morning Herald.* Then on to Manly – an island off Sydney – for a stay at the *Manly Daily,* a free distribution morning newspaper. From there, it was off to Melbourne to spend a week on the *Melbourne Age* before moving on to the *Ballarat Courier.* Next stop was to be Canberra for a four-day stay with the *Canberra Times.*

At that stage, Messrs Teague and Pole-Carew had concluded, I was likely to be a bit tired and in need of a break. So I was then sceduled for a flight from Canberra back to Sydney, where I was to catch a plane to Honolulu for four days' relaxation before flying on to the United States.

Suitably relaxed I was then to fly on to San Francisco to spend four days with *San Francisco Newspapers* – principally the *Chronicle* – then from there by train to Contra Costa to visit another free distribution daily, the *Contra Costa Times.* From there I was to fly to Vancouver where, after another rest and recuperation period beside the lake, I was to visit the *Vancouver Sun* before moving on again to Toronto for three days with the *Toronto Star* and *Canadian Newspaper Publishers*.

At every stage I was booked into the very best hotels.

This incredible adventure was to begin on November 6th, returning home just in time for Christmas. After Christmas there would be visits to be made, with other TBF directors, to look at production and marketing developments in Europe – notably France and Eire.

As we talked through the itinerary Christopher told me, in the most matter-of-fact manner: "Oh, by the way, the Chairman feels it would be most unfair for you to leave your wife behind having just uprooted her from Kent so Pauline is going with you, if she wants to..." Pauline did!

As we boarded our first of many planes to come at Heathrow I had the feeling that I had now well and truly arrived. A jet-setter at the top of the regional newspaper business. I also knew that so very much was about to be asked and expected of me when I took over from Bill Snaith that it was all a bit scary... but very exhilarating.

As we walked around Singapore Airport during a break in the flight to Sydney, it was as real international travellers.

"Are we *really* doing this, Ba?" Pauline asked me.

"We are, mate. We really bloody are! Good innit?"

To get the very best out of this trip I needed to *work* at the newspapers I was visiting rather than just stand around like some visiting dignitary, so I had packed a good working suit. There was no time to take stock of our surroundings after flying in to Sydney and after a good night's sleep I was up and ready for my first day at 7am, "suitably" dressed in a black suit, white shirt and my Guild of British Newspaper Editors tie. As I walked through the bustling streets under a gorgeous clear blue sky and blazing hot sun I realised, with considerable embarrassment, that I was standing out from the crowd like a pale-faced visitor from an undertakers' convention. There was not a jacket, let alone another black suit, to be seen. All the blokes hurrying to their work were wearing shorts, knee-length white socks and open-necked, short-sleeved shirts. They were impeccably smart, with shirts and shorts spotlessly clean, crisp and pressed with precision but it was obvious that, here, in this fabulous sun-drenched country, you went to work dressed with sensible concession to the climate. I had learned *lesson number one* but it was too late to change for my first day, so black suit it had to be. By the time I'd been warmly and enthusiastically welcomed by *Sydney Morning Herald* executive Graham Lee with the greeting:

"Strewth, mate, you look like a pox doctor's clerk!"

I had also learned *lesson number two...* that Australians tell you what they think to your face!

It took no time at all for any misconceptions I had brought with me about the quality of journalism and newspapers in Australia to be banished. The *Morning Herald* was a superb publication with a brilliant set-up and I was immediately struck by what seemed to be a massive editorial staff. There was no national Press in Australia and the big "metropolitans" were as well staffed as the English national dailies.

Lesson number three was soon evident... Even on the best of British regional newspapers, journalists tended to think of themselves and their publications as being poor relations to the nationals. Why? Here in Sydney, it got no better than working for the *Sydney Morning Herald*. There was a great *pride* in that. Were all the journalists on the *Nottingham Evening Post* just as proud to be working for *their* newspaper? Almost certainly not.

But they were bloody well going to be!

Most of my time at the *Herald* was spent working in the features department, for it was there that this newspaper left its British regional counterparts for dead. The lively, happy, noisy, challenging and creative fun factory which was the *Sydney Herald* features department was on a different planet to what I remembered of the *Nottingham Evening Post's* "brains room" with its respectful rituals and library-like silence.

So much to take in and to take back with me...

Manly, island home of the *Manly Daily*, was reached by boat, which left from outside the Sydney Opera House. The concept of a free daily newspaper was an interesting one. With British regional newspaper managements getting increasingly concerned about declining circulations, visionaries like Chris Pole-Carew were prepared to consider giving papers like the *Nottingham Evening Post* away free. Free distribution would retain (considerably enlarge, in fact) existing readership figures – thus ensuring sufficient numbers to sustain the effectiveness of the advertising, which was the biggest contributor to company revenues.

It was going to take a monumental leap of faith to do this and it carried enormous business risk – not least discarding the newspaper sales revenue, which for a big paper like the *Evening Post* (selling 130,000 copies a day six days a week) was very considerable but there was a school of thought which said that this might be the only way to protect your regional evening market for a long term future in which declining sales were, for a variety of demonstrable reasons, absolutely inevitable. Britain had no free dailies – just free weeklies of mixed but mostly cash-strapped and inferior quality – so the opportunity for the new Editor to see free dailies in other countries at first hand was attractive to Chris, who was always at the front of the queue for innovation.

I was, however, going to have to disappoint him on this one. The *Manly Daily* was very much a one-off. It had been free since its formation around 100 years earlier and it was a small paper. It did what it had to do competently and professionally but its editorial content, in proper concession to its market, was mundane. It had plenty of advertising and was obviously a very well run, good, profitable little business – but *little* was the operative word and try as I might I could not see much, if any, relevance to a debate over whether the *Nottingham Evening Post* and similar big English regional dailies should one day go down the free distribution route.

So I just gathered all the financial and marketing information I had promised to return with and bade the very nice folk on the *Manly Daily* an earlier than anticipated farewell, allowing Pauline and I the opportunity to explore Manly and to discover a fish restaurant near the beach which served enormous, exquisite garlic prawns so delicious that 25 years later we still talk about them.

Later on my itinerary was a visit to the *Contra Costa Times* – another free distribution daily in the United States – and I hoped that would give me a more useful comparison to take home for Chris Pole-Carew but meanwhile there was some recreation time on the schedule for us to enjoy the extraordinary beauty of sumptuous Sydney. To see Sydney is to fall madly in love with it and to take in the breathtaking view from the zoo of the harbour and its famous bridge, with the deep blue of the glistening sea contrasting vividly with the gleaming white walls and the purple jacaranda, provides one of those rare enduring images which you carry in the camera of your mind for the rest of your days. Pauline and I had not, at that time in our lives, travelled very much at all and we didn't know God had colours like those in his palette. We were spellbound.

If Sydney and its *Morning Herald* had provided a great experience and some nourishing professional food-for-thought, Melbourne and the *Melbourne Age* were to be of even greater value. There was a lot more time on my itinerary to be spent here and I was so pleased about that.

By now I was acclimatised and no longer looked like the jet-lagged, pasty, alien "pox doctor's clerk" of my arrival. I had adapted to Australia's very different life-style and now went to work jacketless, wearing a smart new white short-sleeved Aussie shirt with the apparently obligatory epaulettes. I was even now sporting a suntan –

not yet to the Premiership standard of the locals but infinitely more impressive than the ones I used to get in Margate!

Australia and Australians make you feel at home very quickly and it was with comfort and confidence that I reported to the *Melbourne Age*, there to be greeted by one of its top editorial executives John Tidey – who was to look after us for the duration of our stay and to become a lifelong friend.

"I don't want guided tours and corporate bullshit," I told John (Australian bluntness being infectious!) "I want to work. Properly."

And – just as it had been in Sydney – it was to the features areas that I was drawn. News is news the world over and while I enjoyed talking to the guys on the news desk and looking at their methods it was clear that I was going to learn little of great significance there. But in features...

The *Melbourne Age* was a great newspaper and what set it apart was the quality of its writing and the innovative ideas in its sections. There was so much to learn here, and no better way to learn than to be one of the staff, albeit only very briefly. So I wrote for *The Age* and I subbed for *The Age*. And I threw myself into being one of the team.

I was asked to write a full page colour piece for the lifestyle section in which I was to contrast England and Australia on the evidence of my visit so far, which I did with great enjoyment and much self-deprecating humour... including an exaggerated account of my first day in the heavy black suit.

The Aussies loved it. Here was a pom taking the piss out of *himself*. Delicious!

This article was also much enjoyed by Chris Pole-Carew, to whom I sent a copy. He persuaded Bill Snaith to publish it in the *Nottingham Evening Post*, which surprised me because it employed a very liberal style that was totally out of character to the normal output of the Nottingham "Brains Room."

Every day and every night spent in Melbourne in the company, professionally and socially, of *The Age* journalists was a joy. I felt like I *belonged* there and it became obvious that I was not alone in that feeling when at the end of my week it was made clear to me that if I wanted to stay there was a job for me.

In just a few weeks, Pauline and I had both grown to love Australia and Australians. Under different circumstances the offer of a job on the *Melbourne Age* and a whole new life in that wonderful country would have been the stuff of dreams for both of us. At that time, British journalists could name their price in Australia and residence and work permits were no problem at all. But, alas, I could not even consider it. Imagine the scenario had I chosen to stay. Here we were, experiencing the trip of a lifetime at the enormous expense of the kindly Colonel Tom Forman Hardy, made possible by the commitment of Christopher Pole-Carew, who had shaken the regional newspaper business to the core by showing such faith in me to be the next Editor of the mighty *Nottingham Evening Post* ... and I ring up to announce, "Sorry, chaps, I'm not coming back..."

What sort of a shit would that have made me?

But, boy, it was tempting!

On our last night in Melbourne the guys at *The Age* threw a farewell party for us in an "English pub". It was a wonderfully warm and typically friendly gesture by the Aussies and it would have been an unforgettable experience if I hadn't got so drunk that the next day I couldn't remember much about it.

For this special occasion I had worn a Kent County Cricket Club sweat shirt in pale cream with a splendid Invicta horse and the italic inscription *KCC* picked out in maroon on the breast pocket. It was a seriously good shirt, of which I was especially proud because it had been presented to me as a leaving gift by the club when I left Kent.

At some stage during this drunken farewell night, a big bloke with black curly hair approached me and in inebriate drawl told me he was an ex-pat and a man of Kent. Tenderly, he stroked the Invicta horse on my breast and as he did so he started to cry.

"Th-aa-sh my coun-teee," he said. "...and ooh I mishh it so-o-o mush!"

Deeply moved and in tears myself, I whipped off my treasured shirt.

"Have this," I told him, "and think of Kent and me every time you wear it."

Now it is said that Melbourne's climate is so variable that you can experience four seasons in one day – and it's true. Having left our hotel to go to the party in sweltering heat and then presented my shirt to the weeping Man of Kent I was to be found waiting for a taxi outside the "English pub" in the freezing cold early hours of the morning half-naked. My nipples were standing out like organ stops, my torso was numb and blue, my teeth were chattering and my prized shirt was on a big bloke with black curly hair who was nowhere to be seen.

"You *are* a prat," said Pauline.

"And I'll bet he's never been anywhere near Kent!" said our taxi driver.

Before we left Melbourne we had a surprise call from my good friend Clive Morman who, with his wife Yvonne, had travelled from Queensland – a hell of a journey, even by Australian standards – to see us. We enjoyed a super get-together, going back over all the good and bad times in the Medway Towns and talking about their life in Australia. It all gave new meaning to the old adage about a small world. When we left our hotel in Melbourne I had accumulated so much useful material from my stay on *The Age* that it was too much to travel with us. I had to arrange for it to be mailed on to Nottingham to await our return.

There was less to learn on the *Ballarat Courier* but I did meet some more very nice people there before travelling on to Canberra to see life on the *Canberra Times*, a very solid and serious newspaper befitting the seat of Australian government.

Here, we encountered a remarkable coincidence. Ian Matthews the Editor of the *Canberra Times* was not only an Englishman but came from Kent, where he had worked on the *Kent and Sussex Courier*. He had emigrated to Australia 20 years earlier and had edited this newspaper for 10 years. Ian was a quiet and reserved but charming chap and his wife Joyce, also from Kent, was lovely. During an afternoon off from my programme on the *Times* Ian and Joyce took us on a trek to see "some real Australia" upon which we encountered our first kangaroos in the wild, watched some extraordinary exotic birds and had our picnic ruined my marauding emus. It was a fantastic experience for us.

During the trip Ian and Joyce told us that Joyce's mother lived at Rainham, where we had bought our first house back in 1971. They were worried about her. She had recently moved into a warden-controlled old people's complex and though she had written to say she was happy they were not at all convinced. Joyce was concerned that mum might just be putting a brave face on things.

"Well, why don't we go visit her and find out for you?" we said.

They were so pleased. It was one of the first things we did when we got back to the UK and we were able to report that mum *was* genuinely very happy in her new abode, had made some very good friends and felt much better about everything now that she was no longer living on her own.

It was so good to be able to put their minds at rest.

Dear old Colonel Tom Forman Hardy had unwittingly done the Matthews family a huge favour! And my visit to the *Canberra Times* had been stimulating, informative and very useful.

When the day came for us to leave Australia it was with heavy hearts that we did so. We had grown so fond of this country. In such a relatively short time we had become so attached to this place and its people that it seemed we had been there forever.

Australia does that to you.

As we boarded the plane that was to take us away from there, possibly never to see it again, I glanced at Pauline and noticed that she was crying. She didn't want to leave – and neither did I.

Such is Australia. A friendly country that truly welcomes and embraces you. A wondrous country whose beauty defies adequate description. A classless country in which meritocracy is benignly endemic. Australia is the dog's bollocks. One day we'll go back

For a couple of council house kids, four days in Honolulu staying at the five-star Waikiki Hilton was just a tad special, but as we "rested and recuperated" in such exotic surroundings we did our best to behave like laid-back, seasoned international travellers, in case too obvious excitement betrayed our novice status and presented a gauche image to our filthy-rich fellow tourists.

Then, it was on to San Francisco...

San Francisco Newspapers and in particular the *San Francisco Chronicle* had a great deal for me to observe during my stay with them. The guys there were friendly and accommodating but I did not feel nearly so much at home as I had in Australia. Here it was impossible to avoid the corporate bullshit and the conclusion that the Americans *talked* great newspapers but didn't always quite succeed in living up to their own extravagant billing.

My visit was meticulously planned from the first minute of the first day to the last minute of the last day, which was so thoughtful and obliging of my hosts that it would have been churlish in the extreme for me to complain that the precision of the itinerary left no time for the sort of spontaneous involvement I had so enjoyed in Sydney, Melbourne and Canberra. So I didn't.

Here I was struck by the comparatively enormous size of the journalistic workforce, the time allowed for assignments and the strict adherence to editorial independence – fine principles all.

Hugely impressive in San Francisco, as it had been in Australia, was the number of sections in these newspapers, all containing excellent journalism and highly lucrative advertising.

In 1981 in the UK not even the quality broadsheet nationals were producing sections this prolifically and successfully and it was virtually unknown in the regional industry. Yet I could see no reason why big regional daily newspapers like the *Nottingham Evening Post* couldn't get into this market and that, along with precisely how to achieve it, was one of many messages I would be taking back with me. Lots of the ideas from Australia and the US were to travel perfectly well.

I returned to our hotel here one evening quite early. Pauline was out exploring San Francisco and as I looked out of the window of our room, high up in the St Francis Drake Hotel, I saw her making her way back. I couldn't explain it then, and still can't, but there was something about the way my darling pretty young wife walked down that busy street in bustling San Francisco, so very far from home but so self-assured, head high, smiling so confidently, so happily, that filled me with such pride and moved me so much it made me cry. Perhaps that one image in that one fleeting moment summed up just how far we had come together. I didn't know, so I couldn't tell her why the hug she got when she came into that room a few minutes later was such an extra special one.

I have to confess, though, that I don't much care for America. It was then – and still is, it seems to me – a very selfish country in which too many people are driven by materialism; in which, to a greater extent than anywhere else in the western world, values have been corrupted by the pursuit of possessions. I concede that this is a generalised impression but so it has to be whenever one assesses a country.

America's values were epitomised for me early on a December morning as I walked to my host newspaper's offices in San Francisco and heard a chilling, witch- like voice, which came apparently from no-where, wailing *"Merry Christmas, sir"*. I looked down and saw what appeared to be a pile of dirty clothes on the sidewalk outside *Woolworths*. Closer inspection revealed that the filthy rags contained an emaciated, hideously ugly old woman. Through a grotesque toothless grin I was offered a second *"Merry Christmas, sir"* and it was then that I noticed that she was holding an immaculate and incongruously expensive ventriloquist's dummy; that the seasonal greeting was supposed to be coming not from the stomach churning old crone but from the beautifully-made, exquisitely tailored male doll and that I was being invited to put some money into the tin mug it held. I put all the loose change that I had, about two dollars, into the receptacle and said *"Thank you"* – upon which the old biddy shot me an aggressive dirty look, so devilishly evil it could have curdled milk, cleared her throat with a horrible gurgle, ***and spat at me.***

It might have been a very unfair conclusion but that one incident, for me, summed up American society – and I'm still to be convinced that I was wrong.

That's not to say that I did not meet some very nice American people, but having been very generously entertained by my hosts at the most lavish venues in San Francisco, I saw, on the way to Contra Costa by train, enough of another, depressed and deprived side to suggest that this was every bit as much a society of extreme haves and have-nots as some of the third world countries which the "rich" US habitually pities and patronises.

Where Australia had cocooned and comforted me, the USA confused and confounded me.

I was welcomed to the *Contra Costa Times* by its stunning blonde publisher Jacqui Lucido – a woman whose good looks were surpassed only by her talent. Here, I soon discovered from this engaging, effervescent and amusing lady that I was going to be taking more bad news back to Nottingham for Christopher Pole-Carew on the free distribution front. Jacqui confided that her newspaper – the very one which Chris had hoped would be a superb example of a *free* daily newspaper for the United Kingdom to emulate – was about to convert to being *paid for!*

Chris was right in that it was a tremendously impressive publication, printed throughout in glorious top quality colour. It was all so good, in fact, that Jacqui and her fellow directors had concluded that to continue giving away such a smart and expensively-produced newspaper no longer made the best business sense.

Oh, dear. Sorry, Chris... You've sent me all the way to Contra Costa in the US of A only to have your pet theory blown out of the water! We were not encountering the best of luck with this particular bit of the revolution. It was, however, by no means a wasted trip. The lovely Jacqui Lucido sent me away armed with so many brilliant, innovative full colour sections to try to adopt and adapt that I had to send off another of those airmail parcel deliveries to await my return to Nottingham.

The *Contra Costa Times* may have been small but it was big on quality. This woman ran one hell of a newspaper and I was privileged to have spent some serious time with her.

On next to Canada and first stop Vancouver where I felt that the *Vancouver Sun* and its journalists were, curiously, closer to their Australian counterparts in culture and conduct than they were to their contemporary cousins in America. Vancouver was quiet. A bit like North Wales on a wet Sunday – but its newspaper was keen and professional. Here, I persuaded my hosts to let me *work* properly like I had done in Melbourne.

In Vancouver I worked with a marvellous journalist-cum-promotions executive, Al MacLellan, a diminuative man with a liking for extravagantly patterned sports jackets and Churchillian cigars. Al was a joy to be with, an inspiring little bloke with infectious enthusiasm and a wonderful sense of humour. He introduced me to a cartoon character called *Herman*, who had taken readers by storm. *Herman* was a Canadian thicko and made me laugh so much the first time I read the newspaper.

The simple cartoon (always the best ones) had *Herman* bent over with a vicious dog hanging by its teeth from his nose. The caption said simply: *"SIT!"* The next day's cartoon had *Herman* lying on an operating theatre table with a very sheepish expression as he looked up at a monitor which, with alarms ringing, was flat-lining. . . The caption said simply: *"Excuse me?"*

"I've just *got* to have this for the *Nottingham Evening Post,* I told Al... and in no time we'd done a unique syndication deal which meant that for a very reasonable sum, *Herman* would be coming to the east Midlands with me. It had become obvious to me early on in this incredible trip that a journalist prepared to *look* and *listen* could *learn* something valuable from every major newspaper on these travels and so it was in Toronto, where I visited the *Toronto Star,* the last newspaper on the itinerary.

This was another class act with much to show me.

On our last day in Toronto it snowed. Real snow. Canadian snow. And that's deep. When we got to the airport we discovered that it was also snowing in the UK. English snow. Not so real, not so deep, but enough, as usual, to cause the cancellation of many flights. In the custody of a Canadian pilot, who wondered what all the fuss was about, we flew out of Toronto but had to be diverted from Heathrow to Ireland. Our trip, therefore, had an unscheduled visit lasting several hours, to Shannon Airport.

We didn't give a damn. It had been such a wonderful, life-changing experience that we didn't want this trip to end.

We eventually made it to Heathrow and back to Nottingham... to a white Christmas. We were home just in time for the *Nottingham Evening Post's* Christmas Party. This was a huge event, attended by the entire workforce of *T. Bailey Forman Ltd. ,* staged in a vast local ballroom and for which no expense was spared. Pauline and I joined the Chairman, the Directors and their ladies on their table for a slap-up traditional Christmas dinner to be followed by dancing, cabaret and general frivolity. It was our first day back in the UK. We were sun-tanned, happy, relaxed and ready to share our experiences with them all. And they all wanted to hear.

After dinner the drink flowed with typical Forman Hardy generosity and style and when, under orders from the DJ, we all stood on our chairs, linked arms and sang loudly along to Wizard's *I Wish It Could Be Christmas Every Day* (including the straight-backed Colonel Tom, bless him!) I had a wonderfully warm feeling of belonging. My cup was overflowing ... in more ways than one.

In the New Year of 1982 it was time for me to start planning for my succession to Bill Snaith's editorial throne. My first task was to convert that wonderful overseas trip into benefits for the *Nottingham Evening Post* and I set about building what I had learned into a programme for my eventual occupation.

In an interview which I gave to *UK Press Gazette* about the adventure I summed it all up thus...

"This tour gave me a once-in-a-lifetime chance to study the methods, the content and the promotion of newspapers in a wide variety of cities and towns in three countries.

I saw much that editors in the UK would find useful and informative. Of course, it is very much a case of horses for courses in the newspaper world but I picked up several specific ideas which can be adapted for use over here and in broad terms, it was invaluable to take a close, first hand look at the way in which managements in those three countries are tackling the problem of producing newspapers which are relative to the 'eighties, capable of fighting the universal decline in sales and facing up to the many threats from rival media sources.

If I have one over-riding impression it is that most of the papers I studied are light years ahead of the provincial industry in the UK in promoting themselves. Far too many of us are still turning out newspapers in the belief that there is some intangible divine right to readership and while there has been a fair degree of progress in promotion in recent years we still have a very long way to go. The best of the papers I visited combine fundamental journalistic excellence with superb promotion. For example, I met a columnist in San Francisco who switched papers and took thousands of readers with him and a topical cartoonist in Australia who is so good he is paid more than his Editor. In both cases, the excellence of those journalists is properly and professionally marketed. Provincial editors in the UK must recognise that promotion does not just mean a float in the local carnival once a year or a cup for a junior soccer league. It can mean the difference between success and failure."

Twenty five years later, that will read, to the initiated, like a "statement of the bleedin' obvious" but back then editorial elitism was rife. Just as many executives on the commercial side of the industry needed to ditch their hostile and jealous attitudes towards editors, so many editors needed to vacate the saddles of their high horses. Lots of editors (mostly the older, longer-serving ones) occupied rarefied ivory towers from which "those grubby marketing types" were excluded. To many of those, the views I expressed in that *Press Gazette* article were heresy.

Already dismissed by several senior fellow members of the august *Guild Of British Newspaper Editors* as a brash young bugger heading for a fall, I had become distinctly unpopular with the old guard when it was reported that not only had I opened up my daily news conference on the *Kent Evening Post* to the newspaper sales people but actually encouraged them to express an opinion on what should go on the front page. This was punishable by tar and feathers!

These prehistoric attitudes *had* to change and eventually they did – though not without a struggle.

While I had been away from Nottingham between 1971 and 1981 a very great deal had happened. Christopher Pole-Carew, the supreme trailblazer, had pioneered the introduction of direct input technology for journalists before most people in our industry even knew it existed. This technology was truly revolutionary. It enabled journalists, using computers instead of the time-honoured typewriters, to deliver their stories, headlines and pictures electronically to printing stage – thus removing several traditional processes and the old jobs that went with them along the way.

Such was *T. Bailey Forman's* principled approach to these matters, always ensuring that employees were treated properly, that despite introducing this enormous change in a heavily unionised environment in 1975, it was all achieved with a minimum of fuss. A whole decade had passed before Fleet Street managements were to grasp the same nettle – and then all hell was let loose with bitter strikes, mass picketing and riots.

Then in 1978, the National Union of Journalists called a national strike over pay. The NUJ still enjoyed virtual closed shops throughout the industry and it had no difficulty in getting effective widespread support for its strike. In Kent I had produced an *Evening Post* of sorts almost single-handedly through all the weeks of the strike (as had most other provincial editors) and that had been possible because the print unions refused to support their "brothers" in the NUJ by striking themselves. ("I'm alright Jack" was never an inappropriate phrase when applied to trade union conduct in newspapers!)

Consequently, although they were pale imitations of their normal content, the regional newspapers continued to publish throughout the strike, thus ensuring that damage to the businesses was kept to a minimum. This, in turn, meant that the striking journalists were able to make their point and eventually to agree a settlement with the *Newspaper Society*, the proprietors' organisation, while still having jobs to go back to... the economic reality of our industry being that prolonged periods of non-publication would **kill** many newspapers.

In Nottingham, however, the situation was dramatically different for two emphatic reasons:

(1) Because of the introduction of direct input technology it would have been absolutely impossible to sustain publication of the *Nottingham Evening Post* without the journalists. Therefore, if *their* journalists had joined the strike the damage to the newspaper caused by prolonged non-publication would have been extreme, possibly fatal.

(2) Because *Nottingham Evening Post* journalists' salaries had always been among the best (if not *the* best) in the country – the NUJ was asking them to go on strike in support of a pay claim for an average £1,500 pa *less* than they were already earning!

There were those in the industry who could recognise and appreciate the trade union philosophy which said that the strong (ie. the very well paid journalists on the *Nottingham* Evening *Post)* had to support their much weaker brethren on, say, the little weekly *Piddlehampton Gazette* but the fiercely determined and independent Christopher Pole-Carew was not among them. Neither were the majority of the journalists on the *Evening Post.*

And who could blame *him* for not wanting to risk disastrous damage to the health and future of his business or *them* for not wanting to subject themselves and their families to the financial hardship of an indefinite period on minimal strike pay when *he* was already paying and *they* were already taking home £30 a week *more* than the NUJ was striking for!

It was a collision course with an inevitable outcome... Christopher Pole-Carew told the *Nottingham Evening Post* journalists that if they joined the strike they would be deemed to be in breach of their contracts of employment and sacked. The NUJ told them that if they did not obey the strike call they would be kicked out of the union and "blacked" – which meant that they would never be able to work anywhere else. They had an unenviable choice to make between loyalty to their company, with which they had no quarrel whatsoever and loyalty to their union. Many of them also had pragmatic issues like keeping up with mortgage payments and other family financial commitments to consider.

Their union should never have put them in that quandary and one likes to suppose that if it happened now any union would be sensible enough to exclude them from the battle, but this was the 1970s, at the height of trade union power in Britain, and nowhere was that power stronger or more frequently misapplied than in the newspaper industry.

Come the awful day of reckoning, 28 of the newspaper's 110 journalists told Christopher they had no alternative to joining the strike, to which the managing director replied that he, therefore, had no alternative but to sack them. And sack them he did.

To say that the shit then hit the fan would be a massive understatement. There was no legislation to control the conduct of trade unions in those days. This was happening under a *real* Labour Government and in the union-dominated (some would have said union *run*) newspaper industry NO management, either in Fleet Street or the provinces, had EVER taken such a stance. Christopher Pole-Carew was either a fool or a very brave man. Events were later to prove that he was, emphatically, not a fool – but in the meantime the wrath of the entire Labour and Trade Union Movement descended on Forman Street, Nottingham, home of the *Nottingham Evening Post*. Their objective was to stop publication of the newspaper.

The whole workforce was subjected to brutal intimidation by thousands of baying pickets, among whom journalists, in whose name the battle was being fought, were a tiny minority. And that mass picketing – shown frequently on national TV news – went on long after the NUJ dispute had been settled. There was no discrimination. You could be a 17-year-old secretary or a little tele-sales girl, totally uninvolved in the dispute, but you still had to walk the terrifying gauntlet of hate and venom, screaming and spitting just to get to your job. The "blackleg" journalists suffered even more, with death threats made to wives and children, appalling hate mail and excrement pushed through the letterboxes of their homes – those extremes were almost certainly not the work of the NUJ, but by now this was a war that went far beyond the initial cause.

Christopher Pole-Carew and the Forman Hardy family became figureheads of the hatred... despised, mocked and presented to the watching world as evil, inhuman capitalist monsters, out to destroy the working classes and eat their babies. The propaganda peddled by journalists whose union membership and vested interest had destroyed any semblance of objectivity painted a grossly biased picture all too readily accepted as real – and not just by partial observers – as the siege of the *Nottingham Evening Post* continued relentlessly for months.

After the pay dispute had been settled nationally, the focal point of the protest was a campaign to "Reinstate The 28". The blacking of the newspaper was to continue unless and until the striking journalists sacked by Christopher Pole-Carew were given back their jobs. It was futile and the NUJ almost certainly knew that, but despite the hate campaign, the mass picketing, the employment of every intimidation tactic in the book (and plenty of new ones!) and all the widespread propaganda, they had not succeeded in stopping so much as *one* copy of the *Nottingham Evening Post* and to give up now would mean enormous loss of face.

That was still the situation when I returned to the paper in 1981. Christopher Pole-Carew had won a famous victory at the cost of acquiring a national reputation as a hard-hearted press baron who abused and exploited his workers. It was complete bollocks. Chris was the best "shop steward" those workers – at all levels and in all facets of the business – could have wished for. They knew it. And he had a great rapport with the guys on the shop floor. They'd have jumped through hoops of fire if he'd asked them to and without the genuinely strong bond between proprietors, management and workforce *T. Bailey Forman Ltd* would not have survived the extraordinary campaign of hatred and vilification which it had endured since 1978.

With the election of Margaret Thatcher, the whole UK industrial scene was about to change and when the national newspaper industry took on its own unions over the introduction of new technology and started a bloody battle, which it was eventually to win, it was often wrongly assumed that the *Nottingham Evening Post's* notoriety as provincial *bête noir* of Britain's Labour movement was due to the same struggle of jobs versus technology. The fact that it never had been and that the Forman Hardy family and Christopher Pole-Carew had achieved that revolution ten years earlier through co-operation and negotiation with the unions was forever lost. Because of the blacking there was now no union presence at the *Nottingham Evening Post* but that had bugger all to do with its state-of-the-art technology and everything to do with the obdurance of a union which, if had not been so drenched in dogma and poisoned by politics, could and *should* have been holding that newspaper and its management up to the rest of the industry as an exemplar rather than a demon in 1978.

The end result of all that, however, was that I was the new Editor of a newspaper that was reviled by the Labour Party, which dominated politics in the city and county of which I was now a prominent citizen. I knew that well enough, of course, when I took the job; my early experience with NUJ cranks way back in 1961 in Shrewsbury had hardened me to any potential difficulty.

They could bring it on… I was ready for them.

And I didn't have to wait long!

At the first public function Pauline and I attended I was introduced to Len Maynard, the Leader of the Labour-controlled

Nottingham City Council. My name meant nothing to him as we shook hands but when the introduction got to *the new Editor of the Evening Post* bit he pulled his hand away and wiped it theatrically on his trousers as if to rid himself of dirt.

That offended me greatly, but it was supposed to, so I wasn't going to let him see that and I just laughed in his face. Then, as we prepared to sit down, the Labour gang moved their chairs around, with much extravagant posturing, so that they had collectively turned their backs on me and my wife in a childish gesture which told us "You're not welcome here."

"Prats!" I said to Pauline.

It was all part of the challenge I had taken on.

Three years after the event, there were still big NUJ posters all over the city showing pictures of the 28 sacked journalists and demanding: **"Reinstate The 28"**. The NUJ knew – as I knew – that this was a farce. The 28 all had other jobs now (mostly better than the ones they'd left because they were good journalists and it was ambition that had persuaded them to hang on to their union cards) and most of them had long since left Nottingham. But Christopher Pole-Carew's "offence" was not going to be allowed to be forgotten.

What a bloody waste of time and effort!

Monday, March 1st 1982 was the day of my succession to the throne of Bill Snaith. It was my first issue as Editor of the *Nottingham Evening Post* and Christopher Pole Carew thoughtfully had a mini-copy of my first front page made into a heavy glass paperweight, which 24 years later sits proudly in my study as I write.

A glance at it brings memories of that day flooding back.

The front page lead story "SNIFF DEN ALERT IN CITY" was an exclusive on what was then the entirely new and disturbing discovery of kids indulging in glue-sniffing.

The main Page One picture was of a gorgeous looking girl in Welsh national costume (March 1st – St David's Day – *gerrit!)*

The blurb at the top of the page promoted four of the *"NEW"* features in the *"NEW LOOK POST"* I had re-designed, re-organised and re-launched the *Nottingham Evening Post* in what could best be described as a "broadloid" format. I had resolved that, despite Christopher's enthusiasm for me to do so, it would have been far too big a step and therefore far too big a risk to "go tabloid"

This newspaper had not changed one bit since I had last worked there 11 years earlier and, brash and young as I was for such a post, even I knew that it would be fatal to change too much too soon. So I had employed a number of tabloid typographical techniques within a broadsheet format while modelling the "new look" paper's style and to some extent its content on the best of those that I had visited on my travels. I had given the paper a much stronger visual impact and I had toughened and livened up the content, with much more comment, strident opinion and humour... led by *HERMAN* the Canadian cartoon character I had laughed so much at in Vancouver.

The paper now had much more personality, with picture by-lines for previously anonymous writers, several of them exceptionally good and previously, I believed, woefully wasted.

The whole new package was bright and modern with strength and depth. We had perfected it and polished it until it shone. I was delighted with it. As pleased as Punch. And so proud of it.

And the readers... *absolutely bloody hated it!*

The telephone lines were buzzing with calls of complaint and protest only minutes after the first edition hit the streets. And they carried on *all afternoon.* So many readers wanted to complain to the Editor personally that Mavis Brand, the wonderful secretary I had inherited from Bill Snaith, took an impromptu and entirely arbitrary decision to protect me from *all* of them – only confessing to me months later that there had been hundreds!

Despite the thoughtful intervention of Mavis, there was no escaping the furore. Nearly every line in the building was jammed. It seemed the whole of Nottingham wanted me run out of town.

Totally dejected, I decided to go for a walk to clear my troubled head and collect my shattered thoughts and as I headed out of the yard next to where the giant press was belching out tens of thousands more copies of this paper which nobody apparently wanted, I was fleetingly tempted to stop it running. Then, as she brushed past me with a severe look of betrayed disapproval, a lady called Rose who worked in the Market Research department snapped:

"Huh! Deserting the sinking ship are you?"

I wanted to crawl away and hide. What the bloody hell had I done! My stomach was knotted. My throat was dry. I was in a cold sweat. Why, oh, why couldn't I have just left things alone and kept it all Bill Snaith's way?

What sweet Mavis could not protect me from was the next day's mailbag. And when I crept in to my office after a sleepless night and saw the mountain of letters on my desk I feared the worst.

I was right to do so. Letter after letter complained bitterly about my "new look "paper and – as Nottinghamians are prone to do – in a sharply blunt manner. One by one I read them. And one by one I scribbled a polite reply for Mavis to type, in which I strove to explain what I was doing with their paper and why. As I was doing this there was a polite knock on my door, upon which a lady I knew to be

Colonel Tom Forman Hardy's secretary handed me a letter and with the air of a judge announcing a death sentence she said solemnly: "The Chairman sent me down with this."

Fully expecting it to contain my P45 I pulled the letter from its envelope with great trepidation and read it.

It was from a lady of 80...

> *"Dear Colonel,*
> *I have been a reader for more than 50 years and I detest this new Evening Post. I hate it. It's awful. Why does a new broom always have to sweep clean and make a mess.*
> *Please sack him."*

Oh, bloody hell! I thought, I wonder if he will?

Months later, I discovered that the Colonel, like Mavis, had decided to spare me some anguish. He had, in fact, received almost as many letters of complaint as I had, but when his secretary had asked if he wanted her to bring them all down the corridor to me he had said: "No – just take one so that he can get the gist!"

As I worked my way through the mountain of protest, one letter stood out, shining like a beacon. It was from a lady called Corrine Fogelman and the fact that her name is etched in my mind 24 years later is testament to how much it meant to me at the time.

She wrote:

> *"May I be the first (she wasn't joking!) to congratulate you on the new look Evening Post. I love it. It is so much better with so much more to read. I particularly appreciate the columnists and I'm still laughing at Herman!*
> *Keep up the good work."*

Corrine was not only the first reader to welcome my efforts. Hers was the ***only*** letter that was not savagely critical.

By far the most common complaint was that I had "moved the deaths". When I was reorganising the pages it seemed to me that the BMD's (the hatched, matched and despatched) page was far too early in the paper. The notices had occupied the whole of Page Four and were, by their nature, just a slab of grey type. I moved them to the back of the paper, as the first page in the classified section – which I thought a far more appropriate position – to allow me to transform Page Four into a lively new features page. Big mistake. In Nottingham, I learned, you bloody well leave the dead where they are. My offence was tantamount to grave robbing!

That night I was invited to go to a Notts County football match as the guest of the directors. They'd heard I was a football fanatic and wanted to welcome me to their club. Nice. And it would be a pleasant diversion from the flak and fury of the paper's re-launch.

Or so I thought.

As I sat in the boardroom having a pre-match drink with the directors it soon became evident that even here, which should have been a haven of sporting escape for me, there was only one topic of conversation... *the new look bloody paper!*

Everybody present had an opinion to give me. And they were all negative. One by one, the directors and their guests tore into me. They all hated the new *Evening Post*. Only one voice came to my rescue and offered support. John Mounteney, a Notts director who was to become a good friend, intervened:

"No, I like it," he said. "I can see what he's trying to do."

But this being Nottingham, not even this positive contribution was going to end on a high.

"Mind you," John continued, "My mum hates it. I was round her house tonight and she had the paper spread across the table. She said 'I don't care for this new *Post*, John. ' I said 'You will, Mother. You'll get used to it. ' She said 'Oh no I shan't. Do you know it's just taken me ages to find the deaths – **and when I'd found them I didn't know one of them!**'"

The next 10 days – the time it took for an accurate analysis of a week's sales performance to come through – were nerve-wracking in the extreme. If I had got it drastically wrong, which the feedback suggested, I might have inflicted serious damage on the circulation of the *Evening Post*. Maybe Bill Snaith's caution and refusal to embrace significant change had been right all along. Maybe my way was the very last thing this newspaper had needed.

When the figures arrived I was able to breathe a huge sigh of relief. They had not moved. So far as people continuing to *buy* the paper was concerned, my changes had produced no effect. Under the barrage of complaints I had endured I had long since abandoned any hope that I might actually have achieved the objective of *increasing* sales. No change was a hugely welcome positive under these circumstances!

One thing I most emphatically would and could not do was to change things back again and restore the paper's previous format, style and content; such defeatism was simply not an option. And when the second week's figures again showed no impact on sales and the protest calls and letters began to subside, I knew I had weathered the storm.

That night I slept soundly for the first time in a fortnight!

Now I began to get phone calls and letters *praising* the new look. I was now able to rationalise the storm of protest and put into perspective the initial mass of complaints and that process was helped considerably when I read a book on Nottingham by Emrys Bryson, brilliant *Evening Post* journalist, local author and broadcaster.

Emrys wrote:

> "Nottingham argues about everything and rarely agrees. The Nottinghamian will never admit openly that he was wrong but after a decent interval of time to save face he will put the matter right and pretend that it was all his own idea in the first place. He might not be strong on tact or diplomacy but he is sincere."

Nottingham's reaction to my revamp of its evening newspaper fitted that scenario like the proverbial glove and when the old dear who had wanted the Chairman to sack me eventually wrote to him again, this time in fulsome praise of the paper, she did not apologise but *did* ask him to pass her gratitude and congratulations on to me!

Emrys was spot on. During my previous, relatively brief spell in this city, I had not learned all about the Nottinghamian character. Now I had. The hard way.

Later, I picked up a couple of apocryphal stories about that character which I used often in after-dinner speeches, never failing to get a laugh from Nottingham audiences who recognised themselves:

> There was a wealthy businessman in Nottingham who died having been a great benefactor to the city. He had spent millions of pounds of his own money unselfishly putting as much back as he ever took out. He had provided money for recreational facilities; put hundreds of thousands into the university and built dozens of hostels for the poor and needy. His death was a grievous loss to his beloved city. Half way through his funeral ceremony, the vicar asked politely who in the congregation was going to give the soliloquy to pay full and proper tribute to this great man. Nobody responded. Again, the vicar asked. And again. And again. But nobody came forward.
>
> Eventually the vicar lost his temper...
>
> "Look," he said, "unless somebody steps forward and pays due and just homage to this wonderful benefactor of the city of Nottingham I will abandon this funeral."
>
> After much embarrassed shuffling of feet and gazing at the floor one chap rose reluctantly, walked slowly to the front of the church, looked down at the coffin and said:
>
> "WELL... HIS BROTHER WERE WORSE."

That is SO Nottingham. As is this...

A couple of Nottingham blokes meet in their local pub on a Sunday lunchtime.
"Owd ya get on last night?" one asks the other.
"Not bad," his mate replied. "I found this place where you can get a pie, a pint and a woman for a pound."
"What were it like?" asks his pal.
"THERE WEREN'T MUCH MEAT IN THE PIE."

My early weeks suffering the slings and arrows of outraged Nottingham could have been very lonely had it not been for two men. Chris Pole-Carew and David Teague stood firmly with me. David in particular was staunchly supportive. He told me one day: "Look mate, you've pierced a boil. You *had* to do it and it was never going to be easy. The paper will come through it and be much the better for it." I really appreciated that. Most directors on the commercial side of our industry would have shied away from supporting the Editor when the flak was flying – the easier to explain poor sales and divert responsibility from their own departments' failings. Not David Teague. Again and not for the last time I remembered Malachi Doyle's words when I was leaving Kent: "You'll be working with a great bloke in David Teague." In just a few months David had shown himself to be not just a superb colleague but a loyal friend and so he remained throughout and beyond my time in Nottingham.

Almost immediately after my arrival, the *Post's* highly talented Chief Sub Editor, George Hunt, the man most insiders had expected to get the Editor's job, left the paper and the profession to run a Post Office in Lincolnshire. He did so without rancour and I understood his feelings. Then his Deputy, Tony Moss, even more talented than George in my judgment, also announced that he was leaving, to start a PR business with a colleague. The loss of these two men was a big blow, but I appreciated their honesty and I'd rather they left than stay on while harbouring resentment over my appointment.

I replaced George with Ian Manning, a stalwart senior sub editor who went on to become one of the most loyal, hard working and committed journalists I ever knew and Tony with Doug Morris – the *same* Doug Morris who had looked after me amid all the NUJ hostility back in Shrewsbury in 1961 and had, by one of life's great coincidences, later moved to the *Nottingham Evening Post.* These two men served me brilliantly as they steered through all the radical changes I was making to the format and typographical style of the paper. This was an extremely difficult and demanding task which required Ian and Doug to have complete faith and belief in what I was doing. They never once let me down.

Accepting the very different ways of the new Editor proved much more difficult, however, for another key executive – the News Editor Bill Ivory. My close hands-on style, so very far removed from the more remote editors Bill had been used to, upset him greatly. He saw it as interference in his domain and an insult to his experience. I was having none of that. And I had to take him on because to give in to him would be seen as a weak climb down by the 114 members of my editorial staff. Bill was a very powerful figure in the newsroom and had been used to running things his way for more than 20 years. He was a tall, handsome, charismatic, intelligent and articulate Welshman who looked much younger than his 50-plus years. He was a good journalist, highly respected, very popular and very proud. But while the newsroom ran like clockwork, I felt it lacked ideas and passion and the newsdesk personnel – all of them around the same age as Bill – had no understanding whatsoever of campaigning journalism and consequently no inclination for what had become an essential part of the role of regional newspapers.

The desk ran with military precision and efficiency but, to me, its output was safe, boring and entirely predictable. I was determined that it would change.

Bill Ivory was determined that it wouldn't.

This collision course soon led to robust exchanges between Bill and I at my editorial conferences, which had become very lively and unrecognisable in style from the days of my predecessor, and after one bust-up over my disagreement with his choice of reporter for a particular assignment Bill wrote a "confidential" letter to the Chairman in which he invoked his distinguished RAF war service (Bill had been a bomber pilot) and told the Colonel he had not been through all that to be "treated like dirt" by a young upstart who showed people no respect. Colonel Forman Hardy did not respond to Bill but sent his letter straight down to me without comment. That couldn't have been easy for him because he had so much more in common with Bill than he had with me, but it was the Colonel's way of supporting me – and letting Bill know that he did.

I was furious. I called Bill into my office, threw his letter at him and demanded to know what the bloody hell he thought he was doing. He looked acutely embarrassed. Clearly, he had believed that the Colonel would back a fellow war hero against this arrogant youngster and sort me out. Clearly, he'd misjudged the Colonel and made a big mistake

Bill bluffed it out. What else could he do? He complained that I showed him no respect and belittled him at conferences. I told him he had to get off his high horse and start being more professional. We had a blazing row. It cleared the air. And we shook hands. But I knew I just had to remove him from the sharp end of the news desk (and his three dyed-in-the-wool lieutenants with him) if I was to impose my ideas effectively and drag this old paper into the new world – and that's what I did.

Nobody got the sack (that *would* have upset the Chairman!) but I had a complete "oil-change" on that newsdesk by appointing Bill Ivory Assistant Editor, finding reasonably important alternative jobs for the others and putting my own hand-picked young team in charge of this – *the* most important area of any newspaper. [3]

My predecessor's Deputy Editor had been Ken Macmillan, who had been Editor of the sister morning paper the *Guardian Journal* until it folded in the late 70s. Ken's first comment to me when we chatted after my appointment was that it was going to take a lot of bloody money to get rid of him! Hardly positive. But he was right. He was very close to retirement and while he and I both recognised that he couldn't possibly be *my* Deputy there was absolutely no point in forcing the issue. I redefined Ken's role (another way of saying I found important things for him to do every day) before appointing Ian Scott as my Deputy Editor.

Ian had been Features Editor of the *Guardian Journal* and a fellow occupant of the "brains room" during my first spell in Nottingham. Ian had also been an internal applicant for the Editor's job and had been very carefully considered for it. He was an excellent, experienced journalist who commanded a lot of respect. A bit dour, I always thought, but a man who always spoke his mind openly and without fear or favour. I like that. And I liked Ian. He proved to be a superb, ultra reliable and intensely loyal Deputy.

A month after I had taken over, Chris Pole-Carew danced into my office waving a set of car keys.

"These are yours, now," he said.

---

[3] Bill Ivory, to his great credit, became a first rate assistant editor. He had a very great deal to offer and his experience and knowledge often proved invaluable to me. Bill and I went on to forge a close, strong and lasting friendship. His wife's tragic illness – she had motor neurone disease – forced his early retirement and he nursed her through to her death, which took a mercilessly long time. His son Billy was later to write a brilliant, moving yet funny, TV play based on his mum's illness.

They were the keys to Bill Snaith's spanking-new, top-of-the-range, pale-yellow Daimler with black leather trim. I'd never been a car fanatic but I felt a huge thrill, great excitement and immense pride as I drove through the city that night in *my*Daimler. Suddenly I remembered riding my *Irwin's* shop bike through Oswestry. And I laughed so much I almost ran tens of thousands of pounds worth of gleaming motor car off the road!

On fairly frequent trips home to Oswestry to see Mum and Dad the Daimler looked absolutely splendid, if a tad incongruous, parked outside their council house and it certainly gave the neighbours a talking point. Mind you, that car was of almost no account as local gossip compared to the Friday night I went for a pint with my dad to the local pub *The Unicorn*. It was a warm night and I was wearing white skin-tight jeans and a pink shirt – forgetting that this was hardly typical or acceptable attire in a bar full of tough blokes, most of whom had come straight from work.

Assorted grimy overalls, sweat-stained shirts and other well-worn working clothes were the customary dress code in this bar and there was nothing whatsoever wrong with that, of course, but I felt and obviously looked a right pansy in my pastel pink and gleaming white. Trying not to look too self conscious, I joined in the banter and the dominoes and I think I'd managed to convince them that Stan's eldest lad hadn't turned into a big girl's blouse... until there was a tap on my shoulder as I stood waiting to get my round in. When I turned around I was really surprised and delighted to see an old pal from my days in Kent.

Mac Ifill, a smashing black bloke who had been an Army officer in Ethiopia before becoming a sub-editor, had been a good friend in Kent and I had no idea he had moved to Oswestry, of all places, to become a sub on the *Oswestry Border Counties Advertiser*, of all papers! We had not seen each other for years and – as blokes do without giving it a second thought in the South East – we gave each other a huge and heartfelt hug.

But this was *not* the South East. It was *Oswestry*. And this was the public bar of *The Unicorn*, where men were men and if you displayed that sort of affection, **you** were **not**. Now, you'd never find two geezers more devoutly straight than Mac and me, but to complement my pastel pink (and to compound the apparent felony) Mac was wearing the prettiest of Paisley shirts and guess what colour his jeans were!

The jaws dropped as sharply as the dominoes and a stunned silence descended on that beer-soaked bar as every pair of overtly heterosexual eyes in the place bore into me and my pal Mac with

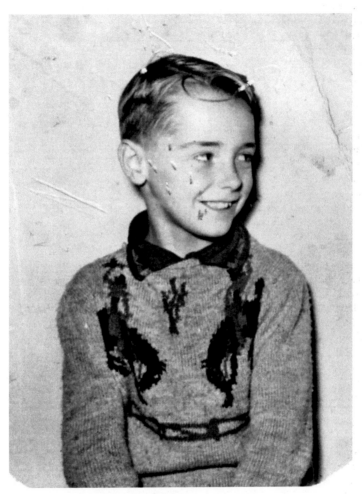

1952 – "I'm going to be a journalist…"

1955 – Not the smartest cricket team! The great Alan Ball is far right on the back row.
Barrie Williams is fourth from the left on the front row.

1961 – "Teddy Boy? Me?"

1967 – "Chronicle News Editor weds."

1971 – First day at work at the Kent Evening Post.

*"Get off our backs!" – **Kent Evening Post** News Editor Barrie Williams is confronted by Alan Mills, Public Relations Officer of South East Gas. Observing the altercation are (from left) Lee Coppack, Local Government reporter, Betty Cole, News Editor's secretary and Geoff Mills, South East Gas executive.*

*In 1979 the **Kent Evening Post** ran a greyhound called "PostSport" at Rochester Stadium. The Editor, in leather coat, watched the dog win its debut race.*

*Farewell to Kent… Pauline bids farewell to **Kent Evening Post** reporters (the late) Jon Ham and Ian "Sniffer" Read at the Editor's leaving party in 1981.*

***Kent Evening Post** Sports Editor Simon Kelner (now Editor of **The Independent**) and behind him **BBC Radio Medway** News Editor Langley Brown at the Editor's leaving party in Kent.*

1983 ~ Appointed Editorial Director of T. Bailey Forman Ltd.

With Pauline at 10 Downing St, welcomed by Prime Minister Margaret Thatcher.

Brian Clough with Pauline at Nottingham Forest's Jubilee Club.

*On a tour of inner city Nottingham with Michael Heseltine
and local MP Martin Brandon-Bravo.*

*Receiving the 1991 Press Gazette **Newspaper of The Year** award
from BBC Radio 4 presenter Brian Redhead.*

*1991 ~ Receiving an award for **Nottingham Evening Post** coverage of disabled sport from HRH the Princess of Wales.*

Interviewing Prime Minister John Major at 10 Downing Street.

*1995 ~ Facing BBC cameras for the **Western Morning News** tabloid re-launch.*

*The new tabloid **Western Morning News** "hot off the Press" after a very long night!
On the right is Andy Gough, then Managing Director.*

*1998 ~ Receiving the Press Gazette **Newspaper of The Year** award (again!) this time from TV presenter Jon Snow.*

"Why do you keep giving us such a f-----g kicking?"
With Alastair Campbell in Exeter in 2000.

2000 ~ Interviewing Prime Minister Tony Blair on TV.

Kindred spirits ... Discussing rural affairs with Prince Charles.

"Come on - let's get stuck in!"
Conducting Western Morning News editorial conference in 2002.

*Going out at the top… With **Western Morning News** journalists
(from left) Clare Jardine, Andy Greenwood, Richard Austin, Lucy Cockcroft, Steve Grant
and Su Carroll and a clutch of awards, including Daily/Sunday Newspaper of The Year
at the glittering Press Gazette event in June 2005.*

*Off you go, boss… How Western Morning News cartoonist **Tom**
saw the Editor on his last day in regional journalism.*

looks of disgust, disdain (and some of sympathy) and it was some time before they could be satisfactorily convinced that Stan's lad wasn't "on the turn"!

After its rocky start the Barrie Williams era of the *Nottingham Evening Post* settled down very nicely. The antagonists in the Labour Party were confused. The more I put myself about the city, the more I wrote articles critical of the Conservative Government, the more Nottingham got to know me personally, the more they began to realise that I was a working-class lad who was in nobody's pocket. Posh Daimler notwithstanding, I simply did not fit the preconceived image they had of an Editor chosen by the mega-rich Forman Hardy's and the despised Pole-Carew. I was supposed to be a brutal right wing Toff who wanted them trodden into the dirt... but, hang on... he's just a normal bloke... "One of us."

First to break the taboo was Councillor Jean Arnold, the Mayor of the city, a splendid woman and a classic true and lifelong Labour supporter. After announcing: "You'll do for me lad," she made up her own rule, that since the Mayor was supposed to be above political bias for a year in office she didn't have to black me and wasn't bloody going to! Her husband and Mayoral consort, John, an equally dyed-in-the-wool Labour councillor and devoted Notts County fan, decided that Jean's new rule applied to him too. Now, when Pauline and I arrived at civic functions it was to an invariably warm and deliberately overt welcome from lovely, feisty Jean and friendly John.

Gradually, most of the local Labour politicians were beginning to realise that by ostracising this big newspaper with its many thousands of readers they were cutting off their noses to spite their faces. But for as long as the NUJ blacking remained there was nothing they could do about it. For my part, I found it intensely frustrating journalistically that while many of them were now talking to me perfectly normally off the record they were excluded from the pages of my paper in a city and county in which they were by far the most widely supported party.

To put it in the Nottingham vernacular... *it were bloody daft!*

As my editorial impact grew and the paper changed even more dramatically in character and style I was approached by the BBC to ask if I would co-operate in the production of a "fly-on-the-wall" documentary. "Highly controversial newspaper, new whiz kid Editor, the whole of Nottingham talking about you – you know the sort of stuff," said the plum-in-the-mouth Beeb girl who came to see me.

"Why not?" I said. And for the next eight weeks I could hardly even visit the toilet without an obtrusive TV crew in tow.

There was lots of "good telly" to be had. One of the main tasks I had set myself was to try to put the newspaper more in touch with the *people* of Nottingham. That bitter dispute, with all its national media coverage, had led most of them to swallow all the NUJ crap. Though many of them still bought the paper every day the "ordinary" people of the city had a pretty dim view of it. To them it was "a Tory rag" that sacked its workers for exercising their rights. I had a massive PR job on my hands and TV exposure could help a great deal.

While I was by no means starry-eyed about appearing on TV (I had done so several times in Kent) and was well aware of the potential banana skins of the "fly on the wall" format – particularly under these circumstances – I figured this documentary could make a big difference.

The producer of the programme, which was to be a half-hour prime time special, was Mike Fitzgerald. I liked him. Immediately. And a lot. The reporter and narrator was Mike Dornan. In those days, TV production was far more cumbersome and labour intensive than it is today. Eight or nine people would accompany me everywhere. Intrusive. Sometimes embarrassing. Often tiresome.

As part of my "get among the real people" campaign I was visiting working men's clubs two nights a week with Don Gray, the *Post's* Newspaper Sales Manager – a talented and likeable Geordie who later rose to the top, becoming Circulation Director of the *Daily Express* and *Sunday Express.*

The routine was that Don and I would arrange to visit each club to set up a feature for the paper. A reporter and photographer would then go to the club on a busy Saturday night, we'd run a big article all about the club, with plenty of pictures of members having fun. They'd all buy a paper to read it. Don picked up a good sale and I'd spread my PR gospel. *Perfect!* I knew this would make good TV because Don and I were of similar ilk and were both totally comfortable chatting away, playing darts and dominoes, drinking pint after pint and getting slightly the worse for wear with the lads and lasses in working men's clubs. And it did. Brilliant.

I had launched a school newspaper scheme. This had come from studying Newspapers In Education schemes in Australia and America. It had not been possible to emulate these to the full because of the uniquely precious approach of UK education authorities (particularly in Labour-controlled Nottinghamshire!) who regarded any commercially motivated presence in the classroom as tantamount to pimping for your grandmother – but I had succeeded in persuading the education mafia to allow me to publish a weekly school newspaper.

The kids from each school chosen would visit the *Evening Post* HQ, have a tour of the operation and a brief training session with some of my staff – then go away and produce their own 8-page newspaper which would go out with every copy of the *Evening Post*. On the day their paper was published the kids were invited back into the building to watch their newspaper coming off the press and have lunch with the Editor in the staff canteen. This, too, gave Don a great newspaper sales opportunity while allowing me to put the paper in touch with youngsters and their parents. I knew this would make good TV because the kids faces as they got their papers hot off the press were a treat to see and the banter I had with them over the bangers and mash was lovely. And it did. Brilliant.

I was launching a campaign against alleged profligacy by the Severn Trent Water Company set against the cost to the Nottinghamshire consumer. It was punchy stuff. They were not going to like it. When the first article in the series hit the streets their PR man was on the phone to me incandescent with rage. I knew this would make good TV. And it did. Brilliant.

Pauline and I were to attend the *Evening Post's* charity Fashion Show, a super sell-out event staged with all the class and flair that you would expect of a David Teague promotions department. Top clothes, top compere (TV comic Ted Rogers), top music, top models; colourful, glamorous, entertaining, sexy. Perfect for denting the stuffy public image of the paper. I knew this would make good TV. And it did. Brilliant.

The fly was on the wall during a particularly hectic and interesting time for naturally breaking news and sport and the Editor was in his element and at his best. I knew it would all make good TV because people have a fascination for our business. And it did. Brilliant.

I agreed to a no-holds-barred interview in which I would be confronted with tough questioning about all the controversy surrounding the *Nottingham Evening Post* and the "devil" himself, Christopher Pole-Carew agreed to be interviewed about his relationship with the new Editor. I knew this would make good TV because I had always been able to see both sides of the NUJ dispute, knew that "our" side had rarely, if ever, been fairly heard, was absolutely confident that I could handle any question they wanted to throw at me and aware that if he was given a decent chance viewers would see that Chris was not the baby eating ogre the propaganda had led them to believe he was. And it did. Brilliant.

The whole TV exposure was going so well and we were nearly at the end of filming when there was a knock on my door. It was Mike Dornan. And he shouldn't have been there because we'd agreed that I'd have a day free of the cameras and paraphernalia to catch up on some boring but essential admin work.

"I know we'd agreed a day off," said Mike, "But we wondered if you'd mind doing a few location shots." I wasn't best pleased because I had a shed load of work on my desk – but I relented.

"Right, where do you want me?" I asked Mike Fitzgerald and the camera crew.

"Could you be walking down the steps to the office at the front of the building?

"Sure... Where now?"

"Could you cross the road and be buying an *Evening Post* off that street seller over there?"

"Like the Editor does every day! OK... Where now?"

"Could we get you walking down into The Square – being among your readers?"

"No problem ... Where now?"

"There seems to be something going on in The Square. Look – lots of people. Can we go and have a look?"

"OK..."

As I walked into The Square, conspicuously accompanied by the ubiquitous TV crew and their loads of equipment, it suddenly became apparent to me that the 'something going on' was a trade union rally.

"Could you be standing here listening and watching?"

Now what! If I stand here somebody might well recognise me and start slagging me off. Someone might even throw a punch at me. But if I turn and walk away it will look like I'm running scared. No option. I just stand, watch and listen...

As I stood being filmed watching and listening to all this I spotted a number of Labour councillors in the crowd who knew me. Would they start making mischief?

I didn't much care by now.

I knew that if they did, THIS would make **bloody** good TV!

It didn't, however. Nothing happened.

Back at the office, my initial feeling was that I should tackle the guys. Had they set me up? And if they did, how **dare** they!

On reflection, I decided against that. It was impossible to say. It could have been entirely coincidental that on a day I was not expecting to be filmed and was, therefore, unprepared there just happened to be such an event in The Square after I'd been persuaded to walk down there. Stranger things have happened!

If I made a fuss it would sour the relationship and maybe influence the presentation of the documentary and if I was totally wrong in my suspicion (and I could well have been) I would look a complete prat.

Instead, I simply said to Mike Fitzgerald, "When this is all over I think I'll write a piece about what it's like to be on *this* side of the TV cameras." It was a clumsy veiled threat to which Mike replied: "How incestuous can we get!"

When the documentary, which they called *Man at the Post*, was completed, the film from The Square was not used. Mike Fitzgerald brought a draft copy of the programme for me to see and as we ran through it I realised that the risk I had taken in agreeing to make it had been worth it.

It was excellent. Exceptionally well made, well edited and fast moving. It had pulled no punches in recognising the controversy over the NUJ battle and featured library shots of the mass picketing but it was entirely objective, fair and well balanced. The NUJ, however, thought otherwise. After the documentary appeared on BBC Midlands TV the union issued a Press statement condemning it as a "whitewash" and "one-sided". There was even a public call for Mike Fitzgerald and Mike Dornan to be kicked out of the NUJ. This was hysterical nonsense. What the NUJ actually meant was that the *Nottingham Evening Post* had not been savagely vilified in the programme as it had been in hundreds of pieces of union propaganda since 1978.

The BBC's failure to follow the party line was, by the NUJ's jaundiced definition, biased reporting. It took quite a while for the flak to die down and it made me appreciate something that in selfish pursuit of my own best interests during all those weeks of filming had never once occurred to me – given their own union's pathological hatred of the newspaper, Mike Fitzgerald and Mike Dornan took far more of a risk in making that programme than I did. It had actually taken considerable bravery on their part but I'd been far too wrapped up in myself to recognise that at the time.

As the row raged around them I made no public comment. To do so would only have made matters worse for them – but I rang Mike Fitzgerald privately and told him how much I admired and appreciated their integrity. And I was so glad that I hadn't turned precious after that incident in The Square!

I was delighted to see as the years progressed that so did the TV careers of both those men. I never saw either of them again but more than 20 years later Mike Fitzgerald turned up in a national news story about *himself*. He had been in the kitchen at his home when a marauding mad *badger* broke in and bit him!

Perhaps Brock had joined the NUJ and the attack was retrospective revenge!

Not long after *Man At The Post* had appeared on TV I started to get messages that the Labour Party might be interested in brokering peace between the NUJ and the *Nottingham Evening Post*. My answer was always the same: "Tell them to come and talk to me." Nothing materialised until one day I was approached by two Nottingham Labour Parliamentary Candidates, Alan Simpson and Graham Allen. They had checked me out with their party colleagues in the Medway Towns, who had told them "He's no Tory" and both were very honest about the fact that with a General Election not far away they thought it bloody stupid to be depriving themselves of the opportunity to reach the *Post's* massive local readership.

A truce was agreed which would allow those Labour politicians who wanted to talk to the newspaper to do so while the NUJ blacking of the paper and its journalists was to continue. I struck an immediate rapport with Alan and Graham, both thoroughly nice blokes. The approach from Alan was particularly surprising and newsworthy in itself because the softly spoken Scouser was regarded as an extreme left-winger. Political labels are invariably irrelevant when you meet people and I liked Alan enormously.

Yes, he was as left-wing as they come but he was also very charming, intelligent, articulate and had a great sense of humour, which was frequently self-mocking. And he was fanatical about football which, as a very young MP, he still played to a good standard. Alan Simpson – you'll do for me, kid.

Graham Allen was more moderate in his leanings but had *Labour* stamped through him like a stick of Blackpool rock. Quiet and deeply serious Graham was very different but just as likeable. Both men went on to win their seats in Nottingham and hold them to this day. Alan became a good friend with whom I spent many enjoyable hours debating the pros and cons of Maggie's Britain.

Eventually I had an approach from the NUJ's Nottinghamshire branch to ask if we could talk privately and provisionally about a deal to re-instate the union at the *Nottingham Evening Post*. This was now getting real and I went to see Christopher Pole-Carew.

Had he lived up to his NUJ legend, Chris would have said: "Tell them, to fuck off – and bring me three of their babies, I'm hungry." But I knew the man behind the mythology and it didn't surprise me one bit when he told me: "Barrie, I was never anti-union, just anti-stupidity. If you feel it's in the newspaper's best interests, you go ahead." The rest of the TBF board were prepared to leave the decision entirely to me... though they did add the rider: "If you let 'em back in here you want your bumps felt!"

I had no doubt about what I should do and it was a conviction based on pragmatic considerations. The union was still powerful and highly relevant and was preventing me from hiring the best young journalists in the field. Nottingham was a Labour domain and I could never see that changing. I was trying desperately hard to forge a relationship between the *Evening Post* and Nottingham's many hundreds of thousands of decent working-class men and women and with the enduring reputation of the paper as anti-worker still a severe barrier, the publicity value alone of a deal with the NUJ would help enormously. I'd learned in Kent that if you were at all times honest, open and decent with your staff. the union presence was incidental and harmless and while my indelible personal experiences meant I could never be a supporter of the NUJ, I knew I could work perfectly well with them.

You had to know the sheer naked hatred which the Nottingham dispute had generated on both sides of the fierce battle to appreciate what it took for the NUJ negotiators, Bob Norris and Alison Simpson, to enter the lions' den and for Christopher Pole-Carew to greet them with a handshake. It was at this stage all being done in the strictest confidence and with the utmost privacy and the mischievous journalist in me wondered how much the picture would be worth.

When both sides had been satisfied that the other was sincere and serious about finding a settlement Christopher withdrew to leave our side of any deal to me and Bob and Alison were joined by the NUJ's tough Scottish leader Harry Conroy and acerbic national secretary Jake Ecclestone as we got down to the hard bargaining.

The union wanted me to write to all 28 sacked journalists and offer them their jobs back in the same positions with commensurate salaries. They also wanted a formal new technology agreement, full recognition, negotiating rights and dozens of other demands accepted. I had no problem whatsoever with re-instatement but I was not going to let them know that because it was **the** big concession for the NUJ. I had done my homework and I reckoned that two or three at most of the 28 would want to come back. The principle of *making the offer* (*victory* as they saw it) didn't bother me one bit because I hadn't been around at the time of the infamous sackings. I had also tested the feelings of the existing staff through a confidential questionnaire and this had told me that while there were inevitably *some* who believed very strongly that the union should never be allowed to darken the doors again there was a pragmatic majority in favour of a deal while only a handful said they would actually want to join the NUJ.

I did, however, have two demands of my own which I regarded as absolutely paramount...

(1)   There was no way I was going to agree to some national new technology agreement when my journalists had been happily using "new" technology for nearly 10 years and already enjoyed excellent rates of pay which more than recognised the added importance the technology brought to their roles.

(2)   I wanted to ensure that *Nottingham Evening Post* journalists would never again be placed between the awful rock and hard place of having to choose between loyalty to an employer with whom they had no quarrel whatsoever or loyalty to their union so I wanted a clause which would remove them from any *national* pay dispute which might arise in the future.

Point One was a very difficult concession for the NUJ because the rest of the industry was only just beginning to catch up with Nottingham and the introduction of new technology, with its heavy implications for *all* the unions in the industry was hugely controversial.

Point Two was so unique and so alien to trade union principles that when I first put it on the table Harry Conroy nearly choked on his coffee!

No matter. I was not going to budge on that. My answer to Harry's dismissive antipathy to the very idea was simple. "Look, Harry – if I'm ever such a crap boss that all my journalists want to go on strike over issues that are *within my control* I'll accept that – but I don't want them ever to have to walk out of here over something on which I can have no influence."

I was content to have an agreement which recognised their right to strike – but **only** over *Nottingham Evening Post* issues. That was anathema to Harry. .

After a long and at times very heated exchange I reminded Harry that it was **him** (or, at least *his* union) who had asked for a settlement, not me, and it looked as if the whole deal was off until Alison intervened and suggested that we should proceed on all the fronts upon which we *could* reach agreement – leaving my two highly contentious clauses for later.

Such was the impasse to be breached on those two issues that our negotiations went on for another **18 months** – with frequently recurring breakdowns and cooling off periods – until finally we arrived at an agreement in which, with one or two concessions to phraseology, my controversial clauses were included. And when, at long last, Harry Conroy and I signed our unique deal to end the NUJ' s long and bitter dispute with the *Nottingham Evening Post* it was in front of national TV cameras, such had been its significance.

In all the years that were to follow I never once regretted making that deal, enjoying entirely constructive and positive relationships with a succession of Fathers and Mothers of the Chapel (shop stewards) – and that happy state of affairs had nothing to do with the introduction of Margaret Thatcher's reforming legislation to control trade union conduct which, had it existed in 1978, would have ensured that Christopher Pole-Carew and the NUJ would never have had their historic conflict in the first place.

When I wrote to each of the 28 sacked journalists offering them their jobs back I had only *one* reply. It was from Lynne Curry, who nobody on the *Post* could remember, which wasn't surprising since Lynne had been employed as a junior reporter in one of the paper's district offices in Newark for only **two weeks** when the strike call came. Into my office at the appointed time of our meeting to reinstate her walked a most delightful, intelligent, talented and funny young woman who went on to become a brilliant writer, one of the best "signings" I ever made and a dear friend.

The most famous supporter of the NUJ throughout the dispute had been Nottingham Forest's hugely charismatic manager Brian Clough. He had, in the blaze of publicity which invariably greeted his every word, joined the "blacking" of the *Post*, refusing to talk to its journalists and pointedly backing the "rival" weekly paper started by the sacked 28 and funded by the union. He never missed an opportunity – and his massively high profile presented him with many – to condemn the *Evening Post* and its "Tory" management in public. Where politics were concerned there were no grey areas for Brian. For an otherwise deep and extremely intelligent man, Brian's political understanding was shallow and simplistic, to say the least, and he saw only the Labour movement's biased one side of this story. But he was genuinely pleased when we made peace.

I have often been asked to relate my own experiences and give my opinion of the truly great Brian Clough, but that is always extremely difficult to do because Brian was such a complex character of so many contradictory parts; I believe my most successful attempt at doing so was in an article I wrote with a genuinely sad heart when he died at the far too early age of 69 in September 2004:

"Brian Clough was the guest of honour at an event to celebrate the achievements of Nottinghamshire's disabled athletes.

As he stood in County Hall with the assembled company of disabled sportsmen and women, their families, friends and supporters and the good and the great of the county the door opened and a mother pushed through a wheelchair carrying her terribly disabled teenaged son.

So awful and visually repulsive were this poor shrunken boy's afflictions that people, as they do in such circumstances, averted their gaze, looking down at the floor, ahead at the walls, up at the ceiling – anywhere rather than towards that wheelchair and its wretched terminally ill contents.

Not Brian Clough.

He strode with deliberately exaggerated gait over to the boy and his mother, lifted him gently out of his wheelchair and gave him a huge kiss. Then, with one arm around mum and the other holding the boy he marched them into the middle of the VIPs and ordered:

"This is a star… Look after him."

That night, as the Editor of the *Nottingham Evening Post*, which organised the event, I was standing next to the great man when he presented all the awards and as one brave disabled competitor after another came forward to meet him Brian Clough cried – openly, unashamedly and without a hint of self-consciousness, he wept. Halfway through the ceremony he turned to me and with tears streaming down that famous face he told me: "I get emotional when I see *real* talent." Then, in more accustomed Brian Clough style, he barked: "Ey, Barrie. Just you make bloody sure I'm doing this again next year."

That was a side of Brian Clough, soccer legend and hard man, that few people ever got to see.

I worked in the same city as Brian for more than 13 years. It was inevitable that we should get to know each other – as well, that is, as anybody outside his family and real, close friends ever knew Brian. Anybody who tells the media, following the great man's death yesterday, that they were his friend is either lying or exaggerating. Brian Clough was the most private of people and the most protective of that privacy. Those genuinely close to him will not be saying that they were. Such was the loyalty he inspired.

So I would never presume even to imply that I was a friend of Brian but I do believe that we liked each other and shared a mutual respect. I was an acquaintance – and outside of his immediately close and private circle that's all anybody was – but I was close enough, often enough to observe the man – his extraordinary motivational powers; his compassion; his great sense of humour. And his less attractive traits – the sheer terror he would strike in some; the temper; the tantrums; the way he would bully and belittle people. Most of the time, those people were big enough to take it – the pretentious, the pompous, hangers-on and journalists were the usual recipients of his occasionally vicious and frequently abrasive tongue.

Brian Clough could be not very nice at all.

But with a warm gesture, an infectious smile, a comical aside, a wicked chuckle he would have you forgiving and forgetting everything.

There are people far better qualified than I to pay tribute to his professional qualities. Suffice to say that I gained immense pleasure from watching his teams play football *his* way – sportingly, fairly, on the ground rather than in the air; natural, fast, free-flowing, a one touch passing game. Disciplined and durable in defence, creative and carefree in attack. They were always a joy to watch.

I saw plenty of the other things for which Brian was renowned, too. Like the day I was lunching in the Forest dining room with him and his Chairman Geoffrey McPherson – a gentleman in both senses of the word. Having joined us typically late Brian announced casually: "Oh, by the way, chairman, I've just sold Justin Fashanu."

"For *how* much?" spluttered the chairman (Fashanu had cost the club £2 million).

"Two hundred and fifty," said Brian.

"Goodness gracious! Who to?" gasped the chairman.

"Notts County!"

That was the first and last time I saw projectile soup.

I remember so fondly the night my wife and I first met Brian. There had been a high profile bust-up between the *Nottingham Evening Post* and Brian Clough over his well-publicised support for the National Union of Journalists in its bitter dispute with the paper, so the reception I was going to get, as the new Editor, when meeting him at a fundraising event at Forest's Jubilee Club was unpredictable to say the very least.

No problem. With charm and courtesy he joined our table and stayed for an hour or so – insisting that the official photographer took a picture of him with my wife Pauline, a lovely photo which we still treasure. He made it abundantly clear that he and I were starting with a clean slate.

Later, he rang me out of the blue and said: "I'd like to come and work for you." This from the man who commanded massive fees, worldwide, for articles and interviews. "Brian, that would be great," I told him, "But you know we can't pay anything like…"

"Oh, bugger the money! Just give me a bottle of champagne every time."

We had a finance director with a straighter bat than Geoffrey Boycott and there was no way he would let me pay the great man in champers, so we ascertained Brian's favourite brand, worked out the cost per bottle and paid him that for a weekly column.

For me, it was an embarrassing pittance to be paying Brian Clough – but for as long as he provided that column it was with the reliability, quality and professionalism for which you would have expected to pay £20,000 a time. Local freelance journalists would park in the streets outside our presses from the early hours of the morning every Wednesday in the hope of being the first to flog the comments in his column to the national papers.

Of my many memories of Brian Clough the most compelling is the last. After a terrible season (which he was later honest enough to attribute to his drinking) Forest were playing out the last few minutes of Clough's last game with visiting opponents Sheffield United coasting to an easy victory, the absolutely unthinkable prospect of relegation for his world renowned double European Champions now a certainty and stunned home supporters subdued in sad eerie silence. Suddenly, Brian jumped from his dug-out and stood, head high, arms folded, back straight, wearing that familiar green sweat shirt. It was a sight which had been synonymous with the City Ground through all the years of glory. The devastated Forest fans managed a chant of "BRIAN CLOUGH, BRIAN CLOUGH" which, initially weak, grew to a deafening crescendo and was even picked up by the thousands of Sheffield United supporters, who all joined in.

Soon, *every* person in the packed stadium was standing in honour of Brian Clough, chanting his name, collective gaze fixed on that famous figure while he stood proud and motionless, as if to attention, with the on-going activities of 22 players on the field of play now reduced to total irrelevance.

With the final whistle seconds away and the cold reality that the great man's fantastic career was ending in relegation sinking in, the Sheffield United supporters started to sing – not the customary, sneering "GOING DOWN, GOING DOWN, GOING DOWN," but the cheerful "ALWAYS LOOK ON THE BRIGHT SIDE OF LIFE." This was not ironic, or mocking. It was totally sincere. Brian, recognising their sincerity, then turned to face those opposition supporters and with his hands high above his head, he applauded them. They – to a man – applauded him back. And I cried. As openly and unashamedly as Brian himself had done that night at County Hall, I wept. Along with thousands of others in that ground.

If they play football for the next 200 years I don't believe anyone else will ever evoke that sort of emotion.

Along with Brian Clough, one of the earliest contacts I made in Nottingham was the new young Governor of Nottingham Prison, John Marriott. John and I were kindred spirits. Both new to our lofty positions; both young to have acquired them. We struck a bond and John, whose wife Marianne and family were staying in Ireland until he got settled with property, etc, became one of our favourite dinner guests. He was a fascinating and entertaining man. His views on the prison service were enlightened and he subscribed heavily to the belief that prisons should be about rehabilitation rather than punishment – but he was by no means soft.

Our friendship facilitated some great exclusive stories and feature articles from Nottingham Prison, for which I was very grateful – and that was why when John asked a favour of me I didn't hesitate to agree. One of his staff was keen to set up a prison newspaper. The benefits were twofold:

(1)   It was a very useful addition to the English section of the prison's educational curriculum, and

(2)   It was an opportunity for the prisoners to express themselves, to get complaints off their chests and to articulate their concerns.

"Can you come in on a purely personal and off-the-record basis and help us set our newspaper up?" John asked.

I was happy to oblige… but it soon became obvious that if I was going to do this properly, it was a considerable commitment. Never mind. It was a fascinating project and John was a good mate.

On my first visit to the prison a group of eight prisoners who had expressed an interest in being part of the project had been gathered together to meet me. The agreement we had struck was that I would not quiz any of the lads about their personal lives, their criminal records or the reasons why they were in prison. If they volunteered any such information, fine – but I was to curb my journalistic curiosity by never asking. Fair enough.

Initially, the lads were sullen and quiet but I soon realised that the way to win their confidence was simply to treat them as equals – which was my natural style, anyway – and it was not long before I'd got them really enthusiastic about *HM PRISON NOTTINGHAM NEWS*. I appointed a team of editorial "executives" led by an editor. That key appointment, the prisoners unanimously agreed, should be a lad called Gary. Gary was a very good-looking young man who seemed less shy and more articulate and intelligent than the rest, but at the same time it was obvious that his mates all liked him very much and respected him. A natural leader, I thought. Chosen as News Editor – and Gary's Deputy – was Garfield, a smashing black lad with a wicked sense of humour and a winning smile. We added a production team then agreed that the entire prison population would be the paper's newsgathering and writing staff. The paper would be printed monthly on our Huthwaite Press and there would be a free copy for every inmate.

In next to no time the prison paper was established, appreciated by the inmates and running very successfully. Like any good newspaper, I had encouraged Gary to insist that there should be no censorship, complete editorial freedom and no input from the Governor or his staff unless they were invited.

The prison newspaper had news of prison events and issues, a sports section in which all the prison's sporting activities were fully reported, submitted articles, a poetry section and letters pages. Poetry and letters were particularly popular – especially the letters because prisoners with a complaint about the prison system, the regimes, the food in the canteen or the Government's penal policies per se were free to write without fear of recrimination and anonymously if they so wished (though it was surprising how infrequently they used that cover).

Once a week at least I would go into the prison and spend two or three hours with editor Gary and his editorial team, planning the next issue. They loved working on their paper – and so did I. Gary and I worked particularly well together and I sensed that he really looked forward to our sessions. Some of the stuff they were producing was well worthy of a much wider audience and I asked John Marriott to let me publish the occasional piece in the *Evening Post* as well. John, with his enlightened approach, saw no problem with that so it also became a source of good material for my own newspaper.

Some months into my prison project I was at a social event at Notts County's Meadow Lane Club when County director John Mountenay brought a middle-aged man and his wife over to meet me. It was prison editor Gary's mum and dad.

"We want to thank you from the bottom of our hearts for what you're doing for Gary," his dad told me. "Deep down, he's a good lad and you've given him a real sense of pride and an interest to keep him going in that place. It means so much to him."

It was a very moving conversation and it revealed that (though I had to abide by my agreement to ask no questions, so I still knew no details) Gary was serving a long sentence, which meant that his offence(s?) were very serious; that he came from a respectable and loving family and that John Marriott's approach to running a prison was absolutely right.

Years later, after John Marriott had moved on and with him had also gone the prison newspaper and my close involvement with it, I had an unexpected visitor to my office. It was Gary and he'd just been released. I didn't recognise him. Prison had aged that lad way beyond his years. He was pale and gaunt and hollow-eyed and the shiny, thick black hair which had added so much to his boyish good looks when I first met him, had thinned and dulled. The enthusiastic, energetic young man I'd left behind in prison looked weary and resentful. He wanted a reference to help get him employment. I could, of course, only refer to his work on the prison newspaper and his great attitude towards that project, but I was more than happy to do that and after we'd had a long chat about what sort of work he might be suited to I implored him to keep in touch with me. But I knew as I said it that he was not going to. It was as if seeing me in my own environment, rather than his own, had destroyed the relationship we'd had and in his eyes made me a part of the establishment which had punished him. It was clear that he regarded his chances of getting a decent job as very slim indeed.

I never saw Gary again. But I've never lost the hope that my reference helped him to get a decent job and that he stayed on the right side of those prison bars.

John Marriott went on to make huge national headlines when he was removed as Governor of Parkhurst Prison after three dangerous inmates escaped in 1995. He always maintained that he had been made a scapegoat and the issue led to the famous BBC *Newsnight* confrontation in which Jeremy Paxman asked the then Home Secretary Michael Howard 14 times if he'd threatened to over rule Prisons Director Derek Lewis and got 14 evasions.

John insisted that his removal had been politically instigated right up to his tragically premature death three years later and writing in *The Guardian*, his widow Marrianne said: "John had written 70 memos to the Home Office about lack of security at Parkhurst. There was no bloody security there, even though it was supposed to be a maximum security jail. John was used as a political football."

I was never close enough to it all to know the truth of that massively controversial affair, but on the day that news of John's death stunned me I **did** know that the prison service had lost a good man; a passionate and progressive advocate who cared deeply about rehabilitating offenders and that prisoners and prison service both could ill afford that loss.

With the NUJ – to the great surprise of everybody in our industry – reinstated at the *Evening Post* and the paper once more recognised by the Labour Movement, I was able to get on with the job of producing a paper that properly reflected all shades of political opinion in the city and county. And it wasn't long before two massive events had the inherently argumentative Nottinghamians at it again...The Falklands War and The Miners' Strike.

The rights and wrongs of Margaret Thatcher's scrap with the Argentines exercised them greatly. They saw it either as a naked attempt by our Prime Minister to bolster her personal ratings or a principled stand for islanders determined to exercise their right to stay British. Either way, many British servicemen were killed or maimed and when it had started, as an almost comic conflict, nobody had expected that. As the body bags and ambulances brought the dead and wounded home there was a desire and determination among Nottinghamshire folk to honour "our boys" and I decided that the *Post* should mobilise that into a local Falklands Fund to raise cash for the servicemen and their families.

It didn't matter on which side of the divide over the rights and wrongs of the war they stood, people responded magnificently and our fund had reached almost £100,000 when the day came for me to hand over the cheque. This was done at a full military and civic ceremony in The Square, in front of a crowd of hundreds of people. Army top brass organised the presentation and I was to hand the *Nottingham Evening Post* readers' cheque over in a symbolic gesture to a wounded local soldier, Danny Blair. Danny, a brave black boy just 18-years-old, had suffered serious head injuries in the conflict but looked unscathed and very handsome in his smart, crisp uniform. The event had been meticulously planned and what happened in mid-ceremony came as a surprise to everyone... down the steps of the Council House immediately behind the stage on which the event was taking place a father dramatically pushed a wheelchair carrying his injured son. The lad, who was dressed in civilian clothes and was clearly not intended to be there, had lost his legs in the conflict and as his wheelchair clattered noisily down step after step, disturbing the ceremony, it became obvious that this was a protest and that the gesture was his dad's way of saying without words:

"Look. *This is what your bloody war did to my boy.*"

If Margaret Thatcher's Falklands War divided opinion in Nottingham it was nothing compared with the Miners' Strike, which split families. To this day, there are fathers not speaking to sons, brothers not speaking to brothers. The emotional scars of this bloody industrial battle will never heal. Never has that fabled obdurate Nottinghamshire character been more dramatically demonstrated than in the stand the local miners made against Arthur Scargill and the National Union of Mineworkers.

You never *push* a Nottinghamian against his will and the majority of lads in our local pits were furious that Scargill had called the national strike over threatened mine closures without a proper ballot. They were as passionate in defence of their threatened industry as any other miners but they believed that an all-out strike was playing into Thatcher's hands and would hasten rather than prevent pit closures. They also felt very strongly that Scargill was too absorbed in his political intent to bring down the Tory Government, which they – rightly – did not see as *their* role. Hence the formation in Nottinghamshire pits of the breakaway Union of Democratic Mineworkers. This was dynamite. And when a majority of Notts lads joined the new union and voted to work in defiance of the strike it became a hell of a story.

The intense, intimidating mass picketing which had engulfed the *Evening Post* in its dispute with the NUJ hit Nottinghamshire again – and bad though *that* had been, this time it was a hundred times worse in its depth and violence. By no means all the Notts miners left the NUM and that put father versus son, brother versus brother, friend versus friend, neighbour versus neighbour in the months of bitter conflict which followed. This presented me with a professional dilemma. Here, on *my* paper's patch, feelings were running incredibly highly. And not just among the miners and their families. This was argumentative Nottingham again – and this time at its most voluble and volatile. *Everybody* had an opinion and Nottingham being Nottingham there were no shades of grey in this often literally violent black or white argument. The *Post* – *ie.* **my own** leading articles – had consistently challenged the Tory Government over the threat of pit closures, supported the miners' case and argued vehemently that the corollary of Mrs Thatcher's policy – the decimation of the UK's coal industry – was economic madness.

So who, now, did my paper support? The majority of the nation's miners who were striking for their survival or the minority in Nottinghamshire who were crossing the picket lines to carry on working? It was a classic no-win situation. Whichever side I supported I was going to anger a lot of people and to experience the intensity of local feeling was to know that this would be no small matter of fleeting upset. Any stance I took was, for better or for worse, going to remain identified with the *Nottingham Evening Post* for many years to come.

This was most definitely not to be rushed and for a while I sat unashamedly on the fence. I got to know the UDM leaders, Roy Lynk and David Prendergast – who had become national household names – really well. I listened very carefully to their arguments. I also listened just as carefully to the arguments of Henry Richardson, the leader of the Nottinghamshire NUM. These were all decent, principled men – just as the miners they represented, from their different sides of the conflict, were decent, principled men.

Finally, I was swayed by two points...

(1)   The UDM miners were exercising their fundamental human right to work in the face of appalling daily violence

having taken a democratic local vote (which Arthur Scargill never did) to do so. Stripped of all the understandable emotion, right was *surely* on *their* side.

(2) I agreed with Roy Lynk and David Prendergast that striking would only eventually weaken the miners and if they were going to stand up to Margaret Thatcher and fight to save their industry they had to be strong. She was, almost certainly, very pleased that they were striking and that they were being led by Arthur Scargill with his transparent ambition to bring her down because that allowed her to present the fight as good old British democracy versus alien Communist oppression and when push came to shove there was only one of those two horses that Joe Public would back.

Therefore, the *Nottingham Evening Post*, from then on and consistently until the long bitter strike eventually crumbled, supported the UDM while continuing to argue passionately against the Government's policy on the coal industry.

Ask me now, more than 20 years later, if I was right to support the UDM and I'd have to say honestly that I don't know.

What did become clear, after those poor beaten strikers had crept like thrashed dogs back to work, was that on one crucial point the much-maligned Arthur Scargill had been right all along... Mrs Thatcher's government **had** been privately determined to rid Britain of the pits and of the coal miners who toiled so proudly in them and all the Conservatives' public protestations to the contrary had been bullshit.

In the event, the bitter feud between the NUM and the UDM, which had irreparably torn apart so many families and friendships, had been cruelly futile. The once vibrant, proud working communities which grew up around those pits have gone forever now and with them a hugely important part of Nottinghamshire's heritage and culture. Deadly dull DIY superstores and characterless car showrooms stand where once there were houses, schools, busy little corner shops and lively miners' welfares. The sad, soulless, dreary emptiness of it all is testament to Margaret Thatcher's callous destruction of a great industry. The UK is *importing* coal and gas and fretting about relying too much on Russia, a country whose ambitions the Iron Lady had always taken great pride in resisting!

In September 1983, there was an event in the career of Barrie Williams which 20 years earlier would have had that pompous despot Alf Exton, Headmaster of Oswestry Boys High School, choking in disbelief. I was formally invited by the Chairman, Colonel T.E. Forman Hardy, to become Editorial Director of T. Bailey Forman Ltd. The "unenergetic and ordinary" youth of Alf Exton's reference who, "given some encouragement might make a reasonable employee" had become a director of a major company in his thirties. The salary increase that went with my appointment to the Board was breathtaking and as dear Colonel Tom made a shy little welcome speech at a special lunch to mark my promotion I was the proudest man in Nottinghamshire. Before the lunch, Chris Pole-Carew had taken time out to brief me on the protocol of the TBF Board and to advise me on how the Colonel would expect me to conduct myself.

Among several useful tips, Chris told me: *"You never talk about profits in front of the Chairman. It embarrasses him."* If you knew Colonel Tom there was nothing surprising about that advice... but more than 20 years later it was to recur in my memory in circumstances which made it sound absolutely extraordinary.

The *Nottingham Evening Post* had a very special place in Tom Forman Hardy's life. Despite his shyness, he enjoyed the prestige of owning the paper while his very substantial wealth meant he was not obsessed with its financial performance. To those old family proprietors of British regional newspapers there was a sense of duty inherent in that ownership, a Victorian ethos about putting something back into the community in which you had created your riches. I'm sure it was that which led Colonel Tom not to want to be seen to be making too much money out of this public duty. He wanted his newspaper to be run as a successful, profitable business, of course, and that's why superb professionals like Chris Pole-Carew and David Teague sat on his board, but his expectations of profit were modest indeed compared with today's corporate greed. What mattered most to him was that we published a decent, respectable newspaper doing a first-rate job for its community. Hence, the Editor was held in special esteem and was expected to keep himself far removed from the slightly grubby business of making money!

Two decades were to change all that dramatically for the worse and most regional editors were to become subservient to the pervasive pursuit of profits, but in the early 1980s being the Editor of Colonel Tom Forman Hardy's esteemed *Nottingham Evening Post* was the best job in the business and one in which you could devote all your time and energy to **journalism.** It was a joy.

Chris Pole-Carew's approach as Managing Director was to protect and shield the Editor from the pressures of the financial side of the business. His view was that others were paid to take *those* responsibilities while the Editor had a unique role away from all that. Chris and I would sit down and agree an annual editorial budget to which I would promise to adhere, unless exceptional circumstances changed my requirements. My budget was always more than adequate to allow me to do what I wanted with the paper and once agreed was never questioned by any other member of the board. At our monthly board meetings, each director would deliver a retrospective departmental report followed by a brief forecast for the month ahead. The Editor's report was always considered to be the most exciting dealing, as it did, with the *"real"* business of the newspaper... followed closely by David Teague's reports on advertisement revenues and on what the combined forces of *my* editorial policies and the flair and innovative initiatives of *his* newspaper sales operation were doing for the circulation of the *Nottingham Evening Post*.

Nobody's report, however, was ever allowed to delay the **board lunch**. This event was a celebration of culinary excellence. Colonel Tom had his own kitchens run by his own chef and the food which came out of them would have graced any five-star restaurant. For Brian, the chef, the monthly lunch was a supreme challenge and his mission was to make every one even better than the one before. Christ, this food was *so* good! On board meeting days you never had breakfast – the better to cope with the fare that awaited. By 12 noon the seductive smells of Brian's cooking would begin to permeate the boardroom, rendering the business of the day a poor second best to the forthcoming delights and leading to much rumbling of directorial stomachs. By 12.30 the arresting aromas would be so distinct that we could guess what we were having, at which point salivation would ensue. At 12.45 sharp, Colonel Tom would declare business done and we would retire to his inner sanctum for drinks while his incredibly efficient staff transformed boardroom into dining room. At 1.15 sharp we would sit down to a meal which could only be described as divine... wonderfully appetising starters followed by Brian's "star" of the show, the main course – sometimes scrumptious succulent roast beef with melt-in-the-mouth Yorkshire pud; sometimes tender, juicy roast lamb; sometimes crispy, crackling pork; sometimes freshly caught trout; sometimes superbly tasty roast pheasant, shot by the Forman Hardys, of course; sometimes a huge whole salmon, poached to perfection – but invariably *absolutely bloody delicious* and always followed by sensational puddings, then a glorious cheese board – starring the imperative creamy Long Clawson Stilton – all washed down by the finest of fine wines. At the completion of each course the Colonel, having satisfied himself that every director's plate was clear, would operate a concealed switch with his foot – the signal for a little squad of smart waitresses to appear as if by magic and clear the table ready for the next treat. Feast concluded, it would be back into the inner sanctum for coffee, served – in best military tradition – by the Colonel himself, brandy or port if you wished and serious cigars. Before we all tottered back to our offices for what little was then left of the afternoon, Brian and his staff would be summoned from the kitchen to receive the fulsome praise and thanks of the Colonel, at which the chef's chest all but burst with pride, his smile as broad as the boardroom table upon which his latest triumphant offering had been so temptingly laid before us.

These were great times.

David had brought so much that was new and effective to the increasingly difficult business of selling newspapers that ours was outperforming the rest of the regional industry consistently. This, in turn, gave me confidence to innovate editorially and we were producing truly ground-breaking newspapers.

Alongside this, Chris was investing in ever improving methods of producing the paper and while we still printed the main daily broadsheet on a 25-year-old traditional mono press he had developed a subsidiary colour press, based at Huthwaite in the north of Nottinghamshire, on which we printed lucrative sub-contract work and colour sections for the *Post*. I had modelled these colour sections on what I had seen being produced very successfully abroad, then added unique local content and they were such trailblazing publications that in 1984 I was invited to address a big international conference titled *PRESS '84* in Berlin to tell the rest of the newspaper world what we were achieving.

It was an extraordinary experience to stand on stage in a huge, state-of-the-art German conference centre and tell an audience of about 500 top newspaper executives from all over the world how bloody good we were in Nottingham!

What we were doing with colour was leaving the national newspapers standing and this was epitomised at that conference by a presentation from Mike Molloy, Editor of the *Daily Mirror* whose title was *The Power of Black and White*.

And Mike's was a deadly serious contribution!

My own speech, in which I used no less than 53 full colour slides of our publications, went down very well – so much so that Sir David English, the Editor of the *Daily Mail* sought me out at dinner that night to congratulate me. And Peter Preston, Editor of *The Guardian*, even took the trouble to write a letter to Chris Pole-Carew to tell him how impressed he had been "by your Editor's speech in Berlin".

Unfortunately, Christopher had once been so infuriated and offended by a piece written by Alan Rushbridger (who is now *The Guardian's* Editor) about the *Evening Post's* industrial relations that he wrote back telling Peter Preston, a lovely bloke, to piss off!

Because of the stand Chris Pole-Carew had taken against the National Union of Journalists in 1978 his company had been booted out of the Newspaper Society. Now that Nottingham was "respectable" again the NS wanted us back in but Chris would have absolutely none of it and he saw the *Post's* trailblazing success, now being widely publicised, as a two-fingered gesture to those who had dumped him when the going got tough. Over his dead body would we re-join the Society!

Some might have found it odd and contradictory that he could forgive the NUJ, his front line foe in that historic fight, to such an extent that he allowed me to bring them back into his business but not his former pals in the proprietors' "club" who he felt had turned their backs on him when he needed their support. I saw no contradiction. Christopher had been an officer in the Royal Navy. An enemy was an enemy, just there to be beaten. The battle with the NUJ had been a bloody one, with both sides employing every tactic in the book (and a good many that weren't!) but once it was over, the decent thing, by officer and gentleman Pole-Carew's creed, was to show respect to that enemy. There could be no such respect, however, for those on your own side who you believed had let you down.

There had been one famous episode in which another leading regional newspaper publisher had invited Chris to speak to his board about the battle with the unions. During that talk, Chris had referred to his resolve to fight fire with fire lest the fierce intimidation from the massed hordes of flying pickets succeeded in frightening his loyal workforce into submission. He gave an entirely hypothetical analogy which said something like, "We told them that if they threw petrol bombs through our chaps' windows we'd go round to *their* houses and do the same."

That comment had then found its way to the NUJ, whose next anti-*Evening Post* publication had a front page headline screaming: **POLE-CAREW SAYS HE'LL FIRE BOMB STRIKERS' HOMES.** It was utter nonsense, of course – he would never have done anything even remotely like that – but it had given the enemy a great propaganda coup and caused Pole-Carew severe embarrassment.

Chris was furious, not with the NUJ, for he figured all's fair in war – but with his hosts at that meeting for not ensuring that what was supposed to be a totally private and off-the-record meeting could not be taped. He never blamed the NUJ for its gross distortion of his throwaway remark but he *did* blame his former friend for dropping him in the smelly stuff. He never spoke to that man again and responded to a long letter of explanation he received from him by tearing it into thousands of tiny pieces and posting it back to him inside the same envelope in which it had arrived!

Against that sort of background, the success which David Teague and I were now bringing to the *Nottingham Evening Post* was doubly sweet for Christopher and such was that success and so revolutionary were many of our innovations that Chris, David and I were in great demand on the international newspaper conference circuit – Vienna, Venice, Rome, Amsterdam, Paris, Seville, Berlin were just a few of the venues at which we strutted our stuff. Except for Venice, when we went on the *Orient Express,* we were flown in our own company jet (or helicopter for shorter flights) by the ultra-reliable Captain Bond. David and I liked Colin Bond a great deal and could not help holding him in high esteem and treating him with great respect. After all, our lives were frequently in his hands – literally!

However Christopher felt the company pilot should be kept in his place. "He's just a chauffeur with wings," he would say – and he treated him as such. We couldn't understand this because Christopher was no snob and Colin Bond was the most affable and likeable of men. Eventually, David and I concluded that Christopher's attitude was down to the fact that he could not himself fly the aircraft. Mr Pole-Carew is a truly remarkable man. There is very little which needs to be done in life that he can not only do himself but excel at. But he didn't have a pilot's licence. Nicholas Forman Hardy did and *he* sometimes took the controls on our many trips abroad, which, we reckoned, didn't help either! So to Christopher Pole-Carew, the superbly accomplished and well-qualified Captain Bond was "just a bloody chauffeur". This attitude was epitomised, it was alleged, the day Colin Bond was very intently and extremely carefully lifting our aircraft and its passengers up through the incredibly congested skies above Holland's Schipol Airport – said at that time to be among the most difficult in the world to navigate. The dials on the control panels were flashing like Blackpool illuminations; the conversation between pilot and air traffic controllers was worryingly animated and intense concentration was etched on Colin's face when Christopher Pole-Carew, hard-boiled egg from a packed lunch in his hand, leaned forward, tapped our pilot on the shoulder and asked him: "Where's the salt?"

Colonel Tom was enjoying all our success too – in his own quiet and diffident way. I had been briefed by Mavis, my secretary, that you could always tell when you had done something that had pleased the Chairman because *he* would come down to *your* office to talk about it. But, beware, Mavis had told me – when he asks *you* to go up to *his* office you're in trouble.

That sage secretarial advice meant that I knew I was pleasing the Colonel. He loved to talk about what I was doing with the paper, the campaigns I was running, the stances I was taking – not in a manner which was in any way interfering (he was an absolute stickler for editorial independence) but out of genuine interest and enjoyment... a sort of vicarious pleasure in what the editor was up to. And our discussions invariably took place in *my* office.

I also knew, however, that there was just *one* area in which the Chairman *would* take issue with his Editor if the need arose... and that was what he saw as smut or sexual innuendo. Given Colonel Tom's age and social background, *his* definition of those sexual no-go areas was just a tad more restricted than that of a thirty-something working-class editor but I was well aware of the parameters.

More than a decade earlier, when I was features subbing on the *Post,* I had allowed through my pages a reference to the shapely knees of the young Princess Anne. In an apoplectic state, the Features Editor Wilf Berry had removed the offending paragraph with a dire warning that: "You'll get the Editor sacked!"

So, I knew the score and given the complete editorial freedom I enjoyed on every important issue it was no sacrifice at all to avoid the Colonel's "smut" – especially since most *Post* readers wanted nothing like that in their paper anyway.

It was, therefore, with much perplexing bewilderment that I walked up the stately corridor to *his* office having been told by an ashen-faced Mavis one day that the Colonel wanted to see *me.*

As I entered his inner sanctum in considerable trepidation I saw immediately why I had been summoned. On his palatial polished desk, opened at its centre spread, was the current copy of *The Message.*

This was another of my trailblazing publishing initiatives. In an attempt to lure the elusive **young reader** I had come up with what I thought was a spiffing idea. Because of the nature of the main market at which the *Post* had to be aimed it was not, with the best will in the world, going to appeal that much to Nottingham's cutting edge teenagers. So I had created their own, separate, weekly newspaper to go out with the *Post.*

To ensure that this publication would hit all the right spots I had recruited a team of teenagers – only one of them a staff journalist – and given them editorial freedom and a pledge of no censorship.

The result was *The Message*, a tabloid for the teenage market. I'd told the young team that if I did not understand the contents of this publication they'd got it right. And so it was.

Because of the restrictions of our press *The Message* could not be inserted into the main paper, but was available in a separate pile in the newsagents with a bold **Free With The Evening Post** emblazoned on its masthead. There it was that my cunning plan had hit a snag. *The Message* was proving hugely popular with the kids. But they were picking it up for free in their thousands – and leaving the bloody *Evening Post* on the counter!

Thus the whole object of this expensive exercise was being lost and David Teague and I were engaged in much debate about how to solve the conundrum. For this particular edition of *The Message* its brightest, best and most irreverent contributor – a local rock musician and photography student Steve Mitchell (now the *Evening Post's* highly respected Chief Photographer) had produced a brilliant centre spread on Janie Jones, a brassy blonde pop singer. The stunning Janie was a controversial girl who had been accused of being involved in high-class prostitution. Clearly, to the lads on *The Message*, with their anti-establishment tendencies, Janie had become a cult figure. And you could be sure that their interest in her would be shared by the teenage readership we were after. Steve had created a seductive spread with a huge cut-out picture of the incredibly sexy Janie wearing a basque and fishnet stockings, brandishing a whip and standing astride a prostrate man who was gazing adoringly up at her credentials.

I'd looked at this raunchy spread (with more than passing interest) and while there was no way it could ever be published in the *Evening Post* I figured that *The Message* could take it... never once thinking that Colonel T.E. Forman Hardy could be counted among its readers.

But he could, dammit! And to say that he did not look best pleased as I walked in to his office was a massive understatement. I'd never seen Colonel Tom angry but Mavis had tipped me off that you could tell when he was because he would brush his moustache from side to side with his forefinger. As I walked towards his desk that forefinger was working overtime; so agitated in moustache manipulation that it was almost a blur.

Oh, Christ... I thought, I'm in deep do-do here!

Pointing at the picture of the jaunty Janie Jones he was all but speechless.

"Just LOOK at her!" he spluttered.

There was only one way out of this. I had to bluff it.

"Yes, sir," I replied, "Not difficult, is it!"

"But it's *obscene!*"

"No, sir. Not by today's standards."

"But she's got a man *underneath* her!"

"Yeah, lucky bugger!"

"But this will *corrupt* the young people!"

"No, sir. You have to understand, it's ironic. It's their way of saying this lifestyle is not acceptable. The whole tenor of the piece is anti-Janie Jones."

I went on in this laid-back, storm-in-a-teacup mode, finally telling the Colonel that *Evening Post* readers were not getting to see *The Message* (which was the truth, if not the intention!) and his moustache finger started to slow down a bit.

I was spared the sack. But it had been a close call.

That was the only occasion in eight brilliant years, before ill-health forced the Colonel into retirement in 1989, that I came even close to falling out with him. I did many things with his beloved newspaper to revitalise and energise it, to move it into the modern world and make it more outspoken and controversial, which I knew he either didn't understand or felt uncomfortable with, but he showed me nothing but support, kindness and generosity.

I loved that gentleman.

In his later years he became frail and forgetful. His lovely wife Marjorie and his son Nicholas did everything to protect him, his pride and his dignity and kept the details of his illness very private but it was clear that his condition was degenerative and that his mind was going. It was tragic to see.

One day in the summer of 1989 Nicholas came to see me with the news that his father had been arrested by the police after driving his car the wrong way down the M1. Luckily there had been no collision with any other vehicle and the police had stopped him before any harm had been done but they might be going to prosecute him.

Sharing his father's absolute regard for editorial independence, Nicholas fully expected me to report the incident. We would report it if anybody else drove towards oncoming traffic on a busy, high speed motorway so there could be no exception made for our proprietor and Nicholas understood and respected that without question. But it hurt like hell publishing that story because I knew how thoroughly ashamed the very sensitive Colonel would be feeling.

Colonel Tom was an intensely private person and notwithstanding his humility and modesty he was fiercely proud of his family's good name. He was incredibly shy and he hated appearing in the newspaper under *any* circumstances. I knew that the mind lapses he was suffering were brief and transient and that he would now probably be feeling deeply ashamed. He would be inconsolable and there would be absolutely nothing his loving family could do or say to alleviate his anguish.

The paradox of his position as a conscientious proprietor was that the very last thing he would expect or want his Editor to do was stifle the story. That would have been futile, anyway because it was being picked up simultaneously by **all** the media, but knowing that did not make me or my staff, who all loved the old boy, feel any better and it was with a pervading sense of betrayal that we published.

But nothing prepared his family or us for what a couple of the national tabloids did with the story. They treated the incident as a great opportunity to ridicule some filthy rich old buffoon. Their tone portrayed a nutty old former Lord Lieutenant of Nottinghamshire, ex-Master of the South Notts Hunt; giddy, galloping old goat nicked for driving the wrong way on the motorway. Yoiks! Tally Ho! Oh, what a spiffing yarn!

God knows how much those tabloids hurt the Forman Hardys when they were already so desperately worried about Colonel Tom. How could those smart-arse tabloid journalists **do** that to him. And why? They didn't know him at all. Yes, he was very rich. Yes, he was steeped in the posh establishment. But he couldn't help it. He'd been born into all that. It wasn't his fault, any more than I could be blamed for growing up in a council house. Reserved and so quiet and shy, Colonel Tom would have preferred to have taken an anonymous back seat in life, but he saw his involvement in all that county set stuff as an unavoidable duty. The dotty old galloping major portrayed in those stupid stories was, in reality, an intelligent, tender and compassionate man who had shown extreme personal courage and selfless bravery protecting his men when fighting on a blood soaked battlefield for the freedom of those piss-taking pricks on the tabloids. Throughout his civilian years in the newspaper business, Colonel Tom had consistently and resolutely defended the Press freedom which they now abused. It made me sick and it reminded me why, all those years before, I had rejected that sort of shit journalism.

A few weeks later, in August 1989, Colonel Tom retired as Chairman of all his companies. In September 1989 he died. He was 70, not a great age at all, and while he was obviously very ill, I have always wondered how much his death was hastened by the shame, disproportionate in his own mind, of that motorway incident and its implications. On October 4th 1989 more than 700 people packed into St Mary's Church, Nottingham to pay tribute to Colonel Tom Forman Hardy, his distinguished military career and his immense contribution to the civic and community life of the county of Nottinghamshire. The national tabloids were not remotely interested in that, of course. But I made sure that his own newspaper, at least, gave him a full and fitting farewell and I wrote his obituary myself, from the bottom of my heart. If he'd been able to read it, I like to think that Colonel Tom would have come down the corridor to **my** office to talk to me about it. Then I'd have known that he'd approved of what I'd written and that mattered so much to me. His family took the trouble, in their grief, to write me a personal note of thanks.

Nicholas Forman Hardy succeeded his father as Chairman of all the *Forman Hardy Holdings* companies in 1989. Nick had inherited a lot of his dad's diffidence and shyness and taking over from Colonel Tom was extremely daunting for him. But of all the business responsibilities now entrusted to him it was the *Nottingham Evening Post* that worried him most. He had come by that particular responsibility through a cruel twist of fate... Colonel Tom had two sons and a daughter. It was said that The Colonel had decreed that upon his demise the eldest boy, William, should take over the newspaper while Nick was to inherit the rest of the businesses. Nick was essentially a farmer. He loved farming and he was happiest when working on the family's green acres. William was, apparently, a born newspaperman. So the old man's plan for his sons' respective destinies was spot on.

Then, tragically, in 1974, William was killed in a motorcycle crash on the Fosse Way. He was only 27. I never knew him but those who did spoke very fondly of him. By all accounts, William was a confident, cheery chap who had learned every aspect of the newspaper business inside out and adored it Nicholas, by comparison, seemed reticent and uncertain among newspapermen. A lovely lad with a genuinely warm and friendly nature, but not best suited, I thought, for the cut and thrust of newspapers.

Ever since the day I took over as Editor Designate in 1981 I had an excellent relationship with Nick. We were roughly the same age and though we were obviously poles apart in our backgrounds we understood each other. There was an instant rapport, too, between Pauline and Nick's wife Jane. The feisty and clever daughter of a Welsh farmer, Jane had been a lawyer before marriage and motherhood and she was great company. The four of us got on tremendously well and we struck a friendship which exceeded professional necessity.

After William's untimely death, Nick had been dropped into the Forman Street maelstrom for a crash course in newspapers. His tutor, mentor (and occasional tormentor!) was Christopher Pole-Carew. Colonel Tom had apparently asked Chris to knock the young Master into shape and I wondered if Chris had taken that too literally. Much as I liked Chris, it seemed to me that he was sometimes too hard on Nick. Dropped, as he had been, into the mad world of newspapers I felt the lad's confidence was too brittle for too much of that sort of treatment and Nick, in turn, seemed to me to have developed a defensive veneer of false, forced toughness and aggression. The upshot was that often when Chris and Nick were together you could cut the atmosphere with the proverbial knife. David Teague appeared to have adopted Chris's approach and attitude to the heir apparent and maybe – for they were both so professional – that *was* the right way to bring him on. I didn't think so. Very likely, I'd got it wrong. But whoever was right or wrong, it seemed that Nicholas Forman Hardy and Christopher Pole-Carew might be on a collision course.

The more I got to know Nick the more it became apparent to me that he'd had quite a sheltered upbringing. Whenever I exposed him to working-class pursuits like a night in a miners' welfare, a bag of fish and chips, a game of pool, an evening at Nottingham Forest's Jubilee Club, he was like an excited child being allowed to get away with being very naughty. His enthusiasm and naivety in that context were charming and endearing, I thought, and one of the few times I got cross with Brian Clough was when he took the piss out of Nick. That's not to say that, as was so often the case with Brian, it was not very funny. It took us more than a year to sell our house in Kent and when, in Nick's presence one night, Brian asked me where I was living and I told him that we were in a company flat at Wilford House he rounded on Nick and with mock outrage told him:

"You're a mean bastard. With all YOUR bloody money you should BUY the lad a bloody 'ouse!"

Nick couldn't recognise the wind-up, looked terribly embarrassed and proceeded to give Brian a verbose explanation as to why that was not possible, upon which Mr Clough barked, "Fuck Off!", turned theatrically on his heels and stormed off in a pretence of disgust, leaving the Young Master red-faced with his flabber well and truly gasted!

"That was cruel!" I protested to Brian later. "Nick's a very nice guy. And he's not the guvnor, his dad is."

"Never feel sorry for rich bastards," was the unrepentant response of football's famous philosopher (conveniently overlooking the fact

that by then he was hardly in poverty street himself!) and he added: *"Just be sure the bugger's paying you enough. Has he given you a contract?"*

Such a detail almost became entirely academic the night Nick and I were going to York to meet Derek Thompson, the TV horse racing presenter. I was driving and to get out of jammed traffic on the Mansfield Road leading north out of Nottingham, I decided to take a detour through some back streets. While stationary at a red traffic light we both spotted, on the adjacent pavement, a stunning looking girl, very sexily attired, talking to a police officer – who had his back to us. It was a very hot summer's afternoon and I had my sun-roof and car windows wide open. As Nick and I looked at this girl (well, any red blooded male would have done) she started to chat Nick up over the police officer's shoulder.

It was only then that I realised I had driven into the middle of Nottingham's notorious red light district, that the girl was a prostitute, that she was being cautioned and that not withstanding the policeman's presence she was attempting to do business with the Chairman's son through the open window of my car...

This would not have pleased the Colonel!

When the traffic lights turned to green I hit the accelerator and sped off with all the pace my Jaguar could muster – and that was fast. It mattered not. A speeding ticket I could take. But a prosecution for kerb-crawling with the Chairman's impeccably brought-up son in my custody was not a good career move!

In Nottingham I achieved the best campaigning journalism of my career. I was at my peak and I had a great team of reporters and writers. I am immensely proud of the work I did there. For example, when it seemed to me that the Tory Government's much vaunted *Care In The Community* project was, in reality, little more than a euphemism for closing down mental hospitals to save shed-loads of money while throwing vulnerable mentally ill people out onto the streets, we ran a campaign called *Who Cares?* in which we told the harrowing stories of patients who were simply not capable of fending for themselves. It was disturbing stuff and hardly designed to sell newspapers, but it needed saying.

Similarly, when fuel costs escalated we alerted Nottingham to the plight of thousands of its old people who were inherently terrified of debt and were depriving themselves of winter warmth to the extent that some of them were literally dying of cold. We found one old boy who was, incredibly, using candles for both light and warmth. The picture of his proud, yet at the same time pathetic, face shot by the flickering light of his candle was one of the most powerful illustrations of a story I have ever seen. I filled the entire broadsheet front page with that compelling image the day we launched our *"Old and Cold"* campaign and the response was phenomenal. That led to the formation of a fund through which the paper raised hundreds of thousands of pounds – all of which went directly to local old folk in need of help with their fuel bills. Nottingham really rallied to this cause and I will never forget the sight of thousands of people of all ages, shapes and sizes gathering at Holme Pierpont for a sponsored run/walk on a cold crisp February Sunday morning. That became an annual event, along with many others, in aid of the *Evening Post's "Old and Cold Fund"*.

Nottingham had escaped the riots that hit several inner city areas, notably Toxteth in Liverpool, in 1981 – but that didn't mean that all the problems which led to those troubles did not exist in our city. They did. And with up to 60 per cent of young men in those deprived urban ghettoes unemployed we were sitting on our own tinder box. So, I embarked on a campaign – with the full backing of the Labour City Council – to highlight the problems and to seek short and long term solutions. We established action groups in all the vulnerable areas made up predominantly of the inner city youngsters themselves but including businessmen, council officials and social workers. Paramount among those solutions was tackling the physical decay and dereliction in which those kids lived – and that's where the businessmen, aided and abetted by a council prepared to reduce red tape to a minimum and hasten good projects, came in. It was a simple but effective method of encouraging pride and purpose where there would otherwise be resentment and lethargy. We would identify a derelict area through the paper then set about trying to improve it, with the full involvement of the young people.

This campaign brought me into close contact with Michael Heseltine, the best Prime Minister this country never had. As Secretary of State for the Environment Michael worked tirelessly on inner city problems until Margaret Thatcher moved him to Defence in 1983. He very much approved of our campaign and – typically – did not allow political differences to prevent him from delivering fulsome public praise of the City Council. After I had been among a small group of big city editors invited by Mr Heseltine to discuss urban regeneration ideas over dinner in the Tower Of London he arranged an unofficial and unpublicised visit to Nottingham, during which I showed him around all our potential trouble spots and particularly areas in which his government could help our action groups by facilitating the release of derelict sites for job creating projects. I got on exceptionally well with Michael Heseltine, who I regard as a giant of a man in intellect and integrity, and he included me in several top level London meetings on inner city issues.

After his big bust-up with Mrs Thatcher over Westland and his consequent resignation from the Cabinet, Michael Heseltine wrote a superb book titled *Where There's A Will* – which he described as "a personal testament, a book of ideas, an autobiographical reassessment." In that book he wrote of the need for a British industrial strategy; the real meaning of the North/South divide; the underlying challenge of the inner cities and the government's proper role in attacking those problems. He sent me an advance copy with a personal inscription and I wrote a full page review of it. Like so much of Michael Heseltine's unrequited brilliance, there were tremendous, innovative ideas in that book and much of it still has resonance and relevance 20 years later.

Around this time, Government started to take regional daily newspapers much more seriously than had ever been the case in the past. The biggest and best local papers had always had a presence in the Parliamentary Lobby but in terms of the time and attention paid to newspapers outside Fleet Street we had always been very much a poor relation. One man changed all that ...

Bernard Ingham, Prime Minister Margaret Thatcher's irascible Press Secretary was – though very different in every respect – the Alastair Campbell of his day. And much of Bernard's own Press background had been regional – with the *Yorkshire Post*. This gave him a better appreciation than most in the Commons of the powerful position of the top regionals in their marketplaces and of the influence they could have on their communities.

He convinced the Prime Minister of that, too. Thanks to Bernard, the top regional editors suddenly found themselves being called to Westminster fairly frequently for off-the-record briefings and to receptions hosted by Maggie at 10 Downing Street. The great Iron Lady was certainly very impressive but she never seemed to me to be genuinely interested in anybody apart from herself. Her successor John Major was totally different. I met him on several occasions and he always went out of his way to talk about *you* and your newspaper; about your city and its issues. His own Press Secretary, Gus O'Donnell – now the exalted Cabinet Secretary – was equally down-to-earth, charming and accommodating. Gus arranged an exclusive one-to-one interview for me with John Major at Downing Street and when I turned up for our meeting the Prime Minister himself took time out to give me a personal tour of Number Ten, describing each painting and possession with great enthusiasm and deep knowledge. He is a truly nice man – which is why, of course, he did not last long as Prime Minister!

So many of my newspaper's campaigns were able to reach full fruition in Nottingham because of the City Council's dynamic young leader John Taylor. Firmly on the left wing of his party, John was of the very opposite political persuasion to Michael Heseltine but they shared the same determination to solve the problems which led to the inner city riots and the same commitment to action rather than mealey mouthed political words.

John Taylor, remarkably, had been elected Leader of Nottingham City Council at the age of 29. There were those in Nottingham who thought that an absurdly young age at which to carry such responsibility. I was not among them. I admired John greatly – not least because, just like Michael Heseltine, he saw inner city regeneration as an issue above politics and worked effectively and efficiently with members of the business community. He and they were poles apart politically but he and they were sufficiently pragmatic to ignore all that and get on with the job. John set up several committees made up of public and private sector people. What those people had in common was a typically Nottinghamian resolve to get things sorted. John asked me to serve on a number of those committees and I was happy to do so. Some journalists might have seen all that as being too close to the Council but John knew – and I often demonstrated it – that our relationship would never stop me giving them a whacking in the paper whenever I felt they deserved it.

Another hugely successful campaign grew out of the need to make the inner city areas of Nottingham more attractive to live in. *"Flower Power"* took the unarguable premise that planting flowers was a remarkably cheap and easy way to brighten up your city. I got the idea from David Welch, a Nottingham man who was in charge of environmental projects in the city of Aberdeen. David had transformed that city through massive floral planting schemes. His thesis, he told me one day, was simple. Plant so prolifically that no amount of vandalism could destroy the effect and the effect, in turn, would have such an impact on people that vandalism would cease.

David told me how he had mobilised people all over Aberdeen to go out and plant bulbs on every bit of waste ground they could find and the results had been phenomenally successful (save for one planting scheme in which members of a local rugby club had endowed a prominent bank on the outskirts of Aberdeen with a terribly rude message to visitors which only became apparent when the daffodils bloomed!)

I took the idea of "Flower Power" to John Taylor, for it could not possibly work without the council's backing, and he loved it. In no time at all the *Evening Post* had motivated and mobilised thousands of readers to plant daffodil bulbs on grass verges, industrial wastelands, scrubby inner city sites – anywhere they felt needed brightening up. In return, the paper gave them a scroll of honour – signed by the Lord Mayor – and recorded their contribution in its columns.

To keep the impetus going I persuaded every celebrity I could to give up an hour or so to go out in the city bulb planting. Nottingham Forest and Notts County soccer stars obliged, as did several stars visiting our local theatres, notably Les Dennis – one of the nicest men you could ever wish to meet. The council bought hundreds of thousands of daffodil bulbs; thousands more were donated free by local garden centres and every Sunday morning for a whole year squads of volunteer planters were out in force.

Almost every Sunday morning for a whole year, Pauline and I were among them, doing our bit… and we loved it. Visit Nottingham in the springtime now and you'll see the results. Wonderful!

That campaign also led to the city winning several honours in the *Britain In Bloom* awards – an achievement it repeats consistently to this day. *Evening Post* campaigns made a significant impact for the better in many ways on those decayed, depressed and dangerous inner city areas of Nottingham and I'm immensely proud of what John Taylor and I achieved together but it needed much more than we could deliver locally. It needed Michael Heseltine and massive injections of government cash and sadly Maggie Thatcher deprived us of both.

Another Nottingham campaign on which I look back with great pride was to get disabled sport treated seriously. This came after I was surprised one day to get a call of complaint about a story which I thought would do nothing but *please* those involved. It was about a blind swimmer being chosen to represent the UK in national paraplegic championship events. The complaint from the young lady's family and supporters was that we had published the story on a **news** page. "She's not some freak," they told me firmly "…that story should have been on a **sports** page."

They were right. Whenever local newspapers published stories about disabled people succeeding in sport they were immediately placed in the human interest category. "Aw, bless 'em. Look what they're doing despite their handicap," was the well-intentioned but patronising and belittling attitude. The reality was, they told me, that serious disabled sport was growing in recognition and impor-

tance around the world and that by treating the sporting achievements of local disabled competitors as news we were stunting that
commendable growth in stature. They were right. And I issued an
instruction that from that day on disabled sport went on our sports
pages. This was not a popular edict with some on our sports desk
but that girl's family had moved me with their plea and I was adamant.

Then, out of the blue one day, I received an invitation to an
awards ceremony at a posh London hotel. It was from the British
Sports Association for the Disabled and the *Nottingham Evening
Post* had been nominated for an award for our coverage of disabled
sport. The honours were to be presented by HRH the Princess of
Wales, the association's patron, who had instigated these media
awards as a means of raising the profile of disabled sport. We didn't
win – but I came away from that glittering ceremony incredibly
impressed by the manner in which disabled sport was now being
conducted and determined to improve our coverage by 100 per cent.

We did. And at the next posh London awards ceremony Princess
Diana presented me with a certificate, a silver cup and a cash prize
to be spent on furthering the promotion of disabled sport in Nottinghamshire. With that money, bolstered by a significant sum from
the *Evening Post* and supported enthusiastically by David Teague
and his promotions team I launched Nottinghamshire's own *Disabled Sports Personalities Of The Year Award* which became a
wonderful annual event with massive publicity, not just in our own
newspaper but on regional TV and local radio, too. The achievements of **every** nominee were featured in the newspaper, as was
every disabled sports event in our county and **every** appearance by
local disabled sportsmen and women in national and international
events. And on **every** occasion the coverage appeared on our **sports**
pages alongside the deeds of able bodied personalities such as Brian
Clough, who became a great supporter of our event.

All this led to the *Evening Post* receiving Princess Diana's award
for newspaper coverage for three consecutive years – after which I
suggested that we should no longer be a recipient lest all the other
newspapers got discouraged!

It's a little known achievement of Princess Diana that the very serious coverage now given to what have grown into really major
disabled sports events such as the Paraplegic Olympics and the
respect and recognition now routinely afforded by national and
local media to disabled athletes is due in no small measure to the
imaginative awards scheme which she initiated and financed. It is a
fact that without that high media profile, disabled sport would not

have grown to anything like the extent it has – but you rarely, if ever, hear the contribution of the tragically deceased Diana mentioned.

Sport played a huge part in my professional life in Nottingham in the 1980s. This was the decade of Torville & Dean but Nottingham's phenomenal Olympic ice dancing champions were never among my best contacts. They seemed to hold no particular regard for their local newspaper, even though Jayne's dad was a newsagent in the city, but their incredible achievements and worldwide fame and acclaim did wonders for the image of their home city – and for sales of the *Nottingham Evening Post!*

It was the decade in which Notts County Cricket Club, with great players such as Clive Rice, Richard Hadlee, Derek Randall, Chris Broad, Tim Robinson *et al* reigned supreme in the English game.

It was the decade in which Brian Clough's Nottingham Forest, having achieved the fantastic European Cup winning double in successive years at the end of the '70s, carried on performing superbly and winning several Wembley trophies.

It was the decade in which neighbouring Notts County, not to be outdone, also made it into the old First Division – giving football fanatics like me the chance to watch the UK's top teams **every** weekend and sometimes even **four** times a week!

I was very close to both clubs, both of which appreciated our coverage and support and I had VIP facilities at both grounds, hardly ever missing a match at either. Directors and players at both clubs were among my friends and – as I had done for Damien Richardson at Gillingham – I got involved in testimonial committees, chairing those of Nottingham Forest's midfield player Ian Bowyer and goalkeeper Steve Sutton.

Often my dad came along to matches with me and he was given all the VIP treatment that I enjoyed myself. That made me so proud and it was a joy to watch him enjoying it so much. I've never forgotten the kindness and warmth of the welcome Dad was always given at both Forest and County. He was made every bit as welcome as I was – and not just by the clubs' management, directors and players. A regular, particularly at Forest, was Ken Clarke, MP for Rushcliffe and prominent member of the Thatcher Cabinet. Ken got on famously with my dad and to hear his greeting at the VIP bar – "Stanley, how *are* you. Come and have a pint with me – bitter is it?" – was remarkable. I mean, Dad was a retired factory worker. Ken was Chancellor of the bloody Exchequer! He didn't have to make a fuss of my dad like that. He was far too big and important to need to curry favour with me and that was never his style, anyway. No. Ken Clarke treated my dad like that because he is a genuinely decent bloke with a sincerely classless nature and the Tories who deprived him of the highest office because he was pro-European were bloody stupid. Like Michael Heseltine, Kenneth Clarke, too, would have made a great Prime Minister. But to my dad, he was just "Ken" a nice bloke with whom you could have a good natter at the bar and to Ken my dad was just Stan, a chap who knew a lot about football and whose opinion on the beautiful game was always worth seeking.

You don't forget things like that – and that's why I've always had a great deal of time for Mr Clarke.

It was while I was driving to a Forest match in 1984 that I heard a magical name from my childhood and from my dad's long gone footballing era... **Tommy Lawton,** legendary footballer regarded by many as the best centre forward ever to play for England, was being interviewed on BBC Radio Nottingham and I was immediately enthralled by this man. That chance hearing led to a friendship which was as remarkable as it was cherished. The story is best told in an article I published the day after Tommy died in 1996. I wrote:

> The schoolteacher in charge of a kids' team was sprinting up and down the touchline like a demented greyhound.
>
> "Run, run, run!" he was bellowing at his young charges. "Move, move, move!"
>
> An elderly man watching this pantomime could stand it no more. He walked up to the teacher.
>
> "Look, mate," he said, "Never mind all this run, run, run. Get them to dwell on the ball; to play the ball; to love the ball; to think."
>
> "Oh yeah," replied the teacher, "and who the bloody hell are you?"
>
> "Nobody, son," said the man softly. "Nobody at all."
>
> The "nobody" was Tommy Lawton, the best centre forward England ever had and he despaired of the way those lads were being "taught" to play football.
>
> Tommy told me that story, among countless others, in many an hour I spent with him enjoying a pint and a fag and talking football.
>
> Tommy died yesterday. We won't have any more of those chats. I won't hear any more of his tremendous yarns. I've lost a dear old friend.
>
> I never saw the great man play. He was from my dad's era. But coming, as I do, from a family with strong Liverpool connections (Everton supporters, all of them) I had heard endless stories about Tommy's days at Goodison Park. I had seen many pictures of him in 1950's soccer albums; the slick Brylcreemed hair with what looked like a half inch parting; the descriptions of the "giant", "fearless", "strong", "brilliant" archetypal old style centre forward. I had read about his incredible playing record – a career spanning 20 years with Burnley, Everton, Chelsea, Brentford, Arsenal and Notts County; 231 goals in 390 league games; 22 goals in 23 England appearances; 24 goals in 23

unofficial war time international matches and an astonishing war time scoring record of 337 goals.

I had heard old boys in pubs drooling about how Tommy headed a ball harder than most men could kick it; I had read Bill Shankly's account of Tommy's headed winning goal in the England v Scotland international match played at a packed Hampden Park in 1939. ..."As the ball went home like a bullet, the swish and ripple of the soaking net made a sound that frightened me. 'Pick that one out,' said Lawton, and it was like a knife going through me."

I knew that Tommy made Burnley's first team at the age of 16; that only 25 games later he was transferred to Everton for £6, 500 (millions in today's money) to replace living legend "Dixie" Dean; that he became the leading goalscorer in the land while still in his teens; that even though he was as hard as nails and built like the proverbial brick outhouse he was such a sporting player that he was never once sent off, never even booked.

Then, in Nottingham in 1984, I went looking for him.

At that time Tommy was a man sadly and badly disillusioned with football. The game had used and abused him, picked him up in his teens and dropped him cruelly from a great height in his 40s.

When his playing career ended Tommy managed Notts County for a while. They sacked him.

He kept a pub which failed, due in no small measure to hangers on who knew what a soft touch Tommy was for free drinks and open ended loans.

Hopelessly in debt, he took a poorly paid job selling insurance, got tempted into fraud in a clumsy bid to end his money worries and ended up briefly but devastatingly behind bars.

The mighty had fallen as far as it was possible to drop. He was ashamed to open his front door. The hangers on disappeared. People who owed him large sums of money crossed the road to avoid him.

The erstwhile super hero of English football was broken and virtually penniless.

Tommy had, in some respects, been his own worst enemy. He had, in many ways, been the George Best of his day. Jack – the – Lad around town, particularly when he was with Chelsea, he had lived as hard as he had played. He had always been generous to a foolish fault and if all those who had borrowed money from him had paid up he would have been a very rich man. As it was, the international superstar who had graced the world's biggest soccer stages, sailed on yachts with millionaires, had an audience with the Pope and appeared in films with Lupino Lane and Diana Dors, stood hunched and alone in the pouring rain at bus stops in Nottingham; that famous, feared head bowed; those great shoulders stooped, unrecognised or shunned and disowned by people who had once lined up in sycophantic file to shake his hand and plead for his autograph.

My own interest in Tommy Lawton at that time was purely and unashamedly journalistic. This was a great story. I tracked him down in order to persuade him to let my newspaper publish his life story. At first he was sullen, uncommunicative and deeply suspicious of me – and who could blame him? Many journalists could be counted among those who had dumped him in the gutter. Eventually, but still reluctantly, he agreed. Then with every meeting that followed he became more relaxed and the real, cheeky, confident, funny and plain talking Tommy began to emerge.

The exclusive Tommy Lawton Story was a genuine scoop. To give our series a suitably high profile launch we staged a *"This Is Your Life"* event for Tommy. Doncaster Rovers centre half – cum – successful TV comedian Charlie Williams did the Red Book bit; more than 200 people packed the Notts County club in which we presented it and we managed to assemble the England team, minus only his best mate Frank Swift who had died in the Manchester United air disaster in 1958, from Tommy's greatest international days to pay tribute to him.

It was a complete and genuine surprise for Tommy, who thought he was just meeting me for a drink at the club.

It was a fabulous night. Tommy grew visibly in stature with the entrance of every famous name from his illustrious past. There was not a dry eye in the house and the event made a great story for us – and great pictures for local TV.

My newspaper duly told his incredible life story and I then signed him up to become a soccer columnist.

Tommy Lawton was back.

The national newspapers picked up the story and ran it; suddenly he was in demand for national TV and radio interviews; fan mail started flooding in from literally all over the world and one of his former clubs, Brentford (where fans thought he had died) organised a testimonial match which raised thousands of pounds for him.

In that match, an England International X1 captained by Gerry Francis played a Brentford side with top star guests in front of a very good crowd and before the match Tommy himself was a star guest on Thames Television. When Tommy (shoulders back, head held high, smiling broadly and now looking nothing like his 64 years) walked proudly on to that pitch through a guard of honour formed by the two star studded sides while a thunderous roar went up from the crowd, it was an intensely moving moment.

Throughout the years that followed Tommy was one of my dearest friends. His columns continued to appear in that Nottingham newspaper, avidly consumed by readers who idolised him, until very recently and though his health constantly gave him problems his mind was as sharp as a razor and his wonderful, mischievous sense of humour intact.

He had had to survive yet another blow when his devoted wife Gaye, who had stood steadfastly and protectively by him through all the bad times, suddenly died but he battled on like the great fighter he always was.

·Tommy was so appreciative of the way in which he said we had re-vived his life that expensive gifts he was given on guest appearances back in the national limelight would appear mysteriously, without explanation, on my desk. Try as I might, I could not get him to take them back. He would not listen to my protestations that he owed me absolutely nothing because he was every bit as good, if not better, for my newspaper as we were for him.

I'm glad, now that he wouldn't take those souvenirs back because they are mine to remind me of a real pal. I shall cherish them (the cut glass bearing the inscription "A Sporting Legend"; the unique and exquisite set of porcelain figures of Britain's eleven "greatest ever players" with Tommy Lawton at centre forward) as much as I will my many personal memories of Tommy and his stories of the big times, the bad times, the sad times and above all the hilarious times which Tommy, with his wicked sense of humour, liked telling best of all.

Tommy Lawton was a gentle man and a gentleman and I consider it an honour to have been granted his friendship.

I was also greatly honoured to be asked by Tommy's family to give the address at his funeral. It was a huge affair. The cortege took a public course through Nottingham, stopping for a while outside the gates of Notts County where fans paid silent tribute. Nottingham Crematorium was packed and the service was broadcast to many more people standing outside. I had no difficulty whatsoever in writing the tribute I was to give at the funeral – but I feared that the emotionally charged task of delivering it would be an entirely different matter.

When I stood at the lectern, looking out at the mourners I saw many famous faces, including Sir Stanley Matthews, looking back at me. And I had to stay sufficiently composed to give my address. I was determined to do so. I told myself: "You owe it to Tommy to get a grip." And I was succeeding – until I glanced down at Tommy's coffin...

His son, Tom Jnr, had tried desperately hard to find one of Tommy's international caps, all of which had been sold by his dad to raise badly needed cash when he was down-and-out, to place on the coffin. I had tried to help in this search and so had several of my reporters. But we'd all drawn a blank. Or so I had thought...

At the very last minute, one of Tommy's caps had been located by Tom Jnr, who had not had a chance to tell me. And there it was, displayed proudly on the great man's coffin. I had just started to deliver my address when I spotted the cap. And I just broke up. The understanding congregation looked sympathetically up at me while I composed myself. Listening to a radio broadcast later, I realised that my debilitating distress had lasted for only a matter of seconds. But at the time it seemed so much longer.

After the funeral, I received a letter from Tom Lawton Jnr...

> *"Dear Barrie,*
> *I would like to thank you for your tribute at the old man's funeral. The words said were brilliant and summed him up perfectly. When you said they were "adequate" you were totally modest.*
> *Did you hear Five Live on the Wednesday? They even played an extract of what you said. It was a wonderful service which truly celebrated his memory.*
> *Dad always referred to you as the "guvnor" so it was entirely fitting that you made such a wonderful tribute.*
> *Thanks once again.*
> *That tribute really made the day."*

I replied to tell Tom Jnr that the gratitude was all mine – for being entrusted with the task of paying tribute to a superstar.

High on my list of great memories of Tommy was the day he had readily agreed to present the trophy at a charity match in aid of leukaemia research organised by my kid brother Les in Shropshire. Pauline and I drove Tommy and Gaye to Shropshire for the event and we called at my mum and dad's house on the way. I'll never forget my dad's face when the great Tommy Lawton walked into **his** front room. He was so chuffed. It was a wonderful moment. And Tommy treated Mum and Dad both with all the courtesy and charm for which he'd been renowned when he was dad's hero.

What a man... and what a story.

I have always believed that Tommy Lawton's life story would make a great piece of TV drama, so much so that some years later I wrote to actor Robert Lindsay about it. There were a number of reasons for doing that: I knew Robert was a great football fan, his mum and dad lived in Ilkeston, just down the road from my own home, and I thought the local interest might draw him. I also believed that Robert, one of Britain's all-time great actors, could portray Tommy through the various stages of his life better than anybody else.

Soon after he received my letter Robert rang me to say he was most intrigued by my suggestion. He'd read the cuttings I'd sent him with great interest and could remember his dad raving about the great Tommy Lawton.

"I've got a lot on just now," Robert told me, "but I'll do my best to get back to you."

I was thrilled. To have Tommy's incredible story told as a TV drama starring Robert Lindsay was a truly exciting prospect – and it would surely mean some nice money for Tommy, too.

Weeks later, I had heard nothing from Robert. Then, as I was relaxing at home one Saturday morning, Reg the plumber who was working on our house suddenly ran, open-mouthed and panting with excitement, into the kitchen where Pauline and I were having a cup of coffee…

"It's HIM – that bloke off the telly. That Woolfie Smith. He's outside. And he wants to see you!"

Robert Lindsay stood at our door with a charming smile.

"Do you know, I've always wanted to see inside this house," he told me. "I used to come scrumping apples in your garden when I was a lad and we never hung around long enough to see inside! I've always wondered what it's like… You must be Barrie."

A cup of coffee and several tales of the young Lindsay's life in Ilkeston later, I was driving Robert through Nottingham to the warden-controlled flats where Tommy – now widowed and not too mobile – lived. Robert and Tommy hit it off immediately. The actor, a truly nice man, put the old fella completely at ease.

Out came Tommy's scrapbooks; his old newspaper cuttings, pictures of himself with film stars Lupino Lane (who Robert had played brilliantly in the West End musical *Me and My Girl)* and Diana Dors. Out came all Tommy's wonderful stories. Robert Lindsay was enthralled. The three of us sat sipping tea and chain-smoking cigarettes for more than three hours and it seemed like three minutes. When Robert and I eventually emerged from the fog of Tommy's little flat (Tommy beaming with pride as the great actor told him what an honour it had been for *him*) it was clear that he was seriously keen on my suggestion. All the way back in my car Robert kept mimicking phrases that Tommy had used in his broad Lancastrian accent. Back at my home, after a gentlemanly insistence on thanking Pauline for his cup of coffee four hours earlier, Robert shook my hand warmly and promised: "I'll be in touch over this."

He said he saw Tommy's story as a one man stage show, using old black and white pictures and film footage – possibly with music. And his final words to me on the subject were: "I like this. I like this a lot."

Several months later, Robert Lindsay rang my office. I was in a board meeting so he left a message with my secretary "Tell Barrie I'm really sorry I haven't been in touch over the Tommy Lawton project but if he watches Channel Four next week he'll understand why."

On Channel 4 the next week was the first episode of Alan Bleasdale's sensational series *Boys From The Blackstuff* about a corrupt council leader – played brilliantly by Robert Lindsay – in Liverpool in the 70s. It was intense, addictive TV drama and became that year's award winning blockbuster. Robert's role was so incredibly demanding and so fabulously played that I could see immediately why the Tommy project had been shelved.

The next call I had from Robert was to say that he was talking to Alan Bleasdale (himself a football fanatic) about the Tommy project but he'd now had an offer to play *Henry V* in a top London production. And so, for the supremely talented and much-in-demand Robert Lindsay, it went on. And our Tommy project began to look dead in the water.

Undaunted and still convinced of its potential success, I next wrote to Bill Kenwright, late of *Coronation Street*, hugely successful theatre impresario and Chairman of Everton Football Club, where Tommy is still worshipped. Mr Kenwright replied with enthusiasm, suggesting that I find a good writer then meet him at his office in London to discuss the project.

Himself making headlines as an extremely promising young writer of TV drama at that time was Billy Ivory – son of Bill Ivory, former News Editor and Assistant Editor of the *Nottingham Evening Post*. Billy – football fanatic and a lifelong supporter of Notts County, for which affliction people are to be pitied rather than blamed – also liked the idea enormously and he and I met Bill Kenwright in Bill's palatial London office.

When I told Bill that Robert Lindsay saw the Tommy project as a one man stage show, he turned to Billy Ivory and said rhetorically "That's not the way YOU see it, is it, son?" Bill Kenwright declared: "It's a play. And I like it." He told Billy: "You go and write it."

Young Billy and I returned to Nottingham raring to go. But there was one huge snag. For some reason (and I couldn't understand it because he's a very likeable lad) Tommy didn't seem to take to Billy, who came to see me one day and told me, "I can't get him to talk freely. He just won't relax with me."

I had a quiet word with Tommy but he had a stubborn streak as unstoppable as one of his famous headers so I don't know if the relationship improved. I do know that Billy, who has since done more absolutely brilliant TV work, postponed the project and there, to this day, it remains, just waiting and crying out to be completed. On his website, Billy, answering a fan who asked why, with his great love of football, he had not written anything related to the sport, did refer to the Tommy Lawton project, so maybe one day he will write it. I do hope so because it is one hell of a story, though my main purpose – to put the icing on the cake of Tommy's comeback and some more money into his pocket – sadly died along with the great man himself.

Editing the *Evening Post* throughout that remarkable and controversial decade was always stimulating, exciting and rewarding. Nottingham being Nottingham we were never short of big news stories. Hardly a week went by without at least one Nottingham story occupying the national newspapers. Our newsroom was a big, busy, bustling blockbuster of a place to be, and in it we reared many exceptional young journalists. The well-publicised community involvement and achievements of the newspaper and its high profile Editor, my frequent radio broadcasts and not infrequent TV appearances, my emergence as an after-dinner speaker in considerable demand on the top local circuit all combined to make me a genuine celebrity in the city of Nottingham – and I loved all that. I was deeply immersed in the community, civic, business, cultural and sporting life of this vibrant, captivating, absorbing city.

Pauline and I had a wonderful home – a delightful 18th century cottage on the Notts/Derbyshire border – many friends, a great social life, a burgeoning interest in gardening and serious walking with Ben, our lovable, loyal Border collie cross; we were travelling the world on both business and pleasure and were able to take Mum and Dad on a really good holiday abroad with us every year; the money I was being paid for doing a job I adored grew even bigger and better annually and much of it was being wisely and cleverly invested by Pauline, our astute family financial manager, in shares and property... including the purchase of a brand new house for Mum and Dad. We were healthy, wealthy and blissfully happy.

No wonder Nottingham has such a fond place in my heart.

While my own star was in the ascendancy, that of the man who was responsible for bringing me to Nottingham was dipping. The inevitable showdown between Christopher Pole-Carew and Nicholas Forman Hardy was looming larger by the week. Nicholas, rightly as the heir apparent, was assuming increasing control of the business in his father's latter years and given the tenuous nature of the relationship between the two men and what I believed to be Chris's somewhat cavalier attitude towards the young Master, conflict seemed inevitable. For me, this was all terribly regrettable. I liked both men enormously. Chris was an absolutely brilliant managing director, occasionally flawed, like all men blessed with genius, but a true visionary and a great leader. Nicholas was (is) the nicest, most thoughtful and considerate of men, but shy, nervous and at that time in his life, afflicted with self-doubt. I felt it was such a tragedy for this most deserving of families that Nick's brother, by all accounts the true newspaperman, had been killed, because if this industry is not in your blood, it can destroy you. Nick lacked absolutely nothing in intelligence and business acumen. He was very bright. But I don't believe he ever had ink in the blood or that he was cut out for newspapers.

Never really comfortable in this environment, Nick tried so hard but for most of the time there were two Nicholas Forman Hardy's – the over-cautious, transparently troubled, tense Nick you saw in the newspaper office and the confident, decisive, happy, relaxed Nick you found in his beautiful home at the heart of his farms and the other family businesses. The difference was dramatic.

My assessment of Nick's unhappiness with the pressures of heading the newspaper business was confirmed (though we didn't realise at the time just *how* significant it was) in a conversation he had with Pauline at the firm's Christmas Party the year before his father's death. Nick and Pauline were standing on the balcony of the huge ballroom looking down on hundreds of newspaper employees who were dancing, chatting and generally enjoying the seasonal spirit.

"You must feel incredibly proud that you're going to take over all this," said Pauline.

"No," said Nick, "I'm just terrified that I'll be the one who loses it all." That was symptomatic of the tortures which this gentle, sensitive young man endured – just because he was who he was.

It was very odd, I suppose, that the son of a factory worker, raised in a council house, actually felt sorry for the posh, public school educated heir to a massive fortune... but I did. I knew Nick well. I was fond of him and I was able to sense his troubles and sympathise with them while I believed that others were intolerant of them.

Also close to Nicholas was Charlie Wright, the company's ageless, jovial Production Director. Charlie had known Nick since he was a child – he'd even bounced the baby heir apparent on his knee – and Nick trusted him and felt safe with him.

As Colonel Tom Forman Hardy's retirement approached, it was clear that two camps were developing and the friction between Messrs Pole-Carew and Wright was becoming dangerously electric. All the clever money was on Charlie being the eventual loser in this battle. As the impartial, objective Editor, I was occasionally sought out by both protagonists for confirmation that the other was in the wrong. Call it cowardice if you like (I do!) but I stayed neutral.

It was only a matter of time before this volcano boiling under the surface at Forman Street blew. One day Chris Pole-Carew called David Teague and I into an office in the bowels of the building to tell us he was no longer our Managing Director. The ultimate clash had come over some big issue or other to do with computers. I never fully understood the details of it all and I never wanted to. I just thought it terribly sad that Nicholas and Chris had not been able to continue to work together while at the same time realising that this was never a professional "marriage" made in heaven.

Chirstopher Pole-Carew, this truly remarkable man, had famously transformed musty old T. Bailey Forman Ltd, with its quaint Victorian ways, into Britain's most progressive newspaper business and become a legend in the industry. Along the way, despite the raging controversy he always attracted, he had changed so many people's lives for the better. The unions had always portrayed him as a monster and he actually enjoyed that reputation (and did nothing to defuse it!) but those close to him knew that among his many qualities was genuine, generous, considerate care for his workforce so long as they were loyal to him.

Nobody owed a greater debt of gratitude to Christopher Pole-Carew than I did and it was with a very heavy heart that I said goodbye to him that day. I just couldn't imagine life on the *Nottingham Evening Post* without him.

Nicholas was as perceptive as he was sensitive. He knew how I felt about Chris and when he came to my office to talk to me about what had occurred he was genuinely worried about how I had taken the news. Such was our relationship that Nick and I could talk candidly to each other. He told me that Charlie Wright would be taking over as Managing Director – "at least for the time being" – and asked what I thought about that. I told him that, in my view, if anybody was going to do that it should be David Teague but Nick seemed to feel uncomfortable with that prospect and Charlie clearly provided the solace that he needed.

This was not good news for the future. I didn't dislike Charlie – it was impossible to do so – but there was no way *he* was going to continue to keep the *Nottingham Evening Post* at the top of the league. Worse than that, David and I knew that Charlie was constantly telling the young Master that the best thing he could do was to sell the newspaper business to one of the big national companies – all of whom had coveted it for years.

Charlie's transparent lack of ambition for our company and Nick's painful discomfort with it were, to say the least, not a pleasing prospect for the rest of the directors. David was particularly pissed off. Charlie just wasn't in the same league as him in terms of talent, flair and management skills. David had done a fantastic job in turning the modest revenue of the pre Christopher Pole-Carew days into many millions. He would have made a superb Managing Director and he should have got the job, but Nick seemed to want a break with the ways of Chris Pole-Carew and perhaps thought that David was inextricably linked to those ways. Whatever, Charlie was now the gaffer… and the company began to stagnate.

There was a glimmer of hope a year or so after Nick had officially succeeded his father in 1989 when he announced out of the blue that he had recruited a new Managing Director. Duncan Currall, only 39, was to join us from the *Hull Daily Mail* where he was Finance Director.

Duncan was from a very different professional culture. He was coming from *Northcliffe Newspapers*, the regional subsidiary of the *Daily Mail* and would bring some new thinking to our boardroom. Duncan's appointment meant that we would have a Chairman and an Editor who were both under 45 and a Managing Director who was under 40, a perfect blend of comparative youth, energy and experience and maybe now I could convince Nick that he **could** thrive in a newspaper environment. My enthusiasm was enhanced even further when I met Duncan and forged an instant friendship with a man I would find very easy to work with.

Others were considerably less pleased. The disappointment of David Teague, passed over for a second time, was as understandable as it was obvious. Charlie Wright clearly wasn't too keen either. He obviously saw Duncan as a cuckoo in the nest and with typical caution Nick had kept Charlie on as Chief Executive. That meant that Charlie had some power of veto over the new Managing Director.

All of which did not make Duncan's job the easiest one in the world!

David was far too professional to be obstructive but, spurned and sullen, he was never going to see any good in the new Managing Director and Charlie was never going to take a back seat!

The task facing Duncan was tough enough without all that undercurrent. The *Nottingham Evening Post* was overdue for major investment. Though we had our small subsidiary colour press which had been relatively inexpensively constructed from bits and pieces at Huthwaite, the paper itself was being rattled out every day on a 30 year old mono press. New full colour presses didn't come cheap. We also needed new premises, so Nick was facing an investment of at least £30 million… in an industry for which he had no real aptitude and in which he seemed to lack confidence for the future. We had travelled around the world with Chris Pole-Carew looking at new presses and state of the art ancillary kit, but the commitment to buy had not been forthcoming from the Colonel or from his son. That was the situation facing our new Managing Director and it was an unenviable one. All Duncan's efforts to move the company on in the direction it needed to take were against Charlie's sage advice to Nicholas to get rid of the newspaper and invest the many millions that would produce into other businesses for which the lad had more inclination and for which there was possibly a better, brighter future. It was a hopeless position for Duncan Currall, not helped by the fact that at this stage, Nicholas suffered a period of ill-health which kept him away from the office for long periods. This had two consequences. It meant that none of the major investment decisions were going to be made and that Charlie Wright was in effective control of the business. This was making an art form of stagnation!

Duncan, frustrated in all his attempts to tackle the major issues, busied himself with minutiae which, in turn, led to totally unjustified ridicule behind his back from middle management and I was furious the night I went to a leaving party for one of the advertising executives and witnessed a piss-take presentation which portrayed Duncan as "Mr Bean".

Thoroughly disenchanted with all that was happening, David Teague, still well short of his 60th year, eventually took early retirement; a premature loss of one of the best intellects in our industry. Selling evening newspapers, which David Teague did more innovatively and successfully than most, had been an increasingly difficult task throughout his time with responsibility for that role. Essentially, they had lost their mass appeal with the arrival of TV evening news and – probably even more significantly – the demise of the 'factory gates'.

Time was when thousands of workers would go through those factory gates in the morning and out again in the evening and the most effective way of finding out what had gone on in the world and in their own locality while they'd been in there was to buy the evening paper. Mass factory employment at the likes of *Raleigh* and *John Player's* had long since declined dramatically and the evening papers had to redefine their *raison d'etre* and strive constantly for new ways of tempting people to buy them. Nobody did that better than David Teague.

One of his many initiatives was to train the *Post's* army of street vendors to smarten up, wear uniforms and be more professional and customer-friendly in their work. He argued that no other business would invest many millions of pounds in talented people and state of the art technology then give the product of all that to "a dirty old man on a street corner" to sell!

This had led to David and I exchanging recollections of newspaper street vendors... As a boy I remembered *Arthur,* who sold the

Liverpool Echo in Oswestry. *Arthur* was just a tiny, dirty old mac under a filthy flat cap, with nothing apparently in between nor underneath. The mac had no visible means of propulsion but would rip along the streets of the town at amazing speed, stopping only to exchange an Echo for the few old pence it cost in those days. Every few minutes, as the mac sped along, a gap would appear under the cap out of which would erupt a cry so loud and blood curdling it belonged in a Transylvanian dungeon.... **Eeeee-cccc-ooooo!** it would go and visitors unused to wailing *Arthur* would jump and turn white with fear. Then there was *Gert* who sold the *Express & Star* (and later, the *Shropshire Star)* from a doorway near Shrewsbury Railway Station for what some locals claimed was about 60 years. *Gert's* sales technique, in stark contrast to *Arthur's*, was mute and entirely stationary. The old girl was not much more than four feet tall, wore a ground length black coat, a big brown floppy hat and a scarf which obscured her face (mercifully, it was said, for it was not something you wanted to see) Buying a paper from *Gert* was a mechanical process. You pulled one from the pile under her arm, upon which, out of the side of the coat would shoot a gnarled, grimy claw – like hand enclosed in a fingerless glove, into which you placed your money which was then deposited robotically into a bit of old blanket which lay on the pavement. This ritual would be repeated hundreds of times a day in complete silence – and few people ever bothered with the change!

Another of my favourites was a big, white haired and bearded old gent who stood outside Broad Marsh bus station in Nottingham selling the *Evening Post* back in the early 1970s. With a cry almost as blood curdling as Arthur's he would announce *"Sssss-eee-eee-veeen-aaahh-poowaahh!"*

"What on earth," I asked back at the office "is that bloke shouting?" The answer was **"Seven 'o' clock Post"** and the explanation was that some 25 years earlier, the Final edition of the *Post* would print at 7pm. (The fact that it now printed at 3.30 pm and he was offering it for sale at 5pm was apparently lost on the vendor and nobody had ever told the old boy that the print time had changed!)

I had a bet with David that he would never win in his battle to smarten up the street vendors. Some of them had been doing it *their* way for a lifetime – and a lot of the best pitches had been handed down through the same families for generations.

But David was determined.

"Don't think that because of the way some of them look they're all impoverished," he said "Some of them make a lot of money out of our newspaper."

I lost my bet. And the *Evening Post* street vendors became a smart army of salespeople – all decked out in the company colours of blue and yellow, though some took to David's sales training with a lot more enthusiasm than others!

He would have had no problem with a street vendor I knew in Chatham – Keith, he was called – a garrulous middle-aged bloke who thought he was Proprietor, Managing Director, Marketing Director and Editor of the *Kent Evening Post* all rolled into one. He was one of those intensely irritating types that you want to punch on the nose every time he opens his mouth. Every time I passed Keith's busy pitch in Chatham High Street, which was almost every day, he would berate me about what I'd put in that day's paper and he would frequently tell his customers: "Those bloody bosses haven't got a clue what they're doing!" One of his biggest beefs was about the usefulness (or *not* as he saw it) of the contents bills (the posters which advertise the top stories in that day's paper). Writing these is a difficult skill (not always practised at its best, I must admit) and one of the many daily duties of the sub editors. Bill writing, like headline writing, has to be very concise because of the limitations of the number of words at your disposal – if bills contain more than four or five words they become too clumsy to be effective and too small to be read at a distance. There was no recognition of these difficulties, however, from Keith who would constantly complain that "these bills will never sell the bloody paper!"

One day, while walking back to the office on the opposite side of the High Street from Keith's pitch I noticed that his contents bill looked more like a page from a novel – impossible to read at anything like a distance. Ready to fire the sub editor who had perpetrated such a monstrosity, I crossed the road for a closer look. The poster was scrawled in blue Biro and read: W*oman of 63 is in hospital with leg and facial injuries after being in collision with a car in Chatham High Street yesterday afternoon.*

It transpired that Keith had witnessed this minor accident, which was reported in a one-paragraph filler deep inside the paper, but because he had seen it, to him it was by far the most important story in that day's issue. So, he had ripped up the poster he had been given and written his own!

I related this tale to David as a warning, but he thought it was a splendid example of marketing initiative. Such is the essential difference between the Editor and the Marketing Director!

Another of David's many ground-breaking sales innovations was two-tier pricing… If you had the *Evening Post* delivered to your door for a minimum of five nights a week you paid three pence less per copy for it. This was hugely controversial within the industry. Many looked closely at emulating it. Nobody had the guts to do so.

With my mate David Teague now gone, Forman Street, Nottingham seemed a very different place. Duncan Currall ploughed on as well as he was able and often confided in me (the only sincere friend he had in the company) over the insuperable barriers he was facing.

For my own part, I escaped the frustrations of these troubled times by throwing myself into my newspaper. Nottingham had some huge stories in this period... including the Hillsborough Stadium disaster when 98 Liverpool supporters were crushed to death at the start of the FA Cup Semi Final against Nottingham Forest (I was there that day, sitting in a stand with David Teague and my dad only yards from where all those people died and we saw things which, to this day, I cannot bear to recall) – and the unbelievable tragedy when a jet airliner crashed onto the M1 near East Midlands Airport, killing 41 people.

We were campaigning as well as we'd ever done and playing a vitally important role in the community, all of which led to our nomination as 1989/90 Daily Newspaper of The Year in *Press Gazette's* Regional Newspaper Awards, the industry's "Oscars".

We were pipped into second place by the *Sheffield Star,* whose coverage of the Hillsborough disaster swung it for them.

This is a hugely prestigious award to win and I was desperately disappointed – the more so since I figured if you can't produce a decent newspaper with **that** sort of story you never will. But that was just sour grapes!

The following year we were again nominated for the award – and Lynne Curry, the superbly talented journalist I had plucked from the Sacked 28 when I did a deal with the NUJ, also won two nominations. Duncan came with me to the glittering ceremony at the Savoy Hotel in London and Lynne, bless her, brought her mum and sister along.

It was an unforgettable day – Lynne was Highly Commended in her two categories, *Columnist of The Year* and *Feature Writer of The Year* – and it was capped magnificently when this time the *Daily Newspaper of The Year* award went to the **Nottingham Evening Post.**

The judges' commendation said:

> "The energy which gives the *Nottingham Evening Post* its appeal runs like a seam of gold throughout the newspaper. It is not just on the front page, or on the sports pages or on the features pages, nor does it appear in various places at various times. Pick it up and it sparkles consistently throughout. Six nights a week it comes out fighting with its fists up, fighting for its readers and fighting for its city. Newsy, cam-

paigning and strongly opinionated – it's rare to find a broadsheet evening which devotes two full columns each night to a well argued leader comment – the *Nottingham Evening Post* takes the award for consistency, for imagination, for flair and for doing it every day. In short, the *Nottingham Evening Post* sets the standards the rest of the regional newspaper industry should follow."

Wow! I was so proud when I took the stage to receive the award from Brian Redhead, the BBC Radio 4 presenter. Duncan was so very pleased for us, too, and when we walked back into Forman Street clutching the trophy the entire workforce was waiting to cheer us into the office. Local TV and radio carried news of our award and my telephone was in danger of melt down from the congratulatory calls, including one from Brian Clough – who knew a thing or two about winning himself!

One of the calls that meant most to me that day was from Mrs Marjorie Forman Hardy, widow of the Colonel and Nick's mother. This lovely old lady was now frail and unwell but she'd heard our news on the radio and she was thrilled to bits. She couldn't wait to ring me.

But from Nick himself? No call. Nothing. Not a word. And I couldn't understand why.

I was, though, genuinely honoured to get a call from *The Times* Media Correspondent, Brian MacArthur – a vastly experienced and highly respected Fleet Street journalist, who had been launch Editor of Eddy Shah's famous *TODAY* newspaper, which broke the Fleet Street mould and the trade union stranglehold and pioneered the use of full colour printing in the nationals.

Brian asked if he could come and spend a couple of days with us to write a profile of the Newspaper of The Year and its Editor. I was delighted – and even more so when his article was published...

Brian MacArthur wrote:

"At 7. 30 on a bright spring morning, Barrie Williams, Editor of the *Nottingham Evening Post,* is driving to work, listening to *Radio Nottingham* and contemplating the leading article he will write as his first job of the day. At the office by 8am he first checks the overnight news stories.

There is a murder and a big fire; the start of a campaign on litter and a story about a man who has been bounced into a surprise marriage.

He claps his hands with pleasure. "It's a good day," he says with the obvious relish of a born newsman. Then he settles down to thunder out his quick 500 words on the litter campaign.

"Litter is a scourge," he writes. "An ugly, blighting blot on the landscape of Nottingham and all its surrounding towns and districts. What validity can there be to Nottingham's claim to be the beautiful 'Queen Of The Midlands' if visitors have to pick their way through litter-strewn streets? Let's face it, there are times when the streets of Nottingham are an offensive disgrace."

That characteristic leader, written in 30 minutes, is one of the main reasons why the judges of the Regional Press Awards decided that the *Nottingham Evening Post* should be the Newspaper Of The Year.

It was a typically forthright expression of opinion for a paper that, night after night, comes out with its fists up fighting for Nottingham – or, as today, since Williams is no sycophant, fighting against its local bureaucrats. The *Evening Post* is a robust paper in a robust city that argues about everything, never admits it is wrong and which is, therefore, never short of strong issues about which to mount campaigns. Since he arrived in Nottingham from the *Kent Evening Post* in 1981, Williams has exploited that bloody – minded streak for all it is worth.

The result is a bright and breezy broadsheet evening paper which expresses every night the campaigning spirit of British regional journalism. Campaigning can seem easy. Select an issue, set a reporter onto it, project the results with powerful display and bingo, you've got a campaign. That sort of ritual campaigning, however, does not win awards. Only a few campaigns get results and the *Evening Post* can now boast several.

Its Old and Cold campaign – the launch of which was illustrated by a picture of an elderly man in an overcoat huddled over a candle as his only warmth – has raised hundreds of thousands of pounds to help the old folk of Nottingham keep warm during the winter cold and is reckoned by experts in social services to have prevented deaths from hypothermia.

When, after a series of stabbings in the city, it persuaded Nottingham police to declare an amnesty so that weapons could be handed in, hundreds responded and the Chief Constable was delighted.

When it declared war on local graffiti vandals, more than 200 were prosecuted and learned the hard way that spraying graffiti wasn't simply middle class fun. Reporter Gill Mullarkey was given two weeks to research her 4,000 word campaign on litter. It was published over two days last week and given most of a page, supported by pictures, graphics and a "Let's Get A Grip On Litter" logo, as well as Williams's leader.

On day two, her plan of action was published in four parts, one for each edition, a typically thorough piece of work.

Ask some of the staff of the *Evening Post* why the paper won the award and the answers come with a confident certainty. "Barrie leads from the front. He must be one of the most hands-on editors in the country," says deputy editor Ian Scott. "We're in tune with the city," says assistant editor Doug Morris. "We're an aggressive, campaigning paper. We take up issues on behalf of the city and we don't pull our punches. And we don't just cram the news in. The emphasis is on being bright and breezy."

"We're not frightened to speak out and we don't sit on the fence," says columnist Lynne Curry. "We're not always right, but we go for it – and if we get a story we're encouraged to take all the time it needs to follow it all the way through." News editor Ian Stewart singles out the paper's in-depth reporting.

The award brought joy not only to the staff of the *Evening Post* but also to the city of Nottingham. On Monday last week, as a Newspaper of The Year logo was used for the first time under the masthead, Williams had a full postbag.

There were several letters from readers but also from major Nottingham businesses, the city council, the universities and Nottinghamshire County Council.

The delight was genuine, said Mr M. T. Lyons, chief executive. "I spend a good deal of time trying to think of ways of making Nottinghamshire better known and more attractive to people who might invest their time, money or careers here and this kind of thing helps no end," he said. "I can only guess at what combination of flair and hard work is necessary to produce so successful a newspaper but my guess is that it comes close to overwhelming."

There was also a fax of congratulations from Keith Parker, Editor of the *Wolverhampton Express & Star.* "Yes, we're as jealous as hell," he said generously.

When Williams arrived at Nottingham, he inherited a paper that was solid, reliable, old fashioned and successful. After the 1979 dispute when 28 reporters were sacked, there was also a residual antipathy to the paper. It was still, for instance, blacked by the Labour Party.

He decided that there was too much of a gulf between the paper and its readers and that the *Evening Post* needed to be less inhibited and more gutsy. He revamped the paper dramatically, adopting a tabloid approach within a broadsheet format. "You don't have to be grey and dull to be authoritative," he says.

Entertainments and BMDs were swept from the front to the back of the paper to clear the front pages for news and he added more national and international news, usually as briefs. They are now displayed prominently on the front page in a two column panel alongside powerfully displayed local stories.

With Don Gray, then the circulation manager, Williams spent 18 months making twice weekly visits to Nottingham's working men's clubs. The aim was not only to discover what they thought of their local paper but also to persuade them that the editor was not a remote middle-class elitist but an "ordinary bloke" who understood the issues that worried ordinary readers.

All the hundreds of pints of Home Ale did the trick: sales of the paper in 1991 are higher than they were in 1981.

Mondays are pretty awful days for news but the *Evening Post* was having a good day when I was there last week. The first edition led on the murder with the fire as the second lead. By the final edition four hours later the splash had totally changed. Now the paper was leading on a city gas blast in which four were injured, supported by a six – column picture; the murder was running as a single column and the fire was relegated to page three.

The taster for the *Post's* litter campaign survived, but at the bottom of the page. There were three strong pictures and a story count of 18 on the front page.

Inside, there was a 12- page school newspaper as well as a 12-page car buyer supplement. Not bad going for a Monday paper during a recession, especially in a paper that sells for 25p, or 22p if it is home-delivered.

Meanwhile, a 28-page Cup Final souvenir selling at 50p was going a bomb at city newsagents as Williams started planning the Post's coverage of the Spurs v Nottingham Forest cup final at Wembley.

When Williams arrived, his aim was to make the *Nottingham Evening Post* an apolitical, campaigning newspaper which rocked the city and county establishment and ruffled feathers. As the award of Newspaper Of The Year demonstrated, he has succeeded."

Soon after our triumph at the awards ceremony, Duncan came into my office late one afternoon looking pale and sombre. He had resigned. This was deeply saddening but not surprising. The activities of Charlie Wright had made Duncan's life a misery. He had been like a lamb to the slaughter and his dream job had become a nightmare. He'd be the better for the experience and he was far too talented not to make it as a managing director somewhere else in the industry but it was not to be with us. And guess what? Charlie Wright was now back in full charge.

Becoming more and more evident in our corridors of power at this time was one Peter Bennett. He was a lawyer, was married to Nick's sister-in-law and had joined the main Forman Hardy Holdings Board, of which ours was a subsidiary, but had started to take more than a passing interest in the newspaper business.

Peter was a nice, good humoured bloke, socially very amusing company and obviously a superb and outstanding member of the legal profession but so far as our very different business was concerned, I couldn't make out where he was coming from, what, if anything, was his brief from Nick, and why he was taking such a keen interest in the costs of our business.

Nick was now much improved in health, which was pleasing because I was genuinely fond of him, as was Pauline. He seemed happier in Forman Street and growing in confidence. And when he announced that he was now seeking a new Managing Director to replace Duncan it seemed to confirm that he was back on track. He made it clear that he was not discouraging internal applications for the job and this set me thinking. Wasn't it time for *me* to stretch myself? There was no way I wanted to give up editorial control of the newspaper but there was a very notable precedent for an Editor also becoming Managing Director.

One Chris Oakley had done it with great success when leading a management buy-out of the *Birmingham Post & Mail.*

I knew Chris well. If he could do it – so could I.

I rang Chris, strictly off the record, and he encouraged me to go for it. So I sent Nick a formal written application. Nick replied, equally formally and properly, to tell me that he had hired a top firm of headhunters to sift all the applications and draw up a shortlist and that I would probably be hearing from them in due course.

I did. And I was invited to Birmingham for an external interview with these guys. To say this was a thorough process was an understatement. My interview took a whole day and involved all manner of tests and interrogation. I didn't mind that. I found this process different and invigorating and I figured that if nothing came of it – and it probably wouldn't – the experience at least would have been valuable. When they had, at last, finished with me I felt that I had certainly not disgraced myself.

Nonetheless, it was a pleasant surprise to then receive another formal letter from Nick informing me that I had been shortlisted for the position of Managing Director of T. Bailey Forman Ltd and inviting me for an interview with the Forman Hardy Holdings Board. For the purpose of the interview this meant Nick, Charlie Wright and Peter Bennett. They began by informing me that the consultants' report on me was very favourable and that congratulations for that were in order.

We then got down to the nitty-gritty ... with Charlie Wright making it loudly and abundantly clear to me that in his view being both Managing Director and Editor was impossible. I resented that because I didn't believe he had given it nearly enough thought and I quoted the example of Chris Oakley. Charlie was having none of it: "Different circumstances," he said, dismissively, and continued his tirade about what an absolute impossibility I was proposing. Then came his killer question: "Would you give up the Editor's chair for this job?"

He knew the answer well enough but I confirmed it for him. "No. I would not."

"And we wouldn't want you to," said Nick.

"Absolutely not," added Mr Bennett.

There followed a set of standard questions about the business which I knew I was answering more than adequately and at the end of all that Charlie Wright repeated his mantra about the sheer impossibility of doing both jobs with the air of a man who could never be wrong about anything and my interview was over.

"How did it go?" Pauline asked.

"I don't know," I said. "And that's the first time *ever* I've not known after an interview. It just felt very odd."

A few weeks later the directors were summoned to the Boardroom for a statement by Nick.

"It's my pleasant duty to announce the name of the new Managing Director of T. Bailey Forman Ltd," he told us. I was, by now, fairly sure that it was not going to be me and I expected an interesting external appointment, but Nick's next line shook me:

"It's Len Simmonds."

Len Simmonds, the Advertisement Director had only joined the Board in 1988. He'd been with the company since he was a lad, having worked as an advertisement salesman before becoming advertisement manager, then director. He was a short bloke of forty something, very competent and likeable, but you would not have picked him out in a crowd. Len was a bloody good advertising man but his working experience of the industry was confined to Nottingham and so in those terms he was Littlehampton Rovers to my Manchester United. I had nothing against "Little Lennie" – as he was known – but this appointment made no sense to me.

As Nick made the announcement, he was looking not at Len but nervously and directly at me – as if he was expecting some violent reaction. His anticipation was well founded. My face must have been a picture of disbelief and anger. I stormed out of the Boardroom and as I marched back down the corridor to my office Nick came after me.

"Have lunch with me later and I'll explain things to you," he said.

"I don't think I want to know," I replied petulantly.

"Oh, come on mate – this is not like you," said Nick.

He was right. I was behaving like a prat.

"OK you can buy me lunch," I told him "…and it had better be somewhere bloody good!"

Over a very good lunch at Nottingham's *Dorchester* restaurant I calmed down considerably as Nick told me: "You know I have the highest possible regard for you – this is purely a business decision." He explained that Len and I had both been on the final shortlist but they felt that he was better equipped than I was for difficult times that lay ahead. When I challenged Nick to justify that judgment specifically he looked flustered and just made vague noises. When I persisted, he got quite cross. I still didn't understand this appointment and I was none the wiser but I was getting nowhere with Nick and I'd never been one to dwell on negatives so I went back to the office to congratulate Len. After all, hadn't I often enough in my own career been a surprising appointment? Give Len a break, I thought, he's entitled to your support. By the time I shook Len's hand and wished him well, I really meant it.

With Charlie Wright the Chief Executive still lurking in the background Len Simmonds started his reign as Managing Director by creating three new Directors: David Crow (Technical); Charles Oskwarek (Advertising) and David Waghorne (Newspaper Sales). All these lads were in their thirties and, just like the new MD, were very competent and likeable – but nowhere near in the same league as Messrs Pole-Carew and Teague.

The three new directors were desperately disappointed to be told that their company cars would *not* be the sleek Jaguars enjoyed by their predecessors but Ford Granadas. They were not to have the Jags they had coveted so much and I was to lose mine since the new directive also applied to the Editorial Director. This move was said to have been instigated by Mr Bennett who, it was rumoured, believed that TBF Directors were overpaid and that their company cars were extravagant. This led me to believe that the new directors were on much smaller salaries than me and that this, plus the downgrading of the cars, was the signal that TBF was to become a different sort of company. But there had been no suggestion whatsoever from Nick that my own salary was to change and the time-honoured TBF principle that the Editor answered to the Chairman and not to the MD remained intact.

While I had enjoyed having a brand new top of the range Jaguar every 18 months for 10 years (who wouldn't!) I was never honestly too fussed about what I drove so long as it was fast, comfortable and got me from A to B, so I kept out of the row that ensued over the cars, but the other lads were bloody furious, saw the removal of the Jaguars as a snub and started a campaign against the new policy. Eventually, a compromise was reached and it was decreed that the directors could choose between a BMW and a SAAB – not as extravagant as the Jaguar but a cut above the Ford Granada. I thought the whole issue was a storm in a teacup but I was right about the message it was sending out... the company was changing.

The message, as translated by Len Simmonds, was that the Chairman wanted a leaner, more profitable company in order to equip it for the huge investment it now required. In 1993 Len unveiled *Project 2000* – "the company's vision of the future".

Len later described it thus:

"Launched with a complete retraining programme and extensive building work, Project 2000 was designed to bring in a new PC based computer system. This was aimed at revolutionising internal communications and operation by extending the networking to link everyone through the system. Exciting changes in the working environment complemented the new equipment. All this was geared to streamlining the workflow, thus equipping the newspapers to respond to future challenges and opportunities. These advances were accompanied by the National Vocational Qualifications linked training programme aiming to encourage quality and personal development. It led, in December 1993, to the company being recognised as an Investor In People company, thus becoming the first major daily newspaper to achieve this award."

My own subjective, cynical, almost certainly unfair and positively liverish assessment of *Project 2000* contained considerably less eulogistic jargon:

"There were some welcome advances in computer technology; the old Victorian building was given a relatively inexpensive cosmetic facelift; the entire workforce (including the directors, for Christ's sake!) were subjected to endless sessions with parasitic business consultants who taught them the nauseating newspeak of corporate crap and the fashionable fads of modern business bullshit, all of which was grafted gratuitously onto our company culture; Len postured and pontificated under his picture in ubiquitous company newsletters which no bugger read and finally we got a flag on the roof and a plaque in reception to say we Invested In People, whatever that was supposed to mean."

Len Simmonds account of *Project 2000* omitted the fact that it also involved significant redundancies in all areas of the company, including 12 members of my own staff. It was devastating for them and painful for me because I had to sack them just to save money. And there was no sign, yet, of what the *Nottingham Evening Post* demonstrably and now desperately needed – the minimum £20 million investment in new colour presses, state-of-the-art printing methods and a modern out-of-town plant to accommodate it all.

It was in the hope that what we were doing was genuinely a prelude to that massive investment that I bit my tongue (well, for most of the time anyway) and went along with much of the consultant-led "revolution" – only occasionally protesting that I thought the emperor was stark bollock naked!

On one of those occasions, Newspaper Sales Director David Waghorne, who, unlike the rest of the new board, had considerable experience of other newspaper companies and had arrived via the *Birmingham Post & Evening Mail*, joined me in a rebellion. "Waggy" and I had a love/hate relationship. We fought like cat and dog over what sold the newspaper (so much so that I once pinned him to the wall during an argument and threatened to knock his block off if he didn't stop trying to edit my bloody newspaper!) but we liked and respected each other. Despite our volatile relationship we had become good mates and allies in expressing some independent opinions against the relentless tide of corporate sewage. We shared an irreverent sense of humour that was lost on our fellow directors.

During one of Len's training sessions, which often lasted for two or even three days, we were being instructed in time management by one of his consultants. As is usually the way with these smart-arse business games, the six directors had been split into teams of two to compete in the task, for which there had be some crappy prize.

The brief was…

It is 11.45am. At 4pm you have to be on a flight from the airport, which is an hour away from your office, to Amsterdam where you are attending a conference. In your in-tray are 32 items (they are listed in detail below) You must work out how many of these 32 items can be dealt with in the time you have available then prioritise them, explain the reasons for your priority list and write your solutions to the issues contained in each of the items you have chosen as your priorities.

As Len licked his lips and his pencil in anticipation of this thrilling examination of our directorial credentials, Waggy turned to me with a resigned sigh.

"Bloody hell, Barrie. More bullshit."

"Yeah. What a load of crap."

"What d'you reckon, then?"

"Well, Waggy, I reckon that with all that work on his desk he shouldn't be swanning off to some bloody conference in Amsterdam."

"Absolutely right. He'll only come back with something unpleasant from the red light district."

"So with so much work in his in-tray, he should really be cancelling the conference?"

"Yeah. That's right. Cancel the bloody conference."

"So is that our answer then, Waggy?"

"Yes, mate. That's our answer."

So instead of prioritising our 32 in-tray items the Williams/Waghorne team simply wrote *cancel the conference* at the top of our test paper and sat back.

The pedantic consultant, patrolling the room like some schoolteacher overseeing an exam, walked over and inquired:

"And what are you two doing?"

"We've finished," said Waggy triumphantly.

"Finished? You can't possibly have finished."

"Well we 'ave, 'aven't we Baz? Ask the Editor – he'll tell you."

"Yes. Waggy's right. We've finished the exercise."

The garrulous jargon merchant was absolutely gob-smacked. He tugged at his rainbow-coloured bow tie and glared at us...

"I simply don't believe you, but there is no point in you two just sitting there doing nothing while the other teams are working. I suggest you go elsewhere in the hotel and we'll call you when we're ready for you."

"Brilliant," said Waggy as we headed for the bar. "What a spiffing wheeze!"

"Nothing of the sort," I replied, "It's the most responsible answer."

Several pints of lager later we were summoned back into the training room by the consultant.

"Right," he said, "I can't wait to hear from you two. Please enlighten us all... What is *your* solution?"

"We cancelled the conference," Waggy announced proudly.

Len glowered at us. The rest of our colleagues roared with laughter. The consultant, eyes bulging in disbelief, looked like he was about to suffer a stroke. Like a Dalek with its complex robotic mechanism buggered by simple human logic he ran around the room spluttering strangulated protest...

"Cancelled the conference! Cancelled the conference! You CAN'T cancel the conference! It's not allowed. It's just not bloody allowed! I've been doing this course for five bloody years and NOBODY ever cancelled the bloody conference!"

"Well *we* did," I said, "and it's the best answer you'll ever get."

I have to admit that my attitude towards Len Simmonds was, for the most part, unfair and unjustified. He proved to be a competent, confident, conscientious, hard-working managing director, very efficient and well organised. He respected the workforce and was deservedly well-liked by the staff. He did not deserve my disdain. I just had no time for all the consultant-speak and my reaction to Len's management style veered between reluctant co-operation and resentful rejection. It wasn't Len's fault and under different circumstances he could well have been very successful, but very little of real substance was happening in the company. This made me irascible and outspoken and I was beginning to see why Nick didn't want me to have the managing director's job!

One day I saw an advertisement for the post of Editor of the *Western Mail* – the national newspaper of Wales – where Duncan Currall was now Managing Director. I rang Duncan: "It's doing my head in, here," I told him. "Why don't I apply?"

Duncan was, as ever, very honest in his reply: "The salary's way below your level," he said.

"I don't mind taking a bit of a drop, Duncan."

"A BIT of a drop!" said Duncan. "You'd be in free fall!"

With the exception of the big, top half a dozen regional newspapers, of which the *Nottingham Evening Post* was one, the sort of salary Duncan was describing would be par for the course in the industry. I was forgetting that when I took this job in 1981 it offered the best salary in the business and that every year since then I had been given a really significant increase – in addition to the chairman's generous Christmas bonus. This was the classic "golden handcuff", and in any event I still loved Nottingham and my job. It was just the management bit that was pissing me off. So, not for the first time in my career I turned a blind eye to all that and threw myself into what I had joined for ... *journalism.*

By now – 1993 – the battle against declining sales of provincial daily newspapers was well and truly joined and theories as to where the solution lay abounded. I had my own – and it was rooted in my background. In the mid 1970s the industry had developed an obsession with graduates. Ever since then, the expectation of academic levels for incoming trainee journalists had risen to the extent that only graduates now applied, which was just as well because with very few exceptions only graduates were now accepted. The reality now was that if I had been applying for entry to our profession I would not have been able to get in!

As a consequence of this I believed that newspapers were losing a lot of their passion and a lot of their relevance to ordinary people. Many of the academic high fliers now predominating in the business had never seen the inside of a council house and wouldn't know the first thing about working-class life. Yet on every council estate newsagents were trying to sell our papers. I was not daft enough to want to throw the baby out with the bathwater and I recognised that many graduate entrants *did* go on to make bloody good journalists but graduates were predominantly middle or upper class and working class kids like me were no longer entering the profession. This meant no real rapport with working class people and that could lead to no readership among hundreds of thousands of decent folk who had either stopped buying our papers or were still doing so out of habit but finding them increasingly out of touch with the realities of their lives.

So what to do about this highly unsatisfactory state of affairs?

I decided to launch the *Nottingham Evening Post's Neighbourhood News* supplements – a weekly insert serving each one of 17 council estates. To fill these 17 supplements I set out to recruit 17 young reporters. The main qualification for each of these 17 jobs was that you had to be already living on the council estate you would be reporting on; the second was that you had to be aged between 16 and 19. The rest – so long as you could demonstrate to me that you had a genuine desire to be a journalist – didn't matter.

This was revolutionary stuff. Yet again, there were editors in the regional industry declaring that Williams had lost his marbles but I knew I was right. I didn't care how arrogant it sounded … if I could find 17 young "Barrie Williams's" out there I knew I couldn't go wrong.

After the recruitment advert appeared in the *Post* I was inundated with replies. Nearly 500 kids applied. We reduced these to a shortlist of 30 then called them in to spend a whole day with the Editor and his Deputy. From those we chose the final 17. These kids were then given three months intensive in-house training conducted by my Deputy Editor Ian Scott – a man with a great gift for training. We then gave them a bicycle and a laptop computer, equipped their home with a telephone (which many did not have) and let them loose on their patches. On the job training continued with the News Desk team as well as Ian going carefully through their copy every day and talking through their errors with them. They were paid just below official trainee journalist level but they were well chuffed with what they were getting and there was a special incentive…

I told them that every trainee reporting vacancy on the main-stream staff in future would be filled by the *Neighbourhood News* reporter deemed to be the best performer of the 17 at that time.

They would then be enrolled for full NCTJ (National Council for the Training of Journalists) training and qualification and if they succeeded they would become fully-fledged senior reporters on the *Nottingham Evening Post*. I had a very sound tactical reason for *that*, too. The corollary was that eventually the majority of our reporters would be *local* lads and lasses and that in itself would, I reckoned, be an enormous advantage. In any regional newspaper newsroom in Britain you would be hard pressed to find any locals on the report-ing staff. This gross anomaly was another manifestation of the raising of the academic standard of entry to the profession and the obsession with graduates and it meant that far too many young reporters were simply passing through with their minds set on "bet-ter things" and "greener grass". This, even sub-consciously, tended to belittle their perception of the importance of the area in which they worked and – unless they were really exceptional – to lessen their genuine interest in the fate of that area and passion for the issues occupying its indigenous residents.

Given time, I argued, my *Neighbourhood News* project could sort out all those shortcomings, lead to increased sales of the *Nottingham Evening Post* and provide a role model for the rest of our industry.

Never known to be afflicted by modesty I spread this gospel far and wide and loudly. This resulted in TV and radio coverage – nationally as well as locally – and in a particularly good half hour programme on BBC Radio 4. "Barrie's Babies" – as they became known – made a very good story in themselves as they worked their council estates on their push bikes, filling their eight pages a week with stories which were frequently good enough to promote to the main paper – even to the front page on occasions. The long-term efficacy of this project needed to be judged over years rather than months but it was looking good.

Despite the pompous protestations of some of the anally retentive editors who wrote to *UK Press Gazette* rubbishing my project, I had nothing against graduates and would always have made exceptions to the rule for specialists and outsiders with genuinely special talents, but I was convinced that what were, after all, *local* newspapers, simply had to be more in touch with the *local* people they purported to serve. Sadly, when I later left the *Evening Post*, my scheme was dropped while still in comparative infancy.

I've always loved an audience and my emergence as a public speaker began when I first arrived in Nottingham and received the customary invitations for the Editor to address WI's, Rotary Clubs, Round Tables and suchlike. I had a big job to do in getting to know this big important patch and its people so I accepted virtually *every* speaking engagement that came in to my office.

This could lead to some pretty uninspiring experiences and I'll remember forever the afternoon I addressed a church ladies club in a tiny wooden hall. Excluding "Madam Chairman", who sat alongside me on two orange plastic chairs behind a flimsy card table at the front, my audience comprised six old women – two of whom looked way overdue for the embalming fluid.

Undaunted by the paucity and short life expectancy of this audience I continued my carefully prepared speech with all the enthusiasm and professionalism I could muster, but my ego was hardly boosted when I looked up from my notes half way through and noticed that all six of them were half asleep. One was snoring loudly and another was farting like an old carthorse.

My concentration wasn't helped, either, by Madam Chairman who, though managing to stay awake (just!) released an incessant stomach gurgle which sounded like dodgy plumbing in a Roman bath house. If Madam Chairman had only dropped off like the rest of her ladies I could have aborted this mission and abandoned my brilliant speech, but every time I looked down at her she gazed back at me with an adoring look which, in someone less than 80, might easily have been taken for lust. So I carried on to the bitter end of my address – upon which one of the two Chapel of Rest cases suddenly jumped up and began applauding in a manner which could only be described as gratuitously extravagant. That woke the rest, one of whom rubbed her eyes and asked, "Is it time for tea?" Madam Chairman then got to her feet and proclaimed, "Ladies – before we take tea would you please join me in asking our speaker Mr Er-um to accept a gift as a token of our appreciation for his most entertaining and stimulating address." At this signal, one of the old biddies emerged from the kitchen clutching a brown paper bag which she thrust rudely into my hands before galloping back to the tea urn. The bag contained six squashed, over-ripe plumbs.

"Well... I thought, *this* isn't going to trouble the tax man!"

There were other occasions, however, when I had larger and more appreciative audiences and I began to polish, in particular, an after dinner routine with which I began to realise I could actually make people laugh quite a lot.

Another good friend and contact was a prominent multi-millionaire Asian businessman, Nat Puri, with whom I attended many a cricket match. Nat owned around 40 companies across Britain and several more abroad but Nottingham was his home and that's where all his company executives would gather for their annual general meeting, followed by a banquet to which Nat always, kindly, invited me. Invariably there was an after-dinner speaker and on one occasion we all sat in embarrassment as the poor bugger died a million deaths. His routine was so flat and the reception it was getting so sterile that half way through he was reduced to telling his audience: "This same material went down very well in Preston last night." That was fatal. The bored dinner guests could just about accept a poor professional speaker but not one who actually apologised! They booed him off.

I turned to Nat and asked: "How much did *he* cost you?"

"Best part of a grand," he replied.

"Bloody hell, mate. You're being robbed. *I'll* do it for you next time – and I'll do it for nowt."

Nat didn't get as rich as he is by turning down that sort of offer and next time it was me who had to entertain around 150 of his business executives. I did, and they loved it. I got a smashing reception that night, and a reputation, which led to many more invitations to be the guest speaker at prominent Nottingham events. I just loved it – and the more I did the better I got and the easier it became. I never charged a fee (foolishly, perhaps); I did it because I enjoyed doing it. I got a real buzz from the laughter and the applause and I reckoned it was bloody good PR for my newspaper.

One of the most memorable of these occasions was the annual banquet of Broxtowe Council, a really big black-tie do. There were about 600 people listening to me that night in a huge venue – the Commodore International – which was accustomed to top professional entertainers. This time I had to be *really* good.

And this – made up of stories (some true, some not), embarrassing moments, cock-ups and jokes I had gathered over the years, was my script...

Ladies and Gentlemen,

This evening brings me – a humble journalist – to you, the pillars of local government. And the links between us are well established. There is a love/hate relationship between local government and the local media. Most of the time you **hate** us and we **love** it when you do.

For years, Nottingham City Council wanted to send me on a cruise... But they couldn't get me over the fence at Greenham Common.

Over the years I've known many local politicians in many parts of the country. Most are hard-working, selfless, intelligent and caring people. But I've also known some right Wallies...

There was a councillor in Wales, Chairman of the Festival Committee, who stood proudly on stage and introduced the London Philharmonic Orchestra, conducted by Sir Malcolm Sargent as "Sergeant Malcolm and his band."

The same man interjected during a committee debate about honouring a local dignitary with the classic question: "But how do we know whether he can PLAY the honorarium?"

There was a Labour elder statesman in Yorkshire who got up when the Town Clerk was retiring to declare: "I'd like the council to stand and pass a substantial motion in this chamber."

There was the dyed-in-the wool true Blue Tory councillor who found himself sitting at a civic dinner next to a typical "Ms" of the very opposite political persuasion. Halfway through the evening she turned to him and said: "I suppose you know I'm a lesbian."

"Oh, really?" he replied. "It must be hell living in Beirut right now."

But to be fair, politicians and council officials themselves have a lot to put up with. Let me share with you some genuine extracts from letters to a local council...

"The toilet is blocked and we cannot bathe the children until it is cleared."

"I need some repairs doing to my cooker as it has backfired and burned my knob off."

"I wish to complain that my father hurt his ankle very badly when he put his foot in the hole in his back passage."

"I request your permission to remove my drawers in the kitchen."

"The person next door has a large erection in his back garden which is unsightly and dangerous."

"This is to let you know our lavatory seat is broken and we can't get BBC 2."

But then as we all know, newspapers themselves are not perfect, nor immune. We have ourselves been known to drop the occasional clanger.

- Like the national newspaper headline saying SIMBAS RAPE TWO NUNS which appeared directly over a tobacco advertisement saying I PREFER THREE NUNS.
- Like the Stop Press item which told *Nottingham Evening Post* readers: 'The Pope is to address Ireland's three Roman Catholics'.
- Also from the *Evening Post:* Parish Councillor Mrs Dottie Flynn has vowed to follow in the footsteps of her husband – who died suddenly on Friday.
- Married with six children, he enjoys displaying his Doberman.
- Cooper told magistrates he had just got married and things were a bit tight.
- The Divorce Court judge said the husband was not in a position to attract sympathy with his own methods of investigation – which included searching his wife's drawers.

One of my old editors once told me: "Accuracy to a newspaper is what virtue is to a lady – but a newspaper can always print a retraction. And such a retraction had to be printed after this wedding report appeared in a newspaper in Staffordshire...

"The bride, who was given away by her father, wore a dress of white figured brocade with a trailing veil held in place by a coronet of pearls. She carried a bouquet of rosebuds and goods vehicles leaving free access to all private parts."

However it was resolved that the best solution was to say absolutely nothing more after another weekly newspaper, reporting the wedding of a girl aged 25 to a bloke aged 78, said that the groom's gift to the bride was an antique pendant!

There was also considerable embarrassment for a London evening newspaper when, in an article on Dame Vera Lynn, it reported: "As the war faded and peace loomed, Vera Lynn was able to advise her husband that she was going to have a baby. It was a symbolic and logical climax to five gruelling years as the Forces Sweetheart."

Court reporting is a fine art and sometimes after sitting through hours of evidence, the reporter can be quite unaware of just how daft his interpretation can look in print. Like this report from the *County Louth Times*:

"Malone said that soon after the party came into his bar Milligan spat at O'Flaherty and called him a stinking Ulsterman. O'Flaherty punched Milligan and O'Rourke hit him with a bottle. Milligan kicked O'Flaherty in the groin and threw a pint of porter in O'Rourke's face. Unfortunately, **this led to ill feeling...**"

There's another little court story, told by the former QC and writer John Mortimer... After a weekend break at the end of a long, arduous and extremely complex fraud trial the Judge resumed on Monday morning only to find that he'd left his summing up in his country cottage hundreds of miles away from the court. Helpfully, the QC for the prosecution suggested: "Fax it up, M' Lud," To which the Judge replied, "Yes, I'm afraid it does, rather."

A well-known local cricketer told me how he was chuckling over a cock-up he'd heard on Radio Nottingham, when a sports commentator had announced that Gary Lineker had pissed a fatness test, until he remembered that the previous week the same commentator had referred to *him* as a shining wit.

Headlines can be another source of embarrassment for newspapers and over the years I've built up quite a collection. Among my favourites is one that was not actually written in error – it was deadly serious – but the image it brings to mind is mind-boggling. It's from the *Bangkok World* and it read:

"WOMAN DIES OF DIARRHOEA AFTER ATTACK BY OWL"

Headlines often have to be written very quickly and under great pressure – and that produced this classic from the *Nottingham Evening Post:* MAN FOUND DEAD IN GRAVEYARD.

And from the *Western Gazette:* MOUNTING PROBLEMS FOR YOUNG COUPLES.

And from the *Kent Messenger:* MASSIVE ORGAN DRAWS THE CROWDS.

But despite the pressures, *good* headlines *are* written. One of my all time favourites is from the *News of The World* and when you hear it you'll realise that it could not have come from any other newspaper. It read: NUDIST WELFARE MAN'S MODEL WIFE FELL FOR THE CHINESE HYPNOTIST FROM THE CO-OP BACON FACTORY

The *News of The World's* slogan used to be "All human life is here", but I reckon that claim applies more to local newspapers – and not just to the editorial columns. A man who was not exactly the sharpest knife in the box rang the tele-ad department of his local paper and inquired about the cost of an advert.

"It's a pound a centimetre," the girl told him.

"Oh, dear said the man. That's much too expensive for what I want to advertise."

"Why, sir?" asked the girl, "what is it?"

"A SIXTY FOOT LADDER!"

There was a Yorkshireman – a typical product of that great county for which the motto is *Brasso In Fisto Intacto* – who rang his local newspaper to place a notice to record the death of his wife. The girl asked him gently: "What do you want the death notice to say, sir?"

"I want it to say Arnold Grimsditch mourns his wife," he replied.

"That's fine," said the girl, "but for the same price you're allowed another three words... why don't you think about what else you'd like to say and ring me back in half an hour."

Half an hour later he rang back.

"Right," said the girl, "have you got three more words?"

"I have," he said, "I want it to say: 'Arnold Grimsditch mourns his wife AND SELLS TELEVISIONS'."

A Derbyshire lad – typically strong in th'arm and weak in th'ead was out to make his way in the world as a haulage contractor and saw an advertisement for someone to deliver a load to a builder's yard in London. He'd hardly been out of his own little Derbyshire village before but he thought he'd give it a go and got the contract. He drove into the middle of London and at Hyde Park Corner stopped a passing pedestrian.

"Excuse me, mi duck," he asked the man "Is this London?"

"Of course it is," said the man.

"Right, then," said the Derbyshire lad,

"WHERE DO YOU WANT THESE BRICKS?"

By the way, how do you know when a Derby lass is getting aroused?
She drops her chips!

A mother was taking her young son to the station by taxi and their journey took them through Nottingham's infamous red light district. The lad spotted a group of girls on a street corner and he asked his mum: "What are those ladies doing, mummy?"

"Oh, they're just meeting up for a nice chat about where they'd all like to go for their holidays," she told him.

At that the taxi driver, a typically blunt Nottinghamian, looked at the mum through his driver's mirror and said: "Oh, come on. Why don't you tell the lad the truth? They're prostitutes and they're waiting there to pick men up."

Later in the cab journey the boy asked his mother: "Mummy – you know those prostitutes. Do they have children?"

"Of course they do," she said, "Where do you think taxi drivers come from!"

Ladies and gentlemen, words are my business. And tonight we've had some fun with words. But I'd like to leave you on a more serious note. I love words because I've always loved reading. When I was a young lad we had no TV set in our house and if we weren't playing football or climbing trees or whatever we were reading – because that's all there was. Now, I see today's kids stuck almost permanently in front of TV sets or computers or some other piece of high technology and I worry: Are we producing a generation of youngsters who are computer literate but brain dead? Are we producing a generation who will not develop the finer feelings of love, of sensitivity, of sadness, of humour that we got from reading? And if the answer is "YES" is that not deeply disturbing for the society of the future?

That's why I always tell my young trainee journalists never to be ashamed of showing true feelings in their work; never to be embarrassed to share their emotions with their readers.

And to illustrate the point I often show them a little piece of writing that I saw years ago in a magazine and I've kept ever since. It was not written by any great famous journalist. In fact, it was advertising copy for posh whisky – *Chivas Regal* if I remember rightly – and I've no idea who wrote it but it describes the feelings of a man of 38 on the occasion of his father's birthday and it goes like this...

Because a red Rudge bicycle once made me the happiest boy in our street; Because our house was always full of books and laughter; Because of countless Saturday mornings you gave up to watch a small boy play football.

Because you used to dance in the kitchen with a tea towel round your waist; Because your cheque book was always busy on my behalf; Because you never expected too much of me or let me get away with too little.

Because of all the nights you sat working at your desk while I lay sleeping in my bed; Because you never embarrassed me by talking about the birds and the bees; Because I know there's a faded newspaper cutting in your wallet about my scholarship.

Because you've always been there when I've needed you; Because you let me make my own mistakes and never once said "I told you so." Because you always made me polish the heels of my shoes as brightly as the toes.

*Because you've remembered **my** birthday 38 times out of 38; Because you've more than your share of grey hairs and I know who helped put them there; Because you made my wife feel one of the family.*

Because you're a marvellous grandfather; Because you wanted to go to McDonalds the last time I bought you lunch; Because you pretend you only need your glasses for reading.

Because you still hug when we meet; Because you still buy my mother flowers. Because I don't say thank-you as often as I should. And because if YOU don't deserve my thanks – who does.

Now, I think that's lovely. Simple words, simply used to describe the sort of love that can only exist between a son and his father.

PLEASE, let's make sure we never lose the ability to express ourselves like that. So, if you've got kids; or grandchildren PLEASE get them to read. PLEASE try to get them to love words as much as I do.

Good night. God bless. And thank you for listening to me."

When I sat down, everybody in that huge venue rose as one and applauded. Some cheered. I could see that one or two in the front were crying.

"Crikey," I thought, "I'm getting a standing ovation."

And boy it felt good!

Word spread, and I became a target for just about every big dinner that required a speaker in Nottingham. I loved it. It made me feel special. And the acclaim it gave me was a wonderful release from what I saw (unfairly but I couldn't help it!) as the endless, intensely boring, industrial democracy drivel I was having to endure at work.

My sanity-saving solution was to keep my head down, concentrate on the "day job" (i.e. the journalism); do my utmost not to get depressed and try not to dwell on the fact that Nick Forman Hardy appeared no closer to making the investment that would move the *Nottingham Evening Post* genuinely forward.

Then one morning I got a phone call from Tony Loynes, the Editor of *UK Press Gazette* and a good friend…

"Barrie, I wondered if you could give me a quote on how you feel about the *Nottingham Evening Post* being sold."

"Piss off, Tony. That's not funny!"

"Oh, Christ. You REALLY don't know? I'm so sorry, mate. I never dreamed you wouldn't. It's true. Trust me. I wouldn't joke about something like this. Your paper is up for sale."

I hung up on Tony. This was a bolt out of the blue. I suppose all the signs had been there… the cost cutting, the slimming down of the staff, the lack of investment, the stagnation – but I hadn't seen this one coming. Nick was selling the bloody company!

I rang Len Simmonds.

"Len, can you come down to my office. I need to speak to you – urgently." Len stood in front of me while I told him of the phone call I'd just had.

"I'll get back to you," he said – and hurried off.

A few minutes later all the directors were summoned to the Board Room for an announcement by the Chairman. The *same* Board Room where Pauline and I, so full of pride, excitement and anticipation had first met Nick's father and mother 13 years earlier. I sat at the *same* highly polished table around which in 1981 we'd talked over that posh lunch with Colonel Tom, Marjorie Forman Hardy, Nicholas and Jane Forman Hardy, Christopher Pole-Carew and his wife Gill as they'd decided whether I was the right sort of person (and Pauline the right sort of wife) to be the Editor of the *Nottingham Evening Post* and Editorial Director of *T. Bailey Forman Ltd*; the same highly polished table around which the original Board that I'd joined, with Chris and David Teague so brave and innovative, had revelled in the triumphs and successes of the early 80s.

Oh, how devastatingly different it all seemed today.

Nick made his announcement and confirmed what Tony Loynes had told me. The *Nottingham Evening Post* was being sold. There were likely to be two or three front-runners and it was a question of assessing the offers that came in and choosing the best. At this stage that was as much as he could say.

I came out of that meeting shocked and saddened and rang Pauline.

"Bloody Hell Paul, Nick's selling the company." It didn't seem real.

The three still relatively new directors had been, understandably, Len Simmonds' men since their appointments and despite my own experience and knowledge of the business they'd rarely sought my advice or opinion, but now they wanted to know what *I* thought we should do, and particularly if we should go for a management buy-out. I was immediately tempted by that prospect but I warned them that this was most definitely **not** something to be entered into lightly. It would involve a lot of risk and commitment – not least financial, I told them. Nevertheless they wanted to pursue that possibility and asked if I could you use my business contacts to set the wheels in motion.

I rang my friend Nat Puri, the wealthiest businessman in Nottingham, who bought companies like other people buy shoes. He was immediately interested and invited me round to his office for a chat. Half an hour later, we had established that a management buy-out, for which he would arrange the funding, was a genuine possibility. He needed to do some more work on it and we'd meet again as soon as he was ready.

At our next meeting Nat was talking detail. He would back a management buy-out bid up to a limit of £50million. He needed to meet all my fellow directors, including Len Simmonds, to test their commitment. And he would be asking each of us for a personal financial guarantee as evidence of that commitment.

I told the rest of the lads and we agreed to meet, along with Len Simmonds, the next morning after we'd all slept on Nat's proposal. At home that night Pauline and I talked the whole issue through in every detail. We could raise the financial guarantee, no problem. And this was a great opportunity. We'd go for it.

The next morning I took Len Simmonds to meet Nat Puri so that he could hear for himself what Nat was proposing and ask any questions he might have before our directors meeting. But it soon became obvious that this meeting was a waste of time. The rest of the lads didn't just get cold feet… they were positively frozen. And I couldn't blame them. Charles Oskwarek was typically blunt and honest. "I'm 34 years old. I've got kids and a mortgage. I've only been a director for a short time. I can't afford the financial commitment and I can't afford the risk," he said. It was clear, too, that Len Simmonds didn't really want to know.

The management buy-out was still born.

Not long after this, two main contenders emerged as likely new owners of our business: *Northcliffe Newspapers Ltd* – the regional wing of the *Daily Mail* and one of the biggest groups in the industry with more than 30 newspapers across the UK – and *Midlands News Group* – led by Chris Oakley, who had staged his own successful management buy-out of the *Birmingham Post & Mail* when the family which owned them had decided, like Nicholas Forman Hardy, to sell. I knew Chris Oakley very well and it was he who had convinced me that it was possible to be an Editor *and* a businessman when I had tried to become Managing Director of *T. Bailey Forman*. I was quite relaxed. I certainly had no problem with Chris – a man for whom I had great respect – acquiring our newspaper and of the big groups, *Northcliffe* was reckoned to have the strongest commitment to editorial.

When it was finally announced that our new owners were to be *Northcliffe* it was also revealed that they had paid £93. 4 million for us. This was universally regarded as one hell of a good deal for Nicholas Forman Hardy and some observers reckoned *Northcliffe* had paid over the top. When it later emerged that the sale did *not* include the newspaper's vast city centre site (worth another £80 million) Nick's deal looked even better.

The speculation was that Chris Oakley had dropped out of the auction at around £50 million, which was, interestingly, the top value Nat Puri had placed on it and, if true, confirmed that it had been a bloody good job that my fellow directors had lost their bottle over a management buy-out bid!

The deal was not, however, to have a smooth ride to its conclusion. The Monopolies Commission got involved because *Northcliffe* already owned the *Leicester Mercury* and the *Derby Evening Telegraph* and acquiring the *Nottingham Evening Post* completed an East Midlands triangle which gave them – arguably – a monopoly of the region. So the Monopolies Commission blocked the sale and it went to appeal.

There were also objections from Labour Party politicians and supporters in Nottingham who feared the influence of the Conservative-supporting *Daily Mail* would turn my newspaper right wing. They wanted assurances that the Editor would not be removed (something of a turn-around from the blacking I had endured at their hands on my arrival in the city!) and that his editorial freedom would not be impaired.

And so it was that I became a crucial witness at the Monopolies Commission hearing in London and absolutely pivotal to a deal worth £93. 4 million! This raised my stock tremendously with my fellow *TBF* Directors – who could only wait, anxiously and uninformed, back in Nottingham while I sat alongside the big guns from *the Daily Mail & General Trust;* the senior Directors of *Northcliffe* and their team of top lawyers as the drama (not an exaggerated word) of the hearing unfolded. This gave me much satisfaction. The special status which the Editor must always be granted on a newspaper had been somewhat eroded by all the "democratising" in Len Simmonds' revolution of our management regime. I hadn't liked that one bit!

Now, our probable new owners and the Monopolies Commission were demonstrating on a national stage just how bloody important the Editor was. They were stressing and underlining that special status. Sweet! Stuff that up your consultant's Khyber, Lennie!

As I gave my evidence through several days of the hearing in London it became clear that if the Editor objected to *Northcliffe's* acquisition of his newspaper it would almost certainly not be allowed. So there I sat – the ex- errand boy from Oswestry – with the fate of a £93.4 million business deal in my hands. Nice one!

As it happened, supporting *Northcliffe* was not a problem for me at all. Of course, given a choice, I would rather Nick was not selling our company but he *was* – and there was no turning back from that. I could object on purely selfish, personal and unsustainable grounds but what on earth would be the point of that? No. I could have no reasonable objection. And I said so in evidence. Moreover, I did not believe for one moment that my newspaper's political impartiality and editorial freedom was under any threat from this company. I based that judgement on sound knowledge of several *Northcliffe* newspapers and their editors. And I said so in evidence.

Nevertheless, when the Monopolies Commission finally granted approval for the deal it was with one unique caveat to protect the Editor... *Northcliffe* could not remove the Editor of the *Nottingham Evening Post,* despite owning the newspaper. The Editor could only be removed by a committee to be made up of selected members of the city's civic and business community. *Northcliffe* could be represented on this committee but had no casting vote and no more influence than any other member.

"What's it like to have the safest job in the industry?" many of my pals asked in phone calls after this condition of sale was publicised.

"You lucky bugger!" But in truth it meant nothing to me. I had never for one minute doubted that whoever acquired the *Evening Post* would want me to remain the Editor. I knew how bloody good I was! The question for me was not if *they* wanted me – but whether *I* wanted to work for them. I had nothing whatsoever against *Northcliffe* and everything I had said in evidence to the Monopolies Commission was absolutely sincere.

But back in Nottingham everything was now going to change so much. This was no longer going to be the dream job it had been in the 80s. I was no longer going to be *the* Editor, sitting alongside *the* proprietor; I was now going to be just one of a mass of *Northcliffe* editors most of whom the proprietor probably didn't even know.

I would still be a director but with very much reduced status, the main directors in this new scenario being on the *Northcliffe* board – men with whom, as a *TBF* Director, I'd been an equal and to whom I was now going to be subservient.

This was not a pleasing prospect. Plus, I had always vowed that I would quit the newspaper industry at 50 because it is so comprehensively demanding of your time. My job had always come first and foremost in our lives yet my wife had never once come even remotely close to complaining about that. I was now approaching 49. During the negotiation period for the sale of the *Post*, Pauline had had a serious health scare and a major operation. She was fit and fine, now, thank God, but the gut-wrenching worry of that had given me a sense of perspective which I'd previously lacked. And thanks to years on a great salary and Pauline's canny handling of our financial affairs we were well off. All of which led me to ask if I really wanted to stick around on the *Evening Post*.

We took ourselves off to our Dorset retreat – a little holiday property on Chesil Beach which we'd bought the year before all this blew up – to do some serious thinking. Pauline was, as ever, entirely unselfish... "What else would you DO?" she asked. "I know how much it's always meant to you. Please think very carefully and don't do anything hastily," she said.

When I got back, *Northcliffe's* Managing Director, Ian Park came to see me. Ian is a legend in our industry, a man of enormous, almost frightening, intellect and deep integrity, a real gentleman. He also has the huge advantage of being a journalist! As we chatted, my (arrogant?) assumption that *Northcliffe* would want me to stay as Editor of the *Post* was confirmed when Ian told me: "You're one of the best editors in the country. You have done an exceptional job here. We'll be delighted to have you with us."

There was no such comfort, incidentally, for my fellow TBF Directors Len Simmonds, David Crowe and Charles Oskwarek. They were offered jobs of reduced status. Len and Charles both refused and left; David Crowe accepted but later obtained a much better job with Johnston Press and has never looked back; Finance Director Barrie Bailey stayed with Nick Forman Hardy. Only David Waghorne was offered a really decent job with Northcliffe and he went on to do very well with them.

I told Ian Park that I genuinely appreciated his warm welcome but I was still far from convinced that I wanted to stay and I tried to articulate my feelings to Ian as well as I could without sounding disrespectful to him or to his company. It speaks volumes for the trust that Ian Park inspires in people that I felt able to speak so frankly to him at our **first** meeting.

"I can't help thinking," I told Ian, "that if I'm going to have a change of circumstances and status, which is inevitable, I'd rather have a *complete* change. After all, I have been here since 1981."

Ian looked thoughtful and paused for some time before telling me: "There's really only the *Leicester Mercury* which would provide a job at your level and there's definitely no opening there."

Then he gave a little punch in the air and exclaimed:

"Aaah... There is *one* possibility. Colin Davison (Editor of the *Western Morning News)* has inquired about going into management. If – and it **is** only an *if* at this stage because Colin has done a worthwhile job – the *Western Morning News* became available, would you be interested?"

Just like Pauline, Ian Park clearly could not see me doing anything but editing newspapers. When I'd referred to a change, I had meant a ***complete*** change – *i.e.* getting out of the profession and doing something entirely different with the rest of my working life. But hang on... This was sounding very interesting. The *Western Morning News* – a highly prestigious quality morning newspaper serving Devon and Cornwall – was completely different from evening newspapers. A real change. A genuinely new challenge. And based in the glorious West Country. Suddenly I was feeling very refreshed, excited even.

I couldn't wait to tell Pauline about my conversation with Ian Park. "That's par for the course," she said, "...we've just had a new kitchen fitted and re-carpeted the whole house!" But she was thrilled at the prospect. We were both ready for a change. And we both loved the West Country.

Ian Park came back with the news that Colin Davison, who had been Editor of the *Western Morning News* for 10 years, **was** still keen on going into management. Ian had found him an opening and the Editor's chair was mine if I wanted it. "But let me stress," Ian added "that we'll be just as happy if you want to stay at the *Nottingham Evening Post.*"

It was now February 1995, nearly 14 years since I took over as Editor of the *Post.* Fourteen tremendous, often exciting, sometimes crazy years. Certainly the most important years of my life. Christopher Pole-Carew and the Forman Hardys had welcomed Pauline and I into their wonderful, wacky family business with warm open arms and in so doing changed our lives dramatically for the better and taken us to heights of achievement and attainment which we'd never even dreamed could be possible when we'd married as a couple of working class kids in 1967. We'd still been young and a bit naïve when we'd moved back to Nottingham in 1981. Now we were a self-assured, well-travelled, worldly-wise and wealthy couple.

"Do you feel bitter towards Nicholas Forman Hardy for selling your newspaper?" I was asked in an interview.

"Don't be bloody silly," I replied. I didn't blame Nick in the least. I'd felt nothing but affection and respect for him when we'd said our farewells. He may have been unsuited to the perilous mountain climb he had inherited with the newspaper but that was not his fault. He was a man of great strength and ability in other areas for which he had a real aptitude and – though his diffidence and true modesty would never allow him to accept that – the success he has since gone on to achieve in those other fields of business proves it.

In any event, there were plenty of industry experts who were saying, with more than a little justification, that his decision to sell his newspaper business was astute, absolutely the right one and that his timing was impeccable. Nonetheless, I knew, because I knew Nick so well, that he would have agonised terribly over it.

In many ways, Nick and I had grown into men together. We had been through a lot along the way. I remembered particularly the note he sent me after I had coaxed and coached him through the ordeal of speaking at his father's funeral...

"I glanced down and saw you willing me on with a look of such kind encouragement," he wrote. "I want you to know how much that meant to me."

Resent him? How could I? Nicholas Forman Hardy is a good man. He showed me and my family nothing but friendship, support, kindness and courtesy through every day of 14 fantastic years. I hope that he is as happy as he deserves to be for the rest of his life and I know that is a sentiment shared by hundreds who worked for him on the *Nottingham Evening Post*, many of whom will have their own personal stories of his kindness to tell.

But that hugely significant chapter in my life was over now. Best have a complete break and bugger off out of there. I accepted Ian Park's offer to become Editor of the *Western Morning News*.

The news came as a huge shock in Nottingham and beyond. For some, the truth that Ian and I had reached a perfectly amicable and mutually acceptable solution to what could have been a very difficult situation for both us was simply not believable and much was made of it by some of the gossip-mongers. That week's *UK Press Gazette* carried a front page splash story with a headline which some people read as a deliberate pun: WILLIAMS GOES WEST IN NORTHCLIFFE RESHUFFLE.

But I was convinced – and so were many of my compatriots – that this move was an excellent one. True, the *Western Morning News* was a smaller newspaper in terms of its circulation – around 44,000 copies a day compared to the *Nottingham Evening Post's* 114,000 copies – but it was by no means the smallest sale of the handful of regional mornings in the UK, all of which enjoyed a prestige that not even the biggest evening papers ever attained and punched way above their weight in important places like the Houses of Parliament. And there were some really big issues brewing in the West Country, to which Ian believed my campaigning instincts could make a major contribution. This really was a very good move for me.

My staff in Nottingham, already reeling from the traumas of the acquisition, were deeply shocked by news of my departure as was the city's civic and business community – not least the protesting politicians who thought their intervention through the Monopolies Commission had secured me a job for life!

My staff produced a special edition of the newspaper for me – 12 pages of tributes, jokes, embarrassing old pictures, piss-takes galore and well-written humorous accounts of some of my escapades. On the front page, I was depicted as Robin Hood in a huge cartoon which was also strewn with daffodils.

This tribute newspaper was funny – as it should be on such occasions – but it was also very moving, particularly the tributes written by Dave McVay, a brilliant writer who I'd plucked from the most unlikely obscurity of Fourth Division football; from my minder when I was a lad, Doug Morris; from my old newspaper sales buddy Don Gray; from Nat Puri, who raved about my performance as an after-dinner speaker; from dear old Tommy Lawton, who wrote, "but for Barrie Williams I probably wouldn't be here now"; and from my mate David Teague, who wrote: "I don't chuck compliments around lightly, but you're the best editor I ever worked with over many years."

The Chief Executive of Nottingham City Council, Ted Cantle, wrote:

> "It is not just that Barrie has been an outstanding newspaper editor and well respected for his independence and fairness. Nor is it that he always had refreshingly robust views – in his case, his fairness has never been associated with blandness! The real blow is that we are losing an energetic and committed Nottingham champion. He has always wanted the best for this city. He has never missed an opportunity to promote Nottingham's case, whether it is tourism, business, regeneration or the arts at stake. And more than that, he has been ambitious for the city, too. Barrie's contribution has not just been in the words spilling across the pages of the Post. He has given freely of his time, ideas and commitment to turn up and participate in many worthwhile causes."

Tory MP Andrew Mitchell, who held the Nottingham seat of Gedling, wrote:

> "A black cloud of depression has descended upon me. Barrie Williams is leaving Nottingham and it will never be the same again! I shall miss Barrie, above all because there was no doubt where his first loyalty as editor lay: it was to Nottingham and the readers. His editorials – often pungent and sometimes uncomfortable – were always designed to bat for Nottingham. I always found that he would listen to a case with fairness and impartiality and give it fair wind, whatever its politics or genesis. I do not know what the transfer arrangements were for Barrie but they ought to have been market beaters! Evening Post readers will miss his spectacular shots at goal – and the fun of seeing us politicians trying to launch equally spectacular saves! Nottingham owes a great deal to Barrie for his campaigning zeal for our city, his wit and humour and his great energy. Nottingham has lost a great champion and I shall miss a good friend."

Andrew also sent me a personal note in which he said that he and left wing Labour MP Alan Simpson had been mourning news of my departure together over a beer in the House Of Commons bar...

"When Alan Simpson and I agree upon something it truly is a bleak day for Nottingham!" he quipped.

Other politicians of both parties (Lib Dems were almost unheard of in Nottingham!) sent nice letters and – just as they had when I was leaving Kent – it was those from readers which were among the most moving.

Like the one from Mrs Corinne Fogelman (who had written to Col Tom Forman Hardy in defence of my re-vamp of the paper back in 1982) who said:

"From the moment your feet were behind the desk in Forman Street there was a marked improvement in the standard of reporting and writing but it is, above all, for the causes you have fought that you will be remembered as the best editor the *Evening Post* ever had. The opportunities you have created for the ordinary man in the street will never be forgotten in Nottingham."

And the one from Mrs Sheila Wheatcroft, who said:

"I have watched the *Post* go from strength to strength under your energetic stewardship and more than anything else I have admired your newspaper's campaigns on behalf of the citizens of Nottingham. You will be missed more than you will ever know by the ordinary people of Nottingham."

That special tribute newspaper my lads and lasses produced listed every one of those campaigns – there were *45* of them!

After Pauline and I had enjoyed a splendid farewell dinner with Nicholas Forman Hardy and his wife Jane at *The Laguna*, Nottingham's finest Indian restaurant, Nick sent me a note to say:

"Your departure is a sad event and I know many will miss you in Nottingham. You brought enormous integrity, fairness and balance to your editorship of the *Nottingham Evening Post* – sadly characteristics that are now almost extinct in the media. Thanks for being such a good steward – and such a good friend."

The highest tribute of all came later when Nottingham City Council made me a Citizen Of Honour – a rare special award granted to very few people – Brian Clough being one of them. At a formal ceremony at the Council House, popular *BBC Radio Nottingham* presenter Denis McCarthy paid humorous, moving and very flattering homage to my years in Nottingham in a speech broadcast by his radio station and the framed scroll presented by the Lord Mayor and proclaiming that *Mr Barrie Williams is made a Citizen Of Honour for Services to the City Of Nottingham* is among my most prized possessions.

Nottingham. Big, busy, bustling, brash, Nottingham. Wonderful, wild and (when you've earned it!) warm and welcoming, Nottingham. Volatile, vibrant, Nottingham. Arrogant, argumentative, amusing Nottingham. You dear, dear city. You'll have a very special place in my heart until the day I die.

10. Go West Young (?) Man

VERYONE FAMILIAR WITH THE DRIVE from the densely populated, industrial Midlands down the M5 and the A38 to the West Country will also know how the vista spectacularly transforms itself into breathtaking wide open spaces – rolling, rising, dipping countryside, becoming ever more gorgeously green, ever more stunningly beautiful, ever more tranquil and empty with every mile that passes after Bristol (which lays claim to membership of this fair region but is in fact an interloper; an ugly, unwelcome urban cuckoo in our pretty rural nest). Such travellers will also know what a bloody long way the *real* West Country is from anywhere. I heard a wit on Radio 5 one day saying "…and then you'll see a sign saying *Plymouth 58 miles* and it's at that point that you lose the will to live."

As I made that long journey to take over as Editor of the *Western Morning News* just two weeks after the announcement that I was leaving Nottingham (Mr Ian Park wasn't one to hang about!) another thought occurred to me…

"How the bloody hell do you sell newspapers down here?"

This area could not be further removed from big, noisy, industrialised Nottingham with its rows and rows of chimney pots or from the densely-populated, urban London commuter land of the Medway Towns – my two previous ports of call at which I'd edited my newspapers with a more than acceptable degree of success.

Looking out from the window of my turbo-charged Saab as it ate up mile after mile, all I could see were cows and sheep (sometimes varying to sheep and cows) and the occasional horse.

A daily circulation of 44,000 for my next newspaper suddenly began to look like a momentous achievement; a minor miracle. I mean ARE there 44,000 people down here! But, God, it was beautiful.

"The Ship", as it is known in Plymouth, is the incredible state-of-the-art building which is the superb home of the *Western Morning News* and *Evening Herald*. Made entirely of glass and steel, it was imaginatively designed by internationally renowned architect Nicholas Grimshaw to resemble an ocean liner.

I had been to "The Ship" once before when Nick Forman Hardy was still serious about staying in the business and we were looking at new colour presses. It is a fantastic building which, along with the machinery it contains, had cost more than £30 million when it was opened just two years earlier. Some in the industry had said "The Ship" was far too extravagant but that was well countered by the view that Ian Park and *Northcliffe's* proprietor, the Lord Rothermere of that time, had wanted to make a statement of faith about doing business in the West Country, which is by no means the *easiest* place in Britain to accomplish that objective satisfactorily.

Fans of *The Ship* and members of the business and civic community in general had really appreciated and warmly welcomed that statement of confidence and commitment to the region and certainly Plymouth loves that iconic nautical landmark a lot more than the succession of bruised and battered local managing directors who have tried to earn profits acceptable to their lords and masters in London – for of all the areas in *Northcliffe's* regional newspaper empire, the West Country, with its vast areas of low-to-no population, was reckoned to be the toughest to crack in terms of advertising revenue and profits.

The Western Morning News was particularly difficult in that regard. In common with a number of other regional morning papers, advertising was hard to obtain because, unlike the evening papers with their relatively compact and largely urban circulation areas dominated by one main city or town and consequently producing impressive penetration statistics, the mornings covered huge territories, much of them rural and containing more sheep than people!

The circulation area of *The Western Morning News* stretched all the way from Taunton in Somerset to the Isles of Scilly – arguably the most beautiful patch of any newspaper in Britain, providing a wonderful source of good material for the Editor but not much to gladden the heart of the Managing Director, whose job was to make money out of it. The incumbent charged with that onerous responsibility when I arrived was Jerry Ramsden, a jolly, rotund, straw-haired, bespectacled Plymothian. A nice man, Jerry. Warm and friendly. Wouldn't wilfully harm a fly. Because he was a Plymouth lad, born, bred and bloody proud of it, *The Ship* meant more to Jerry than it did to anybody else. It was as if that amazing building symbolised his own rise up the ladder of local life to attain the dizzy heights of being boss of the "Mornin' Noos an' 'Erald" and sometimes after work he would sit in the dark at night in the luxurious Board Room – designed so cleverly by Mr Grimshaw as the "Crow's Nest" atop the massive vessel – looking out over the distant lights of his beloved city, sipping a gin and tonic and oozing pride. And why not bless him? Jerry kept an immaculate Visitors' Book in which every visitor had not only to write name, rank and company but also a suitable eulogy to the massive, magnificent glass "Ship". And he was said to have been not best pleased the day some miscreant wag on the staff (almost certainly a cynical reporter) made an entry under the *Comments* column of the hallowed Book which read: *"It's crap! – Joe Bloggs, Window Cleaner."*

Pauline stayed behind, looking after our Lurcher pup Paddy who had succeeded dear old Ben (why can't our dogs live as long as we do?) minding our poultry, tending her fabulous cottage garden and dealing (hopefully!) with masses of people who wanted to buy our house. (Ian Park had kindly offered a bridging loan from the company so that we could acquire a property in the West Country as soon as possible, but we reckoned we'd feel more comfortable if we waited until we'd got a buyer.)

So a lovely country hotel on the edge of Dartmoor became my temporary home while I got stuck into my new job. As I rose every morning and opened the curtains in my large ground-floor room to look out on the glorious Dartmoor scenery, wild ponies would peer through the floor-length bay window at me and after a delicious Devonshire breakfast I would swerve gently to avoid lazy strolling sheep on my drive into work. The contrast with the tense traffic-jammed journey to work through Nottingham's grimy, industrialised and overpopulated inner city could not have been greater.

Every Friday I would drive back up to Nottinghamshire – with my boot packed with scrumptious, freshly baked Cornish pasties for the lads in my local pub – spend the weekend with Pauline and drive back down the M5 early on Monday morning. I didn't mind the long drive both ways at all. I actually enjoyed it and I found it gave me invaluable thinking time.

I reckoned there were a few shirkers on my new staff but in general I was thrilled to bits with them. My predecessor Colin Davison knew what made a good journalist for this type of newspaper. Colin, himself a journalist of the very highest calibre, had left me some real quality. People like News Editor Phil Bowern, Picture Editor Mike Cranmer, Sports Editor Rick Cowderey, Sue Carroll in the Features Department and senior reporters Colin Bradley and Robert Jobson were all Fleet Street standard – indeed, Michael had joined the *Western Morning News* from the picture desk at the *Sunday Times*.

There were some brilliant specialists in the head office newsroom and some first-rate reporters out in the district offices. So, thanks to my predecessor's excellent judgment, the core of the right sort of journalists to take this newspaper on to where I wanted it to be was there. I just needed to sort out one or two areas and add even more quality. My biggest problem was in the sub editors' department, where there were almost as many titles as people, egos as big as the building and not too much sweat and toil. The Chief Sub Editor, a lovely man called Alan Lake, was very close to retirement and happy for me to plan his succession. I knew there was only one man capable of sorting this lot out for me. Tony Moss, who had left the *Nottingham Evening Post* (along with Chief Sub George Hunt) because both were pissed off with my appointment as Editor there, had re-joined me after three years to become a crucial member of my top team. As my Production Editor he had been peerless and priceless, with a great eye for page design, an insatiable appetite for hard work and a tough, disciplinarian management style which suffered no fools and commanded great respect. I thought it extremely unlikely that my successor at Nottingham, Graham Glen, would want to part with Tony so rather cheekily I asked if I could "borrow" him for a couple of months. Graham refused, which didn't surprise me, but confided that Tony was "on the transfer list" which, to put it mildly, did! I contacted Tony immediately, who became my first 'signing' and sorted out the subs desk in next to no time.

With Tony Moss in supreme command of the production area I was free to concentrate all my efforts on the ***content*** of the paper. I was in no hurry. I had learned the hard way in my early days in Nottingham that changes to any newspaper, especially those which have been going for more than 100 years, must not be rushed.

There was an existing plan to turn the *Western Morning News* from broadsheet to tabloid (or "compact" as they were calling it – lest at the very mention of the dreaded T-word they were all turned into pillars of salt!) but I shelved it. Jerry Ramsden was disappointed by that and so was the Newspaper Sales Director, because the *WMN* was labouring under a seven per cent drop in circulation, to which a price war among the national newspapers, resulting in ludicrously low cover prices in the quality broadsheet market in which the *WMN* competed at the time, had contributed greatly. Understandably, a tabloid re-launch was seen by Jerry and his commercial boys as a potential solution and they were keen to press ahead.

However, I was determined that I was going to take my time and get it absolutely right. I figured that two or three years of comparatively poor sales figures did not make the *Western Morning News* a poor newspaper. In fact, for seven of the previous ten years it had recorded a sales *increase*. There was obviously a great deal about this paper with which the loyal readership was perfectly content. I needed to know more about that and I had learned from experience in Nottingham that no matter how much a new editor might believe he can improve a newspaper, by imposing his own, inevitably subjective, ideas and changes, the harsh reality out in the tough marketplace is never that simple or straightforward.

The market research showed some objection to a "compact" format among regular readers – though it was by no means unanimous – but a very strong preference for it among non-readers and casual readers. However, to me, that was not the point. I reckoned that to a very large extent size didn't matter. If what you put into your restyled newspaper is not going to press all the right buttons with both existing and new readers you can tart up its presentation as much as you like and it won't make a blind bit of difference.

Turning a staid, solid, conservative old broadsheet like the *WMN* into a new tabloid would provide masses of free publicity and extensive local interest. The paper's profile would, at least for a short time, be extremely high. It would be daft to waste that heaven-sent opportunity to increase sales by not having your content at the absolute peak of perfection before you took it.

After much consultation with Tony Moss I decided that we would liven up the appearance of the *Western Morning News* in its existing broadsheet format almost imperceptibly – with slightly bolder design techniques, better display of pictures and more imaginative use of the superb state-of-the-art colour printing. I would beef up the content, employ some top-drawer freelance columnists, lift the skirts of this repressed old lady of a newspaper a bit, give her some attitude and cheek and more to say for herself. Then, when we were happy with all that (and it was going to take some time) we would play the ace card of going tabloid if we felt that was still required.

There was another crucial reason for this gradual rather than immediately dramatic approach – I needed to get to know my new patch and its people properly. I had succeeded – not immediately but eventually – in Kent and in Nottinghamshire by acquiring, developing and eventually perfecting a thorough, first-hand *understanding* of the people for whom we were writing; by living among them, sharing their hopes, fears and problems, getting on the same wavelength and striking the right chords for them and together with them. For me, this was an imperative for any new editor and it was irrelevant how good, bad or indifferent at this your predecessor had been because you had no reliable way of knowing and in any event, *you* were the gaffer now.

The extent to which so many new editors did not do this was incredible. The result was that many of them – and by association often most of their journalists, too – sat pompously in remote ivory towers giving readers what they *thought* they wanted instead of living, eating and breathing with them so that they *knew* instinctively. Too many of them produced newspapers for journalists (who were never going to buy one!) instead of for the real people on their patch. In my view, it was one of the biggest single factors in the decline of circulations in this industry. It never ceased to amaze me. And it wasn't going to happen here.

The first columnist I signed up was the incomparable Lynne Curry. This vivacious and superbly talented lady had met and fallen madly in love with Martin on a bike ride to Scarborough when she was working for me in Nottingham and married him a few months later. Martin was a Fleet Street journalist – on *The Independent* – and the last I'd heard of Lynne she'd moved to London to work on Fleet Street herself. In the mountain of mail I received when my move to the Westcountry was made public was a card from Lynne with a view of her house in beautiful Clevedon in Avon and a note which read:

> *Dear Barrie,*
>
> *Bugger me... heard that you were off to the Western Something only to find it wasn't the Western Daily Press (Bristol) but something rather further south and west.*
>
> *Still, Dick Tresder – Richard Tressider (Business Editor of the Nottingham Evening Post) as he prefers to be known – is so unsure of his southern geography that he reckons we'll be virtually neighbours. What's 100 miles or so...?*
>
> *Anyway, just a note to wish you all the very best after so many successful years at the Post and hope you'll like the gentle weather (and manners) down here as much as we do. I lasted in London only a year (hated it) before we bought this rather lovely house up a lane overlooking the sea.*
>
> *Clevedon is delightfully unspoilt – steamers sail from the pier in summer and most of the town is grand and Victorian.*
>
> *The people totally lack any sense of irony – took me ages to put my finger on this – and never say anything to make you laugh, or that's not meant to be taken seriously.*
>
> *As you'll appreciate, this is slightly different from up there and we straightforward types have to learn to be more circumlocutory and stop making fatuous remarks. Still, they get off the pavement for you and you won't need thermals. Daffodils out already. Hope you love it down here and enjoy your new position.*
>
> *All the very best, Lynne*

My reply had been succinct:

> *Dear Lynne,*

Will you write me a Westcountry column please?
I'll be ringing to pester the life out of you until you do.
God bless,
Barrie

I didn't need to pester Lynne. She would be delighted to work for me again, she replied. And she wrote a brilliant, distinctive column, with her special blend of waspish humour, honesty and sound logic, every week for nearly nine years until cancer took her from us, suddenly and senselessly, at the ridiculously young age of 48, leaving Martin, who adored her, utterly devastated and the rest of us shocked and deeply saddened at such a dreadful loss.

Lynne's funeral in a little crematorium in her beloved Somerset – secular, she had insisted, because she had been a frequent critic of religions and could not abide hypocrisy – was unbearably sad, the more so because it was her avowed wish that it should not be. We tried our best to abide by her instructions by not showing too much sorrow but it was impossible because we all loved her so much. I got the opportunity to make a tribute speech to the packed aisles of mourners and I do hope Lynne would have liked what I said about her. Martin wrote to me to say he was sure she would have done.

Lovely Lynne's premature death robbed us of a shining beacon of fun, common sense, perception and a natural talent for writing what her readers would have said had they been blessed with her power to say it. It's an over-used and consequently often devalued word but she was truly unique – as was the rapport she had with thousands of *Western Morning News* readers. She had borne her fatal illness with such typical fortitude and good humour that none of us knew about it and she had continued to write her column with flair, bite and wit for months when she knew she was dying. I only got to know the day Martin rang apologetically to explain that she would not be sending a column that week. She was then just days away from death.

My next signing was Kate Ironside. Kate had worked for me in Nottingham as a Parliamentary Lobby correspondent before moving on to become a political writer for the *Daily Express* then off to Brussels to cover the European Parliament for two years. She was now having babies and freelancing. EU issues were vitally important to the West Country and not only did Kate have a superb grasp of such matters, she was also a gifted writer.

"A weekly column looking at Europe through the eyes of the West Country, please Kate." No problem. Job done.

And so I went on, adding quality to a newspaper which was already starting to raise eyebrows.

There was so much going on in those frenetic final months in Nottingham that I hadn't taken too much heed of the fact that Ian Park was on the point of retiring as Managing Director of *Northcliffe* to be replaced by his Deputy, Alec Davidson. Ian moved up to become Chairman and Finance Director Michael Pelosi became Alec's Number Two. I had met Alec and Michael when I gave evidence to the Monopolies Commission and had a brief encounter over lunch with Alec immediately after the take-over of Nottingham. I hadn't much taken to Alec at that time; he was clearly a very talented and highly professional newspaper executive, with a total and extremely well organised grip on his job, but personally I thought his style was a bit hectoring and patronising – and so it was when he opened the batting for the London Directors at the first *Western Morning News* Business Plan meeting I attended not long after moving to Plymouth.

Perhaps it was because for too long I had been cloistered in the comfort zone of *T. Bailey Forman* board meetings and that they had been totally untypical of the rest of the industry, but as we sat around the enormous Boardroom table in the Crow's Nest of *The Ship* – the local directors on one side, the London team on the other – the comparatively confrontational nature of the proceedings staggered me. Rightly or wrongly (almost certainly the latter!) the whole atmosphere and style of this meeting made me feel angry, humiliated and somehow cheated. I felt that I had not given up the "safest job in the industry" and all that I'd achieved in Nottingham to come down here and be talked down to. I was bloody furious because I reckoned I knew every bit as much about this industry as Alec Davidson did.

I had just had to accept that the day Nick Forman Hardy sold his company was the day my personal circumstances changed dramatically but having lost so much status, then agreeing to move voluntarily to the West Country to tackle this hugely difficult job for *Northcliffe*, I did not feel I had to accept what I saw as Alec Davidson's lack of proper respect for me. I was, I know now, being far too proud, precious and prickly, but the longer this meeting went on the more I began to wonder why the hell I'd left Nottingham. My anger clearly showed because after the meeting Jerry Ramsden told me that Alec had inquired about my body language.

"Body language?" I replied, "he's lucky I didn't smack him in the mouth!"

This was not good. I had two choices:

(1) Swallow my (admittedly over-blown) pride, keep my head down and just edit the paper while pushing the case for *Western*

Morning News development forcibly in the hope of getting my own way.

(2) Just walk out, having first invited Alec Davidson to place *my* job in close proximity to *his* fundamental orifice.

Option Two was almost irresistibly tempting! But I had never been a quitter, so I went for the much more sensible Option One and immediately started to work on a Five Year Plan for the development of the *Western Morning News*. Working closely with the local company's Assistant Managing Director, Mark Johnson, I produced a carefully constructed Business Plan. Mark and I thought this plan, on which we had burned gallons of midnight oil, was a pretty damned fine piece of work but, having sent it to London, it was barely acknowledged – thus adding even further to my frustrating early dealings with Alec Davidson.

That ill-fated start was compounded when Mr Davidson decided to commission a report on the *Western Morning News* and other *Northcliffe* papers by an editorial consultant, David Scott. I'd known David for years. He had edited the UK's first free local daily newspaper in Birmingham in the 80's. This venture had been extremely keenly observed by the whole industry because there were those (Chris Pole – Carew among them) who believed that this could well be where the future lay for all the major evening papers. Given the enormous strength of the existing West Midlands newspapers it had been a hell of a job for anybody to tackle and David Scott, a very good journalist with whom I shared mutual respect, had contacted me in Nottingham for an editors' heart-to-heart chat on a number of occasions. *The Birmingham Daily News* folded and David was now in Torquay where he ran his editorial consultancy.

At a time when it was still far too early to be judging my impact on the *Western Morning News* Alec Davidson handed me a report by David Scott and told me: "I don't think you'll like it." His prediction was an under-statement. I thought David Scott was sitting in second hand judgment, with no real knowledge or understanding of what stage I was at in the gargantuan task of turning around a newspaper and he had delivered to Alec a document which in several parts picked what I considered to be pedantic fault and pointed out things which were transparently obvious to me but needed time and patience – not to mention more money than I had in my budget – to sort out properly. I reckoned that, no matter how talented he was, David Scott was not in a position to criticise the efforts of an editor as experienced and successful as I was and I became very angry because Alec Davidson apparently thought he was.

Newspaper editors are notoriously prickly about criticism and no matter how well-intentioned David's report was, I was incensed.

Again, I was on the verge of walking out. Again I had to remind myself that I had *never* quit when the going got tough. Instead, I sat down and wrote for Alec a critique of a critique, demolishing the critical aspects of David Scott's report point by point. On one section which had particularly irritated me, in which David took me to task for "too many mentions of Nottingham Forest" in a soccer column I was writing for the sports pages, I wrote:

> "I am writing this soccer column because I felt the paper was crying out for one in order to compete with the nationals and we can not afford to buy a celebrity one. I write it in the few spare minutes I can find between editing the paper six days a week; writing the daily leader columns; re-organising the entire editorial structure on a shoestring budget; planning a tabloid re-launch; sorting out myriad staff problems; dealing with the administration of the editorial department on a daily basis; working constantly with my colleagues in the commercial departments to find ways in which we can improve the paper's circulation and advertising performance and attending to all the matters arising from the activities of our board... So I will mention Nottingham Forest as many times as I bloody well like and David Scott can go stuff himself! Incidentally, the readers **love** my column and I've got a mountain of letters here to prove it if you'd like to read them."

I was seriously annoyed by this episode. It would have been an entirely different matter if I had been in the chair for many years and the paper *needed* the benefit of a fresh look – but, for heavens sake, that was precisely what *I* was doing.

I ignored that report and a hundred and one other pieces of unsolicited advice on how to edit the *Western Morning News*, got my head down and proceeded to do it *my* way. I had re-structured the top team – promoting Phil Bowern to Deputy Editor and Jason Clark, the Business Editor, an exceptionally promising, ambitious lad of 24 to News Editor; Tony Moss had re-vitalised those sub editors who had survived his revolution and that department was now trim and efficient; Picture Editor Mike Cranmer, was re-energised, oozing talent and flair and as good as anybody on Fleet Street; the lads in Sport were full of self-belief and using the much bigger section I'd given them to great effect; some of the brighter news reporters had realised that my style of opinionated campaigning and self-expression was not only allowed but bloody enjoyable; the less sparkling hacks had at least doubled their output and those who didn't like the way I did things had, obligingly buggered off; the new writers – both freelance and resident – were bringing quality, depth, humour and pathos to our pages; new appointments such as a full time Equestrian Editor, Farming Editor, Property Editor and Antiques Editor were providing brilliant specialist sections; we were rattling cages and challenging sacred cows around the West Country; the daily editorial conferences became full, lively one to two hours of challenging, arguing, laughing, joking and stimulating sessions out of which came many innovative ideas.

This was slowly but surely becoming *my* newspaper.

After 18 months the *WMN* was unrecognisable from the paper I had inherited but, just as I had planned, the process had been gradual and to a loyal, hardcore readership which would have rejected sudden, dramatic change, almost imperceptible. In fact, the response from readers was hugely encouraging and the most rewarding manifestation of their engagement was a huge increase in the number of letters being submitted for publication.

I was pleased.

During one of those early days of my editorship of the *WMN* my secretary Sheila informed me that there were two men in reception to see me who wanted to tell me they were going to build the world's biggest greenhouse.

"Bloody nutters!" I told her, "That's all I need…"

"Do you want Phil to see them?"

"Yes, please."

Thus, I nearly missed out on one of the biggest stories in the history of the West Country.

Into Phil's office walked Tim Smit and Jonathan Ball with their plans for **The Eden Project.** Tim was a businessman of Dutch origin who had been a millionaire record producer before moving to Cornwall to discover and renovate the *Lost Gardens of Heligan.* Jonathan was a successful Cornish architect.

After they'd left Phil told me: "These guys are deadly serious, boss." And in next to no time I was totally sold on their revolutionary concept of a giant theme park-*cum*-environmental study centre on man's relationship with and dependence on plants. The scale of what these two extraordinary men were proposing was mindblowing. This was a fantastic and exciting idea but they were having great difficulty persuading anybody in Cornwall that they were not dangerous escapees from the funny farm, that this was a deadly serious project with massively positive implications for the county's economy and that if they could succeed in bringing it to fruition it had the potential to become world-renowned.

They needed an ally. They found one.

I devoted an entire broadsheet front page to their plan and two more pages inside and following such heavyweight treatment in the *Western Morning News*, Cornwall began slowly to take this "crazy" idea more seriously. For the next year, as this brilliantly enlightened scheme hit one sceptical snag after another and ran into objections galore the *Western Morning News* stood shoulder to shoulder with these "nutters" – supporting them against the outcry of doubt and derision – until it left the drawing board and began to become breathtaking reality. Tim had recruited Paul Travers, with whom he had worked on record producing and songwriting, to handle the public relations. Paul, a smashing lad with whom I struck an instant and enduring rapport, was a natural – bursting with ideas; a newspaperman's dream.

It was some time later that I first met Tim Smit and we put the wrongs of the world and Cornwall to rights over several drinks, discovering that we were kindred spirits on so many issues. That Eden, which eventually attracted millions of pounds of lottery money, not only matched their expectations but vastly exceeded them to become one of the world's top tourist attractions was a source of considerable satisfaction to me because there was no question that my newspaper had been swimming against a powerful tide of local public opinion.

Although they were later to part company and engage in a high profile legal battle, both Tim Smit and Jonathan Ball have never missed an opportunity to recognise openly and generously the part I played in the hugely successful deliverance of the Eden Project and when Tim made a video of the story of the project, which is seen by all visitors to the fabulous attraction, he made sure that I featured prominently in it.

The friendship which I have shared with the hugely talented and enigmatic Tim Smit ever since is one of my most precious; our comradeship born of standing together against the odds...

And bloody winning!

Another close friendship featured prominently in those early days in the West Country – except this one had been struck some years earlier in Nottingham. Neil Warnock had been appointed manager of Notts County Football Club after achieving great things on the slenderest of shoestrings at non-League Scarborough and getting them promoted to the Football League. Mercurial Notts County were at that time in the old Third Division and Neil took them from there to the First Division in successive seasons, via the play-offs at Wembley on both occasions, before falling out with the Chairman (as he invariably does!) and getting sacked. I was the first friend Neil made in Nottingham and that friendship had endured.

One aspect of my move from Nottingham had caused much mirth among my mates, and that was how on earth I was going to cope watching Plymouth Argyle, a struggling Fourth Division team, after all the glory years with Nottingham Forest and to a lesser, but still significant, extent their neighbours Notts County.

They were right. Incurable footie addict though I was, it was terribly difficult for me to get interested in Argyle until one day, as I was driving back to the office after a lunchtime function in Tavistock I heard a Radio Devon news item:

"Plymouth Argyle have today announced the appointment of a new manager. He is Neil Warnock…"

I was delighted. My mate Neil. Down here. Splendid! Now *this* was different. Now, I *could* get interested in Plymouth Argyle. On his second day in Plymouth I introduced Neil to the delights of a fresh fish lunch by the sea on The Barbican and we talked about his ambitions for what was a sleeping giant of a football club. From then on he would frequently confide in me as a pal – knowing that I could be trusted never to let him down when what he was telling me was off-the-record. True to form, he won promotion in his first season via the Wembley play-off final, which had become his trademark route. Argyle took almost 50,000 supporters with them to Wembley that day. Their opponents Darlington took around 5,000.

My Dad came with me and my pals to that match and he enjoyed it immensely. I was so glad that I had taken him and that it was such a great day out because it was to be the last game of football he saw. He died, not long after.

There was never any greater indication of the huge, unfulfilled potential of this club than the massive support at that Wembley triumph and Neil approached his second season, as did his new army of West Country fans, in a spirit of well-founded optimism for more success.

Unfortunately, it was not to be. Neil and the club's owner Dan MacCauley began to squabble frequently – not least when Mr Mac-Cauley insisted that the players return their Wembley winning shirts to *him*, arguing that they belonged not to them but to the club! This was unheard of. Players had kept their Wembley shirts as souvenirs for as long as matches had been played at the great stadium.

Rows over budgets, travel arrangements (even, Neil told me, over the cost of Snickers bars for the players!) and transfer targets ensued

– culminating in Dan's refusal to sanction the purchase for around £250,000 of goalkeeper Dean Kieley, now a Premiership player, from York City – until finally Neil rang one afternoon to tell me, "Barrie. I've had enough. I'm out of here. There's a Press Conference at six o'clock." My appreciation for the fact that Neil was timing his announcement perfectly for my newspaper was tempered by my huge disappointment that he would not be around the West Country with me any longer. I started a campaign in the *Western Morning News* to get rid of Dan MacCauley – I even went up to Nottingham in a vain attempt to persuade my multi-millionaire friend Nat Puri to buy the club – but Nat had more sense and it was all to no avail!

Despite masses of support from irate fans, our "MacCauley Out" campaign turned out to be my least successful ever! Dan was still there; my newspaper and its editor were banned from the ground; Plymouth Argyle got relegated and went from bad to worse.

Later, Dan sold Argyle to a consortium of local businessmen who were lifelong supporters of the club. They have transformed it into an ambitious Championship club, now, at long last, beginning to realise that great potential – but it had bugger all to do with me!

So far as my campaign to get rid of him was concerned, Dan had won hands down. He beat me well and truly. He did not go until he was good and ready. He always claimed that I was biased because of my close friendship with Neil and he was entitled to believe that, but I was driven, mainly, by belief in the potential of what had now become my favourite football club. For all our rows and acrimonious public exchanges (he often had a go at me on TV) I liked Dan. He is a self-made and very successful local businessman and I've always admired and respected blokes like him. Under different circumstances he and I would probably have been good mates!

Pauline and I were now well settled in our new home – a gorgeous medieval farmhouse, one of the few thatched properties in Cornwall, with our own fields and paddock, the best part of an acre of gardens and stunning views over the River Lyhner – and Pauline was particularly happy to be back in the sort of rural environment from which I'd taken her all those years before. (Neil Warnock bought another beautiful house just a few miles from us which he has kept, so we still see him occasionally.) This was truly the good life... and Paddy our lovely, loopy lurcher was in his element with so many rabbits to chase, catch and eat and so much freedom with which to stretch his long athletic legs.

At the *Western Morning News*, good exclusive stories dug out by what was becoming an extremely impressive team of journalists were becoming frequent and other members of the West Country media who had always referred, affectionately, to the *Western Morning Snooze* were having to revise that description every time we set the day's news agenda, which we were doing with increasing regularity.

At this stage, Jerry Ramsden ceased to be Managing Director of the *Western Morning News Company* and after accepting some administrative group role, which *Northcliffe* gave him, for a while Jerry landed a plumb job as Managing Director of the *Jersey Evening Post*, where he remains to this day. Good for him, such a smashing chap.

Alec Davidson then announced a major change in the structure of *Northcliffe's* daily newspaper business in the West Country. Previously, the *Western Morning News* and *Evening Herald* had operated as a single company with its own Managing Director and Board of Directors, which included the editors – and so had the *Exeter Express & Echo* and the *Torquay Herald Express*. Now, all four newspapers were to be run as one company, to be known as *Westcountry Publications*, with just one MD and one Board, upon which the four editors would also sit. Clearly, this was going to save a lot of money but it also made very good sense – even if being Managing Director of that lot was going to be one hell of a job for one man.

That man was revealed as Andy Gough – who, according to the group gossipmongers, was Alec's blue-eyed boy and destined for a high-flying future in *Northcliffe*. Andy had been a journalist, Assistant Editor of the *Western Morning News*, before accepting the King's Shilling and going into management and becoming Managing Director of the *Exeter Express & Echo*. I liked Andy a lot. He exuded quiet confidence and calm competence. I hadn't had a great deal to do with Andy at Exeter but I'd seen enough of him to know that he and I would get on very well.

We had three things in common: we both came from the West Midlands, we had both worked for the top-drawer *Wolverhampton Express & Star*, and we both had that "straightforward" sense of humour so well described by Lynne Curry as being lost on West Country folk!

With 'Captain' Andy Gough and his no-nonsense Scottish 'First Mate' (Deputy Managing Director Alastair MacColl) now steering *The Ship*, the HQ of the new company, there was a new air of progress about the place and Alec Davidson seemed a bit happier with the inherently difficult West Country region of his realm!

The atmosphere was now right, internally and externally, for me to tackle the biggest change and challenge to the *Western Morning News* since it was founded in 1860… *Going Tabloid.*

The date of the Big Day was set. February 10th, 1997. I'd been working towards this day for nearly two years and quite a lot of the necessary change in content had evolved in the new style broadsheet paper, but there was still a heck of a lot to be done.

We didn't have a whopping budget for this huge day but there was enough for some decent promotion and marketing for the new paper, including TV advertising. My editorial spend would be not much more than it was already. This was fair enough, given that the *Western Morning News* was hardly the biggest earner in the empire. But it was going to be tough.

Having resolved at the outset that merely going tabloid was not going to do anything of significance or permanence to arrest the decline in the sale of the *Western Morning News*. I set about introducing a radical re-appraisal of the market positioning of the newspaper and a much more scientific and structured application of the readership profile to the content of the paper. (e.g. if, say, 70 per cent of the readers lived in rural areas then a proportionate amount of space and editorial emphasis should be placed on rural stories and issues.)

I identified the target market as those people, both indigenous and incoming, who loved the West Country and wanted to keep constantly aware of what was happening in and to the West Country in all its aspects from business to leisure; environment to entertainment. I reckoned that the West Country and "Westcountryness" were extremely marketable and that this gave the *WMN* a distinct and unique selling point which was a very long way short of full exploitation.

The new paper would therefore exude *Westcountryness*; it would be a daily celebration of this beautiful region, including a breathtaking picture, occupying two thirds of a page, of one of its thousands of beauty spots and when you opened the paper every day it would make you proud of living where you did and confirm the wisdom of so doing. The paper would now be re-branded as *The Voice Of The West Country* and would adopt a much more vigorous, aggressive and regionally chauvinistic editorial policy.

It was going to have *balls*. And it was going to have *bite*.

It had to be very much a quality *tabloid*, without hiding behind silly euphemisms like "compact" and it would be aimed at a clearly identifiable target market made up of:

FARMERS, who had always liked us and for whom we could do a very great deal more;

THE BUSINESS COMMUNITY, who rated us very highly and for whom we provided an excellent service which would get even better;

THE CORNISH, a unique people with a unique culture, for whom we were the only local daily paper and for whom we would do a lot more;

OLDER PEOPLE, of which the West Country would always have a much higher than average share because so many retired down there and who presented the mouth-watering additional benefit of being a **reading** generation;

INCOMERS who had chosen to re-locate to the West Country mainly because it **was** the West Country and would be very receptive to our "Westcountryness." and;

FAMILIES, the family unit still being unusually strong in the West Country, particularly in Methodist-influenced Cornwall.

I believed that for as long as we were concentrating on that specific reader profile we could not only arrest the declining circulation but also deliver an audience we could sell to more advertisers, who were almost as rare as hen's teeth in the *Western Morning News* in all but Saturday's edition.

Hitting that readership profile meant strict adherence to a clarity of direction in our newsroom and that meant killing a lot of sacred cows in our reporting activity and very astute use of our limited journalistic resources. I introduced a basic new rule... Whenever a news story, a features idea or a campaign suggestion came into the newsroom it had to be checked against that list of our target readers and a simple question had to be asked. *Is this going to interest these people?* If the answer was *no* we simply did not do it, no matter how important it looked, no matter how often we'd done it in the past, no matter how good a story the journalists thought it was.

This did not apply to what I called the "premiership" stories – a murder is a murder no matter who is reading about it or where – but it **did** apply to the mass of material underpinning the big stuff and it was **that** which would give the newspaper the distinct identity and unique selling point I believed it lacked.

That reader profile was burned indelibly into the schedules for presentation to my two daily conferences and everything on those schedules was checked against it. If ever I felt that one of those groups of readers was being neglected or poorly served on the day I would insist that the team went back and tried again and again until I was satisfied that they were all adequately catered for.

If you present that philosophy to your average marketing man he will say it was just fundamental common sense but, believe me, in the journalistic temple of an important regional morning newspaper in the mid-90s – inherently striving to be all things to all men and relying historically for selection of content on the subjective judgment of senior journalists – this was bloody revolutionary and later prompted many requests from other newspapers to come and see how we did it!

Having sorted the content I needed a *unique* top-drawer design for my *unique* new tabloid and I persuaded Andy Gough to let me invest in the services of top newspaper design consultant Michael Crozier, who had worked on quality Fleet Street papers and several top titles abroad. My investment in this had a cap of £12,000, Andy told me – and that was peanuts to Michael Crozier, who stipulated a limited number of pages to be designed for that sort of fee. However, Michael, a lovely chap, had never worked on a tabloid launch so he got totally carried away with enthusiasm and gave me infinitely more for my money than we'd agreed.

The result was a clean, crisp, classy design, the like of which had never been seen before. Add the typographic talents of Tony Moss and the incomparable picture virtuosity of Michael Cranmer, both working to Michael Crozier's template, and the 'dummy' paper we produced was brilliant. An absolute triumph. So exciting.

When I sent it up to London for Alec Davidson to see his response was that there were too many dots and why wasn't there a television blurb on the front page?

Christ Almighty!

As launch day approached, I had a call from Alex Leys, who was acting as an editorial advisor to Alec Davidson.[4] Alex Leys enthused about the prospect of my tabloid launch then told me: "Alec has asked me to come down to be with you on the night."

My reply was unequivocal: "You can tell Alec to *piss off!*"

But Alex was insistent: "He just wants me to be there to make sure all goes according to plan."

I was equally insistent: "Alex, if you walk through this door on the night, *I'm walking out!*"

---

[4] Alex Leys and I went way back. I'd known him as a bloody good editor of the *Derby Evening Telegraph* and the *Leicester Mercury*. He then ran a national news agency *UK News* – which *Northcliffe* and some other regional industry players set up to replace the *Press Association*, whose charges had pissed them off. *UK News* folded – through no fault of Alex who had performed miracles with the fledgling agency – and he was between jobs, before moving into management and becoming a top managing director.

I wasn't bluffing. I had the utmost respect for Alex Leys but good as he was, he was certainly no better than me, and there was no way he was going to rain on my parade. So many matters of editorial style and judgment are entirely subjective and personally intuitive. Two good editors will inevitably see some things in different ways. Alex and I were both strong-willed (to say the least!) and it simply wouldn't work. And what sort of message would his presence send to my staff? Again I thought that Alec Davidson was treating me like some bloody novice. Again, he had incensed me. Alec seemed to have perfected the art of rubbing me up the wrong way!

I would not budge.

Later, Alex Leys rang me back: "A compromise mate. Can you just have the pages faxed up here for me to see on the night. Just out of interest?"

I had far too much to do to want to continue to argue with Alex: "Oh, all right," I told him. "But only if there's time – and *strictly* for interest only."

News of our conversion to tabloid had spread and there was still mixed feelings among much of the readership... but I was left in no doubt about what one of my neighbours felt about it. The much respected and elderly 'Miss Vera' occupies a rather matriarchal position in the tiny Cornish hamlet in which we live and one night she asked Chris, who farms next door to us, to call and see me.

Chris duly delivered his message...

"About the *Western Morning News* going tabloid," he said, "Vera has asked me to ask you not to do it."

I had been dealing with such objections for weeks and I gave Chris the standard reply, explaining in detail how newspapers had to move with the times, that tabloid did not equate to cheap and nasty and how many people now preferred their quality newspapers in a smaller size.

"Oh, it's not that," said Chris, "She says that if you go tabloid she'll have nothing to wrap her chrysanths in..."

In such moments are one's feet returned to the ground!

Vera must have accepted my explanation because she still takes the *Western Morning News* to this day – though I've never asked how she now wraps her prized blooms.

When tabloid launch night arrived the *Western Morning News* newsroom resembled a film set. Our Big Day had really fired the interest of the rest of the Westcountry media and I had agreed that both BBC *South West* and ITV *Westcountry* could film it. Both were doing it live – with their Business Correspondents in full cry. We also had several local radio reporters on the floor. It had seemed like a good idea at the time. Money cannot buy the sort of publicity this would generate… but they had become a tad intrusive!

We had planned every dot and comma of launch night but it was a massive undertaking. I had agreed with Andy Gough that our first tabloid edition should have a minimum of 56 pages, the better to impress potential new readers and interest in the first tabloid *WMN* had been so great that it had produced an uncommonly large amount of advertising. The result was a 64-page paper. The biggest broadsheet we'd ever done was 24 pages, sometimes it was only 12 and the average was 18. Tony Moss and his brave sub editors were facing a whopping task. For the first two to three hours of the night we were on schedule. Then, as invariably happens on the big occasion, we started to hit problems and miss page deadlines. The longer the night went on, the later we were getting. With TV cameras and microphones following our every move, Tony and I had to be un-characteristically sober in our language but we were beginning to get seriously late.

We could produce the best paper in the world but if it didn't make it to the news stands in time it would all have been for nothing. We were supposed to be on the Press by 12 midnight. And both TV stations had told viewers to be ready for the historic first newspaper off the Press.

No chance! After buckets of blood, sweat and tears we eventually made it on to the Press at 2.30am, mercifully not so late that we'd missed any of our major outletsm but perilously close and certainly far too late to star in the live TV drama they had planned.

In what was scheduled and anticipated to be an intensely moving and historic bit of "theatre" I had arranged for our youngest (Jason Groves) and oldest (Doug Williams) journalists to ceremoniously press the button to start the Press rolling. They did. But everybody was so knackered they couldn't care less and the TV crews had long since gone home to bed!

Andy Gough and I had laid on booze and posh nosh for a bit of a post-launch knees-up in the Boardroom, but only a few diehards bothered to go in there. The rest were so exhausted they just went straight home and crashed out. So did I – as soon as I had thanked everybody.

But we'd done it. And the paper looked great.

Before I dragged my weary limbs out of the building Andy Gough sought me out, a copy of the new *Western Morning News* in his hands: "It's bloody brilliant, mate," he said, and gave me a bear-hug.

There were tears in my eyes as I drove home, because I knew we had produced something really special.

I could not wait to get into work the next day to check the reaction to my new "baby". It was wonderful. I had set up a special hotline to take calls from readers. There were just five complaints, but positive messages of support and congratulations poured in by the hundreds. I recalled the day after I'd re-vamped the *Nottingham Evening Post* (more than 600 complaints!) and I thanked my lucky stars that this time I had been so much more patient.

Andy Gough was thrilled. But from London office and Alec Davidson there was not a peep. "Crafty bastards," I told myself. "They're waiting to see a sales figure (which would not be available for a week) before committing themselves!"

But who could blame them? No point in premature congratulations if it later turned out to be a disaster – and in this business, *nothing* can ever be taken for granted.

When that sales figure arrived it exceeded our wildest expectations... The circulation of the *Western Morning News* had increased by *10.78 per cent!* We had budgeted for an increase of two per cent while quietly hoping we might achieve four or five... but more than ten per cent was phenomenal.

Finally, a message arrived from Alec Davidson acknowledging that the early indications were that we might just have got it right.

I knew that the 10.78 per cent increase would not be sustainable. Our TV advertising campaign (which we couldn't afford to maintain) and the masses of *free* publicity our re-launch had attracted locally would have resulted in a lot of curiosity purchase on Day One.

But if we'd got the paper right we could be confident of holding on to around half of it – which would be a great result. In the event, it settled down at seven per cent up, which was a direct reversal of the seven per cent fall it had suffered before my arrival. A year later, we were recording a plus figure of three per cent and from then on it stabilised – giving us a well-deserved annual ranking among the top five regional daily papers in the UK for sales performance.

Now (at long last!) Alec Davidson seemed to be prepared to accept that I knew what I was doing. (Actually, there followed a number of very pleasant and gracious notes from Alec recognising our achievements. My exchanges with him now ceased to be fractious and mutually point-scoring and we began to get on very well. I now began to think that perhaps his early apparent mistrust of me had been caused by my own arrogance, a character trait that I have never denied and by my nonchalance, caused by my own very high status in Nottingham, towards his position as the boss. I had probably seemed overconfident, even bolshy, to him and he would almost certainly have found *my* attitude towards *him* baffling and irritating, just as I had done his. Whatever the reasons for the early friction, Mr Davidson and I were just fine now and our professional relationship and understanding from then on was excellent.)

In 2001, he wrote me a particularly kind note which said:

"This is to thank you for all you have done. The reception which the *Western Morning News* now enjoys has never been higher. You have taken us a long way down a difficult but promising road."

A few months after re-launch, the *Western Morning News* was voted *Daily Newspaper of The Year* in the *Press Gazette* regional awards. I had won that accolade twice before at Nottingham but this third time was extra special.

The following year the *Western Morning News* was again voted *Daily Newspaper of The Year* and (in a repeat of our achievement with the *Nottingham Evening Post* in 1991) also became the *overall* 1998 *Regional Newspaper of The Year.*

This was the first time that a *Northcliffe* newspaper had ever landed the top industry award – and that brought fulsome recognition from London. I received a formal letter from the *Northcliffe* Board, accompanied by a bottle of extremely expensive malt whisky, recognising my "remarkable achievement".

Chairman Ian Park sent me a personal note:

Dear Barrie,

When I was in Plymouth last month we spoke of your prospects of winning the regional newspaper of the year award. You indicated that you were not overly optimistic because of past successes. I learn today that you were wrong. So may I be quite the last person in the world to congratulate you upon the success of the Western Morning News – the Regional Newspaper Of The Year. May I add a personal congratulation to its Editor. I believe Northcliffe was very fortunate that you so readily undertook to move to Plymouth. You have a remarkable record as a regional editor. I do most sincerely congratulate you on this further success.

As did Managing Director Alec Davidson:

Dear Barrie,

I seem to be writing to you quite a lot to congratulate you on achievements at the Western Morning News. However, my previous letters pale by comparison with your success on becoming Regional Newspaper of The Year. This latest accolade is sought by many but realised by few. May I add my congratulations to the many you must have received."

Recognition also came from the *Daily Mail and General Trust* Board. Finance Director Peter Williams, with whom I had struck a good rapport when we met during the Monopolies Commission hearing into their acquisition of the *Nottingham Evening Post*, wrote:

> *Dear Barrie,*
> *You obviously have not heard that DMGT seeks not to have monopolies (only dominant market positions). I understand that the Western Morning News, however, has secured a monopoly on leading regional newspaper awards! Congratulations to you on the latest.*

The genuinely warm tributes paid to me and my team by the *Northcliffe* and *DMGT* top brass were very much appreciated. And I was equally appreciative of my marvellous journalists. Seeing *their* pride and progress gave me a huge lift every day. We were truly a remarkable team and we were achieving so much together that going into the office every morning was a joy and looking through the pages of that paper every night never ceased to give me a buzz.

That's what it is *really* all about when ink's in your blood...

And there was so much for a good paper with good journalists and a stroppy editor to shout about in the West Country; so many issues which were troubling my community of readers.

Nowhere was there a bigger sense of real and genuine grievance than in the farming community. The badly handled BSE crisis and a myriad of other perceived injustices had led to deep disaffection with the New Labour government – which was demonstrating an appalling ignorance of rural issues in general and the agricultural industry in particular. This was compounded by the demeanour of the Agriculture Minister Jack Cunningham who appeared to revel in hostility towards the farmers whose interests he was supposed to serve. All this had created a real anger among farmers who had taken to demonstrating in the manner previously associated with their French brethren.

My interest in all this had grown from purely professional to fiercely committed. I lived among farmers now. I knew their grievances were real and entirely justified. Farms were going bankrupt by the dozen every day. Very few were making any real money. Farmers who knew no other way of life were having to leave an industry which had sustained their families for generations. The mass depression was palpable and pervasive. The suicide rate was deeply disturbing.

The big *barley barons*; the wealthy arable farmers of the south and east were doing very nicely and it was upon *them* that the Government and the national media appeared to base what limited knowledge they had of the industry. It was the much smaller *livestock farmers* of the South West, Wales, Yorkshire and Cumbria who were fighting a life or death battle to save their farms from extinction... and that fight was on a "playing field" which was not only uneven but stacked grossly unfairly against them.

While their contemporaries in the rest of the EU were enjoying the comfort of concessions and protective policies galore, our poor buggers were being dumped on by Blair's lot. I felt this urban-biased Government really didn't give a damn about them – especially in the West Country where there were next to no Labour votes to be gained or risked. I believed that the agricultural community was disenfranchised, deserted, being abandoned to dangerous decline without care or concern by New Labour politicians who couldn't see beyond their Islington drawing rooms and had no understanding whatsoever of the devastating impact their neglect was having on our farmers, their wives and their children. These farming families desperately needed a champion – somebody to care about them, to articulate their plight, to stand up for them, speak out for them and fight for them.

I didn't ever make a conscious decision to say that this would be *me* and *my newspaper*. That just evolved. Because in the whole of my long career I don't think I had ever been so convinced of the justice of a cause. The *Western Morning News* started to knock seven shades out of Mr Blair's Government on an almost daily basis.

This obviously did not go unnoticed at the highest level because when I attended a business luncheon in Exeter, to be addressed by the Prime Minister, the famous Alastair Campbell slipped into the (perhaps deliberately) empty seat next to mine and got immediately down to business:

"Why are you giving us such a fuckin' kicking?" he asked me.

"Because you fuckin' deserve it," I replied.

To the background noise of a furious demonstration by local farmers going on outside the hotel, Alastair Campbell listened intently and without interrupting as I rolled out one injustice after another and implored him to raise them with the PM. I don't know if people like me are supposed to say things like this, but speak as you find, I say and I *have* to say that on the evidence of this – admittedly my one and only prolonged encounter with Alastair Campbell – I took to the guy. There was none of the conceit of which he is so often accused and he gave me a very good and fair hearing (not that it did any good, but that's another issue!)

At that time I was being followed everywhere by a TV film crew – having again volunteered to be the subject of a documentary, this time in *six* half-hour episodes for *ITV Westcountry* and I'll never know whether it was due to their presence or because I had impressed him with my impassioned pleadings over lunch but on this same Prime Ministerial visit, Alastair Campbell facilitated an exclusive 20-minute interview with Tony Blair for me (that didn't do any good either – but at least I got to make the case!)

My campaigning on our farmers' behalf led to an invitation from the local *National Farmers Union* to speak at a rally which was being staged in Bournemouth prior to a protest march to the Labour Party Conference. There were going to be hundreds – possibly thousands – of farmers there from all over Britain. I was very honoured to be asked to address them and willingly agreed but when the *national* NFU got to hear about it they intervened to stop me speaking. They said it was because there were "too many speakers" and it might well have been no more significant than that. But the local lads were having none of that! Convinced I'd been gagged because of what I might say about the Government, they issued a furious Press Release and prompted a row within the NFU.

I had arranged to go on the march – and not just for journalistic interest. I wanted to *join* this protest. As I waited, with our Farming Editor Carol Trewin and photographer Richard Austin along with hundreds of others assembling to start the march, Richard tugged at my sleeve and pointed across to a group of men who had just got off a coach. They were from Devon NFU and they'd unfurled a huge banner saying: "BARRIE WILLIAMS SUPPORTS OUR FARMERS – WHY CAN'T YOU MR BLAIR?"

I was sincerely flattered and moved but at the same time a bit embarrassed by this gesture. I imagined everybody looking at that banner asking: "Who the bloody hell is Barrie Williams?"

The Devon contingent then asked me to join them on the march and as I strode out along the streets of Bournemouth with them in a defiant parade, led by a huge, handsome Devon Ruby bull, I felt immensely proud and genuinely privileged to be at their side.

Outside the Conference Centre it all got a bit nasty as a bunch of more hot-headed protesters charged the barricades in an attempt to get inside. At this stage, the police moved us on with, to say the least, not much ceremony! I thought: "What a great story if the Editor gets arrested." After the march I sat on a wall while the Devon contingent talked through all their grievances with me. This was filmed for the

TV documentary and I was so pleased about that because there was so little television time being given to the plight and protest of farmers nationally. It seemed that the national media was as ignorant and uncaring about all this as the government.

Just as we finished filming, I heard my name being shouted from across the street. "Barrie! Over here..." It was Labour MP Paddy Tipping, one of Nottinghamshire's finest and among my staunchest allies in frequent battles against the Tory Government when I edited the *Nottingham Evening Post*. "You bugger!" joked Paddy. "I thought you were on *our* side." Then he added, "Where were this lot when the *miners* needed support?"

"Oh Christ Paddy, does it *have* to be so black and white?" I asked him. "These guys are desperate."

Later I received a formal invitation from the South West Region NFU to be the guest speaker at their Annual General Meeting. They wanted me to deliver the speech that I *would* have delivered at the Bournemouth rally if I had not been prevented from doing so. No problem. I'd gladly do that. And in the packed hall in Exeter, I was given a standing ovation. Later, I was presented with a lovely wooden plaque by Devon NFU. The hand-carved inscription says: *Presented to Barrie Williams with thanks for his support for South West farmers.* Never had I felt so close to my readers. I was now so emotionally and deeply involved in this cause. And I couldn't know it – but I'd seen nothing yet...

Back at *The Ship* Andy Gough had started to talk of an "exciting" plan to make *Westcountry Publications* the exemplar of the *Northcliffe* empire. We were going to break the mould, do things differently, find new, more efficient and cost effective ways of running our business. We were embarking upon a management project which, upon successful completion, would provide a revolutionary blueprint which would then be rolled out for a brave new dawn across the whole of *Northcliffe Newspapers*.

Oh, shit! I'd been here before. This was Jargon Land. Nottingham 1993 all over again. The same sort of corporate cobblers I'd had to endure during my last two years as a Director of *T. Bailey Forman Ltd.* Dreadful *déjà vu!* Especially when Andy told me that in producing our master plan we would be working for a year with a business consultant who would guide us through new processes and lead us on a mission to make us better directors while identifying improved procedures to make our business leaner and fitter.

"Andy!" I implored him. "Stop there. It's *all* bullshit!"

"No it's not," said Andy, looking slightly hurt.

"Trust me, mate. I've been there. The emperor's got bloody goosepimples! At best, you'll create an expectation throughout our entire workforce which we will not, in practice, be able to meet. At worst you'll drown us all in a quagmire of jargon."

"No way," said Andy. "That's just the typical reaction of a cynical journalist."

Whichever of us was right, *he* was the Managing Director and he deserved my support so in next to no time, I was going through it all over again. Hour after hour, day after day, sitting in draughty second rate country houses miles from anywhere playing business games and contemplating our characters, testing the quality of our interaction, examining the consequences of our relationships, analysing how we saw each other, how our staff saw us and how we related to them. Basically, all the same business tests and exercises that I'd done before – just brought up to date and tweaked here and there.

There was even another time-management session (hopelessly inappropriate to a totally unpredictable newsroom environment, by the way) though, this time, I didn't cancel the conference!

In fairness, the consultant we were working with – called Simon something-or-other – was a very good bloke with a great sense of humour and a laid-back, self-deprecating style. Simon was intelligent, articulate and very likeable. This made it all more than tolerable and I was determined not to let my scepticism spoil things for him or for Andy Gough, who I regarded as a bloody good managing director and of whom I was genuinely fond.

So this time I tried much harder and when Simon got away from the nebulous business theory and led us in concentrating intensely and methodically on the specifics of what we were doing and where we going with this particular company I even started to amend my view of consultants... *slightly!*

Simultaneously, another firm of consultants – the sort we used to call 'time-and-motion men' – were examining our West Country business, digging into our headcounts, our routines and our procedures, even though they had not the foggiest idea how a newspaper operated. As ever in such exercises, it soon became clear that the project would mean *redundancies* and *economies of scale* and *synergies*. But the work we were doing with our consultant Simon **was** producing some innovative thinking and I had to confess to Andy over a pint one night that even I could see some excellent points in the blueprint we were preparing.

But while all this was going on, a huge disaster was about to hit the West Country...

On March 2nd, 2001 my Farming Editor, Carol Trewin, rang me with devastating news: *Foot and Mouth Disease* had struck in Devon.

You have to live in a farming community to know the gut-wrenching fear those three little words "Foot and Mouth" strike into rural hearts. It's indescribable. In the months that followed the West Country witnessed scenes of medieval carnage and cruelty inflicted upon the animal population on which it depends so heavily as a Government which was totally unprepared for this crisis and hopelessly unsuited to deal with it lurched from one stupid decision to another, causing suffering, misery and heartache on a massive scale.

The Western Morning News was in the middle of all that – doing its best to support our farming communities which were already in severe difficulties and were now brought callously to their knees.

Day after day, week after week *Foot and Mouth* dominated our newspaper. There was no other issue that mattered. No other story that anybody cared about. We published millions of words and hundreds of pictures and narrating all that retrospectively in manageable proportions is impossible.

However, I tried to encapsulate and articulate it as well as I could two years later when I was asked to address a national conference to explore the social and cultural impact of the disaster.

The conference was organised through the Economic and Social Research Council and its title was **Caught Between Science and Society.** And this is what I told that conference…

> "The sense of shock that swept through the West Country on that mockingly sunny morning when Foot and Mouth disease was confirmed at Highampton in North Devon was palpable.
>
> The news from Essex three days earlier had been frightening.
>
> We had breathed a collective sigh of relief when it emerged that the source of the virus was a farm on Hadrian's Wall, just about as far away from Devon and Cornwall as you can get and still be in England. And then this hammer blow.
>
> It could not have been worse. Already severely debilitated by the horrors of BSE and by four years of economic attrition, the most vulnerable region in England had been struck at its weakest point. If ever an event was truly traumatic, this was it. It was as if the entire community had gone into shock.
>
> Even in towns and cities like Exeter, normal life was for a time suspended. Shops and pubs were deserted. Out in the country, schools closed, disinfectant supplies ran out and farming families barricaded their gates, cutting themselves off from the world.
>
> For day after day, week after week nothing else mattered. Foot and Mouth was all-pervasive; interest in it all consuming. As the epidemic unfolded its every twist and turn was followed by a West Country public which was as hungry for information as it was thirsty for comment.

It was the job of the *Western Morning News* to provide both. The sickening slaughter, the huge choking pyres polluting our air and turning our blue skies black with acrid, nauseating smoke; the obscene piles of putrid dead bodies left to rot and stink for weeks because disposal could not keep pace with the rampant killing, the self-serving politics, the questionable science, the bungling, the protests, the fatal impact on businesses and tourism, the injustice, the lies, the human courage and the animal suffering – all were recorded in detail, analysed at length and debated in depth in our pages.

In its coverage of the crisis the *Western Morning News* spoke out for the community. In its Green Wellie Campaign – a fund raising effort to help stricken farmers and their families, **which raised an amazing £1million**, the *Western Morning News* united the community.

Our newspaper was truly in the eye of a storm the like of which had never before been experienced in the West Country; the like of which, pray God, we will never experience again.

In the early days of the disaster the *Western Morning News* was an essential source of information – a commodity which was painfully and shamefully unforthcoming from a Government which took more than a month to wake up to the seriousness of the situation. "It's available on our website," the MAFF spokesmen would say – in urban ignorance of the fact that there were hundreds of vulnerable remotely located farmers who did not even have TV sets, let alone internet access.

In the midst of the disaster the *Western Morning News* was the voice of the West Country agricultural community and the friend it so cruelly lacked in the corridors of power. In the aftermath of the disaster the *Western Morning News* was the champion of the community – battling through the courts in an unsuccessful attempt to force the Government to be called to account for its ham – fisted bungling of the crisis through a proper, open, full public inquiry which, to its enduring shame, it evaded cynically and callously.

Throughout it all, our newspaper was able, in a unique way from its unique position to observe closely the social impact of this dreadful plague. We set up a hotline for people to call and our columns were an outlet for their feelings – feelings of isolation, of desolation, of helplessness and above all of anger over the way the epidemic was being handled…particularly the politically and selfishly motivated, unnecessary and unbelievably cruel contiguous cull policy.

One young farmer's wife sent us her *Diary Of A Stricken Farm*. It is at once a distressing but illuminating, even uplifting, account of a family's tragedy when Foot and Mouth had robbed them not only of their livelihood but of their freedom. It is also a testament to the way in which rural communities will rally to each other's plight in such hours of desperate need.

If I may, I'll read a few passages from that diary….

"As we sit here, two days into slaughter, confined to barracks, the reality of this has hit us like a bolt out of the blue. With carcass upon

carcass mounting up in the sheds the stench started within 24 hours of the first slaughter taking place. My memories of that first day will stay with me for ever. My husband phoning in tears to say they were about to start the killing. Our good friends lifting food for us over the top gate. A deep sense of confinement, unable to hug them as we normally do. The tears that flowed were of temporary relief.

The children and I pushed our wheelbarrow, brimming with food, home in the knowledge that this may be our only supply for the days to come. We felt lucky to have escaped any official warning that may suggest what we were doing was wrong."

Later......

"This is a living hell. As I sit here into the small hours of the morning, unable to rest, the darkness outside is filled with death. A few yards away from where I sit more than 40 pedigree Aberdeen Angus lie dead, sprawled upon each other where they had lain sedated before slaughter. This vision won't move from the forefront of my mind.

We were unable today to get away from the moans and groans of the cows when they were being killed. When their whale – like sounds had stopped the deathly silence was filled with the intermittent pop of a gun. Those poor creatures. Each one my husband knew well.

Only recently he had got up through the night to feed a poorly calf and felt so good that it had survived. Little then did he know this new life would be cut so horribly short.

Our dogs lie quiet outside. There is no work left for them to do now. No more sheep to work; their daily teasing of the cows in the shed is no more. I wonder what they may be thinking. A now haunting silence accompanies the empty fields, a landscape now so void of life."

And later..... .

"Adrian now lies exhausted, mentally, physically and emotionally. Asleep on the sofa next to me, aided only by the alcohol that is needed to calm at this time of night. Although we know this is not the answer to our ever growing problems, at times it takes the edge off the pain we feel. He has to cope not only with the traumas of this horrid disease on a day-to-day basis but with knowing that his beloved father is dying of cancer in a hospice in Cornwall and we can't go and see him as we had planned before this happened."

And at Easter..... .

"Easter Sunday afternoon, the smell now fills every corner of the house and only the burning of oils and joss sticks makes it bearable. In a normal situation, if I had phoned up the environmental health and told them I had 40 decomposing carcasses producing a suffocating stench about 15 yards from our home and my four young children were exposed to this, they would be over straight away but under the circumstances they can be of no help. Compare our Easter with our four children to that of Mr Blair and his four children. The strength we draw from the local village and its people is enormous. I have realised many things through this crisis but the one thing that sticks out is the sheer power of the love humans have for each other. The words of comfort and

---

support, of love and understanding, flow through hour by hour, day af-
ter day.

We have such lovely friends and acquaintances. This makes us feel
extremely privileged people. From the owners of our local post office –
who deserve a medal for the service they give to the community in so
many ways – to the friends who meet us after dark over the top gate with
gifts sent for the children from all sorts of lovely people, to our very close
friends who talk on the phone late into the night, urging us to keep go-
ing. We can't thank them enough."

It became clear that writing to our newspaper, sharing those feelings of despair with the whole community, was cathartic.

All those letters and messages were deeply moving but none
touched us more than a poem we received from a 14-year-old boy
whose father, a farmer on Dartmoor, had just been told his perfectly
healthy animals must die under sentence of the despised contiguous
cull.

William Branfield wrote:

The animals munch on silage and cake
Not knowing of their not so distant fate
On the big fires their corpses will burn
At this thought I weep and turn
On the farm I have lived for most of my days
The animals roamed in their quaint little ways
But now they will be there no more
No cows. No sheep.
Just bare grassy moor.

That little boy's spontaneous poem moved normally cynical journalists to tears when I read it to them.

We published the poem on our front page, with a picture of William
and his dad – who had tears streaming down his face – looking fondly
at their animals and it provoked an amazing response from readers
across our whole territory who wanted desperately to help.

Young William's poem was the catalyst for our Green Wellie campaign to raise funds for stricken farmers and their families.

There was well-spun misconception on two crucial counts:

That farmers in general had brought this plague upon themselves
through bad husbandry and that, despite their own culpability, they
were all being very well compensated so there was no financial hardship.

This was either wilful deception by government to ensure that a
gullible public remained mis-informed or another example of urban
politicians being hopelessly out of touch with rural reality, **but it was
simply not true.**

It conveniently overlooked the fact that at that time it was not just
the farms which became infected with Foot and Mouth disease which
were unable to work, unable to move animals, unable to function, un-

able to make money to put food on the table – but hundreds more bound strictly by the Government's draconian movement restrictions and the enforced closure of markets.

(Those movement restrictions also caused severe animal welfare problems and led to much suffering, particularly among new born lambs drowning in fields which had become seas of mud)

That's why we launched the *Western Morning News'* Green Wellie fund. Modelled unashamedly on Red Nose Day, I introduced Green Wellie Day. Our cartoonist created a wonderful logo – a green wellie with a pair of doleful cow's eyes – and that symbol became as prominent in the West Country as Comic Relief's famous Red Nose.

The campaign united urban and rural communities in a phenomenal fund raising effort. Businesses, schools, offices, supermarkets – all rallied to the cause. Green wellies to be filled with cash appeared on the counters of shops, on the bars of pubs, in car parks and churches.

There were sponsored events and on Green Wellie Day itself people went to work in their offices and shops wearing green wellies and demanding donations from their workmates. Even *ITV Westcountry's* newsreaders joined in – closing their main evening bulletin by lifting their feet up onto their desk to reveal two splendid pairs of green wellies!

The total our appeal achieved – £1 million – was a truly amazing sum for a regional newspaper to raise. And every penny of it went immediately and directly to local farming families who needed it most.

Just as our Green Wellie Day united everybody in support and camaraderie so the Government's gratuitous, cruel and self-serving contiguous cull (the so-called ring of fire policy to kill all healthy animals arbitrarily deemed to be in the vicinity of infected farms) united everybody in anger, disgust and condemnation.

Many of us remain convinced to this day that the policy was introduced because the Prime Minister wanted the epidemic brought under control so the imminent General Election would not be impeded or impaired.

There was mass protest from the Westcountry against that evil mass cull, which produced slaughter of biblical proportions, daily scenes of blood stained horror, mountains of decaying corpses in country lanes, heartbreak for farming families and the instant destruction of irreplaceable pedigree herds bred painstakingly over many generations. But all that meant nothing to the urban based and urban biased New Labour politicians who sanctioned it.

I felt that extreme anger personally. And I don't mind admitting to having used my newspaper frequently to express it.

On April 19th, 2001 – under a disturbing picture of a heap of putrid bodies left at a farm gate and the headline THERE ARE NOW 150,000 DEAD ANIMALS ROTTING IN WESTCOUNTRY FIELDS we reported: -

"It's an image that seems to belong to a darker, more primitive age. Yet this was the appalling scene of dead livestock in a West Country field yesterday, a picture repeated countless times as 150,000 carcases now

await disposal. Sheep, cattle and pigs have been slaughtered without graves in a desperate attempt to control the foot and mouth epidemic. Their stinking bodies are becoming a rich habitat for rats and flies as officials struggle to clear the backlog. Now, fears are growing over a possible threat to human health as farmers report slaughtered livestock lying on fields for weeks. And it is believed that another rash of foot and mouth outbreaks could push the figure up towards 250,000 by next week."

Looking back on that, it's impossible to believe that a British Government could have been so foolhardy in its methods and so inept in its application of them. But it happened. And is it any wonder we were so angry?

I expressed that anger, unashamedly and forcibly, in a front page special article on May 24th after a farming family's brave but futile attempt to halt the contiguous culling of their healthy animals had ended in despair.

My article was illustrated by a harrowing picture of the farmer's beautiful daughter, surrounded by police and cattle killers in anonymous white 'space suits.' The lass was crying hysterically. Horror and helplessness were etched on her pretty young face.

This is what I wrote: -

"The sun is shining, the sky is blue, the grass is green and the birds are singing – yet this is the face of misery in the countryside which politicians are doing their utmost to hide from the eyes of the national electorate. Tina Jones breaks down as police tell her that her elderly father's perfectly healthy herd of cattle is going to be killed.

The Winslade family's brave protest, which took them to court and into conflict with the Ministry of Agriculture through a week long stand – off at their farm in Knowstone, Devon ended in heartbreak yesterday when their 60 organic Charolais suckler cows were slaughtered under the Government's hugely controversial 'firebreak' contiguous cull policy.

It is a policy which has been condemned by one of the Government's own top advisers, Dr Alex Donaldson, Director of the Animal Health Institute, who has said it is resulting in the unnecessary slaughter of thousands of animals.

It is a policy which has been condemned by South West regional National Farmers' Union director Anthony Gibson, who says: "The contiguous cull has been exposed for what it is – one of the most bloody, tragic and disgraceful misjudgements ever committed in the name of science.

It is a policy which farmers and farming communities also condemn as aggressive, callous, inhumane and unnecessary.

Yet it is a policy from which the Government refuses to budge as its Ministers tour the country seeking re-election and giving voters the impression that they have beaten the foot and mouth disaster and that everything is getting back to normal in the afflicted countryside areas.

There was nothing normal about the harrowing scene at Knowstone yesterday as three vanloads of police stood by while MAFF prepared to repel the Winslade family's attempt to stop the cull.

It is not the MAFF officials and vets having to enforce this needless mass killing of healthy animals who are to blame – even though they are the people at the sharp end who have to live with the wrath and hatred of the farming communities.

The responsibility for this policy, the heartbreak and economic hardship it is causing, the serious animal welfare issues it is creating and the callous disregard for the people of the countryside which is at its core, lies squarely with Tony Blair and his Cabinet who decided on this highly contentious course of action before they embarked on their General Election campaign.

The human effect of that policy was epitomised yesterday in the agony and despair of Les Winslade,69, his wife Greta and their daughters Tina and Linda. It is an image that Tony Blair would rather you didn't see.

Surely, no-one outside of Labour Party headquarters can now believe that the Government's handling of the foot and mouth epidemic has been anything other than disastrous. If the disease is "under control" – and with the latest flare- up in the Yorkshire Dales that has got to be in some doubt – then it is no thanks to the work of the Government and in particular the Ministry of Agriculture. They were slow in recognising the magnitude of the outbreak. They prevaricated over calling in the Army. They consistently failed to provide the necessary support to businesses affected by the crisis and they allowed the unburied bodies of animals they had killed to pile up in fields across the West Country, leading to serious public health concerns.

Now, having failed to act decisively in the first few weeks of the outbreak they are using increasingly draconian measures to take out herds and flocks that are almost certainly clear of the disease. There's little doubt that the Government's spin doctors are well aware of just what a disaster their handling of this national emergency has been. That's why, during the election campaign, they have done everything in their power to make it a "non-issue"; to brush it under the carpet while they get on with the job of getting themselves re-elected. And with one or two honourable exceptions the media has fallen for that – leaving the Western Morning News alone in continuing to report the story in any kind of depth and detail.

It is painfully obvious that relations between the rural community and the Government have been severely damaged by this crisis. Those relations were already at rock bottom. Now there must be serious questions over whether the rift can ever be healed.

How, for instance, can the Ministry of Agriculture – or its successor ministry when the election is over – possibly rebuild confidence in its handling of agricultural affairs after the sort of scenes we've witnessed at Knowstone?

*MAFF used a High Court injunction to gain access to Mr Winslade's farm – landing him with a £1500 legal bill when he tried to oppose them. And when he and his daughters manned the barricades in a heart rending but pathetic attempt to try to stop the slaughtermen coming in with their guns they found themselves subjected to the presence of **three vanloads** of police officers. Did they think they were dealing with Bonnie and Clyde? Is this the face of the countryside in 21ˢᵗ century Britain? The full might of the Constabulary and a government Ministry deployed against a frail elderly farmer, his wife and daughters in order to kill their cows? And all that when by any common sense judgment those animals do not need to die anyway?*

So many people who know what they are talking about regard this contiguous cull policy as outrageous. Most people – even Labour supporters – must surely agree that scenes like those we saw at the Winslades' farm yesterday reflect very badly indeed on the Government. And most people must surely agree that this disgraceful, discredited policy cannot be allowed to continue.

*What does Tony Blair **really** think about the continuing crisis in our countryside?*

What do William Hague and Charles Kennedy think about it?

*As all three party leaders criss-cross the country in their election battle buses trying to whip up enthusiasm for their policies from a largely apathetic electorate, what do **any** of them understand of the life – or – death, bankruptcy or survival issues that real people in rural areas like our own are battling with every day? Not much, most country folk would say.*

David Hill, NFU chairman for Devon, asks in an article in today's WMN: - "Has the contiguous cull been an essential tool to combat a virulent disease or the most offensive and cynical use of political will to achieve the background for an election campaign?"

*The true answer to that crucial question can only be found if there is a full, searching, **transparently independent** public inquiry into this whole affair as soon as the election is over and done with. For every country dweller – and particularly those in Devon and Cumbria who have suffered most severely from this heinous plague – such an inquiry is a human right and it is now absolutely imperative that we are given that right."*

That public inquiry never came. The Government set up three so-called inquiries under its own control with very limited parameters and the reports of all three were predictably insipid. None of them had the power to call members of the Government to give evidence and to be cross examined on behalf of their accusers. I was asked to give evidence – in private – to one of those tame inquiries. It won't surprise you to know that I didn't pull my punches but how much of what I had to say got through to those who should have heard it? It certainly did not appear in the published report! The whole neutered "inquiry" ritual was nothing more than a shameful white-wash, cynically designed to look like an open, democratic process of accountability. And most of the urban-biased national media – and as a consequence most of the British public – swallowed it like the placebo it was always intended to be.

But the West Country communities which had borne the brunt of the disaster, suffered the Government's incompetence and seen through its deceit, knew better. They will never forgive and they will never forget and *Foot and Mouth 2001* has built a barricade of deeply scarred emotion between Government and people in those rural communities akin to that which followed Margaret Thatcher's decimation of the coal industry and its mining villages back in the 1980s. And just as residual resentment over that is going to be handed down from generation to generation in what used to be our mining villages so future generations of West Country children will grow up with the legacy of the evils perpetrated upon *their* forebears in 2001.

It's another thesis entirely, but does this Government really want a British agricultural industry or would it be quite content to let it go under and feed us from Europe?

So was there any bright light among all the gloom, anger and deep bitterness of the foot and mouth experience?

Well, yes. There was... It taught our rural communities that they can never expect anything better from a Government which is at best indifferent and at worst downright hostile towards a section of the electorate in which there never had been and never will be any significant Labour votes. That stark realisation has induced a fierce resolve never to be beaten and to stand together in self-determination and self-help.

The countryside has picked itself up, dusted itself off and is doing its very best to start all over again... knowing from bitter experience that in so doing it is on its own."

Among the other speakers at the two-day conference at which I delivered that speech were two lawyers from Cumbria who made a powerful, thoroughly researched and well-conducted case that the contiguous cull had been illegal. Nothing came of that – even though the *Western Morning News* reported that the Government had been forced to admit that 200,000 animals had been unnecessarily slaughtered because of errors in foot and mouth tests...

My London Editor Jason Groves revealed that 600 farms had had all their livestock killed because foot and mouth had been suspected on a neighbouring farm only for that suspicion to be later disproved.

Devon had suffered more than any other county. We'd had 9,551 perfectly healthy cattle and 44.176 perfectly healthy sheep killed for no reason at all. This strengthened even further the mass of calls for a full and proper public inquiry and when Tony Blair finally and irrevocably announced that we were not going to get one I wrote a steaming front page *Comment* attacking the Government for running away and hiding from its demonstrable responsibilities for the whole foot and mouth fiasco. My article accused Tony Blair of cowardice for avoiding a proper public inquiry (subsequent controversial events in Iraq were to prove that while the Prime Minister might have had several failings, being a coward was certainly **not** one of them. But that's another story and the charge seemed to me to be entirely appropriate and justified at the time!)

Our front page grabbed the attention of *ITV Westcountry* and I was invited into their studio to explain my outburst live on their lunchtime news programme. After I had done so with great gusto, the presenter announced that they were then going over to Conservative Party leader Iain Duncan Smith, who was on an official visit to the West Country...

Reporter: "Do YOU think the Prime Minister is a coward for not having a public inquiry into the foot and mouth epidemic?"

Duncan Smith: "I'm not going to use the sort of emotive language we've read in the newspaper..."

At which the presenter turned to me, still live on air back in the studio and barked: "There you are – not even the leader of the Opposition agrees with you!"

Those subsequently asking me what I thought of Mr Duncan Smith as Opposition Leader were well advised to stand back!

I was – and so was almost everybody else in the West Country – so totally and utterly convinced of the justice of the case for a full public inquiry that, along with *Farmers' Weekly* and the *Cumberland News*, the *Western Morning News* backed and contributed financially towards a bid to force one through judicial review.

That didn't work either. And the buggers got away with it.

At the height of the foot and mouth disaster I made an unlikely but subsequently invaluable and much appreciated friend and ally in countryside campaigning... Eminent TV star and supremely successful businessman Noel Edmonds lived on his estate at Jacobstowe in Devon – which was at the epi-centre of the tragedy. I knew all about Noel's West Country connections, but I didn't know that he was an avid reader of my newspaper until on March 14th 2001, after one of my thundering Page One comment articles, Noel wrote privately to me and said:

"Absolutely bloody right! Twice within just four days you have produced powerful front pages and you and your team are to be congratulated upon capturing the mood within our community.

Tears and anger will prove to be a dangerous mix for this Government in the months ahead. Lord knows where this plague will take us and when it will all be finished but I and my family will never ever forget the sense of utter desperation that is spreading around this land which we love.

William Branfield's poem moved me to tears – I have framed it and also Monday's Page One Comment. Please God one day I shall look at them and these dark days will be no more than a distant memory.

I just wanted you to know how much your editorial stance and the quality of your journalism is currently being appreciated by the people around Hatherleigh and Jacobstowe."

I appreciated that so much – and I rang Noel to tell him so.

Later, on Green Wellie Day, Noel had his cherished beard shaved off in a local pub. He'd had the beard for years – his 18-year-old daughter Charlotte told GMTV, which filmed the event and thus gave the appeal priceless national publicity, that she had never seen him without it! Noel's Shave-Off raised more than £6,000 for our appeal fund. His letter had led to a friendship between us that endures to this day and we've done much campaigning on countryside issues together. He's a top man, Noel. Genuine and caring. And it really pisses me off when I read gratuitous ill-informed attacks on him written by Fleet Street smart-arses who aren't fit to lace his shoes.

While its horrendous mis-handling of the foot and mouth epidemic was by far its worst offence there had been other Government policies and attitudes in the first couple of years of the new millennium which were detrimental to the West Country.... the wholesale closure of village post offices which meant nothing in London but was the loss of a lifeline for rural pensioners; escalating fuel costs, which were forcing many rural businesses to close; over-zealous application of EU regulations (ignored by all the other EU governments!) which was driving our fishing industry to the brink of extinction; the virtual disappearance of rural public transport... all combined to add grist to our campaigning mill.

There were other huge issues which could not fairly be laid at the Government's door but were equally important... like the demise of Cornwall's tin mining industry (the day the men on the last shift at the last mine to close, South Crofty, came to the surface with tears streaming down their grimy faces I produced one of my best ever emotive front pages); like the generally parlous state of the Cornish economy, its low pay and high unemployment and the campaign for

EU Objective One status which would bring £500 million to do something about it; like the massive rise in house prices – pushing the cost of a home way above what West Country youngsters could afford... which all helped to keep the *Western Morning News* heavily opinionated.

Then there was the iniquity of the situation in which already hard – up West Country residents, including poor pensioners, were being forced to pay the highest water rates in the UK (and still are!) so that holidaymakers could enjoy clean sea water and safe beaches. Desperately unfair. And boy, did we say so!

There were good, positive campaigns, too – like the one in which, in a matter of months, our readers raised £45,000 to buy fuel for our lifeboats for a whole year.

Then in December 2002 came a singular honour. I was invited to become, gladly accepted and was duly installed as President of the Devonshire Association. For an incomer to be granted this accolade was rare indeed and previous incumbents, since this highly prestigious association was founded "for the furtherance of literature, the arts and science in the county of Devonshire" way back in 1862, had included barons, earls and knights of the realm. I was now such an experienced public speaker that few engagements fazed me but performing a *Presidential Address* in front of such an august body of professional men and women from all over Devon was a tad daunting, to say the least.

No silly headlines, cock-ups and dirty jokes for this lot! This had to be a cerebral speech of substance and passion and it had to reflect the history and time honoured status of the association.

Homework duly done, words polished, the ancient chain of office ("Please don't lose it, Mr Williams, it's worth a fortune") around my shoulders, my *Presidential Address,* delivered in a big civic hall in Plymouth packed with Devonshire Association members, went like this...

Ladies and gentlemen,

It is interesting to learn that your organisation dates from the entrepreneurial days of Victorian England because so does my newspaper. The Devonshire Association was founded in 1862. The *Western Morning News* was launched in 1860 and would almost certainly have reported the birth of your association. Like your own organisation, the *Western Morning News* has been part of the fabric of Devonshire life for nearly 150 years. The story of the *Western Morning News* began in the late 1850s when two young men, brothers -in -law Edward Spender and William Saunders arrived in Plymouth from Bath looking for business opportunities. Spender, born in 1833, was a surgeon's son from a comfortable middle – class background. He was a sensitive young man with literary aspirations who regularly contributed to newspapers and magazines.

By contrast, his brother – in – law Saunders was a far more down to earth character. Born in 1823 – and therefore ten years older than his young business associate – he was married to Spender's sister, Caroline. One thing the two did have in common, however, was that both were fervent teetotallers…a virtue not shared by the present editor!

It was to the Three Towns (as Plymouth, Devonport and Stonehouse were then collectively known) that the pair came from their native Bath to seek business opportunities. After considering various schemes, including a china clay works, the young adventurers eventually settled for the idea of publishing a daily morning newspaper – which would be the first in the West Country.

In the early planning stages they sought the advice of local librarian William Hunt. He was an experienced journalist who, among many other jobs, had been employed by Charles Dickens as a local correspondent for the *Daily News*, which the great man had founded and edited. A former secretary to the Earl of Mount Edgumbe, Hunt at that time was a librarian at Plymouth Library. Another who joined in the early discussions was Alfred Rooker, a solicitor, who later became Mayor of Plymouth. .

In the late 1850s, the Three Towns were served only by weekly newspapers, including the *Plymouth and Devonport Journal*, which dated from 1819. The *Journal* was owned and edited by Isaac Latimer. A friend of Charles Dickens, Latimer had moved to Plymouth from London in 1844. The *Journal* was a Liberal newspaper while another local weekly the *Plymouth Mail* – edited by poet and novelist Mortimer Collins, championed the Conservative cause.

The two newspapers were often at editorial loggerheads and, initially at least, the feuding had some entertainment value for the readers but the row eventually descended into personal attacks and at one stage, after a particularly snide barb in print by Collins, Latimer responded by publishing a complete list of Collins' personal debts and court summonses. The public soon became disenchanted with the sniping and William Hunt, writing in 1887, told how "the persistent bickering were very distressing to thoughtful, influential and public-spirited Plymothians."

Another good reason for Spender and Saunders to suppose that a daily newspaper would be successful was that Parliament had recently abolished the so-called "taxes on knowledge" which heavily penalised newspapers. Almost immediately, in 1855, the *Daily Telegraph* had started up in London, taking its name and its news service from the new invention of telegraphy. That year, also, the weekly *Manchester Guardian* turned into a daily – the first in the provinces. By 1859 five of the six largest provincial conurbations in England had daily newspapers, while the Three Towns were still bereft. Another good omen was that transport was really beginning to open up. In May of that year, the main railway line between Plymouth and Truro had been completed, with the opening of the Royal Albert Bridge at Saltash linking Devon and Cornwall. The Tavistock and South Devon line also opened up from Plymouth. There were many plans under way to extend the railways – all eagerly anticipated by businessmen. Plymouth, then the sixth most important port in England, was a bustling, commercial town with all kinds of new factories opening. Spender and Saunders are said to have been greatly encouraged by the fact that the rapid development of rail travel meant that you could now get from Plymouth to London in thee and a half hours (last week – 142 years of "progress" later – it took me FOUR and a half hours!)

Politically, at Westminster the short-lived Tory government had collapsed after barely a year and Palmerston, the MP for Tiverton in Devon since 1935, was back in Downing Street at the age of 65 with a coalition of left wing Tories and the old Whigs.

It was a world in which executions at county jails were still held in public, sailing ships dominated trade routes and the navy sailed fully rigged ships. The steam yard at Devonport – built to deal with the new fangled steam ships – had only been opened in 1854.

It was an exciting time of new ideas, new inventions, new achievements, new methods of transport – and new means of communication. And people in the West Country wanted to read all about it – **fast.**

Spender and Saunders sensed that here was a real niche in the newspaper market. People now wanted their news daily and they wanted it early. They didn't want to wait until 5pm, when *The Times* (which cost an exorbitant 5d) and the other London papers arrived.

They therefore set about planning a new morning newspaper which would be politically independent and on West Country breakfast tables a good 12 hours before the London nationals arrived by train from the capital.

The first issue of the *Western Morning News* was published on January 3rd 1860 and cost one penny. Its first Editor, Edward Spender, was just 26 years old. It was a four-page broadsheet newspaper measuring, according to the copy held at the British Library, 69 centimetres by 44 centimetres (roughly 27 inches high by 17 inches wide) with six columns to a page. As with all newspapers of that time the front page was given up to advertisements – news was not to appear on Page One regularly until 1949. From the very first, the *Western Morning News* was designed to serve the whole of the West Country.

The stories in that first issue included:

*   *A drunken husband who violently assaulted his wife with an iron bar then hit an intervening police officer with a coal shovel.*

*   *A boy of 10 who was sentenced to seven days in prison with a good whipping – for stealing a "magic lantern."*

*   *A 64-year-old man who – having killed his wife – just dumped her in her night clothes outside their own front door.*

And they may prompt you to conclude that more than 140 years later we haven't made much progress in reducing crime!

Incredibly, in the 142 years that have followed, the *Western Morning News* has had only *eleven* editors. I am the eleventh – and to me, that is a very great honour and privilege.

The first editor, Edward Spender, died while still a very young man. He drowned trying to rescue his two sons who had got into difficulties while swimming off Whitsand Bay in south east Cornwall. All three died – and a stone cross memorial to them still stands looking out to sea over the spot where they perished.

I discovered only recently that, as the crow flies, that memorial is only a mile or so from my house – indeed we look out over that same peninsula – and when you think that I could have bought a house anywhere in the vast West Country region that's a bit spooky, isn't it?

So, the *Western Morning News* in 2002 remains a prestigious regional morning newspaper, still beating the London nationals on late breaking news stories and still adhering to Edward Spender's fiercely independent editorial philosophy.

I have edited the newspaper through one of the most turbulent and troubled periods of Westcountry history. I moved here from Nottingham seven years ago and what I knew about farming could have been written on **half** of the back of a postage stamp. I thought a Devon Ruby was a country lady of ill repute!

Most of my career had been spent in big city environments and from that urban background I found myself thrown in at the deep end of a rapidly escalating agricultural crisis editing a newspaper with a predominantly rural readership, many of whom are farmers.

It was a steep learning curve. What I know about farming now can be written on the **whole** of the back of a postage stamp!

But what I **do** know about, after many years plying my trade as a journalist, is justice. What I **do** have is an inherent sense of fair play and I am deeply offended by injustice in any form. That emotion knows no urban/rural divide. It took only a matter of months down here for me to realise that the agricultural industry in general and the small to medium-sized livestock farming businesses which predominate in the West Country in particular, were being treated diabolically by government at a time when there were so many problems beyond their own control afflicting farmers that what they needed was help, support and understanding.

Then came the unspeakable horrors of the foot and mouth disease disaster and the shameful way in which it was mis-managed by the Government and its henchmen and callously and cynically misrepresented by New Labour politicians

In Nottinghamshire, I had witnessed a Tory government, through a mixture of deliberate political intent, indifference and ignorance, presiding over the death of our coal industry and the disgusting decimation and demise of our proud mining communities.

Now, in the West Country, I was getting a chilling sense of *deja-vu*. Was I, in the West Country, now about to witness a Labour government, through a mixture of deliberate political intent, indifference and ignorance, presiding over the death of our agricultural industry and the disgusting decimation and demise of our proud farming communities?

Not if I could help it. Not if my newspaper and its marvellous team of journalists could do anything to try to stop it. That is what has driven me, my journalists and my newspaper through this unprecedented period of turbulence, trouble and strife in rural life.

When you are arguing with national politicians, there is never any substitute for personal experience and my wife Pauline and I are privileged to live next to a dairy farmer and his family. They are a lovely, proud, hardworking and uncomplaining farming family – typical of so many in Devon and Cornwall. While I was hearing all the craftily spun political clap-trap about whingeing farmers, with plenty of money, hooked on subsidies, expecting the Government to do everything for them, I was watching this exceptionally hard-working family, putting in all the hours God sends, soldiering on through the exhaustion barrier and through the night, battling against massive and ever worsening odds with never a word of self-pity – just to make a living and to maintain the farm which is their heritage and their consuming passion.

To hear smug, slick-suited, self-serving, superficial and ignorant, urban MPs sniping and sneering publicly and remorselessly at brave, undemanding farming families like these filled me with an anger so intense that I find it difficult to articulate.

The eldest boy in that family, which we are proud to call our neighbours, wants no more than to eventually take over that farm from his dad – just as **he** did from **his** father – and to continue the family's farming heritage and self-sufficient work ethic. To deprive him of that birthright through no fault of his own or his parents would be the greatest of injustices. But that's just what's happening to farming families all over the West Country.

The average age of farmers in Devon is now 58 and rising. New blood is essential – not just to the future of food production but to the very fabric of rural life as we know, love and cherish it. That future is in the hands of the young people of Devon and hundreds like them all over rural Britain.

It is tremendously encouraging to those, like me, who believe that there is now a vital mission to be accomplished in our beloved countryside that there are – despite all the trials and tribulations besetting and bashing this crucial industry – lots of committed youngsters who want to do it.

These committed young people want to do it without subsidies – and let's remind everybody that, despite what politicians would have us all believe, **governments** introduced and maintain subsidy systems – **not farmers!**

These committed young people want to do it fully equipped with finely tuned business, communications and IT skills. And above all, they want to do it on a level playing field and on equal terms with their foreign competitors – a basic right of fair play of which their parents have been cruelly, cynically and shamefully deprived.

That's not too much to ask is it?

There is one area of Government thinking with which I *do* agree – and that is that the modern farmer should be a land manager, paid for the essential task of managing and maintaining our countryside while at the same time producing food and being engaged profitably in diversified rural business activities. That makes sense – and would banish forever the unfair and largely inaccurate tag of the "subsidy junkie". On this, the Government is starting to make the right noises by suggesting it wants to switch traditional support payments to initiatives which have a public and/or environmental benefit. That surely has to be the right way – but while supporting the Government in that resolve, we should also urge caution and patience. In New Zealand in 1984 they went "cold turkey" on subsidies and that caused irreparable damage. We simply cannot stand another body blow.

So, the proud and ambitious young people of rural Devon are not afraid of the future. They **are** prepared to work in a different way. They **know** that food production is going to have to change. They **know** that the food producer of the future is going to need more control over what happens to that food; that it will no longer be enough just to leave it at the farm gate. They **know** that the challenge which lies ahead of them is an enormous one. And it is the duty of everybody who lives in this beautiful county and wants it preserved in the way we know and love it to help them meet that challenge. How?

Well, for a start we can all insist on buying and consuming **local** produce. Let's be unashamedly chauvinistic about that because if enough of us do it we can make a massive difference.

The *Western Morning News* is running a major campaign to persuade people to buy local. At a recent summit meeting we called together all the existing food promotion agencies, producers, distributors, retailers – including, encouragingly, one national supermarket chain – to pool all existing efforts together in one big concerted coalition campaign so that we can hopefully achieve a huge impact on the amount of local produce bought and consumed locally in the West Country.

We hope to involve not just individual consumers, vitally important though they are, but businesses, local authorities and schools. In short, a huge effort unprecedented in its scale and reach. "Accept no substitutes" we are saying. "**Insist** on local produce" – in supermarkets, shops and restaurants; on canteen menus at work; in your local pub. And if it's not local – leave it on the shelf until they get the message. .

I implore you all to join in our campaign and get all your friends and family to do the same. The only cauliflower available to buy in my local supermarket last week was German. Yet I look out from my bedroom window at fields full of them, while Westcountry farmers are leaving their industry in droves; many more are going bankrupt and suicides are at an all time high because they can't make ends meet. Has the world gone mad?

The next time you're in a supermarket, check out the shelves. Find the local produce and if you can't (and you probably won't) find the manager instead and tell him: "Your cauliflowers are from Germany; your carrots are from Spain; your apples are from France; your beans are from Kenya; your lamb is from New Zealand; your beef is from Argentina. I'm FROM DEVON. I'm IN DEVON. And this bloody basket is staying empty!"

We can *all* make a difference. If the population of Devon does not believe passionately in a successful future for agriculture and if we are not prepared to fight with every bone in our bodies to secure that future, we are not only betraying our optimistic young people, who are prepared to devote their lives ahead to it, we are betraying ourselves, we are betraying the West Country and we are betraying rural Britain.

Let's not do that.

Recently, I was very privileged to be invited to give the keynote address and present the awards at Bicton Agricultural College's graduation ceremony. Because of the horrors that Devon had been through with foot and mouth disease and as an act of defiance, they decided to combine the graduation ceremony with a service of celebration for farming and the event was staged, not at the college as usual but in the grandeur and serenity of Exeter Cathedral... which was absolutely packed out with people who wanted to demonstrate sympathy with the sentiments.

This was one of the most moving experiences of my life. Those youngsters and their families were so brave, so defiant and above all, so optimistic about the future, despite all they had been through.

One of my favourite songs is *The Greatest Love Of All*.

After the horrors of BSE and foot and mouth disease; in the wake of arguably the worst decade in the history of Devon farming and in the context of the recovery which our young people symbolise so positively and hopefully, there cannot be a more appropriate sentiment than a verse from that song.

So I read it out that night in Exeter Cathedral.

It goes:

I believe the children are our future
Teach them well and let them lead the way
Show them all the beauty they possess inside
Give them a sense of pride to make it easier
Let the children's laughter remind us how we used to be

Let the children's laughter remind **us** how **we** used to be.

But first **we** have to help **them**. We have to help them to re-create an environment in Devon which will ensure that laughter is no longer the luxury it has become in the countryside. It is up to each and every one of us to fight for the preservation of this beautiful county the way it is. The way we want it to stay.

Can you even begin to imagine Devon without agriculture and particularly without the dairy industry with which it is internationally synonymous? Can you even begin to imagine the fields of Devon without cows? Yet that very fabric and tradition; yes, even the continued presence of those animals is now under very serious threat.

I grew up in Shropshire and I'm old enough to remember the previous foot and mouth epidemic in 1967 – the eye of the storm of which was in Shropshire, Cheshire and Mid-Wales. The fields of Shropshire used to be just like those here in Devon. But after foot and mouth so many livestock farmers gave up, allowing big companies to come in and gradually buy up all the land that it changed the landscape of much of rural Shropshire forever. Now there are massive, flat, industrial-sized fields running as far into the distance as the eye can see – mile after mile of silent open space yielding Euro crops for the multi – nationals. No hedgerows; no wildlife; no birdsong; no cattle; no sheep. No laughing children.

Let's not allow that to happen to Devon. Let's fight to keep the Devon we love the way we love it for the children – for they **are** our future."

That speech was, according to the report in the annual magazine of the Devonshire Association, "received with acclaim". I know that I had a lump in my throat as big as an apple as the standing ovation its audience gave me went on for several minutes.

Later, I had a letter from Ian Park, Chairman of *Northcliffe Newspapers*, congratulating me on becoming President of the Devonshire Association. Ian wrote:

> *I hope you are pleased by the compliment to your work this represents. To be so elected after only seven years in the South West seems to me a significant recognition. I thought it took a lifetime to belong. As you know I am an admirer of your editorship and your newspaper and I do not believe you were ever better than at the stressful time for Devon that was foot and mouth. Your Presidential Address was moving – and clearly deeply sincere.*
> *Every good wish,*
> *Ian.*

There had been another round of management musical chairs in *Northcliffe* and at *Westcountry Publications*. Alec Davidson had departed – to be replaced as Group Managing Director by a young *DMGT* high flier, Kevin Beatty. The gossipmongers reckoned that Kevin, an ebullient and extremely impressive Irishman, was a Trojan horse – a temporary appointment with a brief to bring the regional wing more under main board control. They were probably right.

Andy Gough was next to go, later to become Managing Director of the *Cambridge Evening News*. His successor was none other than Duncan Currall, the man with whom I'd worked so well in Nottingham. Knowing of our previous relationship, Kevin Beatty asked me to meet Duncan and welcome him to *Westcountry Publications*. It was my pleasure. And that night, over a curry at my favourite Indian restaurant, I found myself marking Duncan's card... for the **second** time in our respective careers. However, this time there was absolutely no doubting Duncan's staying power! Since we had last worked together in Nottingham, more than ten years earlier, Duncan had matured and strengthened considerably. This man was now a top class MD and relishing what was arguably the toughest management job in the *Northcliffe* portfolio.

It took Duncan no time at all to get a grip at *The Ship*. Paramount in his brief, just as it had been with every other incumbent of his new chair for more years than anybody cared to remember, was the hoary old chestnut of trying to make the *Western Morning News* more profitable. Duncan did.

Kevin Beatty and the young Lord Rothermere (Jonathan – in his early 30s – had inherited upon the death of his father) appeared to be quite pleased with the way in which *Westcountry Publications* was being run and we seemed set fair for that most luxurious, rare and elusive of newspaper industry commodities – a period of sustained stability.

Duncan and I spoke the same language. Always had done. I'll wager there's never been a more open, constructive, harmonious and productive relationship between a managing director and an editor than the one we enjoyed. I had no problem with any of the financial constraints under which he placed my department and he had no problem with any of the editorial demands I made of his office. The result was that the *Western Morning News*, slowly and sympathetically, began to produce a better bottom line while I was able to continue to produce an excellent, award winning newspaper playing as prominent a role in its West Country community as ever.

We were producing cracking editorial campaigns, notably against the criminally destructive march of giant wind turbines across the West Country's cherished environment under the demonstrably daft pretence of protecting it (a crusade in which Noel Edmonds played a prominent, powerful, articulate and extraordinarily well-informed role); against the grossly discriminating pricing policy for milk which (as if dairy farmers did not already have more than enough problems) was now costing more per litre to produce than it was bringing in; against the absurd, badly drafted and politically motivated fox hunting ban – another batty and blinkered manifestation of Labour's "revenge for the miners"; against the detrimental dumping of dredged waste from Plymouth naval base into the sea along one of Cornwall's most beautiful and environmentally precious coastlines (*stupid* or what!) and against just about everything that Margaret Beckett said or did! (Mrs Beckett seemed to make an art form of conflict with and neglect of the farming industry whose interests, as Secretary of State she was supposed to represent).

Another campaign which won the hearts of our readers was against speeding drivers on Dartmoor, where there is a 40mph limit, whose selfish behaviour was killing wild ponies by the score. The picture with which we launched our *Take Moor Care* campaign was one of the most emotive I ever saw. It showed a beautiful little white and tan mare very gently prodding the motionless body of her dead foal with her foot as if to say: "PLEASE get up." Her foal had just been hit by a speeding car. That picture was a real heartbreaker and as well as giving it the whole of our front page under the tear-jerking headline *PLEASE DON'T DIE* I also used it for a chilling poster which was displayed prominently across Dartmoor.

The number of ponies killed fell dramatically as a result.

Most prominent and effective was our *Buy Local* campaign, which I launched in the aftermath of the economic ravages of the foot and mouth disaster. This developed a tremendous momentum... more than 500 West Country restaurants and pubs now display the *Western Morning News Jeff Chef* seal of approval (Jeff Chef is a cartoon caricature of a rotund West Country cook and when you see his cheerful countenance in the window you know that establishment serves only local produce). Schools in the West Country adopted our campaign and hundreds of our schoolkids had been pestering the life out of everybody for good, nutritious locally produced food long before Jamie Oliver so brilliantly captured the nation's attention with his own crusade. The *WMN* produced a roll of honour of the best local suppliers, sponsored a competition for young trainee chefs, produced glossy magazines with mouthwatering recipes, all using only local ingredients, staged the UK's biggest farmers' market in Plymouth and launched a search – backed and televised by *ITV Westcountry* – for *The Best Local Food Town In The West* ... and that is by no means to list *all* this campaign's activities.

Among our *Buy Local* campaign's many prominent supporters was the Prince of Wales. Its sentiments and objectives were music to Prince Charles' own campaigning ears and he gave us enthusiastic support from Day One. I became a member of the Prince's *Rural Action Group* – a countryside spin-off of his extremely successful

Business In The Community scheme – and I was honoured when my work for that group led to my receiving an award as HRH's "Ambassador for the West Country" and a beautiful book on the Gardens of Highgrove with a personal inscription recording "*My gratitude*" from the Prince.

These activities led to quite frequent visits to Highgrove, St James Palace and later Clarence House for Rural Action Group leadership team meetings which were, more often than not, hosted and chaired by Prince Charles. This man gets an unjustifiably bad Press. He is extremely intelligent and well-informed – particularly on the rural issues which are so close to his heart – and he *cares* with a passion which is infectious. He seemed always to be genuinely grateful to us for our work and often said thanks with pleasant informal lunches, dinners or receptions at which he would make a point of talking at considerable length to all the group's members – around 16 of us. I never did let the royal presence or the grandeur of the surroundings restrict the bluntness (for which I've always been known!) of my contributions and HRH appeared always to appreciate that. Several of my colleagues looked horrified the evening Charles asked us over dinner for any criticism of how the group was functioning and I told him: "There's not enough cow shit (by which I meant *working farmers*) around this table!" The discomforting embarrassment that induced in some of the dinner guests was immediately quashed by Prince Charles who replied enthusiastically: "I agree with that!"

As well as popping into Charlie's assorted pads for my dinner I was, around this time, also seeing quite a lot of his mum!

During the Queen's Jubilee Year in 2002 I was introduced to Her Majesty on three occasions... which included a splendid and unforgettable reception for selected members of the media at Windsor Castle. Impressive though that was, however, it was nothing compared with the experience of being invited to a private luncheon with the Queen and the Duke of Edinburgh at Buckingham Palace in February, 2003.

I was one of just eight guests. They included Lieutenant General John Reith, Chief of Joint Operations; Professor Mohamed Wahab, Professor of Electronic Engineering at the University of Glamorgan; Lord Watson of Richmond, International Chairman of the English Speaking Union; Jane Sixsmith, the Olympic hockey player ... and my good mate Tim Smit, Chief Executive of the Eden Project.

As lunch appointments go, this one really was different class and as I crunched my way over those pristine pebbles (which most of the rest of the world only gets to see on TV or through the railings of Buckingham Palace) to keep it, I realised that this was truly something special. Yet – and this is surely a tribute to everybody concerned, not least the Queen and the Duke themselves – at no stage of the proceedings did I feel anything other than completely at ease. It sounds like a joke, but those world-famous corgis and dachshunds (and "dorgies" – the product of some incestuous over-familiarity between the two!) really did play around our feet as the Royal hosts chatted away to their guests for half an hour before lunch was served.

The Queen has the most gorgeous sparkling eyes, which entrance you. She also has a sense of humour almost (but not quite!) as wicked as her husband's and the ability to make you feel that sharing a conservation with her is just a normal occurrence. The Queen and the Duke both put you so much at ease that it was only when we walked into the dining room and I saw the magnificent gold cutlery laid out on a huge table which shone like a mirror that it really sunk in. Bloody hell! I and just seven other guests were sitting down to lunch with the Queen of England!

Suddenly, fleetingly, I was back in the prefab in Oswestry with Mum and Dad, eating our free rabbit, then in *Irwins'* grocery shop in Oswestry loading my bike. And now I was in the Queen's dining room! And to think that we used to hide from the rent man under our dinner table! Who d'a' thought it!

What a shame that my dear Mum was, by now, too ill and frail to appreciate fully an honour bestowed on her lad which a year or two earlier would have seen her bursting with pride. One of **her** boys sitting at The Queen's table! My word, she'd have been overjoyed if she'd been fully fit and well, but in the event, it didn't really sink in. She died soon after, while on holiday with us in Cornwall. Very suddenly and painlessly, thank God, in Pauline's arms.

That brief flashback was broken by a familiar gruff voice coming from the other side of the palatial table:

"Hey, Barrie – what's THIS for?"

It was Tim Smit, being characteristically relaxed about his surroundings and trying to work out the purpose of the exquisitely decorative little bowl of water placed in front of every guest.

"Don't know, mate!" I mimed back, as inconspicuously as I could.

At this, an attentive flunky sidled discreetly up to Tim and whispered in his ear. That was the signal for Tim, delightfully unabashed, to holler across the table:

"HEY, BARRIE. IT'S TO WASH YOUR FRUIT!"

Bear in mind that while this little interlude was taking place he was sitting only three places from the Queen and it will give you some idea why I love Tim Smit to bits! The man is an absolute star.

By the way, in 1997 my mum's sister, our much-loved Aunt Eileen, had published a book, which perhaps explained why I too should have felt perfectly comfortable in royal company (!) as well as discovering some coincidences which I found decidedly spooky...

Eileen's book was the result of many years of painstakingly tracing her family tree. This revealed that mum's family, the Kerr's, were from a line which can be traced back to 15th century Scottish landed gentry and that among the activities of some very exalted descendants was the ownership and editorship of the *Northampton Mercury* in the early 18th century (newspaper proprietors in the family!) My mum's great grandfather rejoiced in the splendid name of Marmaduke Plantagenet Errington Winter Kerr (*Marmaduke* was my first boss Jack Cater's nickname for me!) and had been born in Shrewsbury (where my career began!)

Marmaduke was killed in an horrific train crash when he was only 22 and his son Henry (mum's grandfather) was disgracefully done out of his share of his mother's very considerable inherited fortune by a mean step-father who had then eased at least some of his deservedly guilty conscience by giving Henry a menial job in one of the family's chain of shops, of which the poor cheated bloke was rightfully an owner! So, up until the late 1800s my mum's family had been extremely wealthy people among whom could be counted Scottish noblemen and landowners, including the Earls of Lothian and Ancrum; military top brass, including one General John Manners Kerr (Brigadier General in the West Indies in 1800); William Kerr MD (acclaimed surgeon and a founder of Northampton Hospital in 1793) and James Winter, a character who would have done justice to *The Onedin Line*, having run away to sea from his home in Charmouth, Dorset (a stone's throw from where Pauline and I bought a seaside property!), settled in Newfoundland and founded an 18th century shipping line which gave him massive wealth with which he retired to Devon (now part of our home patch!)

Mum's father, Charles Kerr, having lied about his age when only 17, fought in the Battle of Ypres and the Somme and after discharge from the army on medical grounds in 1917 became a railway worker in Oswestry in the Depression-ridden 1930s, a job in which he remained until he retired in 1961 – the year I started work as a journalist. Mum, bless her heart, always had a polished air about her. Now I understood why.

Back at *The Ship* it seemed things had never been better. My newspaper had never been better; its marvellous team of journalists had never been better; its reputation in the West Country had never been higher. We were at our peak.

When Kevin Beatty moved back into *DMGT* – as everybody expected he would – and Michael Pelosi was appointed Managing Director of *Northcliffe* I gave it barely a thought. Michael, a small, quietly spoken, refined Scot, had always been very pleasant, easy to deal with and like Ian Park, who appeared to be his mentor, a stickler for good manners and gentlemanly conduct.

Michael Pelosi had been Finance Director under Ian then Assistant Managing Director under Alec Davidson and Kevin. I thought his time had come and that he was overdue for the top job. A nice man, Michael. I was pleased for him.

But some of the gossipy doom merchants among the *Northcliffe* editors were less pleased.

"Beware," they warned glumly. "The bloody money men have taken over…"

Always a stranger to pessimism, I paid this no heed.

Events were to prove that I should have done…

I figured that the *Western Morning News* was now in reasonably good nick. Advertising revenue was attaining a level of consistency which would have been welcomed as a real achievement when I had first joined *Northcliffe* a decade ago and our circulation performance was good.

Assistant Managing Director Tim Saunders – a close friend of mine who had trained under David Teague at the *Nottingham Evening Post* – was responsible for our commercial departments and he had put a brilliant, predominantly female, team led by an impressive manager, Lorraine Barnett, in charge of *Western Morning News* newspaper sales and promotions.

We worked so well together, those girls and I. I just loved them and I believe that affection was mutual. This was genuine teamwork. And we always found the time to have a good laugh. The result was a sales performance which was consistently among the top five in the UK regional industry. And that took some doing! The girls frequently returned from industry awards ceremonies with arms full of trophies awarded for sales and promotion achievements – and they couldn't wait to get to my office to show them off to me.

Journalistically, we were consistently receiving accolades and winning awards – the latest being *NFU Countryside Rural Newspaper of The Year* and *EDF Energy South West Daily Newspaper of The Year*. All of this led to an invitation from *BBC Radio Devon* for me to be the guest on John Coates *Afternoon Show* and be interviewed in depth for more than half an hour (a lot of radio time) about my newspaper and myself. This had never been a problem for me!

I'd never felt more confident, more relaxed, more on top of my job, more passionate about my newspaper's campaigning causes and all that came across in an interview enjoyed immensely by both subject and questioner. I'd done loads of radio over the years but this one felt special. And John Coates thought so, too. So did his listeners who called and e-mailed in appreciation – one saying that she'd never bought the *Western Morning News* but would now.

Pauline, so used to me being on radio that she was as blasé as me about it, had been "knocked out" by this one. She rang me on my car phone as I drove out of the BBC car park.

"That was just brilliant," she told me. "The best you've ever done."

The final exchange between John Coates and I on that programme had gone like this:

> John Coates: I sense this great passion, this enormous commitment, this huge enjoyment of what you do. But what next? Where does Barrie Williams go from here?
>
> Me: Right now I can't imagine doing anything other than editing the *Western Morning News*. I still go to work every morning with a feeling of excitement. I can't wait for every day to start. For as long as I feel like that there's nothing on earth I would rather do.

Just a few weeks later I was no longer the Editor of the *Western Morning News...*

There had been rumblings about the top brass not being happy with the profits predicted by the annual business plans of all the group's regional newspapers. Even though *Northcliffe* had just recorded an annual profit of around £104million, it was on a margin which was some 10 per cent below those now being achieved by the other major players in the regional industry field like *Trinity Mirror* and *Johnston Press* which were hitting 30 per cent margins.

There had been mutterings from the gossips about how this was going to be a year of painful cost-cutting but I'd not been bothered by that. What was new? And in any event, these crises had a habit of being mountains made out of molehills on the gossip circuit.

Pauline and I had been down at our Dorset retreat for a holiday, enjoying the sea and the sunshine and walking with Paddy. During the week, Phil Bowern had phoned to tell me that there was big news from Bristol, where *Northcliffe* had appointed an Editor-in-Chief (Mike Norton from the *Derby Evening Telegraph*), whereupon the Editor of the *Bristol Evening Post*, Mike Lowe had resigned and that *Western Daily Press* Editor Terry Manners had been told that he would now have to answer to Norton. (Terry was later to leave, too.)

I was shocked to hear about Mike Lowe – a bloody good editor and a blunt northerner in the same mould as me, but apart from wondering briefly if I might be asked to become Editor-in-Chief of *Westcountry Publications* I hadn't wasted any valuable holiday time wondering whether this had implications for Plymouth.

When we got back, I went into the office, as I always did the night before returning from a break, to check the e-mails and internal documents, sort the postbag and catch up on all the papers so that I could get off to a flying start the next day.

On my way in, I rang Duncan Currall for a chat – and mentioned the Bristol business. Duncan's reply was strange...

"I wanted to talk to you before that leaked out," he said. "Can you come and see me when you get in?"

When I walked into Duncan's office he looked apprehensive and troubled.

"What's up, mate?" I asked.

"They want to do the same here as they've done in Bristol."

"You mean appoint an Editor-in-Chief?"

"Yes."

"And...?"

"They want you to stand down."

The shock was deep and instant. This was like a kick to my stomach. I simply couldn't believe what I was hearing.

"You mean they want me *out?*"

"I'm told you'll be getting a very generous settlement."

"Settlement? This isn't about bloody money!"

"I know. I've said that with you it's pride, not money."

"And *why* do they want me out?"

"I'm to ask you to ring Michael Pelosi. But I wanted to talk to you first."

"And will there be an Editor-in-Chief here?"

"Yes."

"And who will *that* be?"

"Alan Qualtrough." (Alan was the Editor of the *Plymouth Evening Herald*, a former *Daily Express* man and a good editor who did a more than competent job on the evening paper but he had only been in the chair for about three years and he had nothing like my own vast experience and incomparable achievement record in our regional industry. In fact, nobody had!)

Now I was not only severely shocked – but badly hurt.

"Oh, for fuck's sake, Duncan!"

"So, will you ring Michael Pelosi?"

"No I won't. I've got nothing to say to him!"

With that I stormed out of Duncan's office.

"Wait! Barrie! What are you going to do?" he called after me.

"They can fuck off!" I shouted, as I ran down the stairs and out of the building.

When I got home, Pauline was gardening.

"You haven't been long. I wasn't expecting you," she said.

"You're not going to believe this…" I said.

Nor did she! Pauline just laughed – incredulously.

"No. Don't be silly. You're having me on… Aren't you?"

"No. I wish I was. It's true. They want me out… *Me!*"

I opened a bottle of wine and we sat in silence, looking out over the estuary. Paddy, with that uncanny sense which dogs have of knowing when you're feeling down, sat between us – his head in my lap. It was a warm sunny evening. The view was as beautiful and tranquil as ever and it calmed me.

We sat there for hours, both of us in shock.

Now and then I broke our silence, each time repeating,

"I'm not upset – just so bloody *angry.*"

And each time Pauline replied: "How *could* they?"

Early the next morning I rang Duncan at home. I felt bad about the way I had talked to him and I wanted to apologise. None of this had anything to do with him. He hadn't needed to insist on breaking the news to me himself. He had done that as a friend – and my violent reaction had abused that friendship.

By now, I had calmed down considerably. I still didn't know the official reason for last night's bombshell news but I'd already rationalised it. I just knew that it would have *nothing* to do with my ability and performance as an editor or as a journalist and *everything* to do with that infernal bloody bottom line. I told myself that if they were prepared to get rid of the best editor in the regional business to save money that was *their* problem, not mine. I had no wish to continue working for them. There would be no shouting match. I was not going to demean myself. I would retain my composure and my dignity – even though I was inwardly seething with anger and indignation.

I rang Michael Pelosi…

"Oh, hi Barrie. How are you?"

"How do you *think* I am?"

"Sorry. That was just an expression."

"So what have you got to say to me Michael?"

"We want you to retire. It's nothing personal…"

"It's pretty bloody personal to *me!*"

Michael Pelosi went on to say that he simply had no alternative but to try and increase the profitability of the newspapers and that he was having to identify meaningful ways in which to approach that task. Getting me to retire was a purely financial decision and it was no reflection whatsoever on me. There would be a generous financial settlement.

He would be identifying areas where there could be a "common spine" between the *Western Morning News* and the *Plymouth Evening Herald* and synergies with Bristol.

I pointed out that he seemed merely to assume that I would not co-operate with cost-cutting measures when the reality was that I had already reduced the editorial running costs I inherited at the *WMN* by many thousands of pounds. He said he knew that, that he didn't expect me to agree with what he was doing and that I was welcome to go up to London and shout at him – but this was going to happen.

I told Michael Pelosi that my greatest concern was for my newspaper. I said I knew I couldn't go on forever and that I'd talked previously to Kevin Beatty and to Duncan about the need to identify the right successor and for me then to groom that successor carefully and slowly over a prolonged period because the *Western Morning News* was a difficult and delicate newspaper. I believed that the Editor **had** to have a deep understanding of the readership and the region and a thorough grasp of all the nuances which were inherent in this unique job. It had taken me the best part of two years to get on top of it.[5]

I had to try to convince myself that the *Western Morning News* should no longer be *my* concern but I'd nursed that paper like a baby. I'd devoted 15 hours a day, six days a week for 10 years to its reborn transformation. Walking away from it was always going to be a huge wrench when the time came – but this? This was like rearing your child with love, care, devotion and years of bloody hard work then just turning your back and walking away without a minute's warning or preparation. It was awful. But I was determined to keep calm and composed – outwardly, at least.

My next call was to a lawyer. I needed one to carefully go through the paperwork which *Northcliffe* had prepared to seal my departure and financial settlement. There was something awfully formal and final about that and I was not looking forward to it. But Steve Allen,

---

[5] This was typically arrogant of me – and a bit pompous. What I was *really* saying was that nobody else could possibly understand *my* newspaper, which overlooked the fact that there had been *ten* other editors in its history – all of whom probably felt exactly the same! The harsh truth is that *nobody* is indispensable and if that wasn't so, newspapers like the *WMN* would not have survived the inevitable departure of editors over nearly 150 years!

the lawyer who accepted the task, was superb. Steve made me laugh and restored my sense of perspective. I needed that. He told me that if I was to take this to an industrial tribunal I would almost certainly win hands down. But even if I was to "hit the jackpot" of the top level of compensation available on every count it would be very much less than the money that Michael Pelosi was going to give me if I just buggered off.

"Let's face it, old son," said Steve, "I do not see before me the most impoverished client who will ever sit in that chair!"

He was right. I had always found *Northcliffe* to be an honourable company and this was no exception. They were being much more than fair to me financially. Many people at this stage of their career would have jumped for joy, snatched their hand off and dashed for the door! Even so, I still had a gut feeling to resist. I was not short of money. Far from it. And on a matter of principle…

Then I remembered what a much valued friend in Nottingham, a lawyer called Martin Suthers, had once told me over a pint:

"When people talk principles, logic dies and only lawyers get rich!"

No. Fighting this would be a pointless and futile gesture. It was time to vacate the saddle of my high horse, and when I told Steve Allen that I was going to accept *Northcliffe's* generous financial settlement, so let's get on with the paper work, he nodded silently in unspoken approval.

I then had to go into the office, face my staff and tell them that I was leaving. And I had to tackle what seemed like 101 other bits of bureaucracy bound up with my removal from employment. It was a desperately daunting business. I'd been a journalist for 44 years. Apart from that one very brief spell of exhaustion way back in Wolverhampton I had not even had so much as *one* day off sick since 1961! Having to sever that lifelong link and love affair with what had always been so very much more than just a job to me was always going to be tough when the time came. Having to do it under these circumstances was much worse.

I sat down in my office and opened my briefcase, in which I'd put a carefully prepared list of all the severance matters which I had to attend to that day. Pauline had helped me compile that list the night before and she had secretly pinned a note to it.

It said: "Me and Paddy love ya, babes."

And the rest can go to hell!, I thought.

Michael Pelosi had prepared a statement which said simply that I was retiring, but quite apart from the fact that I was barely sixty and wasn't simply retiring, nobody who knew me was going to believe it anyway! I told Michael Pelosi so and I asked if the statement could say that I was retiring *early* "because of a major change of policy and structure within *Northcliffe Newspapers*."

Michael agreed to that immediately.

The news hit my staff like a bolt from the blue. They were shocked to the core. Some were in tears. Some of them were clearly afraid for their own futures. I'd always had a unique style and with that went some unique appointments. A different editor might well take a different view. Suddenly I found myself acting as a counsellor for worried journalists – one after another knocking on my door to ask me if I thought *their* job would be safe. Under my own considerably less than cheery circumstances I could have resented that – but I didn't at all. After all, I'd *had* my career, while some of these people had barely *started* theirs.

Just a few days later we were due at the *Press Gazette Regional Newspaper Of The Year Awards* in London, at which we'd yet again been nominated for *Daily/Sunday Newspaper Of The Year*.

Phil Bowern observed: "Wouldn't it be a piece of pure Hollywood if we won it, boss?"

And we did win it.

Michael Pelosi sent me an e-mail to congratulate me.

I didn't feel that a reply was appropriate!

When news of my imminent departure hit the *Western Morning News* readership the reaction was overwhelming. People in all walks of life were shocked. I'd been moved and flattered by the public reaction when I'd left Kent and Nottingham. The fact that this – the end of my *third* editorship – produced the strongest response of all was hugely gratifying and confirmed for me that I was going while at the very peak of my power and performance; not shuffling away like some boring old fart way past his sell-by date, but bowing out while at the top; at my award-winning best. I had always said that was how I *wanted* it to be. More importantly, it also confirmed that all the effort I'd put in to combine the professional requirements of my newspaper with the interests and problems of West Country people, so badly served by government, had been worth it...

People like Anthony Gibson, South West Regional Director of the National Farmers' Union, who wrote:

> "I was genuinely very sorry to hear that you are no longer at the helm of the WMN. The fact that under your leadership, the paper was prepared to highlight and champion agricultural and rural issues has made a huge difference, not just to the mo-rale of the farming community (and one should never

underestimate the importance of that) but to the development of policy. That influence reached its peak during the foot and mouth crisis when your newspaper became a beacon of hope and understanding for beleaguered rural communities frustrated beyond belief by the incompetence surrounding them. I cannot think of any issue at any time in which a regional newspaper has been such a force for good as the WMN was at that terrible time. But there is another area where your influence has come to have an even more lasting impact and that is in the local food movement. The fact that an ever – growing proportion of consumers are not merely prepared but positively enthusiastic about paying a bit more for something a bit special is transforming the food market, to the benefit of producers, processors and consumers alike. Some of us had been fighting an uphill battle for years to change our food culture. What turned the tide was the spirited and imaginative intervention of the WMN. Within the space of a few short years the Westcountry has become a region that people visit because of, rather than in spite of, the food they will find there. That has potentially huge economic benefits and it simply would not have happened had it not been for you and your newspaper. Thank you for all you have done for farming and for the rural community. You have made a real difference to the lives and livelihoods of hundreds of thousands of country people and we will always be grateful for it."

Like Tim Jones, Chairman of Devon and Cornwall Business Council, who wrote:

"Along with the entire business community, I am greatly saddened and disappointed at the news of your departure. You have single-handedly championed so many wonderful causes and you have been unquestionably the greatest advocate for a wide range of massive issues for the South West region. You have been instrumental in achieving major changes for the better on so many issues that they are difficult to summarise. On behalf of the business community and personally, I would like to extend my deepest thanks and appreciation for the massive effort you have made on behalf of our region."

Like David Fursdon, Chairman of the Country Land and Business Association, who wrote:

"It was a great shock to hear that you are leaving the WMN. I am so sorry to see you go and I am very grateful for all you have

done for rural communities generally and for those in the South West in particular during your time as editor. We have so much to be grateful to you for. On a personal note, I have much enjoyed our working relationship and I am sorry that it is being brought to an end."

Like Lord Clifford of Chudleigh, who wrote:

"I wish to express my gratitude to you – particularly for your tremendously wholehearted support of the conference I organised at Bicton Agricultural College in 1998. Like so many others – offshore fishermen, farmers, those wishing to protect the values of West Country life – I praise you for the sound and balanced judgements and the directions made during your tenure as Editor of the most interesting and challenging newspaper in England. Well done."

Like Lady Mary Holborow, Lord Lieutenant of Cornwall, who wrote:

"This is to thank you for all you have done during your years as Editor to help me and the different projects that I have wanted to support. I know how hard you have worked for Devon and Cornwall and you will be a hard act to follow."

Like Spencer Gammond, Head of Communications for the Royal National Lifeboat Institution, who wrote:

"I was very sorry to read about your retirement. Under your stewardship the WMN has been such a stalwart supporter of the RNLI – for which we owe you a huge vote of thanks. I am delighted that we were able to mark our appreciation by presenting you with an award last year."

Like Tim Smit of the Eden Project, who wrote:

*"I have had the privilege of knowing you for ten years and not once in all that time has your support for Eden wavered. I want you to know how deeply grateful I feel for your friendship and support. You made the journey feel fun and never lonely, but – most importantly – you **believed.**"*

Like James Morrish, of the Rural Stress Network – which has helped hundreds of desperate farmers – who wrote:

"Thank you for all you have done. There are some of us who do not forget."

Like the Countess of Morley, who wrote:

"I have cheered you on through your tremendous efforts to help the farmers of the West Country against the lack of understanding and interest of the present Government – the plight that small traditional family farmers find themselves in saddens me deeply. Devon and Cornwall have been so fortunate to have had you as a champion with a voice loud enough to have been heard in Westminster! I do hope that your successor will carry on all your good work and that the WMN will continue to be what you have made it – a force for good for the people of the West Country."

Like the NFU 's Ian Johnson, who wrote:

"We have been through an awful lot together, what with the horrors of BSE and Foot and Mouth; the collapse of farm incomes – not to mention Bovine TB and Defra incompetence. You will be sorely missed and I have already had expressions of concern over the departure of such a great champion of country folk, tackling issue after issue often neglected as being too unsexy by less committed media."

Like Methodist Minister Rev. David J. Harding, who wrote:

"Thank you so very much for all that you have done for and with the Western Morning News. I was disturbed to read between the lines of the announcement by Northcliffe Newspapers. Please ensure that more information about your apparent conflict with them is made public when appropriate!"

Like Hillary Weatherley, Communications Manager of South West Water, who wrote:

"I was deeply saddened that you will be leaving the Western Morning News after so many years of splendid work. You did a really brilliant job and you can go out with your head held high."

Like Vice Admiral Sir Louis Le Bailly who (in addition to a personal letter in which he said he was "...shocked and devastated to read that you are leaving the helm of a newspaper I have come to regard, since you took it over, as one of the most informative and helpful in this increasingly crazy world.") wrote this tribute, published in the *Western Morning News:*

"In these difficult days, as more and more TV and radio channels evolve and the quality of output deteriorates, it is to a few remaining Press outlets that we have to look for truth and the reasoned sustenance of those freedoms and responsibilities won for us by our ancestors. Barrie Williams, with the first class team he has gathered around him, has played a notable part in this battle and most of us will be saddened by his departure. It was a fitting ending to his distinguished editorship to read last week, in a famous and reputable national newspaper with no commercial relationship, that the Western Morning News is the most effective campaigning regional newspaper in Britain. Many of us will wish Mr Williams well – coupled with the hope that he will not for long lay down his pen or his sword."

Like Michael Howard, then Leader of the Conservative Party, who wrote:

"...you have done such a fantastic job in holding the Government to account on their rural policies."

There was an e-mail from Peter Williams, the Finance Director of the *Daily Mail and General Trust*, which said:

"From a DMGT and a Northcliffe point of view, I was disappointed to learn that you were moving to a life of greater leisure, but delighted on your behalf. You have made a great contribution to Northcliffe, the Western Morning News and to the West Country and I gather that you fully intend to continue with the last of these. It's been great that you've taken to the area with such enthusiasm. Congratulations, also, on your award of Regional Daily Newspaper of the Year. Nothing like going out at the top!"

Just as had been the case when I had left Nottingham and Kent, I found letters written to me by the "ordinary" readers very moving and – in the case of at least one of them, Kevin Pyne from Dartmouth, remarkably supportive. Kevin – a man I had never met and did not know – wrote:

"I was saddened to read in the Western Morning News about the imminent retirement of Barrie Williams, the editor in charge of what I consider to be the best newspaper in the country, after ten years at the helm. As an avid reader of the paper I am inclined to ask: Do I smell a rat? I am just an old ferryman but I have an uncomfortable sense of foreboding. It begs me to ask the question: What's going on? I do hope I'm not looking at a "profit

is best" scenario. I can't say that I understand the ways of big business. I will say, though, that I started to read Mr Williams' *Western Morning News* because I grew tired of other newspapers which will print anything just to sell copies. The WMN, on the other hand, treats every story with a journalistic excellence sadly now missing in many papers. Who does not marvel at the excellent photography, for example – and the authoritative reporting and guidance which it so often offers its readers? I have been known to get so interested and involved in an article while stirring my morning porridge that I have set alight the newspaper on the gas cooker more than once. There you have the key to this newspaper's success – it's always interesting and often exciting. I thank you, Mr Williams, for this. It deals with the affairs of a penniless poet and the wealth of the Duchy of Cornwall with equal informative precision and without bias to either. May I suggest to whoever is the new editor that if you alter the formula of my favourite paper then I'm off. The Western Morning News is a way of life to those who read and value our nationally acclaimed morning newspaper. Many causes and campaigns would have gone unnoticed if it were not for the honest, unbiased reporting of the Wessey staff and long may it stay that way. Be ever vigilant, readers. Something tells me this good man is going for the wrong reasons."

Mrs J. Gill of Okehampton wrote:

"We are so sorry to hear you are leaving the WMN. You have made it a very good paper. Your understanding of the difficulties the countryside is facing today is always expressed clearly and factually and I just hope your successor has the same interest."

Michael Ashton of Torrington, wrote:

"We are very sorry that we are to lose our editor, Barrie Williams. He has been a great supporter of everything we love in the West Country and he has told many truths that have made the Government and authorities feel very uncomfortable."

Ron Boswell of Looe, wrote:

"I read with dismay and sorrow that you are taking early retirement. We are often poles apart in our opinions but, nevertheless, I hold you in great respect for all that you have achieved and attempted to achieve for the people of the West Country and Cornwall in particular."

Vic Ellery of Brixham, wrote:

"Like thousands of other loyal readers the news that Barrie Williams, editor of the WMN, is taking early retirement came as a huge shock to me. Mr Williams says a major change of policy has instigated his departure but Northcliffe has given no further explanation. Will the paying punters ever know?"

Tess Nash of Helston, wrote:

"I am devastated to learn that you have been "persuaded" to take "early retirement." I hope that my fear that the unique "People's Forum" – which is what you have made the Western Morning News – will now be lost to us proves to be wrong. Sadly, I very much doubt it. The South West has lost a great champion."

Dr Edward Hamlyn of Ivybridge, wrote:

"We may never know why we have lost you, but we all know it is a serious and grievous loss. You must take our loss as a huge validation of what you have achieved. There can be no higher acclaim for a man in your profession than the affection of your readers, which you have in abundance."

There were many more letters like those. There were also lots of letters, e-mails, notes and cards from fellow media professionals...

Like Simon Read, Editor of *BBC South West* who wrote:

"...You'll be greatly missed by all at BBC Spotlight. Many congratulations on an extraordinarily successful ten years in charge of the Western Morning News. It's been a great read every morning for those of us in the business and the leadership you showed during and after Foot and Mouth was outstanding. I always felt you richly deserved the many awards and tributes you attracted as editor."

Like Jane Blanchard, Head of Features at *ITV Westcountry* who wrote:

"What a terrible loss. You completely turned the Western Morning News around and transformed it into a must-read and a real champion of the West Country."

Like Alastair MacColl, Managing Director of the *Middlesbrough Evening Gazette* (and former assistant managing director of *Westcountry Publications)* who wrote:

"You had a magnificent ten years as editor of the Western Morning News. You turned around this title and transformed it into something with direction, passion and a real sense of what the West Country means to the people who live and work there."

Like columnist Kate Ironside, who wrote:

Jon (Kate's partner Jon Smith, Political Editor of the Press Association) and I were horrified to hear that you are taking early retirement... You've been a marvellous editor to work for, both at Nottingham and in the West Country, and I think that what you have achieved with the Western Morning News in particular has been nothing short of remarkable. Few editors can claim to have driven through such a transformation of a newspaper."

Like Andrew Porter, Deputy Political Editor of the *Sunday Times* (and now Political Editor of *The Daily Telegraph*) who wrote:

"...Thank you so much for giving me my first job in journalism and then giving me an even bigger break by making me London Editor of the WMN a year later. I still refer to the WMN as "we" when talking to people and that loyalty comes from the way I felt about working for such a great paper and the leadership you gave it. You gave me the best grounding in journalism that any aspiring reporter could get."

Like Andrea Kuhn, one of the WMN's best journalists, who wrote:

"I have had a great four and a half years with you at the paper and I've learned so much. I feel very lucky to have worked for an editor who had guts – an increasingly rare breed. We've had some fun, caused some mischief and hopefully helped a few people along the way. What better job is there?"

There were lots more expressing similar sentiments from journalists across the country – many of whom I had lost touch with years since – and to read them all was both moving and uplifting.

One of the most touching letters came from Duncan Currall, who wrote:

"I have found it very hard to adequately put into words my feelings over all that has taken place here in the last few weeks. It could – and should – all have been so very different, given your outstanding achievements throughout your long and distinguished career. Throughout all the recent turmoil you have typically retained your professionalism and integrity when

many a lesser man would not have done. I am so delighted that the Western Morning News won the Newspaper Of The Year award, particularly in these circumstances. It is richly deserved. It is unique that you, as editor, have been recognised so many times in this regard at Nottingham and here and it seems extraordinary how history has repeated itself from when we worked together in Nottingham and I left just after you had won the award there. Thank you for all your personal support. I have very much enjoyed working with you again."

Duncan (what a gentleman. And what a loyal friend) was keen for me to have a "proper send off" from *Westcountry Publications* but I was adamant that, under these circumstances, I wanted to go without pomp and ceremony. It would have been altogether different and one of the big retirement parties attended by your family, your colleagues, the good and the great of your community and the London directors which *Northcliffe*, used to stage at some plush local venue to pay tribute to retiring editors might have been appropriate if I had been taking normal retirement at the time of my choice but I wasn't and I had no stomach for a "celebration" which would have been false and forced.

I told my staff, too, that there was to be no fuss. When the time came, I just wanted to walk quietly away.

And that's what I did.

A career which had spanned 44 years, 30 of them at the very top of my profession as an editor, was ending with no more ceremony than the day it had all started...

In 1961, as a boy of 16, I had walked into the *Shrewsbury Chronicle* alone and unnoticed. In 2005, as a man of 60, I walked out of the *Western Morning News* alone and unnoticed.

Rather a lot had happened in between.

Meanwhile, there had been much speculation in the industry about what *Northcliffe* was up to. *Press Gazette* quoted "an insider" as saying that in order to smooth the progress of its project to achieve radical increases in profit margins, an "awkward squad" of experienced editors who might resist it had been targeted for removal. That might indeed have been at least a contributory factor in the departures of myself, Mike Lowe from the *Bristol Evening Post* and David Gledhill from the *Bath Evening Chronicle* – because we are all renowned straight talkers! Whatever the reason(s) I had become much less angry by the day as the date of my departure had approached.

After all, I had enjoyed ten unforgettable years of fabulous journalistic achievement in the West Country and I would be genuinely forever grateful to *Northcliffe* for giving me the opportunity to do that. Had they not come into my life in such a dramatic way back in 1995 I would never have known the *Western Morning News*, its marvellous journalists, its wonderful loyal readers and the breathtakingly beautiful region it serves. I owed our splendid life in the glorious West Country entirely to *Northcliffe*, a good company which, in many ways, had treated me very well indeed. Much as recent events had offended my pride and hurt my heart, my head now told me that I really did not have much to complain about.

Eventually, by the time I received an invitation from Michael Pelosi to a private farewell lunch at Claridges with members of the London board, I had rationalised the whole situation to such an extent that I was very happy to accept. My attitude, now, was why not go and have their posh nosh and say farewell to *Northcliffe* with all the pride and dignity with which I'd managed to greet them when they had first invaded my precious domain in Nottingham?

Then, I had – rightly – controlled a burning desire to tell them to piss off! Then, I had behaved in a professional, polite and good humoured manner. Then, I had kept cool, calm and collected. Now, I would do all that again.

And, damn it, despite everything, I still *liked* Michael Pelosi and the rest of them! After all, Michael was just doing his job. And just as I had always done, he had every right to do that *his* way.

This attitude clearly got through to *Press Gazette's* Jon Slattery when, a few weeks after I'd left my job, he came down to my home in Cornwall to interview me for his magazine. Spread across two pages, with several shots of me receiving awards to contrast with the main picture of me now relaxing in our lovely rural Cornish acres, under the headline DON'T MENTION PROFITS IN FRONT OF THE COLONEL, Jon's article traced the story of my career. He wrote:

"When Barrie Williams was editor of the *Nottingham Evening Post* in the 1980s he was asked to join the board. One bit of advice he was given was "don't mention profits in front of the chairman, he doesn't like to talk about profits."

What a contrast to the regional press today, when the pursuit of ever higher profit margins is seen by some as the major force shaping the industry.

Williams was one of three high-profile editors who left *Northcliffe* in the summer ahead of its plans to make substantial savings and increase its margins. He made it clear in July why he was taking early retirement from the *Western Morning News* at 60. In a statement, Williams said his decision was because of "a major change of policy and structure within *Northcliffe.*"

Those changes included plans to appoint an editor-in-chief in Plymouth, where the *WMN* and the *Evening Herald* are published. Few in the industry could imagine Williams – well known for his bluntness – answering to an editor-in-chief!

His departure ended a near 30-year run as a regional editor. He was editor of the *Kent Evening Post* for five years, the *Nottingham Evening Post* for 14 years and the *WMN* for 10 years.

Going to see an editor just after he's left his newspaper is a bit like death-knocking, but Williams is in a far from sombre mood. Maybe it's because he was able to watch the Ashes series uninterrupted by the stress of an editor's job or because he lives in a very beautiful part of Cornwall.

Swigging tea from a mug emblazoned with the *Western Morning News* masthead, Williams speaks proudly of his record at the paper.

"When I joined, its sales figure was seven per cent down. In the eight years since we went tabloid the worst sales figure we ever recorded was minus 2. 5 per cent and there were a number of ABC periods in which we achieved an increase, including last year.

"Every year since 1997, the WMN has been in the top five for regional newspaper sales performance. We built a reputation for quality, campaigning regional journalism and every year we have won top industry awards, including *Press Gazette* Newspaper of the Year and daily/Sunday Newspaper of the Year three times. The WMN is the current holder of that title and of *EDF Energy South West Newspaper of the Year* and of *NFU Countryside Rural Newspaper of the Year*. It also holds numerous national and regional newspaper sales awards.

"I've never been renowned for my modesty, but I reckon that's a recent record second to none in the industry and I'm very proud of it."

So does he miss it?

"Was I sad to leave all that behind? Of course I was," he says. "But *Northcliffe* has decided on a new structure to achieve higher levels of financial performance and it is perfectly entitled to do that.

"After 25 years as a director of newspaper companies there's enough of the businessman in me to understand the situation, even if I don't agree with what they're doing. It's not like they've said, "Williams, you're a crap editor, bugger off!" It's a purely financial scenario. While I don't agree with it, I respect entirely their right to run their own company the way they see fit. I owe *Northcliffe* a great deal. If they had not offered me the opportunity to edit the *Western Morning News* I would not have enjoyed arguably the best, most challenging and rewarding years of my career. They entrusted me with a prestigious morning title and left me free to edit it in my own way."

Williams wanted to be a journalist from the age of 11. It had a lot to do with when he was growing up in Oswestry and lived next door to a journalist who regaled him with stories about his working life. His first attempt to join a paper at 16 failed when the editor of the Oswestry paper told him "We don't employ Teddy Boys." Williams admits to having had a Brylcreemed quiff at the front and a "duck's arse" flip at the back.

However, he was offered an apprenticeship on the *Shrewsbury Chronicle*. Three years later he joined the *Impact Press Agency* in Shrewsbury and had his first brush with Fleet Street journalists.

"The idea of being a reporter in Fleet Street was everyone's Mecca, but there were an awful lot of talented small fish in that big pond. I decided for that and other reasons that I'd rather be a big fish in a small pond."

He returned to the *Chronicle* as News Editor before working on the *Wolverhampton Express & Star, Stoke City Times* and *Nottingham Evening Post*. In 1971 he joined the *Kent Evening Post* where he became editor for five years. He left Kent in 1981 to become editor of the *Nottingham Evening Post*.

Both Kent and Nottingham were family-owned titles. In Nottingham, the proprietor was Colonel Tom Forman Hardy, whose family had substantial farming, brewing and property interests. Williams remembers: "He was happy as long as the paper was ticking over. He just loved owning a newspaper. He was a stickler for editorial freedom and independence but he loved to sit and talk about the issues and what we were campaigning about.

"People of my generation of editors had the best years. There were almost no financial pressures. You submitted a budget each year and it was approved. About a year after I joined Nottingham I was appointed to the board and became editorial director." This was when Williams was advised not to talk about profits in front of the chairman. "You've gone from that to a situation where editors now have to think about their contribution to a 30 per cent profit margin, or whatever."

Extraordinarily, the *Evening Post* had what Williams described as "its own air force." This comprised a helicopter and a company jet. "We even had our own pilot, called Captain Bond."

Another bit of company largesse came before Williams took up the editorship at Nottingham. He and his wife were sent on a round-the-world trip. The idea was for Williams to look at newspapers in Europe, America, Canada and Australia. "It was all first class travel and must have cost thousands of pounds, but I learned a lot," he says.

Northcliffe took over the *Evening Post* for £94million in 1994.

Politically, Nottingham was a strong Labour Party city and there was a lot of opposition to the local paper being owned by a company with links to the *Daily Mail*.

The Monopolies Commission at first blocked the deal, but it went through after appeal. As part of the appeal Williams gave evidence in favour of the takeover: "I am convinced that if I had said a bad thing it wouldn't have happened."

A condition of the takeover was that the editor of the *Evening Post* could not be fired or hired without it going before an independent committee of "the great and the good" of Nottingham. Williams says: "People joked that I had the safest job in the world."

Nevertheless, he quickly took up the job of editor of the *Western Morning News* when offered the chance to move on by Ian Park, then managing director of *Northcliffe*.

The *WMN* became a strong campaigner on rural issues under Williams, who believes "the maltreatment of rural areas is appalling" The paper became a thorn in the side of the Government, especially in the aftermath of the foot and mouth crisis. Alastair Campbell once asked Williams: "Why do you give us such a f---ing kicking?" He replied: "Because you f---ing deserve it!"

Williams has been approached to continue his campaigning on rural issues in the political arena, but is undecided about taking up the offers. However, he adds: "No way am I going to sit in the bath counting toe nail clippings."

Williams believes his near 30-year record as an editor will never be repeated. "People are starting in the business so much later. I was brought up in a council house and I joined a paper straight from school at 16."

Williams thinks the stress on academic qualifications has "cut the council house kids out" from entering journalism. At Nottingham he pioneered a scheme employing kids on council estates to write for the paper and supplied them with laptops.

"I wouldn't get in to the profession nowadays," he claims. "A lot of regional papers have lost touch with their readers. You have middle-class journalists writing for people who aren't on the same wavelength. They have lost the common touch." Williams believes the switch to graduates began in the 1970s because of an "intellectual arrogance" that journalism, as a profession, was akin to law or medicine and should have a similarly high academic level of entry.

"...But it's a people business. It is all about getting on with people in all walks of life. The academic bit is non-essential unless you want to be a specialist. We have a lot of well-educated but bland people who, when looking for a job, stopped at "j" for journalism and thought 'that might be rather fun.'"

For Williams the job has been more than just "fun". He says the kick he got out of being an editor was "making a difference" to people. He has a huge file of letters from organisations and individuals who feel they were helped by the *Western Morning News*. One said: "You can't leave it at that."

It is unlikely that he will."

I was grateful to Jon Slattery for that article. Condensing a 44-year career into a couple of magazine pages and doing it anything like justice was far from easy. Jon did it very well indeed.

In the same issue of *Press Gazette* that week was a news item announcing that the editor-in-chief of the *Western Morning News* and the *Plymouth Evening Herald*, Alan Qualtrough, had also been made

Editor of the *WMN*. Alan's deputy on the *Herald*, Bill Martin, became its editor – thus saving the very considerable salary and all the other expenses of the newly departed *WMN* editor.

A couple of weeks later, I went to my farewell lunch at Claridges. The *Northcliffe* directors came, which I expected. So did Lord Rothermere and *DMGT* Finance Director, Peter Williams, which I didn't. I really appreciated the effort made by Lord Rothermere and Peter to attend... even if I was somewhat less than impressed by the fact that they all turned up at around 1.25pm for an event that was supposed to be 12.30pm for 1pm, leaving me (the guest of honour) sitting alone with only the waiters for company for the best part of an hour before my hosts arrived. Dear old Colonel Tom Forman Hardy would have been mortified by such timekeeping!

To be fair, they had come straight from a board meeting through heavy London traffic and there was a great deal going on in the company at the time, but still I felt that the whole event was more rushed than was appropriate and when it came to what passed as the formal bit, Mr Pelosi's "speech" went thus:

> "Barrie, we thank you for what you have done for the *Western Morning News* and before that in Nottingham. I won't go into your achievements because they've been well documented elsewhere – but thank you."

And that was it. A unique and unparalleled 44 year career in British regional journalism described with all the emotion, eloquence (and economy!) of a true accountant. Just 34 words.

*Well, **that won't need much subbing!** I thought.*

Afterwards, Lord Rothermere and Peter Williams were kind and gracious in their good wishes as they bid farewell to me.

Then they went for a pee and Michael Pelosi announced:

"Barrie, your car's outside."

Then he hurried me down the stairs, onto the street and into his chauffeur-driven vehicle. "Take Mr Williams to the station, please," he told his driver, shaking my hand through the open window. Then he dashed back into Claridges.

And so, with abrupt finality, the career which had been my life since I was just a boy was flicked aside like a discarded cigarette on a busy London street.

I felt no anger, no bitterness; I bore no grudges, no ill-will.

But I was not prepared for the emptiness.

London never felt more lonely. It was not a good feeling.

Earlier on that same day in London I had been to the House of Commons to meet Andrew Mackay, Deputy Chairman in charge of Tory candidates. It was a meeting set up by Michael Howard after he and I had corresponded on the possibility of my becoming a Conservative MP. Many of the people with whom I had come into contact over the years (particularly Tories) would have been absolutely gob-smacked by the mere suggestion of "Barrie Williams, Conservative MP!" but it was by no means as daft as it sounded. I had built up a very high reputation in the rural areas of the West Country and that achievement was recognised and respected by the Leader of the Tory Party who had on several occasions expressed his admiration of the way in which the *Western Morning News* fought for the rights of our country communities against the appalling ineptitude and occasional hostility of the destructive urban Blairites.

And (without a hint of immodesty!) I had suggested to Michael Howard that if I stood as a West Country General Election candidate I could almost guarantee success... particularly in one of the constituencies which were ravaged by Foot and Mouth.

My meeting with Andrew Mackay was, therefore, a serious one.

We talked through which West Country seats might be available and he felt – while stressing, quite rightly, that I would have to go through the local selection process like anybody else – that I had a really excellent chance of obtaining a winnable seat to fight. I left the House of Commons quite inspired by the prospect but later, after giving it a great deal of thought, I decided it was not for me. The trouble was that having been politically agnostic as a journalist for 44 years I simply could not see myself as a genuine Tory. Yes, I believe absolutely sincerely that this Labour Government is disastrous for rural Britain. True, I could campaign better than anybody on those country issues so dear to my heart – especially the wicked treatment of our farmers – but what about the rest of it? Could I *really* be a 100 per cent Conservative? Could I *really* preach the Tory gospel with total sincerity and conviction on issues outside of those affecting the rural areas? The answer was "no" and so that had to be an end to the matter.

My next visit to London was to enjoy, at a big posh ceremony, the very real honour of being awarded a place in *Press Gazette's* **Hall Of Fame** – of 40 journalists who had contributed most to our industry in the last 40 years. That was nice.

Some weeks later, the business pages of the national newspapers dropped a bombshell for everybody connected with *Northcliffe Newspapers Ltd*. All the regional newspapers were being put up for sale. It was a move that stunned the industry. The very idea that the young Lord Rothermere could be prepared to sell the family silver was unthinkable, particularly since *Northcliffe* comfortably made more than £100 million annual profit.

But selling he was.

The *Northcliffe* newspapers were up for "auction" with a "reserve price" of £1.5 billion. It was reported that *DMGT* said it had decided to sell because it would not be able to take *Northcliffe's* profit margins of some 20 per cent up to industry-leading margins of 30 per cent or more without compromising editorial standards.

Inevitably, industry gossip was rife. One trade press report speculated that when Lord Rothermere – who is a genuinely nice bloke – saw how much pain was going to be involved in achieving the holy grail of a 30 per cent profit margin he simply would not do it.

Much gossip also centred around who the likely buyers were.

There ensued weeks of worry and uncertainty for *Northcliffe's* employees, not knowing who their next owner was going to be, how that owner would run their newspapers, how many would keep their jobs, how many would be thrown out of work.

Then, just as suddenly and shockingly, as the sale announcement had been made, came another: *DMGT* had decided *not* to sell *Northcliffe* after all.

Writing in *The Independent* business section, Jeremy Warner observed:

> "Oddly for a company that lays claim to such a fast moving news operation, Daily Mail and General Trust seems to have left it too late in putting its regional newspaper titles up for sale. The mouth-watering valuations that tempted Lord Rothermere into considering a sale in the first place evaporated before his eyes the moment they came under the auctioneer's hammer. In the end, they didn't even make the reserve price. DMGT may have done the right thing in withdrawing the titles from the market but there is no disguising the embarrassment. In the end, the titles were judged to be worth more to DMGT, which says it has identified further significant cost and revenue opportunities, than they apparently are to anyone else. Better to admit embarrassment than to sell at an undervalue, DMGT would say."

The Independent article reckoned that there was growing alarm in the City over the damage new media might do to traditional sources of newspaper revenue. According to Jeremy Warner the sort of classified advertising which is the lifeblood of the regional Press was particularly exposed to the advance of Google, broadband and multi-channel TV. And Jeremy Warner concluded:

> "Are we already witnessing the slow, or even quite rapid, death of the newspaper industry? This seems to me an exaggerated view, yet there is no doubt that in deciding to out bluff Northcliffe's lowball bidders, DMGT is taking quite a gamble."

While national newspaper pundits like Jeremy Warner contemplated the regional industry's future, for the employees of *Northcliffe* the huge initial sense of relief that they were no longer up for sale was tempered by the prospect of the next round of cost savings.

For the last few years, ever since other big groups had embarked on the pursuit of profit margins of 30 per cent and more there had been an uneasy feeling among those of us still trying to believe in the long term future of the regional industry that the corporate clever money was on our slow but sure death by a thousand new media cuts and that, meanwhile, the overriding objective was to screw as much money as possible out of regional papers before the lid was finally nailed down on their coffin. It was an entirely unproved theory which could well be totally wrong but under all the circumstances and with the evidence of constant cost cutting set against the inexorable march of the multi-headed new media monster it had never seemed ridiculously fanciful.

Northcliffe, however, had resisted the 30 per cent route. And in the previous couple of decades it had invested many millions in state of the art colour printing facilities and top class technology – all to keep its regional newspapers at the forefront of the industry. If even *Northcliffe* was now joining this dash for bigger and bigger profits, hadn't all hope of a long term future for this once proud and defiant industry to be abandoned?

The major cost-cutting and re-organisation plan for *Northcliffe Newspapers*, which had resulted in my own departure, had apparently been put on ice when the company had been put up for sale.

Now, almost certainly, it would come back... And it did.

DMGT announced that it was going to merge its national (*Associated Newspapers*) and regional (*Northcliffe Newspapers*) divisions into one company and increase the on-going cost cutting savings of £30 million to £45 million. The new merged business would be headed up by Kevin Beatty, the managing director of *Associated*. Michael Pelosi would now report to Kevin and *Northcliffe's* London office management structure (often considered, in the somewhat less than impartial view of many of the regional managing directors, to be an expensive and unnecessary tier and a heavy drain on *their* hard earned profits!) would cease to be. At the same time, *Northcliffe's* regional management structure would be streamlined into six regional areas. A *Northcliffe* spokesman was quoted as saying that although the workforce had reduced from 7,500 employees at the start of 2005 to 6,600 in March 2006, further redundancies could not be ruled out. In May 2007, the newly re-named *Northcliffe Media* recorded an operating profit of £42.5m, up by £5.4m, or 15 per cent –

even though advertising revenues fell by nearly £4m, or 2.6 per cent and circulation revenues dropped two per cent.

In financial terms – and I am perfectly prepared to concede that in the cold, hard reality of big business that is what *really* matters – the mission had clearly succeeded.

And doing without Barrie Williams as Editor of the *Western Morning News* had presumably done its bit to contribute.

Glad to have helped, chaps!

11.   Don't Let It Die

AND SO, I BELIEVE, IT WILL GO ON for the UK's regional newspaper industry in general. Costs will be screwed to the floor. Ever-increasing profits will be the driver. Investment in print journalism will be minimal. Any businessman will tell you that this looks like classic *management of decline*.

Meanwhile, there will be growing corporate interest and investment in new media. Even veteran national media columnist and former *Daily Mirror* editor Roy Greenslade told a conference:

> *"I have been a print journalist for 42 years and up until, say, three years ago I expected to die a print journalist. But there is no point in looking backwards, in being an inky dinosaur, so I have come to accept that the only way forward for the media industry and for me is to embrace the revolution – of becoming an internet revolutionary."*

There are those who believe that in future people will watch their news and sport on mobile phones; that a new generation of consumers wants immediate access to news through their computers.

And who can argue with them? Right now, there cannot be much doubt that the long-term future of newspapers does not look good and that the regionals – always the poor relation to the nationals when it comes to essential corporate investment – are the most vulnerable.

Yet there are those who will tell you that the regional newspaper industry has been through similar periods of crisis before and survived; that first local TV and then local radio and then Teletext, etc, were all considered at the time to be sounding the death-knell of the local Press. These people believe that there will *always* be a place for the printed word, despite the march of new media; that newspapers are such an inherent part of our culture in the UK that they will never die. They believe that the industry is in a fascinating transitional stage with regional newspaper businesses evolving into community media companies, following their audience by providing local content through the delivery method of their choosing, but retaining the ***printed newspaper*** as the lynch pin of the operation.

There's no disputing the first stage of that assessment – but retention of the printed word? In the long term? I think I can subscribe to that optimistic prognosis if applied to the newspapers owned by the smaller companies but can those (the majority) belonging to the big groups survive the rigours of their owners' relentless pursuit of the *Three Ps* – profits, profits and more profits?

I could not, rationally, blame the big companies if they are, in fact, seeking the highest possible short- and medium-term profits at potential risk to the long-term survival of their local newspapers, while staying ahead of the pace on the development of new media. Stripped of emotion, that probably makes a very great deal of business sense.

For them, there can be no room for sentiment. They are competing in the "Premiership" of big business amid the insatiable demands of shareholders and the vicissitudes of the City. That's the league they play in and there's absolutely no point being bottom of that league. Once the bar of annual profit margins had been raised to that greedy 30 per cent all the other competitors had to try to jump it.

That's the nature of the business they are in. Keeping up with the pace, no matter how painful that can sometimes be, is absolutely unavoidable and it's pointless for emotive journalists (the majority of whom were at the back of the queue when business nous was handed out!) to scream and wail about it. That ain't going to change a bloody thing.

No. The crunch question, for me, is:

Do we have to accept that the majority ownership of such a vital component of British democracy as our local and regional Press has to remain with these big, bottom-line-driven corporate companies?

With the exception of a handful of MPs, led by Austin Mitchell, who tabled a Commons question on the issue, very few people in this country are aware that there is a strongly held view among some observers that most of our much-loved local Press is at risk of being driven into extinction by the unavoidable profit demands of its owners and the inexorable growth of new media.

If the optimists are right, the current frenetic activity will settle down and all our regional newspapers will carry on bringing local news, views, information and campaigns on crucial issues to our communities for a very long time to come, bolstered by burgeoning new media alternatives for new generations of consumers.

I hope they are right. I really do. But count me among the pessimists (and that is entirely contrary to my nature) because I just cannot see how the current pursuit of huge and ever-increasing profits can be commensurate with a passionate commitment to strong local *journalism* – the industry's *raison d'etre* nor, consequently, with the long term survival of our local newspapers.

I would dearly love to be proved to be wrong on this and one big company which can do that is *Northcliffe* – which in July 2007 returned to acquisitive ways by buying 25 titles in the south east of England from *Trinity Mirror*! But if I *am* right, I also believe that the life expectancy of both local journalism and local newspapers *could* be extended very considerably if the big groups got out of regional newspaper publishing and sold their newspapers individually to new *local* proprietors or consortia.

It's not likely to happen in the short term but the time *may* come when the big companies will be prepared to sell their titles in other than one big, hugely expensive block and that is when the prospect of local ownership could be opened up. New local owners, with just one or two newspapers each and different motivation and financial expectation, would have dramatically lower costs and could afford to have much less demanding and escalating profit targets while still getting a more than decent return. This would mean that the local owners could invest more in editorial quality and promotion which, in turn, would mean that the newspapers would be far better equipped to survive than they might be under the constant cost cutting of the big boys who have no real alternative to staying in the rat race.

Such a solution would be turning the clock back to the days of the old Victorian founders – many of whom wore the ownership of their newspapers like a local badge of honour and prestige and saw it as putting something *back* into the communities out of which they were making their fortunes. That philosophy endured for many years until, one by one, the newspapers were swallowed up by the expansive big groups (indeed it still endured at the *Nottingham Evening Post* with Colonel Tom Forman Hardy and is still alive and well in Edwin Boorman's *Kent Messenger)* and I do not believe it would be impossible for that same spirit of local ownership of our local newspapers for motives other than profit to return in a modern business setting.

In fact, a government which cared genuinely about preserving this great industry for future generations could smooth a transition back to local ownership. This is not pie in the sky, nor the ramblings of one of Roy Greenslade's inky old dinosaurs. What I propose would be ultra-modern, lean and lively local businesses, well managed and profit *making* but not profit *driven* – thus re-igniting the local altruistic spirit which played such a prominent part in the culture of regional newspaper ownership before huge corporate profits came to rule all. In this context small could be beautiful and profitable for many more years than the current mass ownership may be able to sustain unless profit demands are reduced drastically – and I just cannot see that happening.

Most communities served by local newspapers have their wealthy local champions who could be persuaded to retrace the pioneering footsteps of the Victorian local Press founders and would get enormous personal satisfaction and a great sense of civic contribution out of so doing.

I would gladly get involved in such a counter revolution and if it succeeded, as I believe it would, it could mean that the demise of local newspapers, which have been an integral part of our communities for 150 years or more, can be dramatically decelerated – if not avoided altogether.

Why should our communities *care* about that?

Because if we lose our local newspapers I do not believe any other form of media can ever replicate adequately their unique watchdog role. A very great deal of accountability to the public will be lost in all sorts of places, many local misdemeanours, crimes and corrupt practices will go unreported and consequently unexposed to the communities in which and against which they are perpetrated, the immensely powerful deterrent factor and fear of being *named and shamed in the local rag* will be lost and with it will go a great deal of the self-discipline which shapes decent local society.

The sustained pressure for essential change in policies on local issues by government (local and national) which these newspapers are able uniquely to exert will evaporate. Governments (local and national) will no longer be called publicly to account for their actions against the best interests of local communities to anything like the extent to which they are now because TV and radio simply cannot perform that function even half as well or as often as local newspapers do. TV and radio's local role, valuable and welcome though it is, is different and their time too condensed. (Half an hour of TV news equates to just two columns of newspaper type.)

Say what you will about Britain's regional Press, I can affirm that it remains politically un-affiliated and totally independent. *Never,* in all my 44 years in this industry, did any boss or proprietor *ever* put any pressure whatsoever on me to follow any political line or to show any political favour. I know that surprises a lot of people but it is absolutely true and other regional editors would confirm it. Lose that freedom, that fierce independence, that relentlessly challenging attitude and your community will lose so much that can never be replaced.

The local "rag" is taken so much for granted that few people will realise just how badly it will be missed until it is too late. And if, in the meantime, the fundamental structure and the journalistic skills and aptitude employed in that vital local service are lost they will – like so many other lost trades in the UK – never come back.

I reckon that is what the irreversible pursuit of ever-bigger profits by the big corporate owners is putting at risk. And it is why I believe that only by reverting to *local* ownership of the *local* Press can that essential community role be protected from the extinction which, I believe, is at least the potential corollary of the current situation.

Of all the changes I've seen in nearly half a century working in local newspapers none carries anything like the seeds of self destruction as the reduction of status, gradually over the last 20 years, of the essential stock-in-trade... the *journalistic* role and function. Lose that and local newspapers have lost everything, including the reason for their very existence. Yet, by unintended default and collateral damage from ceaseless bottom line improving cuts, I believe that is happening.

According to *Press Gazette*, the average annual salary for journalists in the regional Press in 2007 is £17,750. That is disgraceful for an industry that counts the yearly profits from the work of those journalists in hundreds of millions. That figure is well *below* the national average wage. And these salaries are being paid to talented people who, by any measure, are way *above* average. Regional journalists have to be academically well qualified, intensively well trained, and so dedicated and committed to their craft that they are prepared frequently to work ludicrously long and antisocial hours, often sacrificing their home lives. And multi-tasking (which means that they will have to include internet and video skills in their repertoire *for no extra pay*) is now an essential part of the mission of the corporate managements. How long can this poor pay be tolerated before youngsters will no longer want to know about a profession which once held so much allure?

It seems to me that consuming new media will be like eating fast food. It will satisfy the hunger without stimulating the senses. It will be a robotic routine rather than an enriching experience. Thus, new media input may require a minimum of journalistic skill, heart and soul but that will *never* be the case with the content of the best of our local newspapers which, without the essential nourishment of journalistic excellence and passion, can only wither and die.

So, deprived of the levels of financial investment in journalism which will, in my view, be incompatible with the profit demands of the big companies, the future of the printed word in the regional industry will be very bleak indeed.

All of which makes it hard to escape the conclusion that, left as it is, our much loved and long cherished local Press is in the early stages of its death throes. Its demise would not be wilful but it would be an outrage nonetheless. And it's tragically ironic that a once great and proud industry in the essential *communications* business could be slipping away from us without the knowledge of the vast majority of British citizens because what's happening to it is not being effectively *communicated* to them.

Viewed alongside that disturbing big picture it is utterly inconsequential that my own career was prematurely sacrificed on the altar of ever bigger profits. Of that personal matter I now think, *Hey, what the hell!*

I had a bloody good innings. I hit plenty of runs.

I had lots of excitement and thrills along the way.

And so much fun. And so many laughs.

I helped a few people and I made a bit of a difference here and there by rattling cages and righting wrongs.

I gave hundreds of journalists a helping hand in a profession which gave me so much myself.

And Barrie and Pauline Williams, those two council house kids from Shropshire who met on a dancefloor in the swinging Sixties, now enjoy a lifestyle which our dear parents could never even have dreamed of.

The nature of the unique and special profession which made all that possible was articulated most succinctly for me by one of the best writers I ever worked with.

Neil Young joined me at the *Western Morning News* as a subeditor but I felt he was wasted in that job. Neil is Irish and, like me, from a working class background. His work is of the highest intellectual standard and he writes with flair and passion, all of which probably means that, to the accountants currently running like ravaging ants all over our newspapers, he will be seen as a luxury, so I hope the buggers don't sack him!

Among the mountain of mail I was so moved to receive when I left the *Western Morning News* was a note from Neil. His brief message meant so much to me because in just a few words it managed to sum up not only the way one of my best journalists felt about me, which was deeply gratifying, but also the way I had always gone about my job, how I felt about regional newspapers and why I believe that we should all do everything within our power to save the local Press.

Neil wrote:

Barrie...

Just a note to say it has been a privilege working with you over the past nine years. I've learned an enormous amount under your editorship and from the vision and campaigning style you've brought to the Western Morning News. I'm especially appreciative of the opportunities you have given me to develop in varied areas of journalism. I doubt that many other editors would have done the same, spotted the dormant talent, or taken the risks. I've worked for quite a few editors, but none by a country mile with such guts and talent or who believed so passionately in the principle that we're here to champion the readers, the underdog, and give them a voice. That's our job and when we get it right it feels like the best job in the world."

It did, mate. It really did.

~ End ~